CANNED ART

Clip Art for the Macintosh

Second Edition

Erfert Fenton
&
Christine Morrissett

Peachpit Press
Berkeley, California

CANNED ART: CLIP ART FOR THE MACINTOSH, SECOND EDITION
© 1992 by Erfert Fenton and Christine Morrissett

Peachpit Press, Inc.
2414 Sixth Street
Berkeley, California 94710
Phone: 510/548-4393
Fax: 510/548-5991

This book is set in Adobe Systems' version of ITC Galliard. Aldus PageMaker was used for page layout. The text was printed on a Varityper 5300 PostScript imagesetter at 1200 dots per inch; the graphics were printed on a QMS PS800+ PostScript laser printer at 300 dots per inch.

Notice of Liability:

Trademarks:

ISBN 0-938151-78-9

0 9 8 7 6 5 4 3 2 1
Printed and bound in the United States of America

PRINTED ON RECYCLED PAPER

CONTENTS

INTRODUCTION

In the olden days (say, the 1970s or so), if you needed some artwork to put in a newspaper, newsletter, or the like, you'd buy a book of *clip art*. These books were filled with illustrations that were in the public domain, meaning you could freely use them without obtaining the artists' permission or paying royalties to the owner of the publishing rights. When you saw a drawing you liked, you'd simply clip it out with scissors and affix it to your publication with tape, glue, wax, or some such messy substance.

Many people still use these traditional methods, of course. But the Macintosh has brought us a new kind of publishing: desktop publishing. These days, anyone with a personal computer, the requisite software, and a knack for design can turn out decent-looking documents with a minimum of training. Today's publishers cut and paste chunks of data rather than pieces of paper, and an electronic clip art industry has sprung up to accommodate them.

Like its predecessor, computer clip art encompasses a wide variety of themes and drawing styles. The illustrations may be original pieces drawn by artists employed by a clip art company, or they may be scanned images of existing artwork. Some companies even offer scanned photos in digital format. While subject matter, drawing style, and illustration quality differ from one company to the next, all Macintosh clip art has one thing in common: once you buy a disk, you're free to use the artwork it contains in your publications (read the license agreement that comes with your clip art for details). As with any other software, however, you may *not* give away or resell the digital versions of the artwork you purchase.

Clip with Care

A word of caution: While the manufacturers listed in *Canned Art* are responsible for obtaining the rights to use the art they publish, clip art you find on electronic bulletin boards isn't always carefully screened. Nowadays, anyone with a scanner can convert a piece of art into a format that can be viewed and printed with a computer. How can you tell if a picture you find on a bulletin board is OK to use? In general, anything published in the United States before 1906 can safely be assumed to be in the public domain. Most European works, and works published in the U.S. after 1977, are copyrighted for 50 years after the creator's death. Therefore, if you see a digital version of your favorite character from the Sunday comics, chances are it's an unauthorized copy and shouldn't be used in a publication you distribute, whether you charge for the publication or not. To use copyrighted artwork, you should write to the publisher and request permission to reprint it; most copyright owners will charge a small fee for reprinting their material.

Why Go Digital?

Electronic clip art has many advantages over its paper-based ancestor. For example, a digital image can be electronically "cut" and "pasted" an unlimited number of times; electronic publishers won't confront a hole in a page once they've used an image, nor will they have to resort to making photocopies of images they want to use more than once. And unlike clip art on paper, electronic clip art can be easily modified by the user; with the appropriate software, even a relative klutz can resize, rotate, or reshade an image. Finally, digital clip art is easy to store; hundreds of images can be placed on a 3.5-inch disk, or thousands on a CD ROM, reducing clutter in your office or studio. Unfortunately, the last advantage is also a disadvantage: because many clip-art vendors don't publish catalogs of their wares, buyers have to depend on samples shown in ads or on packaging, and often don't know what they're getting until they purchase a disk. With *Canned Art,* we've taken on the task of bringing together a centralized, comprehensive catalog of Macintosh clip art (much of the artwork in this book is available for the IBM PC as well, as noted on the introductory page for each company).

Is It Really Art?

Clip art has always gotten a bad rap. Alas, clip art has never enjoyed the prestige of its sister arts, Painting and Sculpture, and has therefore been woefully absent from the curricula of our institutions of higher learning. Hence, skilled practitioners are rare. The problem was compounded when clip art came to the Macintosh, since clip artists had to learn a new medium: MacPaint. Because a free copy of MacPaint was included with every Mac, many amateur artists felt compelled to enter the fledgling clip art racket. Although some of the early Mac clip art was good, much of it was substandard stuff. Once the Mac became established, however, and a larger pool of artists became available, the overall quality of Mac clip art took a turn for the better.

The advent of digital scanners gave the clip art business a shot in the arm, since piles of artwork already created by professional artists could be transformed into digital format—provided it was in the public domain. Still, certain types of images didn't lend themselves to being rendered as a pattern of dots. Line art, for example, lost a good deal of crispness when scanned.

About two years after the Mac appeared, the Mac clip art industry was given another boost with the introduction of Adobe Illustrator, the first PostScript graphics program. PostScript will be described in the next chapter; for now, suffice it to say that PostScript gives Mac artists precise control over lines, curves, shading, and color, allowing them to produce high-quality artwork that rivals that created by traditional means.

Today's clip art customer can choose among thousands of illustrations, many of them quite impressive. Mac owners who scoffed at Macintosh clip art in the early days may have a change of heart when they thumb through this volume. If you're still skeptical, look at the printer's ornaments from The Underground Grammarian, near the end of this book. Now that's art!

Who Uses Clip Art?

If you were participating in a word-association test and heard the term "clip art," chances are you'd respond in a flash with "newsletter!" This is a typical response, and the professional who was administering the test would peg you as normal. But it's a limited response. Now that a good deal of high-quality clip art is available for the Mac, it's showing up in a wide spectrum of applications, including newspapers, books, maps, technical papers, presentations, office documents and reports, and advertisements. Figure I-1 shows just a few of the potential uses for Macintosh clip art.

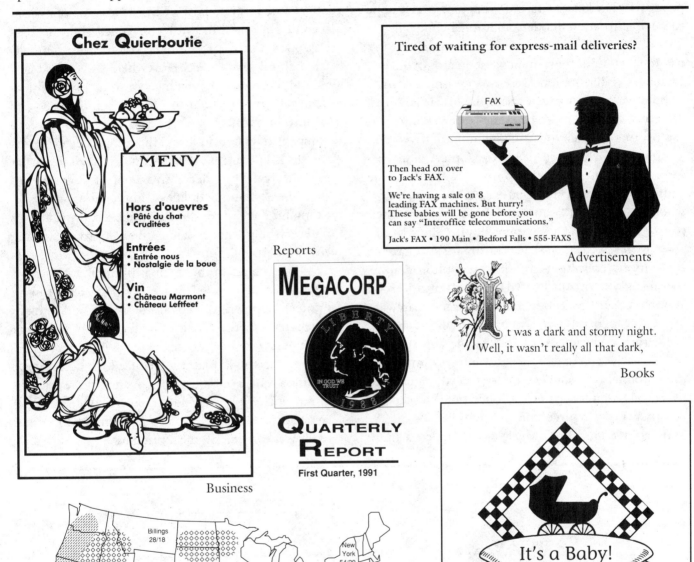

FIGURE I-1. Examples of how clip art can be used.

About the Clip Art In this Book

We did our best to contact all the Macintosh clip art vendors. *Canned Art* features artwork from 35 companies. If we've left anyone out, we apologize; we hope to be able to accommodate additional companies in future editions. To be included in this book, artwork had to meet the authors' minimal standards of quality. In general, if illustrations were amateurishly drawn or sloppily scanned, they were rejected. Only a handful of companies didn't make the grade. A few companies, for reasons of their own, chose not to have their illustrations included in this book. Others didn't respond to our queries. In the appendix, we've listed the addresses and phone numbers of a number of vendors whose images aren't shown in this book; interested readers can contact these companies for information.

(Note: Because of space constraints, we haven't reproduced collections of digitized photographs, specialized volumes such as 3-D images or medical clip art, or the many collections of freeware and shareware clip art offered by user groups and online services. Numerous companies are listed in the appendix, in case you wish to contact them for information about their products. We suggest you contact your local Mac user group for information on noncommercial clip art. Another good source for inexpensive clip art is Showker Graphic Arts, which has compiled a huge collection of freeware and shareware drawings. Showker's address and phone number are listed in the appendix.)

Needless to say, a catalog of this type can't stay up-to-date forever. That's why we've come out with a second edition. But with companies churning out artwork at a rapid rate, even this volume will eventually fall behind the times. Nevertheless, *Canned Art* should be a valuable reference for some time, both as a central source for company names and addresses, and as an indication of the type and quality of art each company offers. In addition, the comprehensive index should help you find the art you need in a particular subject area, be it decorative elements, musical instruments, religious holidays, international symbols, or mythical creatures. Finally, the book provides tips on everything from resizing a drawing to organizing your clip art collection.

The clip art in this book is printed at 25% of its original size. Figure I-2 illustrates what 25% means in printer's terms, since a logical person would think of the figure on the left as a reduction to 25%. For example, if you have an image that's 4 inches square, you might think that the reduced version should occupy a square one-quarter of the size of the original, or two inches on each side. However, when a page-layout program reduces our sample image to 25%, it reduces *each side* of the bounding square to 25%,

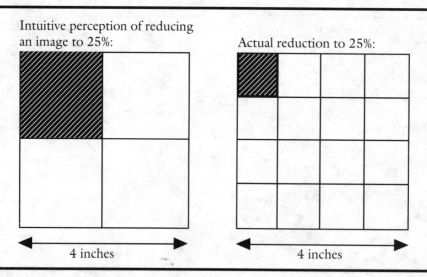

Intuitive perception of reducing an image to 25%:

4 inches

Actual reduction to 25%:

4 inches

FIGURE I-2. Will the real 25% reduction please stand up?

resulting in the one-inch-square image shown on the right. We want to clarify this point so you'll have a good idea of the original size of this book's images.

The artwork in this book is printed at a resolution of 300 dots per inch. We chose the relatively low resolution not only because the cost of setting such a large book at a higher resolution would be prohibitive, but also because several clip art vendors expressed the concern that if the reproduction quality were too high, people might use *Canned Art* as a traditional clip art book and cut out illustrations with non-digital tools (i.e., scissors) rather than buying their art disks. Keep in mind that some of the images have lost a fair amount of detail from being reduced, and that they would look cleaner and crisper if printed at a higher resolution, such as the 1200 or 2500 dpi offered at your local typesetting service bureau. This book is intended as a buyer's guide, not a coffee table book.

If you want to get a better idea of how each company's artwork looks, send the coupon in the back of this book to Peachpit Press to receive two disks full of sample artwork.

How This Book Is Organized

Canned Art consists of three basic components: introductory text, reproductions of artwork, and an index. Chapter 1 describes the various file formats a clip art collector is likely to encounter and notes the advantages and disadvantages of each. Chapter 2 is a collection of tips for getting the most out of your clip art collection: cutting and pasting hints, tips for modifying artwork, and a description of your printing options. Chapter 3 discusses several methods for organizing a large clip art collection. The appendix gives information on additional clip art vendors, as well as the utilities described in this book. The index is organized by subject, rather than by image name. For example, if you're looking for a picture of a lobster (and what desktop publisher doesn't occasionally need a reproduction of a lobster?), you'd look under "lobster," since one of the collections offers a lobster under the somewhat cryptic title "In Deep Places #2," and other companies might choose still other names.

Many index items are listed as subentries under subject categories. If you're looking for lobsters, for example, you'll also find "lobster" listed as a subentry under the main entries "Food" and "Sea life."

For your shopping convenience, the artwork in this book is arranged alphabetically by company. To leave room for revision or expansion, the pages are numbered separately for each company, rather than consecutively throughout the book. Each company has been given a three-letter code (for example, SUN for SunShine) to facilitate listing page numbers in the index.

An introductory page for each company lists basic information: the company's name, address, and phone number; collection names; artwork format (file formats are discussed in Chapter 1); and other relevant information. The pages that follow depict the company's artwork, arranged alphabetically or numerically by package, depending on the company's naming scheme (some companies use the "Volumes 1-*x*" approach, while others give each package a name, such as "Realistic Reptiles & Amphibians"). The images in each package are listed in alphabetical order by image name (a few companies identify their illustrations by number instead of name; since the numbers would serve no purpose in this book, we've left them out). If a package consists of more than one disk—which many do—the contents of each disk are listed in alphabetical order, by image name. If the artwork on a disk is arranged in folders, the folders are presented in alphabetical order, with their contents alphabetized by image name. Figure I-3 shows a sample page and how it's organized.

For most companies, we've shown all the artwork available at press time (November 1991). If a company's entire repertoire isn't shown, we say so in the introductory page for that company. Space constraints prohibited us from showing the complete collections of several companies with exceptionally large libraries. For example, showing every image offered by companies like SunShine and Metro ImageBase would have required more than a hundred pages per company. In these cases, we've shown only samples from each volume; footnotes indicate when we've done so.

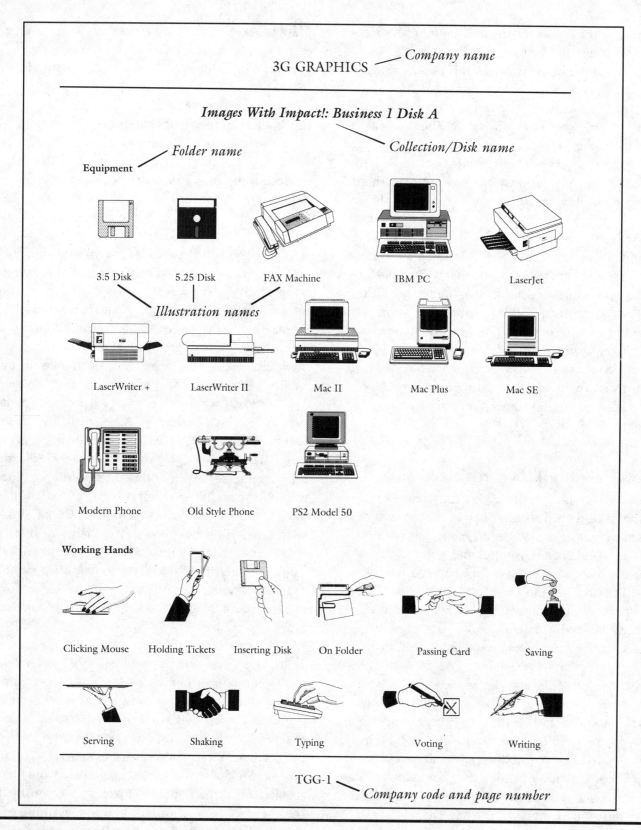

FIGURE I-3. *The components of a typical page of this book.*

1
FILE FORMATS

aper-based clip art has one advantage over its computerized counterpart: you don't need to know terms like TIFF, PICT, or EPS to cut out a picture with a pair of scissors. Macintosh clip art comes in a variety of formats, which may seem confusing if you don't have much experience with Macintosh graphics. Don't worry; in most cases you don't need to know the format of the artwork you're pasting into a page-layout program. Mac page-layout programs automatically accept most popular formats.

But if you intend to modify an illustration, it's a good idea to know some basic facts about each format: how it works, what its strengths and weaknesses are, and how it compares to other Mac graphics formats. This chapter provides a sketch of each of the graphics formats in which Mac clip art appears.

Paint

Among the most popular Macintosh graphics programs are the *bitmapped graphics programs*. Why are they called bitmapped graphics programs? Because

drawings are made up of a map of bits. Ahem. A less tautological explanation is in order. The Mac's screen is laid out as a grid of dots, 72 dots to an inch. (These dots are sometimes called *pixels,* which is short for picture elements.) In the Mac's memory, each dot in the grid is represented by a bit, which is computerese for binary digit, the 1's and 0's that make up computer instructions. Bitmapped drawings are very straightforward; a value of 1 turns a bit on (black), while a value of 0 turns it off (white). To create shades of gray, bitmapped graphics programs use patterns of black and white dots.

Fortunately, Mac artists don't have to deal with 1's and 0's. Instead, they use on-screen brushes, pencils, airbrushes, erasers, and other tools to paint with pixels. A pencil lays down black pixels, for example, while an eraser tool turns black pixels white. Because the tools found in bitmapped graphics programs resemble the tools you'd find in an artist's paintbox—and because the first such program was named MacPaint—these programs are also known as *paint programs.*

Figure 1.1 shows an image created with a paint program.

Programs that produce bitmapped graphics include MacPaint, SuperPaint, FullPaint, Canvas, and DeskPaint. Some paint programs support color. Painting in color involves more than simply turning pixels on or off; color paint programs use eight—or even 24—bits to set the color of each pixel. Like black-and-white paint programs, color paint programs provide tools such as paintbrushes and erasers to make painting on the screen similar to painting on paper or canvas. Color paint programs include PixelPaint, Studio/8, Modern Artist, PhotonPaint, and Cricket ColorPaint. The images shown in this book were created in black-and-white paint programs. If you wish, you can paste black-and-white images into a color paint program and colorize them.

The advantages of bitmapped graphics are as follows:

• Because images are made up of a pattern of dots, they can have fine-grained detail reminiscent of antique etchings or engravings. In fact, many of the illustrations in this book are reproductions of turn-of-the-century prints.

• The metaphor of artist's paintbox makes paint programs easy to learn and use. Once you've mastered the mouse, you can immediately pick up an electronic pencil and start drawing. Therefore, anyone can modify bitmapped clip art without investing a lot of time learning a graphics program.

FIGURE 1.1. *As you can see from the enlarged portion of this picture, paint images are made up of a series of dots. These programs use different dot patterns to simulate shades of gray, as seen in the cherub's face.*

The disadvantages of bitmapped graphics are as follows:

• Although the dot-by-dot approach has its good points, bitmapped images can be tedious to edit. You could compare a bitmapped image to a needlepoint design; to alter an object you have to remove stitches and replace them with new ones. If you want to change an area from one shade of gray to another, for example, you have to erase the original gray before adding the second shade.

• Unless you're careful, bitmapped images can become distorted and muddy when reduced, stretched, or rotated. The following chapter discusses techniques for cleanly reducing bitmapped art.

• Since bitmapped drawings have a resolution of 72 dots per inch—the resolution of the Mac's screen—they don't take advantage of high-resolution printers like the LaserWriter, which prints 300 dots per inch. (You can improve the appearance of bitmapped images by printing them at a reduced size on the LaserWriter, however.)

• Bitmapped text doesn't take advantage of the high-quality PostScript typefaces found in printers such as the LaserWriter. Like bitmapped graphics, bitmapped characters are composed of maps of dots.

PICT

A second type of Mac graphics applications are the *draw programs,* which produce *object-oriented graphics.* Just as paint programs are named after Apple's pioneering MacPaint, the term "draw programs" comes from Apple's MacDraw, the granddaddy of all object-oriented graphics programs. Unlike the dot-by-dot approach of paint programs, draw programs describe illustrations using mathematical expressions to describe the lines and curves that make up an image. If you draw a line, for example, an object-oriented graphics program notes the line's starting position, ending position, and other attributes such as its width and fill pattern. A bitmapped graphics program, on the other hand, would record the screen position of each pixel in the line.

Figure 1.2 shows an illustration created with a draw program.

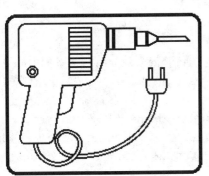 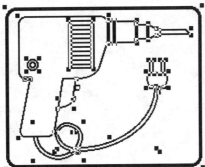 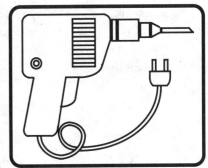

Draw image displayed on screen   Draw image with elements selected   Printed image

FIGURE 1.2. Draw images are composed of a series of objects made up of lines and curves. You can change an element's shape or size by dragging control points displayed on the screen.

Unlike a static bitmapped image, the components of an object-oriented drawing can be edited at any time. When you click on an object, tiny "handles" appear on each line or shape that makes up the object. You can grab these handles and stretch or shrink an object's outline as if it were a rubber band. Draw programs also let you change the width and shading of lines, move objects behind or in front of other objects, and change a filled area from one shade or pattern to another without first erasing the original shade or pattern. And if your change doesn't look right, it's not set in stone; even after you've saved a drawing, you can go back and edit it until it suits you. Once you're satisfied with your changes, you can group the objects that make up an image to prevent them from being changed (even then, you can ungroup them later and make further changes).

Although object-oriented drawing programs can save files in a variety of formats, the most common format is PICT. Many graphics programs either automatically save documents in PICT format or have an option that lets you save them in PICT format. Most graphics, word-processing, and page-layout programs can open PICT files. You could look at PICT as the Mac's native graphics language, since PICT files are written in QuickDraw, the set of graphics routines that produces the text and graphics you see on the screen. When you cut or copy a drawing and save it in the Mac's Scrapbook, it's saved in PICT format.

Programs that produce object-oriented graphics include MacDraw, Dreams, and MacDraft. SuperPaint and Canvas, which were listed as paint programs in the previous section, also provide tools for creating object-oriented drawings.

The advantages of object-oriented graphics are as follows:

- The PICT format is a universal format that allows you to transfer graphics among different programs.

- Object-oriented drawings are dynamic; you can edit an image at any time.

- Unlike bitmapped graphics, object-oriented graphics are *resolution-independent;* instead of being tied to the screen resolution of 72 dots per inch, these graphics let you take advantage of high-resolution printers.

- Like object-oriented graphics, the text created in object-oriented drawing programs can be edited at any time. Also, these programs let you use the high-quality typefaces found in printers such as the LaserWriter.

- Object-oriented graphics files are generally smaller than bitmapped graphics file, so they use up less space on disk.

The disadvantages of object-oriented graphics are as follows:

- Although object-oriented drawing programs provide freehand drawing tools, these programs don't offer the dot-by-dot precision of bitmapped graphics programs.

- Many object-oriented drawing programs use patterns of dots to simulate shades of gray, rather than taking advantage of the subtle gradations that high-resolution printers can produce.

PostScript

The PostScript language, which was developed by Adobe Systems, offers an alternative to QuickDraw for creating graphics on the Mac. PostScript graphics are composed of paths made up of Bézier curves. To edit a PostScript graphic, you grab either the curve itself or one of the control points that make up the curve, and drag to reshape the curve. Figure 1.3 shows a PostScript illustration.

Like the draw programs just described, PostScript graphics programs let you edit an image at any time, changing attributes such as size, line width, or shading. PostScript offers several enhancements over

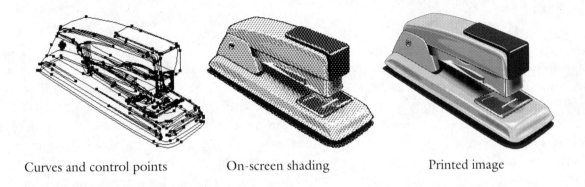

Curves and control points   On-screen shading   Printed image

FIGURE 1.3. PostScript graphics programs give artists precise control over lines and shading.

QuickDraw, however. For example, PostScript treats text as just another graphic object, allowing you to rotate a character, change its outline weight, or fill it with a shade or pattern. Some of the clip art collections in this book include alphabets that are saved as Post-Script outlines.

PostScript offers other capabilities not found in QuickDraw, such as precise control of line width, access to subtle shading variations (up to 100 shades of gray, rather than the draw programs' simulated-gray patterns), the ability to place text on a curved path, and the ability to rotate, stretch, or skew text or graphics.

PostScript graphics programs include Adobe Illustrator, Aldus FreeHand, and Cricket Draw. Illustrator and FreeHand offer sophisticated color-separation capabilities, allowing you to separate a drawing into cyan, magenta, yellow, and black plates for color printing.

EPS

Most PostScript drawing programs use QuickDraw to display images on the screen. Therefore, when you save a drawing in PostScript format and paste it into another application, such as a page-layout program, the second program won't have access to the original program's instructions for mapping the PostScript graphic to QuickDraw. In this case, the program into

which the graphic is pasted displays a gray box that's the same size as the PostScript image and shows the image's title, program of origin, and creation date (see Figure 1.4). The PostScript graphic will print just fine—you just won't be able to see it on the screen.

An ingenious enhancement called Encapsulated PostScript (abbreviated as EPS or EPSF) lets you see PostScript graphics on the screen. EPS saves a drawing as a PostScript file that includes a QuickDraw component that enables other applications to display the graphic. EPS is an invaluable aid for positioning graphics in relation to other text and graphics in a publication. PostScript drawing programs offer you the option of saving a file in the program's native format or in EPS format.

The advantages of PostScript drawing programs are as follows:

- Drawings are dynamic; they can be edited at any time.

- PostScript's Bézier curves offer precise control over an object's shape.

- PostScript offers graphics effects such as rotation, gradient fills (blending from one shade of gray to another), skewing, and text on a path.

• PostScript takes advantage of the high-quality typefaces found in printers such as the Laser-Writer.

• PostScript is resolution-independent; the same drawing can take advantage of a LaserWriter's 300-dpi resolution or a Linotronic L300 imagesetter's 2500-dpi resolution.

• Programs include utilities for creating color separations.

The disadvantages of PostScript drawing programs are as follows:

• PostScript graphics programs are somewhat more expensive than most other Mac graphics programs, and require a good deal of time to master. Unlike a paint program, you can't be up and running in ten minutes with a PostScript graphics application.

• PostScript graphics can take a long time to print, especially if they contain certain types of special effects, such as radial fills. In addition to being annoying, slow printing can be expensive

if you're paying by the hour to use a service bureau's high-resolution PostScript imagesetter.

TIFF

Some Mac clip art companies use digital scanners to convert existing artwork into a form the Mac can use. Scanners save files in a format called *TIFF*, which stands for Tagged-Image File Format. TIFF was developed by Aldus Corporation to allow images with gray-scale information to be placed into page-layout programs and printed as halftones that take advantage of high-resolution output devices such as the 2500-dpi Linotronic L300 imagesetter. Because many scanners scan images at a resolution of 300 dots per inch, TIFF images look good when printed on a 300-dpi laser printer such as Apple's LaserWriter.

Some clip art vendors offer black-and-white TIFF images; others take advantage of gray-scale scanners to create images with a wide range of tonal values. Unlike the pixels in a paint image, which can be either black or white, each pixel in a TIFF image can store eight bits of information, meaning it can be any of 256 (2^8) values of gray. (To display gray-scale TIFF images on your Mac, you need an 8-bit graphics card—one that supports 256 levels of gray.)

PostScript file:

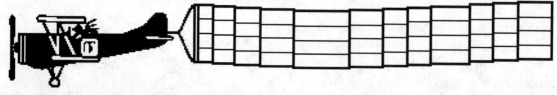

EPS file:

FIGURE 1.4. Encapsulated PostScript combines the best of both worlds, PostScript and QuickDraw, allowing PostScript images to be displayed on the screen. Without EPS, the biplane is displayed as a gray rectangle.

You can paste a TIFF image into a page-layout program and print it from there, or alter the image first with a program that accepts TIFF images, such as DeskPaint, LaserPaint, or SuperPaint 2.0. To alter an 8-bit TIFF image, you need a gray-scale graphics editor such as ImageStudio or Digital Darkroom.

Figure 1.5 shows a piece of Mac clip art in TIFF format.

The advantages of TIFF are as follows:

• TIFF format allows you to save and print continuous-tone graphics that approximate the quality of those created by conventional graphics cameras. With TIFF, you can use your Mac as a photo-retouching station.

• Because TIFF images are scanned at 300 dots

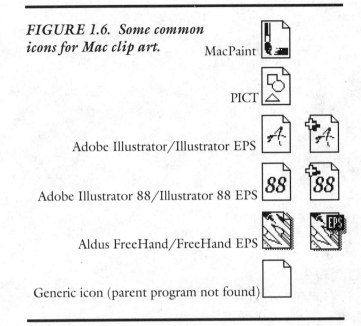

FIGURE 1.6. *Some common icons for Mac clip art.*

MacPaint

PICT

Adobe Illustrator/Illustrator EPS

Adobe Illustrator 88/Illustrator 88 EPS

Aldus FreeHand/FreeHand EPS

Generic icon (parent program not found)

per inch, they create crisp images that make full use of a laser printer's capabilities.

The disadvantages of TIFF are as follows:

• Because they contain so much information, TIFF files can take up a considerable amount of disk space. Some TIFF files won't fit on an 800K floppy disk.

• Modifying gray-scale TIFF files requires a fairly large investment in hardware (an 8-bit graphics card) and software (a program that supports gray-scale editing).

There. Now you know the basics of Mac graphics formats. You can toss around acronyms like TIFF and EPS with the best of them. Figure 1.6 shows some of the icons associated with the formats discussed in this chapter. Keep in mind that you'll see the generic icon at the bottom if you don't have the program that created the illustration. The next chapter delves deeper into Mac graphics, offering tips for cutting, pasting, modifying, and printing clip art with various programs.

FIGURE 1.5. TIFF *images take advantage of high-resolution printing.*

2
CLIP TIPS

This chapter presents tips for using clip art in the various formats that were introduced in the last chapter. For those who are new to the Mac, we'll begin with a brief overview of cutting and pasting. More experienced users can skip to the tips for the specific formats that interest them. A final section offers miscellaneous tips for using clip art.

Because readers will be using a variety of graphics programs to modify their clip art, most of the tips in this chapter are general-purpose; they apply to a given format rather than a particular program. For example, the tips for paint programs will work with most Macintosh bitmapped graphics programs. A few of the tips are program-specific, however.

Cutting and Pasting

Apple Computer, in its infinite wisdom, has always encouraged Macintosh software developers to adhere to a set of user interface guidelines. Consequently, you can pull down the Edit menu of almost any application and find commands called Cut, Copy, and Paste. This section explains the basics of these commands.

When you *cut* an image, it's removed from your document and placed in a temporary file called the *Clipboard*. When you *copy* an image, the original graphic remains in place and a duplicate is placed in the Clipboard. It's important to remember that the Clipboard is used for *temporary* storage. If you cut or copy a second item, that item replaces the previous contents of the Clipboard. Although the Clipboard's contents remain intact if you switch from one document or application to another, they're lost when you turn off the Mac. Once something is cut or copied to the Clipboard, it can be pasted into a different location in the document where it originated, or pasted into another document. The destination document can be created with a different application than the source document; for example, you might copy a MacPaint illustration, exit MacPaint, and paste the graphic into a document created with a word processor.

The Clipboard is fine for cutting and pasting on the fly, but for permanent storage you'll use a desk accessory called the *Scrapbook*. While the Clipboard

ART TO GO

If, by some chance, you scan the thousands of graphics in this book and still don't find just the image you're looking for—or if you have an existing illustration that you want converted to Macintosh format—you can go the custom clip art route.

• Showker Graphic Arts & Design has compiled a mammoth library of public-domain and shareware clip art. The company offers a service called Clip Art to Go. You can call Showker and ask for artwork in a particular subject area. If they don't have what you want, their artists will create custom artwork on request. The company also converts logos or other drawings to EPS or PICT format.

Showker Graphics is a nonprofit organization. Proceeds go to the Johnny Appleseed Award, a series of prizes given to user group members who perform public services.

• A company called Wordscapes will convert a logo, technical drawing, or just about any type of graphic into EPS format. They converted the Peachpit Press logo you see on the title page of this book from a pen-and-ink drawing to an EPS file.

See the appendix for information on contacting these companies.

holds only one image at a time, the Scrapbook can hold hundreds of pictures. To place an image in the Scrapbook, you simply cut or copy the image, select the Scrapbook desk accessory from the Apple menu, and paste in the image. (If you do a lot of cutting and pasting, you'll find the following shortcuts handy: ⌘-X for cutting, ⌘-C for copying, and ⌘-V for pasting.)

The Scrapbook provides an easy-access storage area for clip art, but it has its limitations. For example, even though the Scrapbook can hold hundreds of pictures, you probably won't want to store more than a few dozen, since the Scrapbook provides no way to

find images other than scrolling through its contents. In addition, the Scrapbook deals only with PICT images (both draw and paint images are stored in the Scrapbook in PICT format); if you paste a TIFF image into the Scrapbook it's converted to PICT, and you can't paste EPS or PostScript graphics into the Scrapbook at all. Since the Scrapbook can't hold all types of artwork, some applications provide a Place or Import command that allows you to paste in non-PICT artwork.

☞ You can get around the Scrapbook's organizational limitations by placing your clip art in multiple Scrapbooks, one Scrapbook for each subject area. Look in your Mac's System folder, and you'll see an icon named "Scrapbook File." In order to be recognized by the Mac, the Scrapbook must have this name. If you give the Scrapbook file another name (say, "Scrapbook File-1"), the Mac will no longer open that Scrapbook, but will instead create a new one, automatically naming it "Scrapbook File." To access your original Scrapbook, go back into your System folder and give the new Scrapbook File another name, such as "Scrapbook File-2." Then change the name of the first Scrapbook File back to "Scrapbook File." The original Scrapbook will then appear when you choose Scrapbook from the Apple menu. You can make as many auxilliary Scrapbooks as you like, although you can use only one at a time.

Unless you're on a tight budget, you might prefer to use a more sophisticated method of organizing your clip art collection. Several companies offer alternatives to the Scrapbook; these are discussed in the following chapter.

Paint Programs

The following tips apply to bitmapped graphics programs such as MacPaint, FullPaint, DeskPaint, and SuperPaint's paint layer.

☞ The biggest mistake clip art neophytes make is resizing artwork in a paint program. Because paint programs operate at 72 dots per inch—the Mac's screen resolution—thay have to tack on pixels to enlarge an image or subtract them to reduce it, often with less-than-pristine results.

To resize an image in a paint program, you surround it with the marquee, hold down the ⌘ key, and drag to enlarge or reduce it. You can retain an object's proportions while resizing it by holding down both the Shift and ⌘ keys as you drag the image.

If you must scale an image in a paint program, your best bet for avoiding distortion is to resize it in powers of two (50% or 200% of its original size, for example) if your program has a Scale command. For best results, however, you should paste a paint image into another program—such as a draw program or a page-layout program—and scale it there. If you don't have such a program, you can paste a graphic into a word processor document and use the word processor's Page Setup or Print command to print it at a reduced size. Paint images look crisp and clean when printed at a reduced size.

☞ Don't panic! If you just filled the entire screen with paint, accidentally erased part of a drawing, or committed a similar atrocity, don't worry, you can undo it—*if* you act immediately. If you make a mistake, immediately go to the Edit menu and select Undo. You must select Undo before performing any other action, including clicking the mouse button while the pointer is anywhere other than in the menu bar.

☞ Mac paint programs offer variations on two selection tools, the lasso and the selection rectangle, also called the marquee. The lasso shrinks to hug the outline of an object it surrounds, while the marquee selects the object and a rectangle of white space that surrounds it.

A rule of bitmapped graphics is: "As it is cut, so it shall be pasted." If you copy a selection with the marquee, the surrounding white space is copied as well, and can obscure underlying objects when the selection is pasted on top of another graphic. To avoid this problem, select images with the lasso before cutting or copying them.

Note: In some paint programs, holding down the ⌘ key while you select an object with the marquee causes the marquee to shrink to fit the selection, à la lasso.

☞ Lassoing can be a delicate operation. You don't have to painstakingly surround an entire object to select it, however. You can lasso most of the object and then release the mouse button; the tail end of the lasso will automatically join up with the starting point, closing the loop around the object.

☞ To make a quick copy of a piece of artwork, select it with the lasso or marquee, hold down the Option key, and drag to "peel off" a copy. You can make multiple copies by repeating this procedure while the object is still selected.

☞ Paint programs provide an eraser tool that's about the size of a real-life pencil eraser. If you need to erase a large area, you'll find the standard eraser too small. On the other hand, for detail work you'll find it too large and cumbersome. Fortunately, you can easily create custom erasers large and small.

The easiest way to create a small custom eraser is to select the paintbrush tool, modify its size, and make it into an eraser by painting in white.

To erase a large area, select the rectangle shape tool and set its border to "none" and its color to white. Then, simply drag the white rectangle over the area you wish to erase.

☞ To keep patterns intact, hold down the ⌘ and Shift keys when resizing bitmapped graphics in Page-Maker.

☞ When you paste a bitmapped graphic into a word processor document, the picture automatically shrinks—if necessary—to fit within the document's margins. If this happens to you, delete the image, adjust the document's ruler to widen the margin, then repaste the graphic.

☞ When you paste a graphic into a word processor document, it lines up with the document's left margin. To move the graphic, click anywhere on it and drag it to the right. (Be careful not to grab one of the "handles" at the corners of the graphic, however, or you'll stretch the image rather than move it.)

☞ Many Mac programs offer an option called "Smoothing" in their Page Setup or Print dialog box. This option applies an algorithm that places intermediate pixels in bitmapped graphics, smoothing their jagged, stairstep appearance when they're printed on a laser printer (see Figure 2.1). Depending on the effect you want, you can select or deselect the Smoothing option before printing.

You should note that the Smoothing option doesn't work with high-resolution imagesetters such as the Linotronic L100 or L300. Therefore, if you print a paint image at a service bureau, it will retain the jaggies. If you want to include smoothed graphics in a document output by a service bureau, you may have to print them on a laser printer and employ old-fashioned pasteup techniques (i.e., real paste).

Draw Programs

Many of the following tips apply to graphics created with object-oriented graphics programs such as MacDraw, MacDraft, DeskDraw, and Dreams, or draw/paint programs such as Canvas and SuperPaint.

☞ If you have a draw program, you can edit clip art that comes in PICT format. In most cases, you'll have to ungroup the image in order to edit it. Once an image is ungrouped, you can reshape curves and change attributes such as line weights and fill patterns. Once you've made your changes, group the image to protect it from further changes.

☞ When you move an object in MacDraw, the object is replaced by a rectangle with a gray border. This technique speeds up the program, since the object doesn't have to be redrawn on the screen as it's moved, but it makes it hard to accurately position the object in relation to other objects. To see the object as you drag it, hold down the ⌘ key when the object nears its destination.

Smoothed:

Not smoothed:

FIGURE 2.1. Your laser printer's smoothing option can improve the appearance of bitmapped graphics.

☞ Dragging small objects in a draw program can be difficult; it's all too easy to accidentally grab a handle and stretch the object instead of moving it. To avoid this annoying occurrence, draw a larger object—such as a rectangle—near the tiny object, select both objects, and drag them in tandem. You can callously delete the helper rectangle when the move is complete.

☞ To "white out" an area of a drawing you don't need, use your draw program's freehand tool to draw a shape on top of it. Select white from the pattern menu and choose the No Border option, and you've blotted out the area.

☞ If you paste a draw image into a paint program, it becomes a series of dots like any other paint image. If you resize the image after pasting it in, patterns will become distorted. You can, however, stretch or shrink an object-oriented graphic in a paint program without distorting the drawing's patterns. First, copy the draw image to the Clipboard or the Scrapbook. Then, open your paint program and use the marquee to draw a rectangle the size you want your graphic to be. The pasted graphic will be resized to fit the selection rectangle, but its patterns will be intact.

☞ Oddly enough, MacDraw doesn't include a scale command. There is a way to reduce a clip art image by a precise percentage, although it involves what's known in computer circles as a *kludge*. This trick entails teaming up the illustration and a square.

First, select the Show Size command, which will display the dimensions of any object you draw. Next, use the Shift key and the rectangle tool to draw a 1-inch square. Select both the square and the graphic, hold down the Shift key to keep the graphic's proportions intact, and drag one of the square's handles; as you resize the square, the illustration is resized along with it. To reduce the graphic to 50% of its original size, for example, you'd shrink the square to 0.5 inches, to reduce it to 75% of its original size you'd shrink it to 0.75 inches, and so on (see Figure 2.2).

☞ If you place a PICT file into a PageMaker document and find that the edges of the image are lost, return to your draw program and surround the image with a box. You can then crop the image to hide the box when you place it into PageMaker.

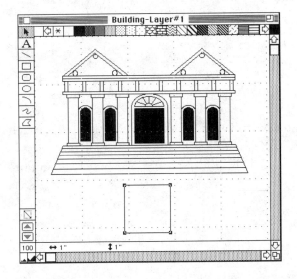

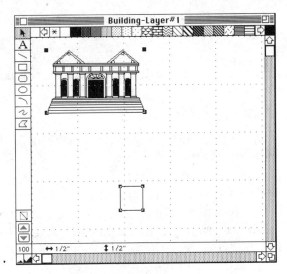

FIGURE 2.2. To proportionally reduce a graphic in MacDraw, select Show Size and resize a square along with the image.

ART AT YOUR FINGERTIPS

You've probably noticed the little pointing hands (☞) sprinkled throughout this chapter. (Such gizmos are known to publishers as *dingbats*.) The hand comes from Adobe Collector's Edition I, a collection of PostScript images. It would have been extremely tedious to place each and every pointing hand into PageMaker when laying out the book; fortunately, we didn't have to.

Instead, we used Art Importer, a nifty utility from Altsys Corporation that converts artwork in PICT or EPS format into a PostScript font. With Art Importer, you simply open a graphics file and assign the image to any key on the Mac's keyboard. You can place up to 256 graphics in a single font, since you can access additional keystrokes with the Shift and Option keys. Art Importer automatically creates a screen and printer version of the new font. You then load it as you would any other font, and type graphics instead of text from your keyboard.

Art Importer is great for dingbats, but it's not limited to tiny graphics. You can print a graphic character at any size your applications will support. This feature makes Art Importer a valuable tool for adding many types of graphics to your documents, including letterheads and logos.

PostScript Programs

The following tips apply to clip art created with Adobe Illustrator or Aldus FreeHand.

☞ If you place an EPS graphic into a document created with a page-layout program such as Quark XPress or PageMaker and take the document to a service bureau to be printed, be sure to take the original EPS graphic with you. If the EPS file isn't included, the graphic won't print.

☞ While FreeHand or Illustrator graphics can be placed in a page-layout program such as PageMaker or Quark XPress and printed from there, not every Mac owner has a page-layout program. Some people use word processors for publishing, and word processors accept artwork in PICT, but not EPS format. Fortunately, a workaround exists. First, open a PostScript clip art illustration with Illustrator or FreeHand. Choose Select All from the Edit menu, then hold down the Option key while you select Copy. This transfers PostScript as well as PICT information to the Clipboard. You can then paste the drawing into a word processor document and print it as you would from a page-layout program.

☞ Illustrator doesn't allow you to rotate a scanned image that you're using as a tracing template. If you're converting a bitmapped or TIFF image to PostScript format, rotate the image in another program, such as DeskPaint, before placing it in Illustrator.

☞ If you're editing a PostScript graphic and add a graduated fill, you're in for some long screen refreshes—and some long waits at the laser printer if you're running periodic proofs. Therefore, you should add graduated or radial fills as the last step in your editing process.

TIFF

The following tips apply to clip art that's in the TIFF format.

☞ If you place a TIFF graphic into a document created with a page-layout program such as Quark XPress or PageMaker and take the document to a service bureau to be printed, be sure to take the original TIFF graphic with you. If the TIFF file isn't included, the graphic won't print.

☞ Some image-processing programs don't include rulers. If you need to see the size of a scanned image on screen, you can scan a ruler and add it to the image before you edit it. You can then delete the ruler when you're finished editing the picture.

Using Mac Art on an IBM PC

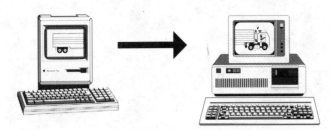

If you want to convert Macintosh clip art into an IBM PC format, you have several options for transferring your Mac art onto IBM PC disks. Once you've made the conversion, you can load graphics in many common Mac formats—MacPaint, EPS, PICT, and MacDraw—directly into PC programs such as PageMaker, Ventura Publisher, WordPerfect, and Microsoft Word.

A number of products can transfer files between the two machines. These include:

• MacLink Plus. This product from Data Viz includes a cable and software for both the Mac and PC end.

• TOPS. To use Sitka's TOPS, you'll need an AppleTalk board in the PC, an AppleTalk network connecting the PC to the Mac, and TOPS software.

• SuperDrive. The easiest way to transfer Mac art to 3.5-inch PC disks is to equip your Mac with Apple's SuperDrive. (This drive is standard equipment on the Mac IIcx and SE/30.) You'll also need the Apple File Exchange utility, which is included on a utilities disk that comes with the Mac.

Because SuperDrive is both the easiest and the most widely available of the file-transfer methods, we'll look at this option in detail.

To transfer a file, you'll first need to copy the clip art onto your Mac's hard disk. Next, you'll need to format a 3.5-inch disk on the PC. Place an unformatted disk in drive A: of the PC, and type **FORMAT a:/t:80/n:9** (or, if the 3.5-inch drive on your PC is drive B, type **FORMAT b:/t:80/n:9**).

Before you insert the PC disk into the Mac's drive, start up the Apple File Exchange utility. When you open Apple File Exchange, you'll see boxes containing lists of files. On the left are the files and folders on your hard disk. Click on the folder that contains your clip art, then click on the image you want to transfer to the PC.

Now insert the PC disk into the Mac's drive. Its contents—if any—will be listed in Apple File Exchange's righthand box. To transfer the file from the Mac to the PC, select the file and click Translate. When the transfer is complete, the file's name will appear in the righthand list.

Eject the disk, insert it in the PC's drive, and place the graphic into a word processor or page-layout program.

Note: Read the licensing agreement that came with your clip art to see if you're permitted to use the artwork on multiple computers.

Miscellany

The following general-purpose tips should increase the efficiency of many a clip artist.

☞ Make sure you work on a copy of an illustration, not on the original. Most clip art companies ensure this practice by locking the contents of a disk, preventing the original drawings from being altered.

☞ To avoid the effort of cutting an image from a page of clip art and placing it into PageMaker, you can simply place the entire page of artwork on PageMaker's pasteboard and use the cropping tool to block out all but the image you need. You can then resize and position the graphic that's still visible.

3
ART ORGANIZERS

nless your clip art collection consists of only a few disks, you'll need to come up with a scheme for organizing your artwork. You don't want to find yourself rattling through a pile of floppy disks every time you need a particular image. Fortunately, you can choose among several art-management approaches, choosing one that fits your work style and budget.

The simplest—and cheapest—approach is the hard-copy technique. If a clip art company offers a catalog along with its wares, you can flip through it to find the image you need. Or you can use the graphics and index in this book for reference. The catalog approach can become cumbersome if you own artwork from dozens of sources, however. Finding the right floppy disk, accessing the illustration you need, and pasting it into a document can take more time than you'd care to spend.

You could, of course, store all your clip art on your hard disk, but a large collection can occupy a good deal of valuable hard-disk real estate. Besides, you're not likely to use every image in every collection

you own. Let's say you publish a newsletter on wildlife conservation, for example. You'll want to browse through pictures of plants, animals, and outdoor scenes, and not clutter up your disk with images of aircraft, office workers, holidays, and other items not pertinent to your project. Since you're using computerized clip art, you may as well let your computer help you sort and retrieve it. You'll have to do some work up front, culling the images you need and placing them in an electronic archival system, but your initial efforts will be rewarded by speedy searches later on. Macintosh art-management tools range from Scrapbook enhancements to full-fledged art organizers that let you search for drawings by name or keyword. In this chapter, we'll look at the entire spectrum of art organizers.

Scrapbook and Clipboard Alternatives

The Mac's Clipboard and Scrapbook were described in the previous chapter. These utilities improve the clip art collectors' lot, but they're not perfect. For example, it would be handy if you could temporarily store more than one image in the Clipboard, enlarge the Scrapbook's window to see an entire picture, save images in formats other than paint or PICT, or edit a Clipboard or Scrapbook image before pasting it into a drawing. Fear not! Several developers have addressed these shortcomings—and others as well—and offer enhancements to Apple's original cut-and-paste duo.

Art RoundUp

Included with Dubl-Click Software's WetPaint clip art series is a nifty desk accessory called Art RoundUp. Unlike the Scrapbook, Art RoundUp doesn't store a collection of drawings for you. Instead, it enables you to search existing collections of MacPaint illustrations by filename until you find the one you need. The utility then lets you open the image you want (whether it's stored on a hard disk or a floppy disk), select the entire image or a portion of it, and paste it into a document— all without leaving the application you're working in.

For example, if you're typing along in Microsoft Word and suddenly feel the urge to insert a graphic, you can simply mosey up to the Apple menu and select Art RoundUp. When you select the DA, you're presented with the window shown in Figure 3.1.

FIGURE 3.1. Art RoundUp.

The desk accessory's menu opens a copy of a MacPaint image and displays it in a resizable window complete with scroll bars. (A grabber tool (the hand icon) lets you nab an image and move it quickly around the window if you find using the scroll bars too slow.) If you find both the grabber and the scroll bars too slow, a Show Page command lets you see a reduced version of an 8 1/2-by-11-inch page and move the viewing area to any part of it.

Art RoundUp offers a small but serviceable collection of tools for modifying a drawing before you copy and paste it. (Since you're working on a copy of a drawing, the original will remain intact.) The lasso and marquee let you surround a portion of an image— an improvement over the Clipboard and Scrapbook, which force you to copy and paste the entire image they contain. The lasso lets you surround an irregular shape, while the marquee selects a rectangular area. The pencil tool allows you to add lines or shading to a drawing, while the eraser wipes out sections you don't need.

The DA's menu offers several editing options as well. Invert changes black to white and vice versa in a selected area, and Flip Horizontal and Flip Vertical change the selection's orientation.

Art RoundUp saves you the trouble of filling the Scrapbook with images, since you can simply insert a disk of artwork and copy an image on the fly. This utility conserves hard disk space as well, since each image you place in the Scrapbook eats up memory.

SmartScrap & The Clipper

Solutions International decided to improve on both the Scrapbook and the Clipboard, replacing them with two custom desk accessories. Solutions' enhancements are packaged together as SmartScrap & The Clipper II. SmartScrap is indeed smarter than the original Scrapbook. In addition to letting you cut, copy, and paste graphics, SmartScrap offers the following capabilities:

☞ You can create several scrapbooks and give each its own name, switching among scrapbooks when necessary.

☞ You can give each scrapbook page a name and search for pages by name, rather than using the original Scrapbook's hit-or-miss method of scrolling through its contents to find a particular picture. You can also search for a drawing by means of a pictorial table of contents, which shows a miniature version of each drawing in the scrapbook.

☞ As with Art RoundUp, you can resize the window, move horizontally or vertically with scroll bars, and cut or copy a portion of an image with a lasso or marquee tool. If the image you're copying is larger than the displayed window, the selection tool scrolls when you hit the window's edge, allowing you to select large drawings.

☞ You can print some or all of the pages in a scrapbook.

You install SmartScrap as you would any desk accessory, and it's waiting for you in the Apple menu from within any application that supports desk accessories. To create a SmartScrap scrapbook, you select the desk accessory and choose New Scrapbook in the SmartScrap menu that appears. SmartScrap opens a blank scrapbook file, which you then proceed to fill with pictures. You can copy and paste images one by one, or use the ScrapMaker utility, which lets you add an entire folder's worth of MacPaint or MacDraw images to a scrapbook at once.

Once you've pasted an image into a SmartScrap scrapbook, you can assign the image a name to help you locate it later with the utility's Find Page command (see Figure 3.2).

When you need an image from a SmartScrap scrapbook, you select SmartScrap, switch to the scrapbook you need, flip through the scrapbook's pages or use the Find Page command to find the appropriate image, and copy all or part of the image with the lasso or marquee. Since SmartScrap is a desk accessory, you can do all this without leaving the application you're using.

SmartScrap's companion program, The Clipper, lets you modify an image in the Mac's Clipboard

FIGURE 3.2. *SmartScrap lets you name images to help you find them later.*

before you paste it into a document. With The Clipper, you can trim or scale drawings to a specified size before you paste them into a document, or use a special command to exclude extraneous elements—such as text—that you don't want to paste into your document.

You might use The Clipper to scale a large MacDraw image to fit within the margins of a MacWrite document, or to trim an unwanted area from a MacPaint image before pasting it in. Unfortunately, The Clipper's scaling function can distort bitmapped graphics, so this DA is most useful for PICT-format drawings.

MultiClip

While SmartScrap gives you access to multiple scrapbooks, Olduvai Corporation's MultiClip lets you create multiple clipboards. But MultiClip improves on Apple's Clipboard in a number of ways. The Mac's Clipboard, as you'll recall, can store only one item at a time. MultiClip lets you place numerous items into a clipboard; an item is added to the clipboard's collection rather than replacing the previous contents (see

Figure 3.3).

MultiClip is an INIT; you simply drag its icon into your Mac's System folder, and the utility appears as a desk accessory in the Apple menu when you start up your Mac.

MultiClip actually resembles the traditional Scrapbook more than it does the Clipboard, in that it stores multiple images and its contents won't disappear when you turn off the Mac. But it offers one advantage of the Clipboard: each image is automatically added to MultiClip when it's cut or copied, whereas with the Scrapbook you must cut or copy an image, open the Scrapbook desk accessory, and paste the image into the Scrapbook. MultiClip, then, offers the best of both utilities: the speed of the Clipboard and the permanent storage capabilities of the Scrapbook.

Like SmartScrap, MultiClip lets you save several MultiClip files and select among them, as well as select a portion of a graphic to cut or copy.

The latest version of MultiClip lets you copy, store, and paste sounds as well as graphics.

Art Organizers

Utilities like Art RoundUp, SmartScrap, and Multi-Clip can reduce the chaos of your clip art collection,

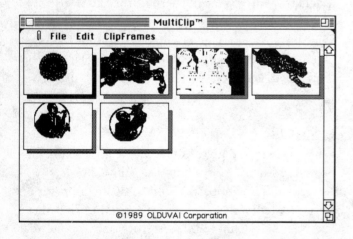

FIGURE 3.3. MultiClip combines the capabilities of the Clipboard and the Scrapbook.

but to efficiently access images in a large collection, you might want to graduate to a full-scale art organizer. Art organizers have several advantages over the Clipboard and Scrapbook alternatives just described. Among their pluses are the ability to deal with multiple graphics formats—including TIFF and EPS—and their ability to search for drawings using keywords that you assign.

We'll look at three art organizers in the section that follows.

Mariah

Mariah, from Symmetry Corporation, is billed as a "multimedia organizer." This utility lets you keep track of graphics, sound, text, and animation files. With Mariah, you can organize your clip art into collections that contain Paint, PICT, PICT2, TIFF, and EPS files. Each collection can contain as many as 32,000 items (whether you have enough space on your hard disk to accommodate 32,000 items is another matter). Several collections can be open at once.

You can set up collectionss any way you want, giving each a title that describes its contents. You might create a separate library for each project you're working on, or create libraries devoted to subjects such as "Dingbats" or "Transportation." Mariah creates postage-stamp-size miniatures of each illustration you add; you can flip through the miniatures in each library or page through full-size drawings until you find the image you want. To augment its electronic archives, Mariah can print catalogs of the thumbnails in each of your collections, or display them as a slide show (including sounds and animations if you've archived them).

You can also search for a drawing by title, or by keywords you assign. Mariah allows you to search either a single library or all libraries on disk.

When you find the appropriate drawing, you can select all or part of it, copy it to the Clipboard, and paste it into a document. A Place button transfers a copy of the selected drawing directly into programs that have a Place command, such as Quark XPress or PageMaker; you don't have to copy the image to the Clipboard and then paste it into the document.

As a bonus, Mariah lets you convert one file format to another (EPS to TIFF, for example). This feature can come in handy if an application doesn't support a certain type of format.

PictureBook+

Loop Software's PictureBook+ lets you catalog images in a number of scrapbook files.

PictureBook+ can be used as a stand-alone application or installed as a desk accessory if you prefer. Both versions offer the same features. When you open PictureBook+, you're presented with a resizable, scrollable window like the one shown in Figure 3.4. When you add an image, an "Untitled" icon appears, and you can then name the image.

Like Mariah and SmartScrap, PictureBook+ lets you create as many graphics libraries as your hard disk space will allow. You can open all of your Picture-Book+ libraries at once, so you can easily cut, copy, and paste among them. The utility's Finder-like interface lets you drag picture icons into other libraries, or into a trash can icon if you wish to delete them.

With PictureBook+, you can view thumbnails of your images, or search by image name or keyword. You can print a single image or an entire catalog.

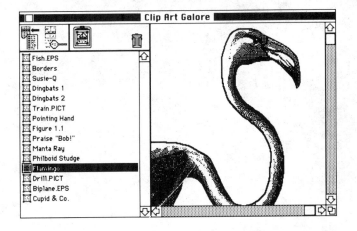

PictureBook+ accepts graphics in paint, PICT, TIFF, and EPS format. The program can import graphics from the Scrapbook or SmartScrap as well. A handy option treats EPS files as though they were PICT files, allowing you to copy them to the Clipboard and paste them into various applications. The PostScript data in the EPS file is included with the PICT image, and the graphic will print as PostScript.

Multi-Ad Search

Multi-Ad Search lets you build a database of up to 32,000 images in paint, PICT, EPS, TIFF, or RIFF format. You can search for an image by file name, keyword, volume, or file type.

Like the other utilities described in this chapter, Multi-Ad Search lets you view thumbnails of graphics once they're located and print a catalog of images if you wish. You can copy and paste the image you need, or place it directly into a layout program like QuarkXPress or Multi-Ad Creator.

One More Option: Stuff It!

It's up to you to decide which—if any—of the art organizers meets your needs. If you're not the organized type, the least you can do is save yourself some disk space. An indispensible utility called StuffIt can compress your graphics files, allowing you to cram more artwork onto a hard disk or floppy. You can store clip art libraries in compressed form until you're ready to use them, then use the utility to decompress the graphics. StuffIt is not only a space saver, but is invaluable for transferring files electronically, trimming your phone bill and online service charges.

The original version of StuffIt is available as shareware from your local Mac user group. An enhanced, commercial version called StuffIt Deluxe is available for $99.95 from Aladdin Systems.

FIGURE 3.4. PictureBook+ offers a Finder-like interface that allows you to drag filenames from one graphics library to another.

APPENDIX: VENDOR INFORMATION

Additional Clip Art Companies
The following companies are not shown in this book. You may wish to contact them for information about their clip art.

Advantage Computing
1803 Mission St., Suite 416
Santa Cruz, CA 95060
800/356-4666
(Misc. subjects)

Alpha Telecommunications
1245 16th St., Suite 100
Santa Monica, CA 90404
800/736-1567
(Medical)

Applied Microsystems
3111 C St., Suite 325
Anchorage, AK 99503
800/327-2588, 907/261-8702
(Misc. subjects)

The ArtMaker Company
500 N. Claremont Blvd.
Claremont, CA 91711
(Misc. subjects)

BBL Typographic
52A Mt. Stuart Rd.
Mt. Stuart, Tasmania 7000, Australia
Phone: 002-312382 (from US: 011-61-02-312382)
Fax: 002-312385 (from US: 011-61-02-312385)
(Ornaments from antique Bibles)

BudgetBytes
1647 SW 41st St.
Topeka, KS 66609
913/266-2200 or 913/266-2288
(Misc. subjects)

Dream Maker Software
7217 Foothill Blvd.
Tujunga, CA 91042-9988
Phone: 818/353-2297
Fax: 818/353-6988
(Misc. subjects; flags)

Educorp Computer Services
7434 Trade St.
San Diego, CA 92121-2410
Phone: 800/843-9497, 619/536-9999
Fax: 619/536-2345
(Misc. subjects)

Empire Berol USA
Rapidesign Division
P.O. Box 990
San Fernando, CA 91340
800/323-2454
(Architecture, electronics)

Farcus Cartoons
Box 3006, Station C
Ottawa, Ontario
K1Y 4J3 Canada
Phone: 613/235-5944
Fax: 613/230-3873
(Business cartoons)

Imagine That! Publications
12200 Marion Ln., Suite 5120
Minnetonka, MN 55343
612/593-9085
(Clothing design components)

MacMedic Publications, Inc.
5805 Westheimer
Houston, TX 77057
Phone: 800/477-0717, 713/977-2655
Fax: 713/784-3759
(Medical)

Nova Cube
14 Jarrell Farms Dr.
Newark, DE 19711
302/234-1098
(Military)

One Mile Up
7011 Evergreen Ct.
Annandale, VA 22003
800/258-5280
(Government; military)

Pacific Rim Connections, Inc.
3030 Atwater Dr.
Burlingame, CA 94010
Phone: 415/697-0911
Fax: 415/697-9439
(Oriental images)

Pleasant Graphic Ware, Inc.
P.O. Box 506
Pleasant Hill, OR 97455
503/345-5796
(Misc. subjects; heraldry)

Showker Graphic Arts & Design
15 Southgate
Harrisonburg, VA 22801
703/433-1527
(Misc. subjects)

So-Cal Graphics
8340 Clairemont Mesa Blvd.
San Diego, CA 92111
800/368-3823
(Trademarks)

Software-of-the-Month Club
2180 Las Palmas Dr.
Carlsbad, CA 92009
Phone: 619/931-8111, Fax: 619/931-8383
(Misc. subjects)

TechPool Studios
1463 Warrensville Center Rd.
Cleveland, OH 44121
Phone: 800/777-8930, 216/382-1234
Fax: 216/382-1915
(Medical)

Totem Graphics, Inc.
5109-A Capitol Boulevard
Tumwater, WA 98501
206/352-1851
(Misc. subjects; animals)

TS Graphics
108 Shrewsbury Ave.
Red Bank, NJ 07701
Phone: 908/530-5959, Fax: 908/219-0822
(Misc. subjects)

Wayzata Technology Inc.
P.O. Box 807
Grand Rapids, MN 55744
Phone: 800/735-7321, 218/326-0597
Fax: 218/326-0598
(Misc. subjects; nature)

Wheeler Arts
66 Lake Park
Champaign, IL 61821-7101
Phone: 217/359-6816, Fax: 217/359-8716
(Misc. subjects)

3-D Clip Art

The following companies offer clip art created with 3-D graphics programs.

NEC Home Electronics (USA) Inc.
Computer Products Division
1255 Michael Drive
Wood Dale, IL 60191-1094
708/860-9500

MacroMind/Paracomp
600 Townsend, #310-W
San Francisco, CA 94103
Phone: 415/442-0200
Fax: 415/442-0190

Digitized Photos

The following companies offer digitized photos on CD-ROM.

Discimagery
18 East 16th St.
New York, NY 10003
212/675-8500

D'pix
1570 Fishinger Rd.
Columbus, OH 43221
Phone: 800/238-3749, 614/451-4372
Fax: 614/451-5899

Image Club Graphics
#5, 1902 11th St. SE
Calgary, Alberta
T2G 3G2 Canada
Phone: 800/661-9410
Fax: 403/261-7013

NEC Home Electronics (USA) Inc.
Computer Products Division
1255 Michael Drive
Wood Dale, IL 60191-1094
708/860-9500

Tactic Software
11925 SW 128th St.
Miami, FL 33186
Phone: 800/344-4818, 305/378-4110
Fax: 305/232-7467

Wayzata Technology Inc.
P.O. Box 807
Grand Rapids, MN 55744
Phone: 800/735-7321, 218/326-0597
Fax: 218/326-0598

Custom Clip Art Services

The following companies will create custom clip art for you. Showker also offers a wide array of images culled from public-domain sources and Mac user groups.

Showker Graphic Arts & Design
15 Southgate
Harrisonburg, VA 22801
703/433-1527

Wordscapes
4546 B-10 El Camino Real
Los Altos, CA 94022-1041
415/968-8737

Utilities

This section lists the various utilities mentioned in this book.

Art Importer
Altsys Corporation
269 W. Renner Rd.
Richardson, TX 75080
Phone: 214/680-2060, Fax: 214/680-0537

Art RoundUp
Dubl-Click Software, Inc.
9316 Deering Ave.
Chatsworth, CA 91311
818/700-9525

MacLink Plus
Data Viz, Inc.
55 Corporate Dr.
Trumbull, CT 06611
203/268-0030

Mariah
Symmetry Corporation
8603 E. Royal Palm Rd. #110
Scottsdale, AZ 85258
800/624-2485, 602/844-2190

MultiClip
Olduvai Corporation
7520 Red Road, Suite A
South Miami, FL 33143
Phone: 800/548-5151, 305/665-4665
Fax: 305/665-0671

Multi-Ad Search
Multi-Ad Services
1720 W. Detweiller Dr.
Peoria, IL 61615
800/447-1950, 309/692-1530

PictureBook+
Loop Software
P.O. Box 1249
Menlo Park, CA 94026
415/326-4803

SmartScrap and The Clipper II
Solutions Inc.
30 Commerce Street
P.O. Box 783
Williston, VT 05495
Phone: 802/865-9220
Fax: 802/865-9224

StuffIt Deluxe
Aladdin Systems
165 Westridge Dr.
Watsonville, CA 95016
Phone: 408/761-6200
Fax: 408/761-6200

TOPS
Sitka
950 Marina Village Parkway
Alameda, CA 94501
510/769-9669

Animated Clip Art

The following company offers "animation clips" for multimedia presentations.

Media In Motion
P.O. Box 170130
San Francisco, CA 94117
Phone: 800/395-2547, 415/621-0707
Fax: 415/621-1724

CLIP ART CATALOG

Adobe Systems, Inc.

1585 Charleston Road
Mountain View, CA 94039
415-961-4400
800-344-8335 orders, U.S. and Canada

◆

Collection	Format	No./Size Disks	Price	Computer
Collector's Edition:				
Patterns & Textures	Illustrator	8-800K	$225.00	Mac
Symbols, Borders, & Letterforms	Illustrator	2-800K	$125.00	Mac

Patterns and Textures Disk 1

Dot Patterns

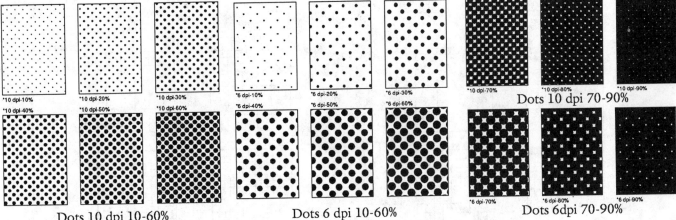

Dots 10 dpi 70-90%

Dots 10 dpi 10-60%   Dots 6 dpi 10-60%   Dots 6dpi 70-90%

Gradations

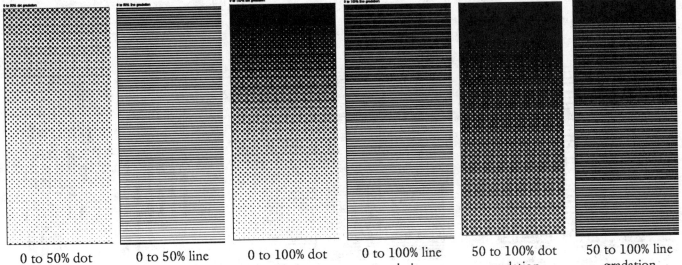

| 0 to 50% dot gradation | 0 to 50% line gradation | 0 to 100% dot gradation | 0 to 100% line gradation | 50 to 100% dot gradation | 50 to 100% line gradation |

Undulating Gradations

Patterns and Textures Disk 1 (continued)

Line Patterns

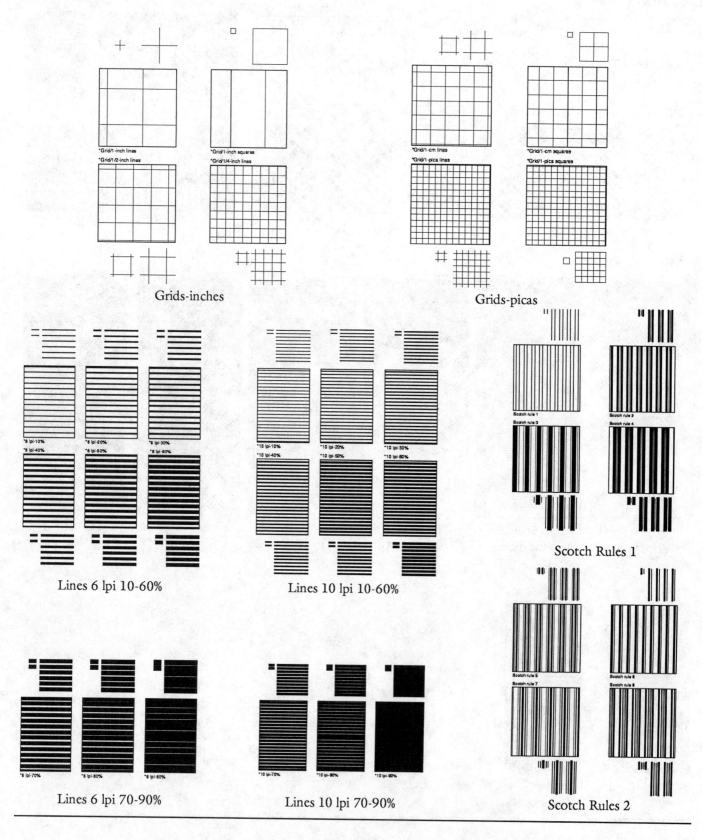

Grids-inches

Grids-picas

Lines 6 lpi 10-60%

Lines 10 lpi 10-60%

Scotch Rules 1

Lines 6 lpi 70-90%

Lines 10 lpi 70-90%

Scotch Rules 2

Patterns and Textures Disk 2

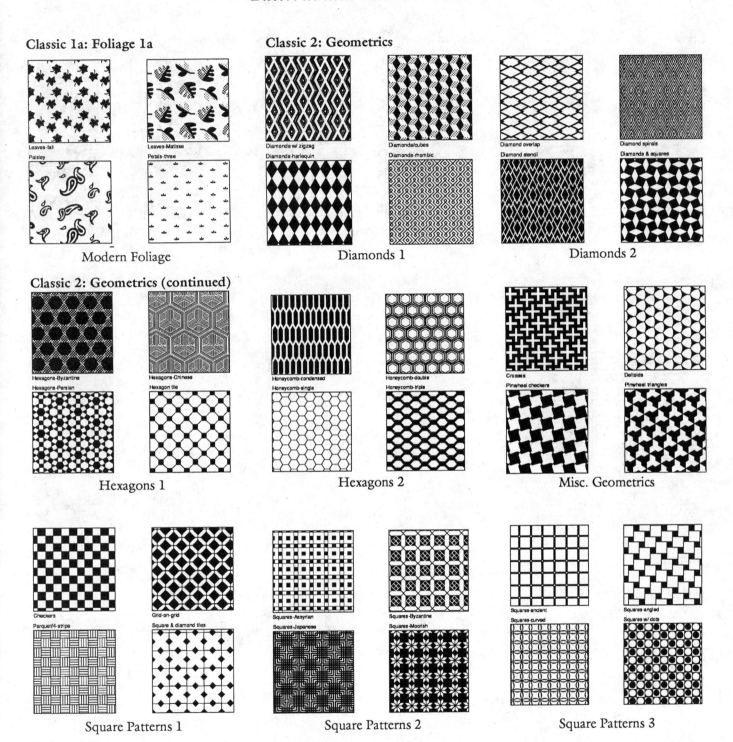

Classic 1a: Foliage 1a

Leaves-fall | Leaves-Matisse
Paisley | Petals-three

Modern Foliage

Classic 2: Geometrics

Diamonds w/ zigzag | Diamonds/cubes | Diamond overlap | Diamond spirals
Diamonds-harlequin | Diamonds-rhombic | Diamond stencil | Diamonds & squares

Diamonds 1   Diamonds 2

Classic 2: Geometrics (continued)

Hexagons-Byzantine | Hexagons-Chinese | Honeycomb-condensed | Honeycomb-double | Crosses | Deltoids
Hexagons-Persian | Hexagon tile | Honeycomb-single | Honeycomb-triple | Pinwheel checkers | Pinwheel triangles

Hexagons 1   Hexagons 2   Misc. Geometrics

Checkers | Grid-on-grid | Squares-Assyrian | Squares-Byzantine | Squares-ancient | Squares-angled
Parquet/4-stripe | Square & diamond tiles | Squares-Japanese | Squares-Moorish | Squares-curved | Squares w/ dots

Square Patterns 1   Square Patterns 2   Square Patterns 3

Patterns and Textures Disk 2 (continued)

Classic 2: Geometrics

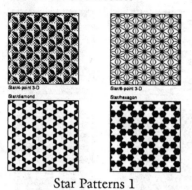

Star/4-point 3-D · Star/6-point 3-D
Star/diamond · Star/hexagon

Star Patterns 1

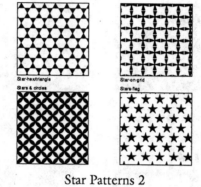

Star-hex/triangle · Star-on-grid
Stars & circles · Stars-flag

Star Patterns 2

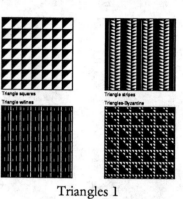

Triangle squares · Triangle stripes
Triangle wflines · Triangles-Byzantine

Triangles 1

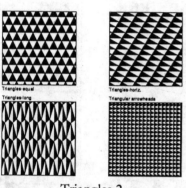

Triangles-equal · Triangles-horiz.
Triangles-long · Triangular arrowheads

Triangles 2

Patterns and Textures Disk 3

Classic 3: Misc. Classic

Arrows-Arabian
Arrows-fat tail
Arrows-reverse
Arrows-tricolor

Arrow Patterns

Cloth-woven
Herringbone 1
Herringbone 2
Houndstooth

Fabrics

Knit
Lattice-thin
Lattice-thick
Links

Interlocks 1

Links-Japanese
Perl
Weave-cane
Weave-Y

Interlocks 2

Plaid 1
Plaid 2
Plaid 3
Plaid 4

Plaids 1

Plaid 5
Plaid 6
Plaid 7

Plaids 2

Scallops
Scallops-dotted
Scallops-Japanese
Scallops-pointed

Scallops

Waves-scroll
Waves-smooth
Waves-water

Waves

Zigzag
Zigzag-nervous
Zigzag-stripe

Zigzags

Patterns and Textures Disk 3 (continued)

Classic 3: Modern Art

Laguna

Lanterns

Deco 3-D boxes

Deco diamonds

Op checkerboard

Op eyes

Spiked scallop

Deco half-circles

Deco spiked arch

Op rectangles

Op squares 1

1950's

Art Deco

Op Art 1

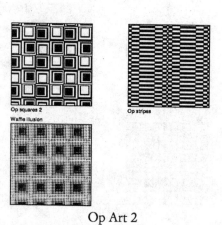

Op squares 2

Op stripes

Waffle Illusion

Op Art 2

Patterns and Textures Disk 4

Classic 4: Ornamentals

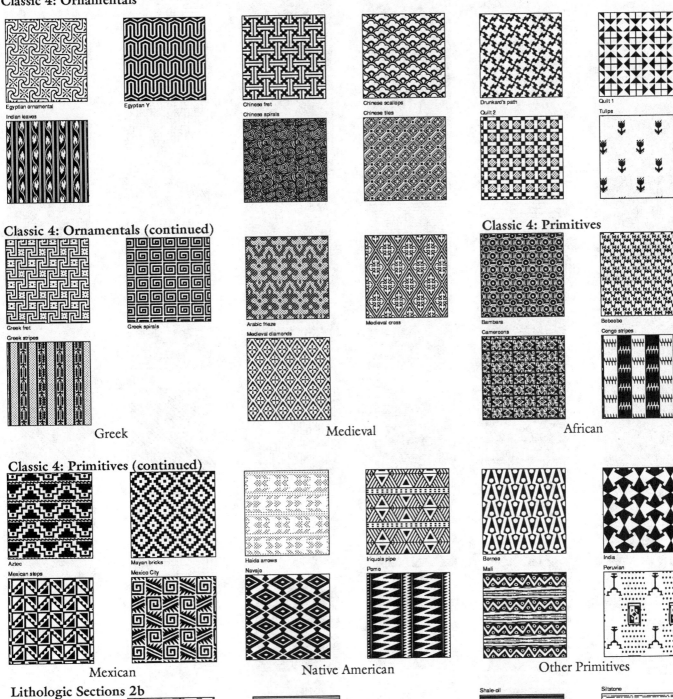

Egyptian ornamental · Egyptian Y · Chinese fret · Chinese scallops · Drunkard's path · Quilt 1
Indian leaves · Chinese spirals · Chinese tiles · Quilt 2 · Tulips

Classic 4: Ornamentals (continued)

Greek fret · Greek spirals · Arabic frieze · Medieval cross · Bambara · Boboobo
Greek stripes · Medieval diamonds · Cameroons · Congo stripes

Greek — Medieval — African — Classic 4: Primitives

Classic 4: Primitives (continued)

Aztec · Mayan bricks · Haida arrows · Iriquois pipe · Borneo · India
Mexican steps · Mexico City · Navajo · Pomo · Mali · Peruvian

Mexican — Native American — Other Primitives

Lithologic Sections 2b

Shale-calcareous · Shale-carbonaceous · Lithologic 11 · Shale-oil · Siltstone

Patterns and Textures Disk 5

Architectural Graphic Standards: Architectural Sections

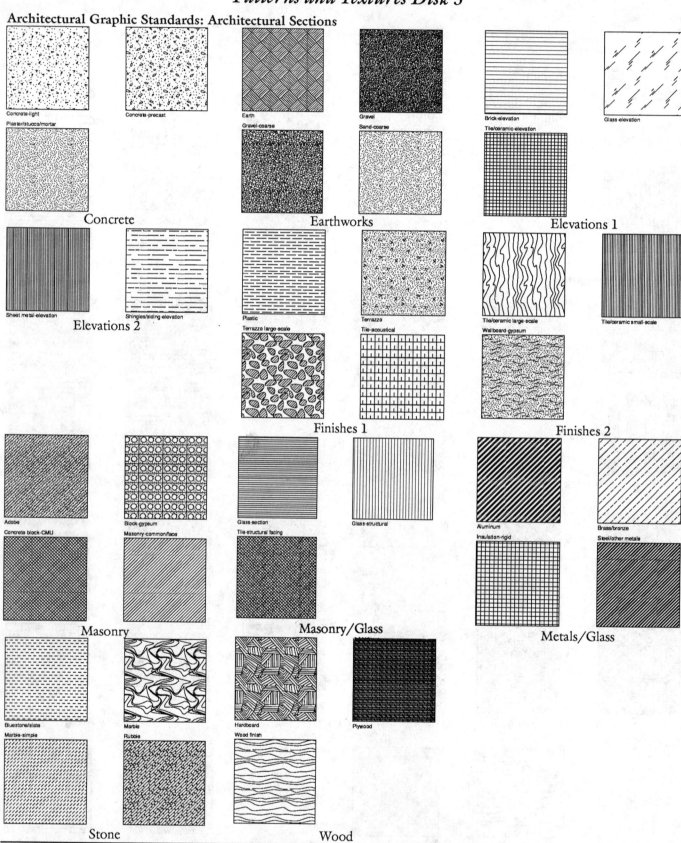

Concrete-light

Concrete-precast

Earth

Gravel

Brick-elevation

Glass-elevation

Plaster/stucco/mortar

Gravel-coarse

Sand-coarse

Tile/ceramic-elevation

Concrete

Earthworks

Elevations 1

Sheet metal-elevation

Shingles/siding-elevation

Plastic

Terrazzo

Tile/ceramic large-scale

Tile/ceramic small-scale

Elevations 2

Terrazzo large-scale

Tile-acoustical

Wallboard-gypsum

Finishes 1

Finishes 2

Adobe

Block-gypsum

Glass-section

Glass-structural

Aluminum

Brass/bronze

Concrete block-CMU

Masonry-common/face

Tile-structural facing

Insulation-rigid

Steel/other metals

Masonry

Masonry/Glass

Metals/Glass

Bluestone/slate

Marble

Hardboard

Plywood

Marble-simple

Rubble

Wood finish

Stone

Wood

Patterns and Textures Disk 6

Architectural Graphic Standards:
Architectural Surfaces

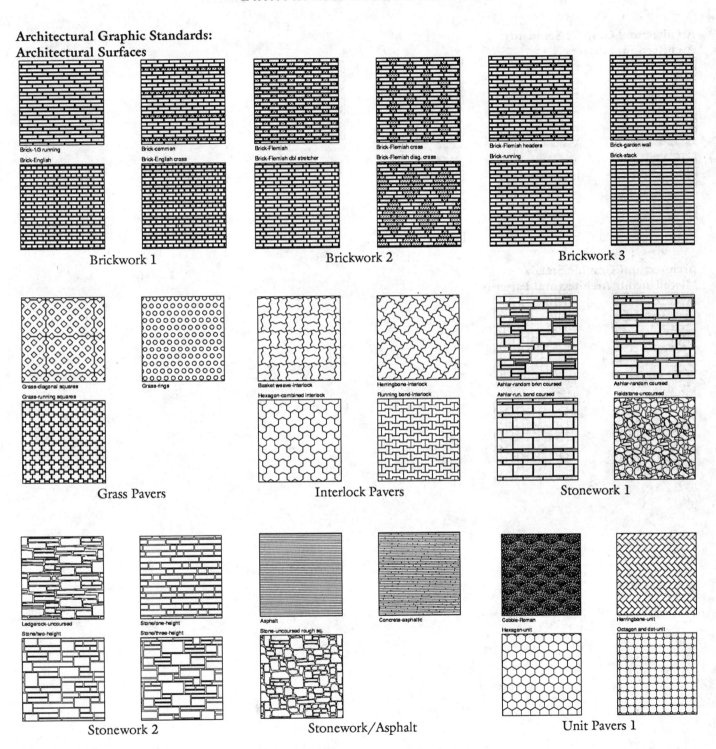

Brick-1/3 running Brick-common Brick-Flemish Brick-Flemish cross Brick-Flemish headers Brick-garden wall

Brick-English Brick-English cross Brick-Flemish dbl stretcher Brick-Flemish diag. cross Brick-running Brick-stack

Brickwork 1   **Brickwork 2**   **Brickwork 3**

Grass-diagonal squares Grass-rings Basket weave-interlock Herringbone-interlock Ashlar-random brkn coursed Ashlar-random coursed

Grass-running squares Hexagon-combined interlock Running bond-interlock Ashlar-run. bond coursed Fieldstone-uncoursed

Grass Pavers   **Interlock Pavers**   **Stonework 1**

Ledgerock-uncoursed Stone/one-height Asphalt Concrete-asphaltic Cobble-Roman Herringbone-unit

Stone/two-height Stone/three-height Stone-uncoursed rough sq. Hexagon-unit Octagon and dot-unit

Stonework 2   **Stonework/Asphalt**   **Unit Pavers 1**

Patterns and Textures Disk 6 (continued)

Architectural Graphic Standards:
Architectural Surfaces

Parquet/bskt weave-unit

Running bond-unit

Parquet/bskt weave-inter.

Running bond diag.-interlock

Running bond diag.-unit

Stack bond-unit

Stack bond square-unit

Unit Pavers 2

Unit/Interlock Pavers

Architectural Graphic Standards:
Miscellaneous Architectural Patterns

Roof-slate

Roof-tile

Shingle-rough

Tile-Spanish

Roofing

Patterns and Textures Disk 7

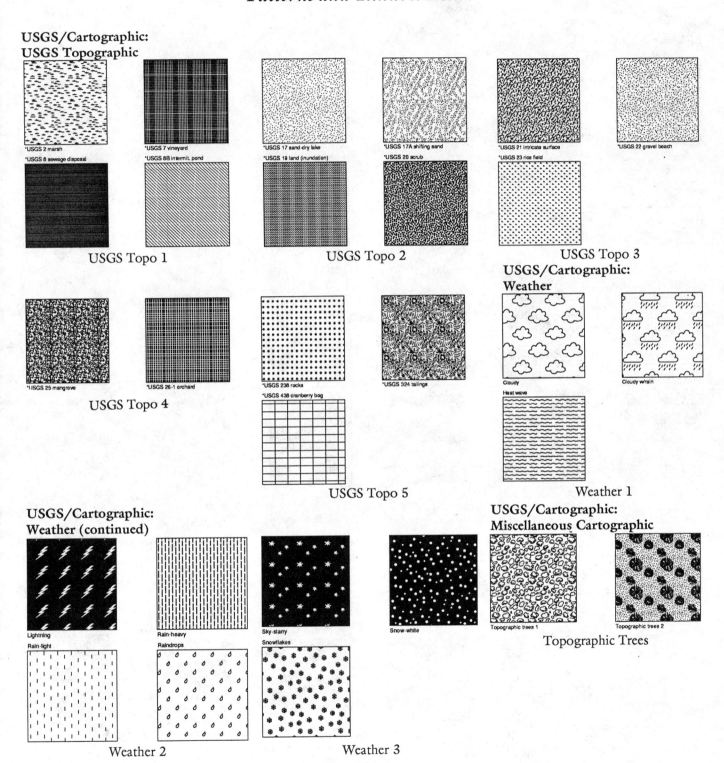

USGS/Cartographic:
USGS Topographic

*USGS 2 marsh
*USGS 7 vineyard
*USGS 17 sand-dry lake
*USGS 17A shifting sand
*USGS 21 intricate surface
*USGS 22 gravel beach

*USGS 8 sewage disposal
*USGS 8B intermit. pond
*USGS 19 land (inundation)
*USGS 20 scrub
*USGS 23 rice field

USGS Topo 1
USGS Topo 2
USGS Topo 3

USGS/Cartographic:
Weather

*USGS 25 mangrove
*USGS 26-1 orchard
*USGS 238 rocks
*USGS 324 tailings
Cloudy
Cloudy w/rain

USGS Topo 4
*USGS 438 cranberry bog
Heat wave

USGS Topo 5
Weather 1

USGS/Cartographic:
Weather (continued)

USGS/Cartographic:
Miscellaneous Cartographic

Lightning
Rain-heavy
Sky-starry
Snow-white
Topographic trees 1
Topographic trees 2

Rain-light
Raindrops
Snowflakes
Topographic Trees

Weather 2
Weather 3

Patterns and Textures Disk 8

Lithologic Sections 1

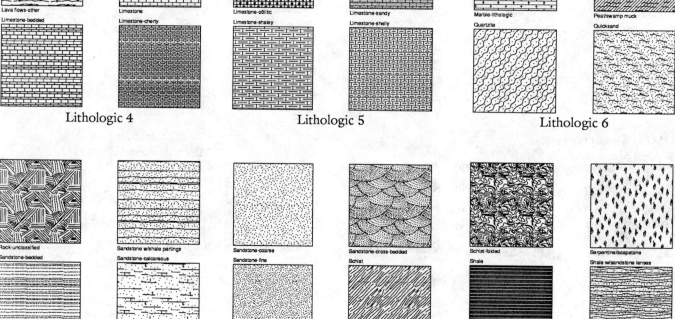

Anhydrite | Breccia | Chert-bedded | Chert-shaley | Dolomite | Gneiss
Breccia/tuff | Chalk | Claystone | Conglomerate | Gypsum | Lava flows-basic

Lithologic 1   Lithologic 2   Lithologic 3

Lava flows-other | Limestone | Limestone-oölitic | Limestone-sandy | Marble-lithologic | Peat/swamp muck
Limestone-bedded | Limestone-cherty | Limestone-shaley | Limestone-shelly | Quartzite | Quicksand

Lithologic 4   Lithologic 5   Lithologic 6

Rock-unclassified | Sandstone w/shale partings | Sandstone-coarse | Sandstone-cross-bedded | Schist-folded | Serpentine/soapstone
Sandstone-bedded | Sandstone-calcareous | Sandstone-fine | Schist | Shale | Shale w/sandstone lenses

Lithologic 8   Lithologic 9   Lithologic 10

Patterns and Textures Disk 9

Basic Graphics 2:
Textures/Mezzotints

Mezzotint-dot

Mezzotint-shape

Mezzotints

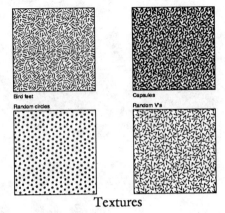

Bird feet

Capsules

Random circles

Random V's

Textures

Classic 1b:
Foliage 1b

Leaf-triple

Pansies

Thistle

Water lilies

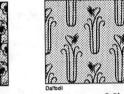

Daffodil

Floral vines

Misc. Florals 1

Morning glories

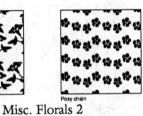

Posy chain

Misc. Florals 2

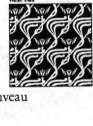

Art Nouveau

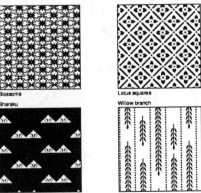

Blossoms

Lotus squares

Sharaku

Willow branch

Japanese Florals

Lithologic Sections 1b

Rock-granitic

Rock-massive igneous 1

Rock-massive igneous 2

Rock-porphyritic igneous

Lithologic 7

Symbols, Borders & Letterforms Disk 1

Font Outlines

 Punctuation 1.1
 Punctuation 1.2
 Punctuation 1.3

Punctuation 1.4   Punctuation 1.5   Punctuation 1.6

Punctuation 1.7   Punctuation 1.8   Punctuation 1.9

Punctuation 1.10   Punctuation 1.11   Punctuation 1.12

Punctuation 1

Punctuation 2.1   Punctuation 2.2   Punctuation 2.3

Punctuation 2.4   Punctuation 2.5   Punctuation 2.6

Punctuation 2.7   Punctuation 2.8   Punctuation 2.9

Punctuation 2.10   Punctuation 2.11

Punctuation 2

Special Punct. 1.1   Special Punct. 1.2   Special Punct. 1.3
Special Punct. 1.4   Special Punct. 1.5
Special Punct. 1.6   Special Punct. 1.7
Special Punct. 1.8   Special Punct. 1.9   Special Punct. 1.10

Punctuation for Special Effects

ABCDEFGHIJ KLMNOPQRST UVWXYZ abcdefghijklm nopqrstuvw xyz .,:!? 1234567890 $¢£¥ƒ(){}[] &

Sans Serif

ABDOPQR abdegopq 46890&£

Sans Serif for Special Effects

ABDOPQR abdegopq 46890&£

Serif for Special Effects

ABCDEFGHI JKLMNOPQ RSTUVWXYZ abcdefghijk lmnopqrstuv wxyz.,:;!? 1234567890 $¢£¥ƒ()[]{} &

Serif

Graphics

Arrow 1.1 ... Arrow 1.12   **Arrows 1**

Arrow 2.1 ... Arrow 2.12   **Arrows 2**

Arrow 3.1 ... Arrow 3.12   **Arrows 3**

Symbols, Borders & Letterforms Disk 1 (continued)

Graphics (continued)

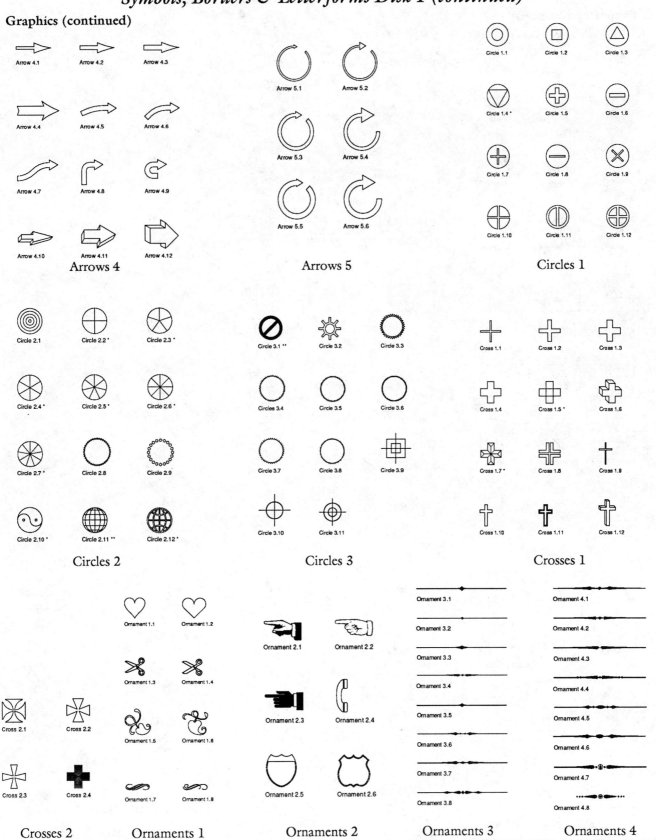

Arrows 4

Arrows 5

Circles 1

Circles 2

Circles 3

Crosses 1

Crosses 2

Ornaments 1

Ornaments 2

Ornaments 3

Ornaments 4

Symbols, Borders & Letterforms Disk 1 (continued)

Graphics (continued)

Polygon 1.1	Polygon 1.2	Polygon 1.3
Polygon 1.4	Polygon 1.5	Polygon 1.6
Polygon 1.7	Polygon 1.8	Polygon 1.9
Polygon 1.10 *	Polygon 1.11	

Polygons 1

Polygon 2.1	Polygon 2.2	Polygon 2.3
Polygon 2.4	Polygon 2.5	Polygon 2.6
Polygon 2.7	Polygon 2.8	Polygon 2.9
Polygon 2.10 *	Polygon 2.11 *	Polygon 2.12 *

Polygons 2

Polygon 3.1	Polygon 3.2	Polygon 3.3 *
Polygon 3.4	Polygon 3.5	Polygon 3.6 *
Polygon 3.7	Polygon 3.8	
Polygon 3.9	Polygon 3.10	

Polygons 3

Square 1.1	Square 1.2	Square 1.3
Square 1.4	Square 1.5	Square 1.6
Square 1.7	Square 1.8	Square 1.9
Square 1.10 *	Square 1.11	Square 1.12 *

Squares 1

Square 2.1	Square 2.2	Square 2.3
Square 2.4	Square 2.5	Square 2.6
Square 2.7	Square 2.8	Square 2.9
Square 2.10	Square 2.11	Square 2.12

Squares 2

Square 3.1 *	Square 3.2 *	Square 3.3 *
Square 3.4	Square 3.5 *	Square 3.6 *
Square 3.7 *	Square 3.8	Square 3.9
Square 3.10	Square 3.11	

Squares 3

Square 4.1	Square 4.2
Square 4.3	Square 4.4

Squares 4

Star 1.1	Star 1.2 **	Star 1.3 *
Star 1.4	Star 1.5	Star 1.6
Star 1.7	Star 1.8	Star 1.9 *
Star 1.10	Star 1.11	Star 1.12

Stars 1

Star 2.1	Star 2.2	Star 2.3 *
Star 2.4	Star 2.5	Star 2.6 *
Star 2.7	Star 2.8	Star 2.9 *
Star 2.10	Star 2.11	Star 2.12 *

Stars 2

Symbols, Borders & Letterforms Disk 1 (continued)

Graphics (continued)

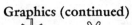

Stars 3

Stars 4

Textboxes 1

Special Effects Examples

Drop Shadows

Multiple Outlines

Offset Outlines

Reverse Effects

ADOBE®

Symbols, Borders & Letterforms Disk 2

Building-Block Borders

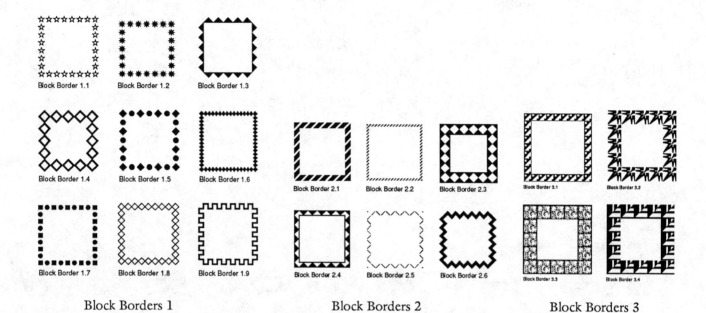

Block Borders 1   Block Borders 2   Block Borders 3

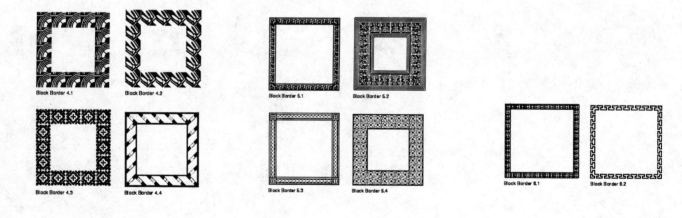

Block Borders 4   Block Borders 5   Block Borders 6

Symbols, Borders & Letterforms Disk 2 (continued)

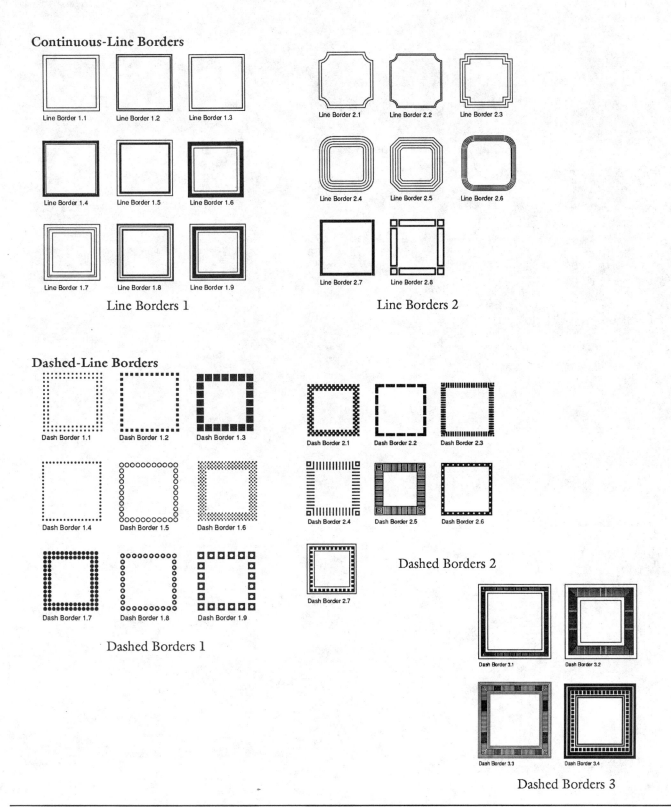

Continuous-Line Borders

Line Borders 1

Line Borders 2

Dashed-Line Borders

Dashed Borders 1

Dashed Borders 2

Dashed Borders 3

Alsek Productions, Inc.

5051 Boston Way
Chandler, AZ 85226
602-961-3686

Collection	Format	No./Size Disks	Price	Computer
Techman Vol. 1	PICT/EPS	1-800K	$59.95	Mac
Techman Vol. 2	PICT or EPS	1-800K	$59.95	Mac

Techman Vol. 1

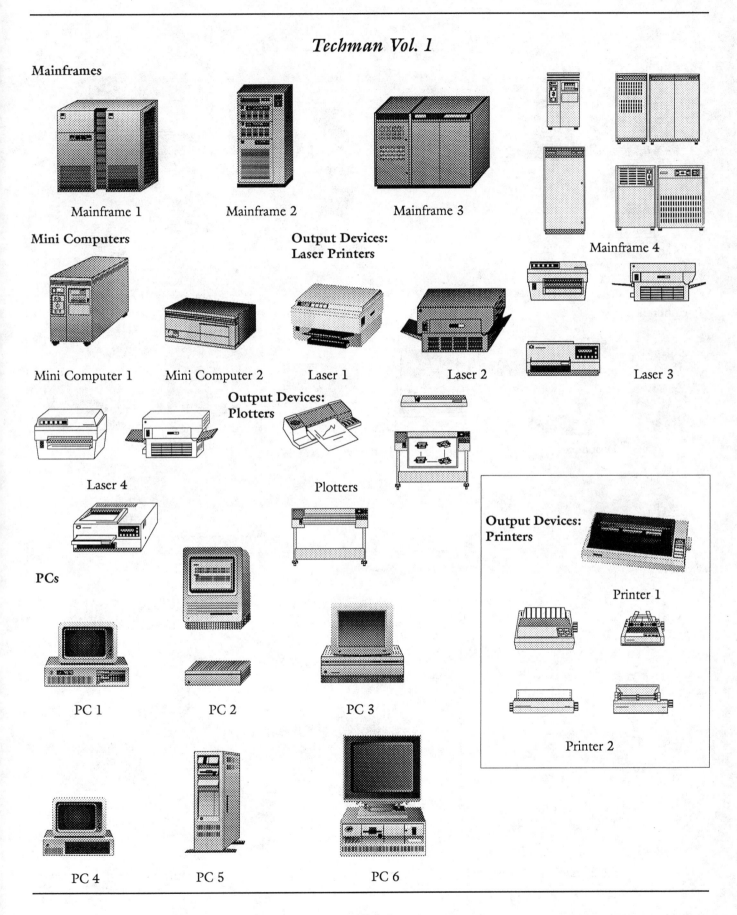

Mainframes

Mainframe 1

Mainframe 2

Mainframe 3

Mainframe 4

Mini Computers

**Output Devices:
Laser Printers**

Mini Computer 1

Mini Computer 2

Laser 1

Laser 2

Laser 3

**Output Devices:
Plotters**

Laser 4

Plotters

**Output Devices:
Printers**

Printer 1

Printer 2

PCs

PC 1

PC 2

PC 3

PC 4

PC 5

PC 6

Techman Vol. 1 (continued)

PC's

PC 7

PC 8

PC 9

Peripherals

Peripherals

Portables

Portables

Scrapbook File

Symbols

PROCESS

INPUT

DECISION

OUTPUT TO SCREEN

TERMINATE or INTERRUPT

OUTPUT TO PRINTER

CONNECT

OUTPUT

TAPE ARCHIEVE

CARD INPUT

MERGE

DISK STORAGE

DP Symbols

Workstations

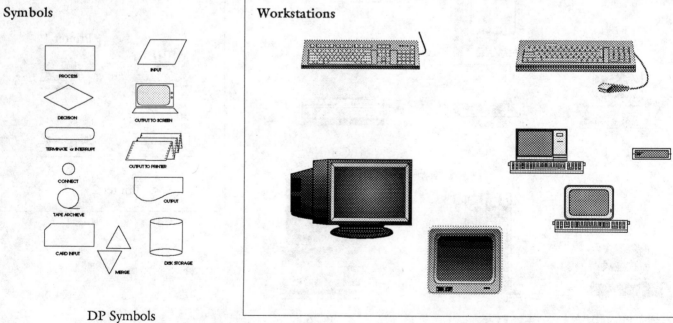

Artbeats

Box 20083
San Bernardino, CA 92406
714-881-1200
714-881-4833 fax

◆

Collection	Format	No./Size Disks	Price	Computer
Dimensions Volume 1	EPS	3-800K	$79.95	Mac/IBM
Dimensions Volume 2	EPS	4-800K	$99.95	Mac/IBM
Natural Images Volume 1	EPS	5-800K	$99.95	Mac/IBM
Natural Images Volume 2	EPS	4-800K	$129.95	Mac/IBM
Potpourri Volume 1	EPS	4-800K	$99.95	Mac/IBM

Notes:

• Full Page Images CD-ROM $509.75.
• Also available: Backgrounds for Multimedia, 40 different images that can be placed into any animation, presentation, 3D rendering or image manipulation program that imports 8-bit PICT format including Aldus Persuasion, MacroMind Director, and Adobe Photoshop.

Dimensions Volume 1

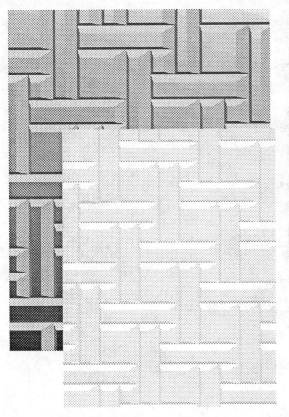

Bevels (High Contrast and Low Contrast)

Film Grid (Light and Dark)

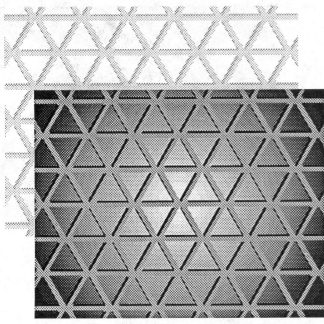

Triflection (High Contrast and Low Contrast))

Vanishing Points (Light and Dark)

Dimensions Volume 1 (continued)

Laser Edge (Light and Dark)

Mirror Tile (Light and Dark)

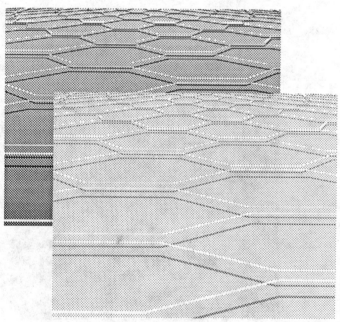

Network (Light and Dark)

Line Mesh (Light and Dark)

Dimensions Volume 1 (continued)

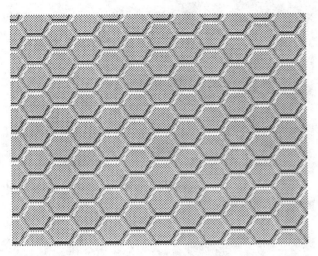

Hexagons (Dark)

Hexagons (Light)

Line Mesh (Dark)

Line Mesh (Light)

Dimensions Volume 2

Banded Steel (High and Low Contrast)   Beveled Glass (Dark and Light)

Burst (High and Low Contrast)   Ceramic Tile (Dark and Light)

Dimensions Volume II (continued)

Horizon (High Contrast and Low Contrast)

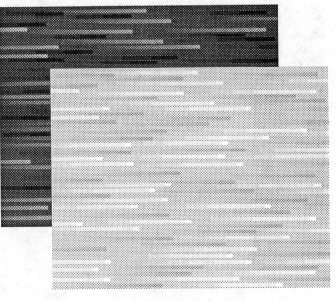

Speed (Dark and Light)

Gridwork (High Contrast and Low Contrast)

Parquet (Dark and Light)

Dimensions Volume II (continued)

Concave Bricks (Dark and Light)   Shaded Bricks (Dark and Light)

Natural Images Volume 1

Currents (Light and Dark)

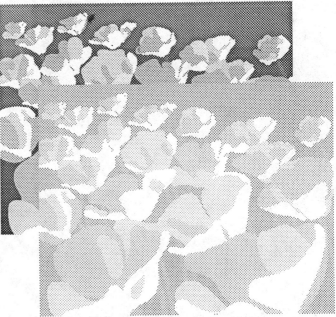

Poppies (High Contrast and Low Contrast)

Starlight (Low Contrast and High Contrast)

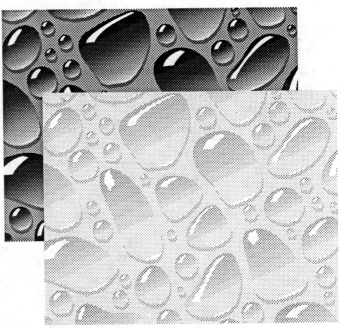

Droplets (Low Contrast and High Contrast)

Natural Images Volume 1 (continued)

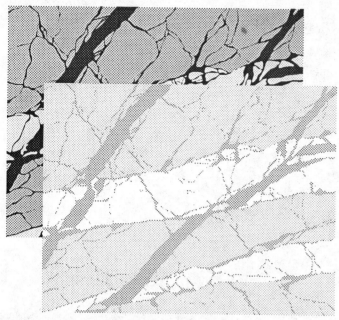

Marble (Low Contrast and High Contrast)

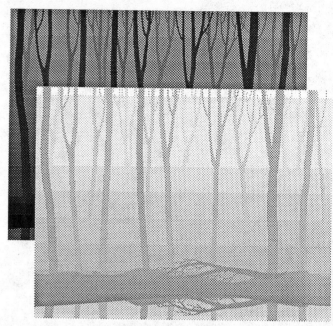

Forest (Dark and Light)

Wheat (High Contrast)

Wheat (Low Contrast)

Natural Images Volume 1 (continued)

Mountain Tops (High Contrast)

Mountain Tops (Low Contrast)

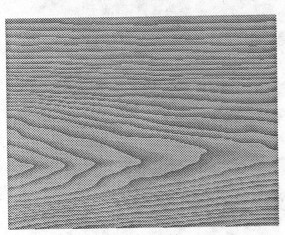

Wood (Dark)

Tree Silhouette (High Contrast)

Wood (Light)

Tree Silhouette (Low Contrast)

Natural Images Volume 2

Canyon (High and Low Contrast)

Dusk (High and Low Contrast)

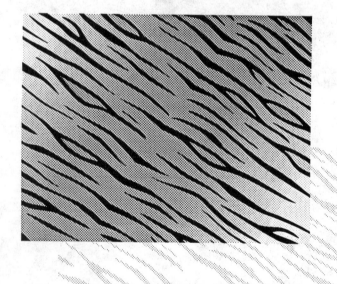

Tiger Skin (High and Low Contrast)

Grass (High and Low Contrast)

Natural Images Volume 2 (continued)

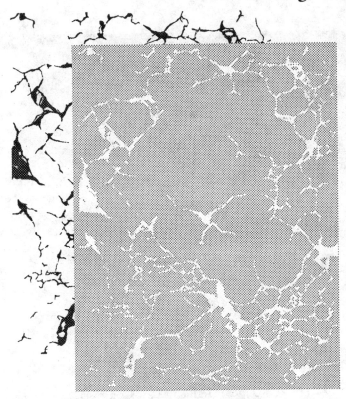

Cloud Silhouette (High and Low Contrast)

Marble 2 Dark and Light
(Screen placed behind light image to expose white elements.)

Palm (Dark and Light)
These images both have transparent backgrounds; an
opaque rectangle has been placed behind the light image
for production purposes.

Olympic Range (High and Low Contrast)

Natural Images Volume 2 (continued)

Azalea (Dark and Light)

Dunes (High and Low Contrast)

Angled Grad (High and Low Contrast)

Bottom-Top Grad (High and Low Contrast)

Natural Images Volume 2 (continued)

Left-Right Grad (High and Low Contrast)

Right-Left Grad (High and Low Contrast)

Top-Bottom Grad (High and Low Contrast)

Undulating Grad (High and Low Contrast)

Potpourri Volume 1

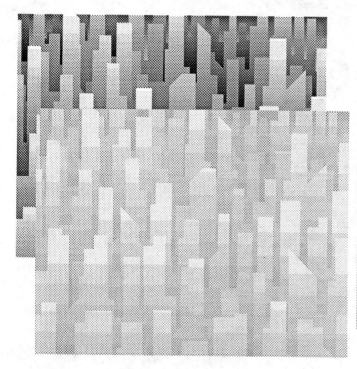

City (High and Low Contrast)

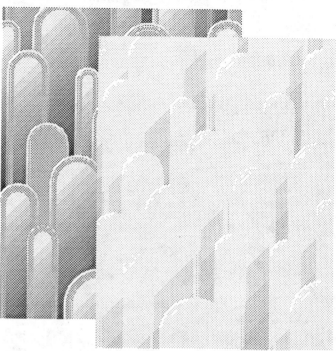

Deco (High and Low Contrast)

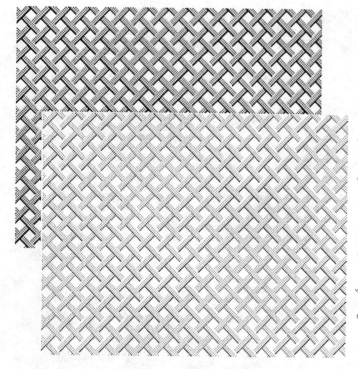

Lattice (High and Low Contrast)

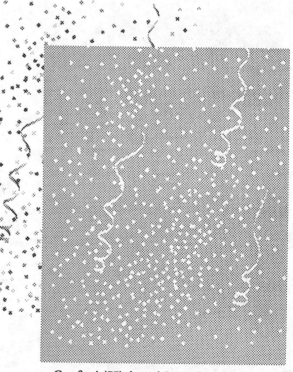

Confetti (High and Low Contrast)
(Screen placed behind light image to expose white elements.)

Potpourri Volume 1 (continued)

Floorboards (High and Low Contrast)   Transition (High and Low Contrast)

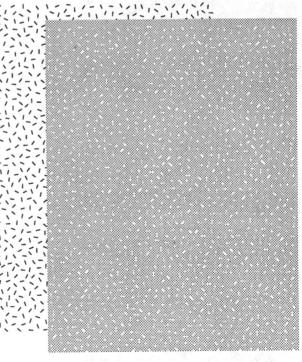

Fibers (Light and Dark)   Scratch (High and Low Contrast)
(Screen placed behind light image to expose white elements.)

Potpourri Volume 1 (continued)

Arizona (Dark)

Arizona (Light)

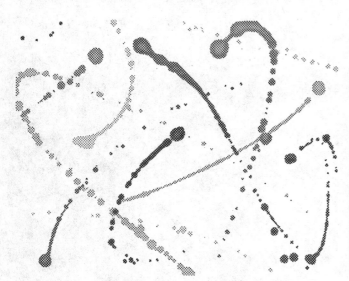

Splatters High Contrast

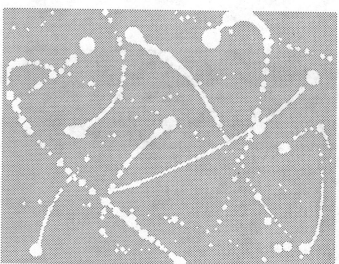

Splatters Low Contrast
(Screen placed behind light image to expose white elements.)

Potpourri 1 also contains all of the Graduated Fills found in Natural Images 2, seen on pages ART-12 and ART-13.

Berkana International, Inc.

216 Downing Avenue North
North Bend, WA 98045
800-488-9448 orders only
206-888-5353 information
206-888-5363 fax

◆

Collection	Format	No./Size Disks	Price	Computer
Designer's Toolkit: Initial Caps	EPS	5-800K	$129.00	Mac

Initial Caps Disk 1
Each image is a separate EPS file.

ABCDEFGHIJKLMN
OPQRSTUVWXYZ

Deco Caps

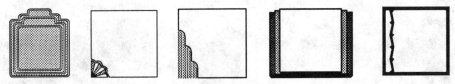

Deco Tiles 1 through 5

ABCDEFGHIJKLMN
OPQRSTUVWXYZ

Engraved Caps

ABCDEFGHIJKLMN
OPQRSTUVWXYZ

Engraved Sans Serif Caps

Engraved Tiles 1 through 5

Initial Caps Disk 2

Each image is a separate EPS file.

ABCDEFGHIJKLMNOPQR
STUVWXYZ

Embossed Caps
(Screen placed behind alphabet to expose white elements.)

    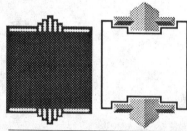

Embossed Tiles 1 through 5   Horizontal Tiles 1 and 2

  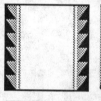 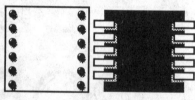

Horizontal Tiles 3 through 5   Vertical Tiles 1 through 4

Vertical Tile 5   Riveted Tiles 1 through 5

ABCDEFGHIJKL
MNOPQRSTUV
WXYZ

Riveted Caps

BERKANA INTERNATIONAL, INC.

Initial Caps Disk 3
Each image is a separate EPS file.

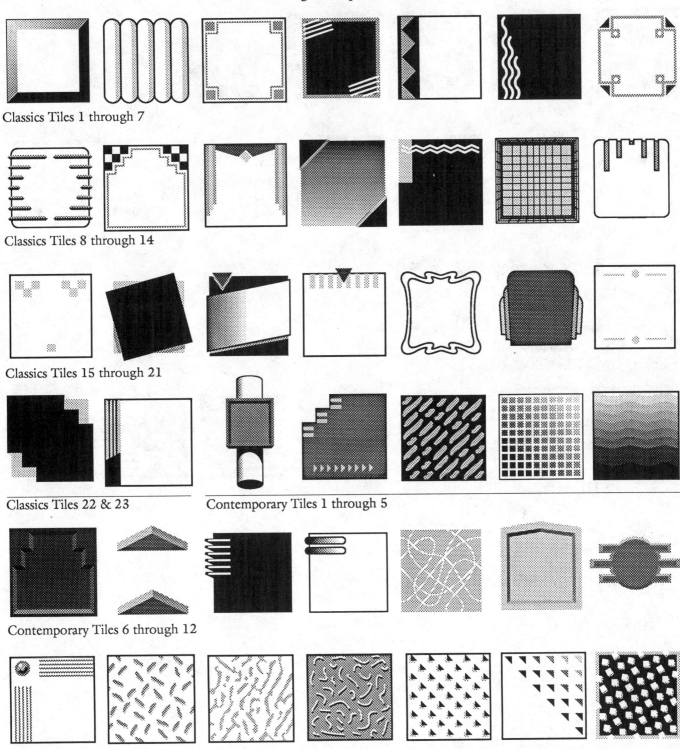

Classics Tiles 1 through 7

Classics Tiles 8 through 14

Classics Tiles 15 through 21

Classics Tiles 22 & 23

Contemporary Tiles 1 through 5

Contemporary Tiles 6 through 12

Contemporary Tiles 13 through 19

BERKANA INTERNATIONAL, INC.

Initial Caps Disk 3 (continued)
Each image is a separate EPS file.

   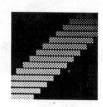 

Contemporary Tiles 20 through 24

Familiar Objects Tiles 1 through 7

Familiar Objects Tiles 8 through 10

  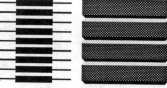  

Hi Tech Tiles 1 through 7

Hi Tech Tiles 8 through 10

Initial Caps Disk 4
Each image is a separate EPS or TIFF file.

Abstract Tiles 1 through 7

Abstract Tile 8

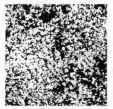

Daubing BW.tif

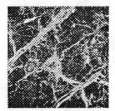

Marble 1 Gray.tif

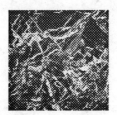

Marble 2 Gray.tif

Scribbles BW.tif

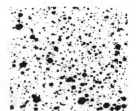

Stipple BW.tif

Wood Gray.tif

Initial Caps Disk 5

Each image is a separate EPS file.

Variety Caps

Best Impressions
800-487-1753

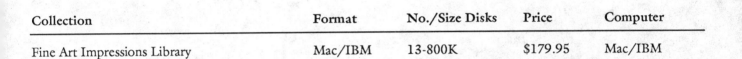

Collection	Format	No./Size Disks	Price	Computer
Fine Art Impressions Library	Mac/IBM	13-800K	$179.95	Mac/IBM

Notes:

• Best Impressions indicates that they will be shipping several new art packages after publication of this volume: First, Designer Tiles & Custom Borders, available in EPS format in both black-and-white and color. Also, 2 other packages are planned for release: Business Concepts and Holidays, which will also be EPS graphics in black-and-white and color. Contact Best Impressions for more information.

BEST IMPRESSIONS

Disk 1: Illustration Showcase

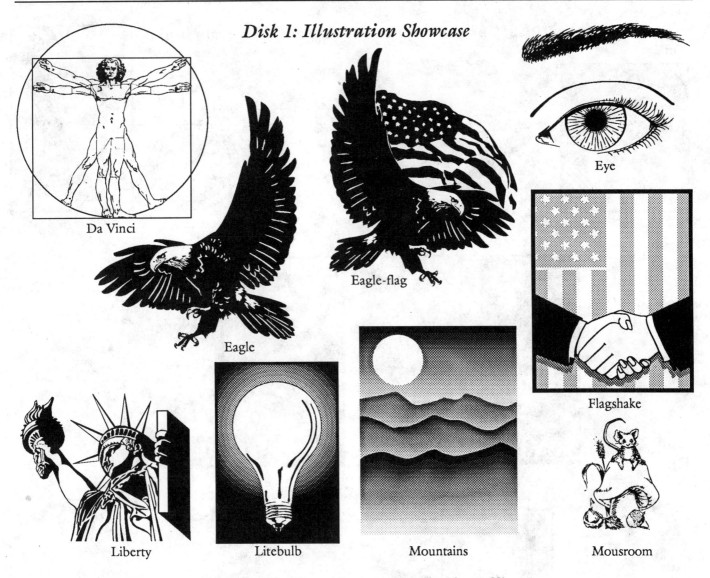

Da Vinci

Eagle

Eagle-flag

Eye

Flagshake

Liberty

Litebulb

Mountains

Mousroom

Disk 2: The Four Seasons & At the Office

Office

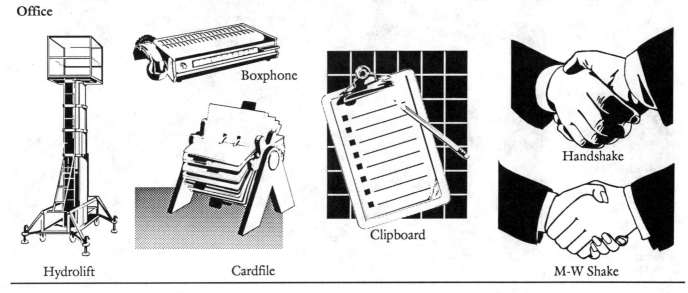

Boxphone

Clipboard

Handshake

Hydrolift

Cardfile

M-W Shake

Disk 2: The Four Seasons & At the Office (continued)

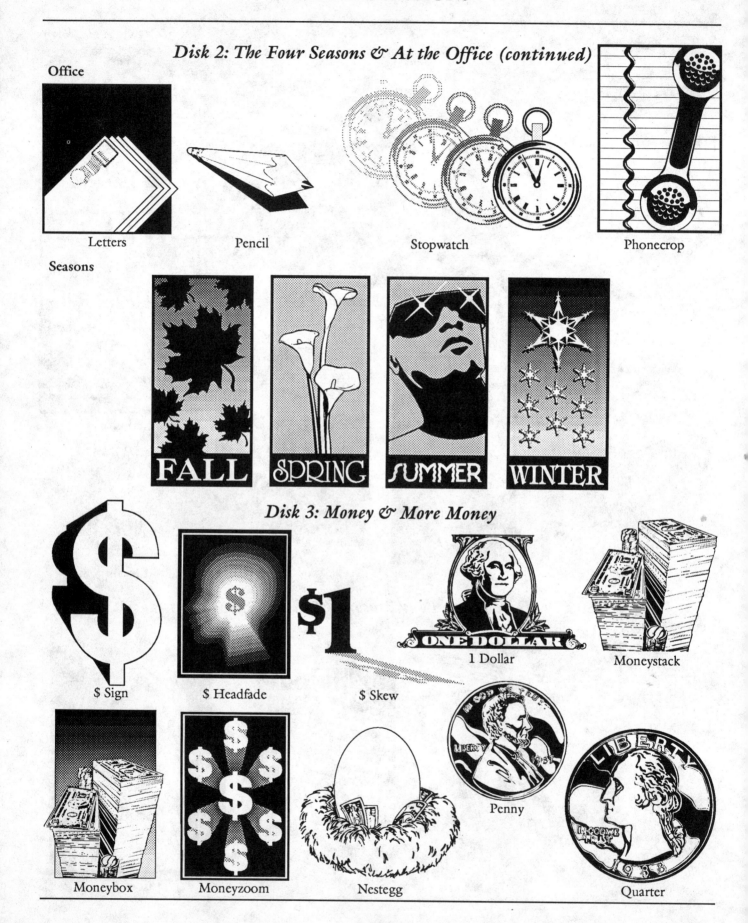

Office

Letters

Pencil

Stopwatch

Phonecrop

Seasons

FALL

SPRING

SUMMER

WINTER

Disk 3: Money & More Money

$ Sign

$ Headfade

$ Skew

1 Dollar

Moneystack

Moneybox

Moneyzoom

Nestegg

Penny

Quarter

Disk 4: Professional Workforce 1 & Making Headlines

Headlines

Datadisk

F-Y-I

Forecast

Memo

Schedule

Salesbox

Outlook

Thank You

Professional Workforce I

Display

Execujet

Gearman

Growth

Mancase

Manchart

Disk 5: Professional Workforce II

Manclock

Manphone

Mantalk 1

Meeting 1

Meeting 2

Phonegirl

Reader

Receptionist

Stressed

Teamwork

Workgirl

Disk 6: Art & Entertainment, Borders & Boxes

Arts & Entertainment

Clapboard

Corkpop

Dress-up

Masks

Mona Lisa

Music Staff

Borders 1

$ Corner

Burst 1

Burst 2

Burst 3

Burst 4

Checkerbox

Columns

Disklabel

Disk 7: More Borders & Boxes, Making the Mark

Borders 2

From the desk of

From Desk

Ribbon Box

Note

Leaf Box

Sale Tags

Leg Box

Making the Mark

Bull's Eye

Place-1st

Place-2nd

Place-3rd

Disk 8: Going Places

BMW Sedan

Footsteps

Palm Trees

Cypress

Testarosa

Globe-USA

Disk 8: Going Places (continued)

Truck 1

Truck 2

USA Map 1

USA Map 2

Disk 9: World Cup Sports

Baseball

Biking

Football

Golf Man

Horserace

Run to Win

Skiing

Tennis

Slam Dunk

Victory

Disk 10: Occupational Themes

Banking

Building

Farming

Law Scales

Management

Manufacturing

Medicine

Pharmacy

Police

Disk 11: Symbols & Signs

Arrows 1

Arrows 2

Car Phone

Cat

Checkbox

Ear-Lines

Eye-Lines

Fax

Greyhound

House-3D

House-Black

House-Family

Disk 11: Symbols & Signs (continued)

Mindpower

Maple Leaf

Modem

No Smoking

Peace Dove

Phone

Remember

Stop Sign

Disk 12: Portraits

Beauty

Boydream

Girlbear

Glamour

Grad Kids

Lil Kids

Pucker Up

Puzzled

Disk 13: Silhouettes, Credit Line, Personal Computing

Credit

Card-Amex Card-Diners Card-Discover Card-Hand Card-Master Card-Visa

Personal Computing

Floppies  Hand-Mouse  Keyboard  Manydisk

Silhouettes

Bikini

Hand Hold  Couple  Jump-Girl  Jump-Man

Muscle Man  Run-Jump  Shapely  Sidebend 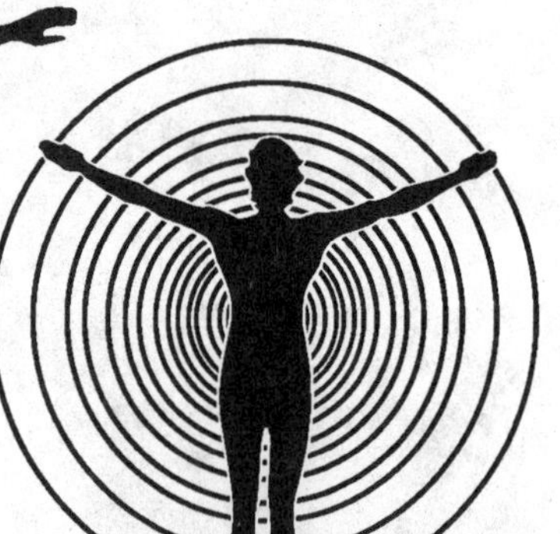 Whole Man

CAR Inc.

7009 Kingsbury
St. Louis, MO 63130
314-721-6305
314-863-7212 fax
800-288-7585 orders & information only

———————◆———————

Collection	Format	No./Size Disks	Price	Computer
Clipables: Animals	EPS	2-800K	$39.95	Mac/IBM
Clipables: Borders	EPS	2-800K	$39.95	Mac/IBM
Clipables: Business	EPS	3-800K	$39.95	Mac/IBM
Clipables: Dingbats/Symbols	EPS	6-800K	$89.95	Mac/IBM
Clipables: Display Banners	EPS	1-800K	$39.95	Mac/IBM
Clipables: Figures	EPS	2-800K	$39.95	Mac/IBM
Clipables: Holidays	EPS	3-800K	$39.95	Mac/IBM
Clipables: Humor	EPS	2-800K	$39.95	Mac/IBM
Clipables: Maps	EPS	4-800K	$39.95	Mac/IBM
Clipables: Medical	EPS	2-800K	$39.95	Mac/IBM
Clipables: Ornaments	EPS	1-800K	$39.95	Mac/IBM
Clipables: Portfolio	EPS	11-800K	$89.95	Mac/IBM
Clipables: Sports	EPS	4-800K	$39.95	Mac/IBM
Clipables: Transportation	EPS	2-800K	$39.95	Mac/IBM

Notes:

Clipables is sold in a variety of other packages as well:
- 45-disk set $299.95
- Clipables I: Animals through Holidays (19 disks) $169.95
- Clipables II: Humor through Transportation (26 disks) $169.95
- CD-ROM (all 45 disks): $299.95

Animals 1

Angelfish

Bassett Hound

Blue Whale

Butterfly

Cockatoo

Crab

Dalmatian

Dolphin

Eagle

Elephant

Giraffe

Goldfish

Guenon Monkey

House Cat

Animals 2

Jaguar

Kangaroo

Killer Whales

Koala

Ladybug

Lion

Lobster

Ostrich

Partridge

Penguin

Shark

Swan

Turtle

Borders 1

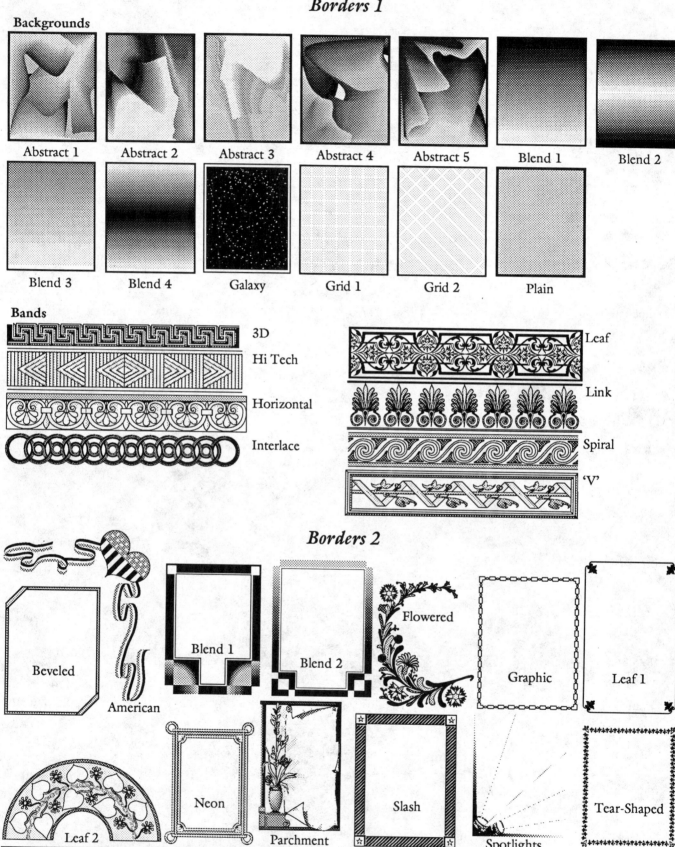

Backgrounds

Abstract 1 · Abstract 2 · Abstract 3 · Abstract 4 · Abstract 5 · Blend 1 · Blend 2

Blend 3 · Blend 4 · Galaxy · Grid 1 · Grid 2 · Plain

Bands

3D · Hi Tech · Horizontal · Interlace

Leaf · Link · Spiral · 'V'

Borders 2

Beveled · American · Blend 1 · Blend 2 · Flowered · Graphic · Leaf 1

Leaf 2 · Neon · Parchment · Slash · Spotlights · Tear-Shaped

CAR INC.

Business 1

3D Pie Chart 1, 2 · **Attache Case** · **Barchart Downward, Upward** · **Business Discussion** · **Business Machines** · **3.5 Disk** · **Big Mac**

Black Mac · **Black PC** · **Computer (A,B,C)** · **Computer Network** · **Computer Terminal** · **Copier** · **Mac SE**

Fax · **Film Projector** · **Hand on Keyboard** · **Hand on Mouse** · **Keyboard Draw** · **Mac II/IIFX**

Computer Peripherals · **Overhead Projector** · **PC** · **Phone** · **Slide Projector** · **Video Camera**

Business 2

Calculator · **Calendar** · **Call Bell** · **Com. Paper** · **Fever Chart** · **File Folder 1** · **File Folder 2** · **Filing Cabinet**

Fire Extinguisher · **Gavel** · **Handshake** · **Hand Truck** · **Hourglass** · **Man at Podium** · **Man With Glasses** · **Money Bag**

Paper Cutter · **Pencils 1, 2, 3, 4** · **Pie Chart** · **Presentation-Listening**

Presentation-Looking · **Presentation** · **Pie Cylinder** · **Pushpins** · **Reference Books** · **Rolodex**

Business 3

Rubber Stamps

APPROVED   CANCELLED   OVERDUE   PAID   SOLD

Safe   Salesforce, Man, Woman   Water Cooler

Situations

Agreement   Argument   Car Phone   Checking Time   Coffee Break   Computing

Handing Over   Late Night   Stress   Thinking   Woman 1   Woman 2   Woman 3

Dingbats & Symbols 1

3-D Icons

Arrow, Circle, Diamond, 4-Headed Arrow, Hexagon, Pentagon, Star, Triangle, 2-Headed Arrow

Acrylic Pt. Tube   Act II   Airbrush   Apple

Arrows

Chrome

Straight 1, 2   Curved/Black   Straight 3   White/ Drop Shadowed   Wraparound

Awards

Places: 1st, 2nd, 3rd, 4th, Grand Prize

Artist's Palette   Baby Block   Baby Bottle   Baby Buggy   Back to School   Band Aid   Barrel   Bell   Bevel   Bird   Black Cat   Bones

Book   Camp Fire   Candle 1, 2, 3   Bowtie Collar   Bullet   Cactus   Camera 1, 2   Car Shop   Car Symbol

Car Wash   Cards: Clubs, Diamonds, Hearts, Spades   Cents Sign 1, 2   Change Purse   Citrus   City   Clipboard

Dingbats & Symbols 2

Clock A, B — Clothespin — Cocktail — Comb — Computer — Crayon — Cross A, B, C — Cup & Saucer — Cup A, B, C

Clock C — Decline — Diamond/Gem — Disk/3.5 — Disk/5.25 — Dish

Doghouse — Dollar Sign 1, 2 — Dollar — Camping 1, 2 — Checkmark — Crosswalk — Detour — Do Not Enter — Don't Forget

Fragile — Handicap — No: Camping, Food & Drink, Left Turn, Littering, Right Turn, Smoking, U Turn — One Way — Picnic Area 1, 2 — Railroad

School Crossing — Seat Belt — Slippery — Smoking — Stop — Traffic Signal — X Mark — Yield

Drum — Ear of Corn — Eiffel Tower — Electric Outlet — Envelope — Eye — Family Unit — Faces: Angry, Happy, Sad, Surprised

Dingbats & Symbols 3

Environment

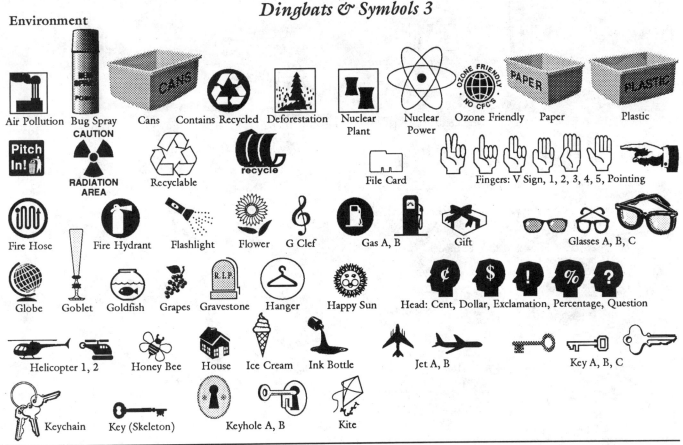

Air Pollution — Bug Spray — Cans — Contains Recycled — Deforestation — Nuclear Plant — Nuclear Power — Ozone Friendly — Paper — Plastic

Pitch In! — CAUTION RADIATION AREA — Recyclable — recycle — File Card — Fingers: V Sign, 1, 2, 3, 4, 5, Pointing

Fire Hose — Fire Hydrant — Flashlight — Flower — G Clef — Gas A, B — Gift — Glasses A, B, C

Globe — Goblet — Goldfish — Grapes — Gravestone — Hanger — Happy Sun — Head: Cent, Dollar, Exclamation, Percentage, Question

Helicopter 1, 2 — Honey Bee — House — Ice Cream — Ink Bottle — Jet A, B — Key A, B, C

Keychain — Key (Skeleton) — Keyhole A, B — Kite

Dingbats & Symbols 4

Logo Symbols

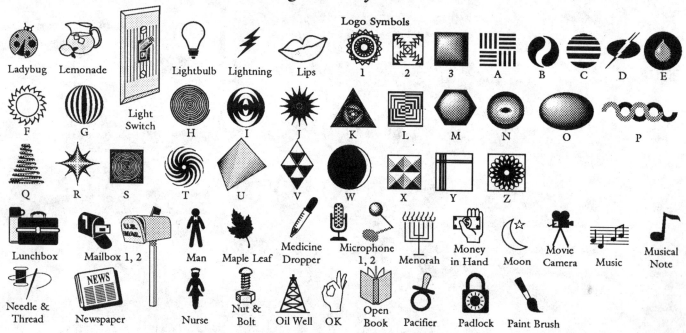

Ladybug, Lemonade, Light Switch, Lightbulb, Lightning, Lips, 1, 2, 3, A, B, C, D, E, F, G, H, I, J, K, L, M, N, O, P, Q, R, S, T, U, V, W, X, Y, Z, Lunchbox, Mailbox 1, 2, Man, Maple Leaf, Medicine Dropper, Microphone 1, 2, Menorah, Money in Hand, Moon, Movie Camera, Music, Musical Note, Needle & Thread, Newspaper, Nurse, Nut & Bolt, Oil Well, OK, Open Book, Pacifier, Padlock, Paint Brush

Dingbats & Symbols 5

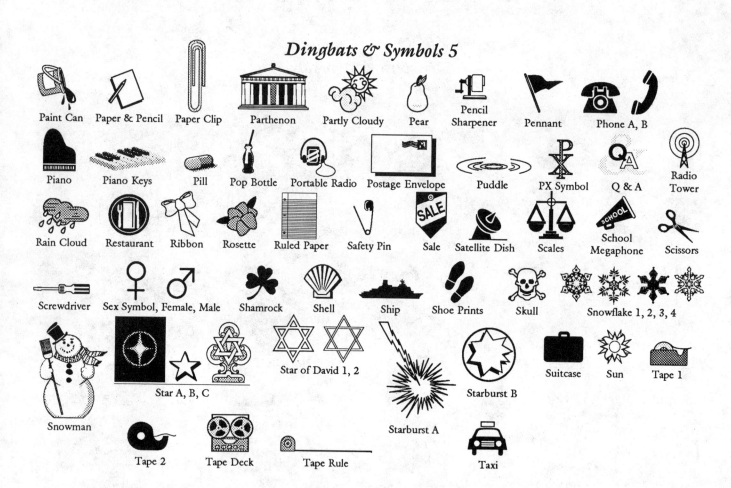

Paint Can, Paper & Pencil, Paper Clip, Parthenon, Partly Cloudy, Pear, Pencil Sharpener, Pennant, Phone A, B, Piano, Piano Keys, Pill, Pop Bottle, Portable Radio, Postage Envelope, Puddle, PX Symbol, Q & A, Radio Tower, Rain Cloud, Restaurant, Ribbon, Rosette, Ruled Paper, Safety Pin, Sale, Satellite Dish, Scales, School Megaphone, Scissors, Screwdriver, Sex Symbol, Female, Male, Shamrock, Shell, Ship, Shoe Prints, Skull, Snowflake 1, 2, 3, 4, Snowman, Star A, B, C, Star of David 1, 2, Starburst A, Starburst B, Suitcase, Sun, Tape 1, Tape 2, Tape Deck, Tape Rule, Taxi

Dingbats & Symbols 6

Sports

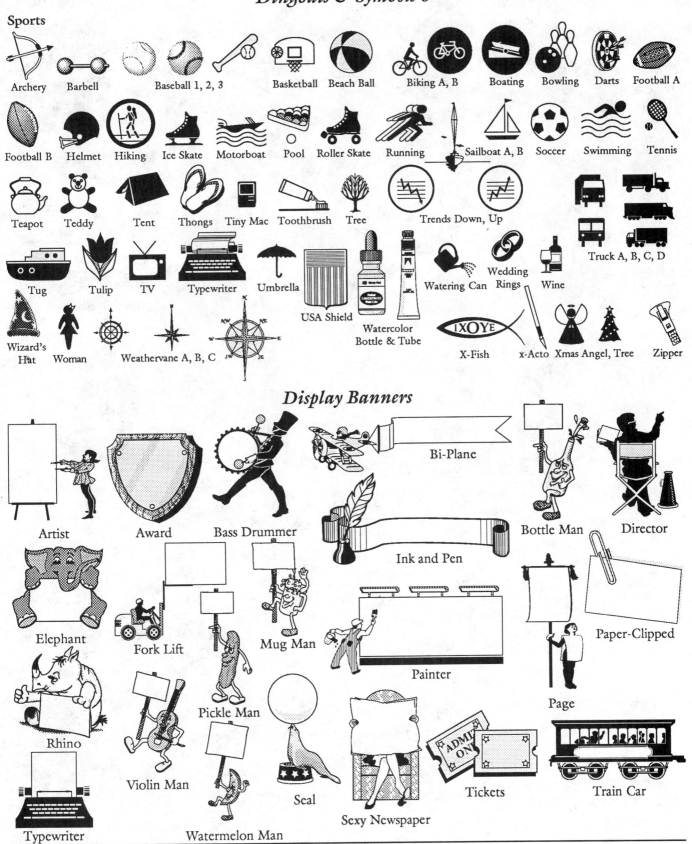

Archery Barbell Baseball 1, 2, 3 Basketball Beach Ball Biking A, B Boating Bowling Darts Football A

Football B Helmet Hiking Ice Skate Motorboat Pool Roller Skate Running Sailboat A, B Soccer Swimming Tennis

Teapot Teddy Tent Thongs Tiny Mac Toothbrush Tree Trends Down, Up Truck A, B, C, D

Tug Tulip TV Typewriter Umbrella USA Shield Watercolor Bottle & Tube Watering Can Wedding Rings Wine

Wizard's Hat Woman Weathervane A, B, C X-Fish x-Acto Xmas Angel, Tree Zipper

Display Banners

Artist Award Bass Drummer Bi-Plane Bottle Man Director

Elephant Fork Lift Mug Man Ink and Pen Painter Paper-Clipped

Rhino Violin Man Pickle Man Seal Page Tickets Train Car

Typewriter Watermelon Man Sexy Newspaper

CAR INC.

Figures 1

Bath

Bowl 1, 2

Chinese Person

Clown

Drummer

Fashion 1, 2, 3

Fighters

Horn Player

Japanese Person 1, 2

Figures 2

Mexican

Peruvian

Trumpeter

Warrior

Wedding

Holidays 1

Barbeque

Birthday

Bow 1, 2

Carolers

Celebration

Cherub

Christmas Horn

Doves

Drummer

Easter

Father's Day

Firecracker

Flag Twins

Holidays 2

Fireplace

Gifts

Graduate

Graduation

Halloween

Happy Birthday

Holiday Cheer

Holly Leaves

Jack-O-Lantern

Love

New Year

Holidays 3

Mother's Day

Nutcracker

St. Patrick's Day

Trick or Treat

Valentine Heart

Xmas House

Xmas Piper

Xmas Sweater

Xmas Wreath

Xmas Town

Humor 1

Accountant

Ball and Chain

Banker

Barber

Baseball

Car

Chemist

Cookbook

Couch Potato

Envelope Man

Grocer

Handyman

Happy Doggie

Hunter

Kitty

Listener

Little Fibber

Little Man

Miss Fish

Mr. Baseball

Mr. Calculator

Humor 2

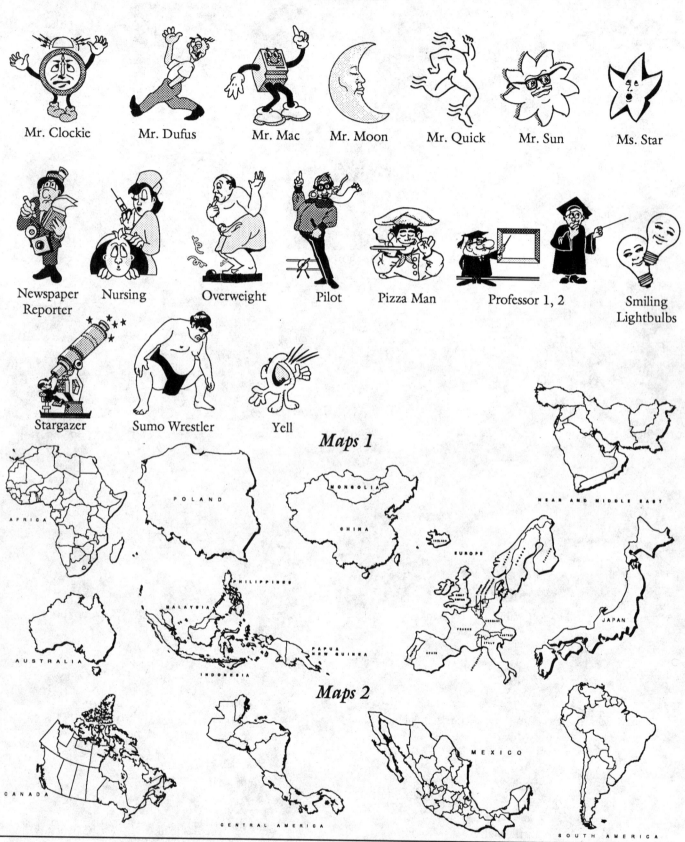

Mr. Clockie

Mr. Dufus

Mr. Mac

Mr. Moon

Mr. Quick

Mr. Sun

Ms. Star

Newspaper Reporter

Nursing

Overweight

Pilot

Pizza Man

Professor 1, 2

Smiling Lightbulbs

Stargazer

Sumo Wrestler

Yell

Maps 1

AFRICA

POLAND

MONGOLIA

CHINA

NEAR AND MIDDLE EAST

ICELAND

EUROPE

JAPAN

AUSTRALIA

PHILIPPINES

MALAYSIA

PAPUA NEW GUINEA

INDONESIA

Maps 2

CANADA

CENTRAL AMERICA

MEXICO

SOUTH AMERICA

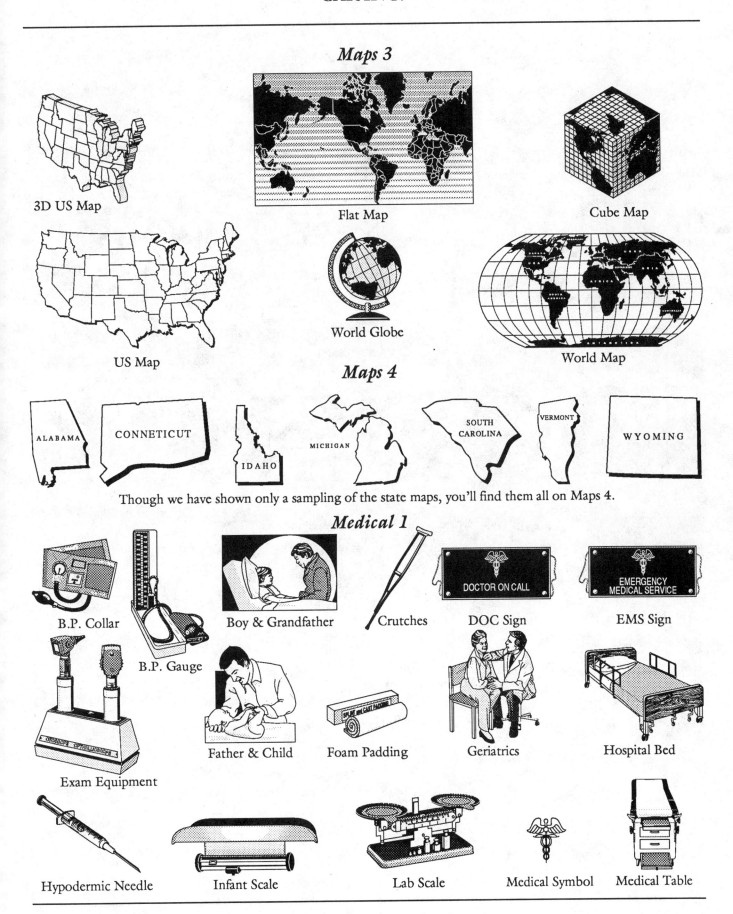

Maps 3

3D US Map

Flat Map

Cube Map

US Map

World Globe

World Map

Maps 4

ALABAMA CONNETICUT IDAHO MICHIGAN SOUTH CAROLINA VERMONT WYOMING

Though we have shown only a sampling of the state maps, you'll find them all on Maps 4.

Medical 1

B.P. Collar

B.P. Gauge

Boy & Grandfather

Crutches

DOC Sign

EMS Sign

Exam Equipment

Father & Child

Foam Padding

Geriatrics

Hospital Bed

Hypodermic Needle

Infant Scale

Lab Scale

Medical Symbol

Medical Table

Medical 2

Medicine Dropper

Mortar & Pestle

Paramedics

Quad Cane

Scissors

Snellen
Eye Chart

Stethoscope

Stretcher

Sundry Jar

Throat Exam

Walker

Wheelchair

Ornaments

Round & Square

A

B

C

D

E

F

G

H

I

J

K

L

M

N

Spacers

1

2

3

4

5

6

7

8

9

10

11

12

13

14

Portfolio 1

Anchor

Artist

Birdcage

Book

Buddha 1

Buddha 2

Chemistry & Engineering

Candle Holder

Cat Face (Shown at 50%)

Cats & Window

30-60-90 Triangle

Beakers (Shown at 50%)

Chemistry

Compass

Drafting Chair

Drafting Table

Engineering

Ink Bottle

Mechanical Pencil

Microscope

Roll File

T-Square

Template

Taboret

Portfolio 2

Chess

Coins (Shown at 50%)

Dragon

Dolphin

Children

Abacus

Children Faces: Angry, Happy, Sad, Surprise (Each a separate file.)

Hockey

Jump Rope

Jumping

Kick Ball

Little Brother

Prayer (Shown at 50%)

Rainy Day (Shown at 50%)

Reading

Dietary

Dairy

Fruits & Veggies

Grains

Meats

CAR INC.

Portfolio 3

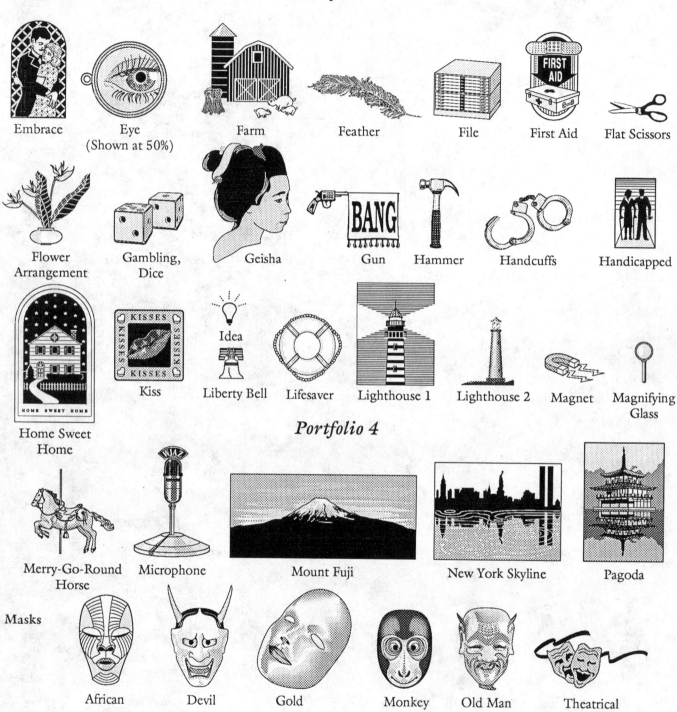

Embrace

Eye
(Shown at 50%)

Farm

Feather

File

First Aid

Flat Scissors

Flower
Arrangement

Gambling,
Dice

Geisha

Gun

Hammer

Handcuffs

Handicapped

Home Sweet
Home

Kiss

Idea

Liberty Bell

Lifesaver

Lighthouse 1

Lighthouse 2

Magnet

Magnifying
Glass

Portfolio 4

Merry-Go-Round
Horse

Microphone

Mount Fuji

New York Skyline

Pagoda

Masks

African

Devil

Gold

Monkey

Old Man

Theatrical

Numbers, Digital

1234567898O

Digital Numerals (Each a separate file. Shown at 50%)

Portfolio 5

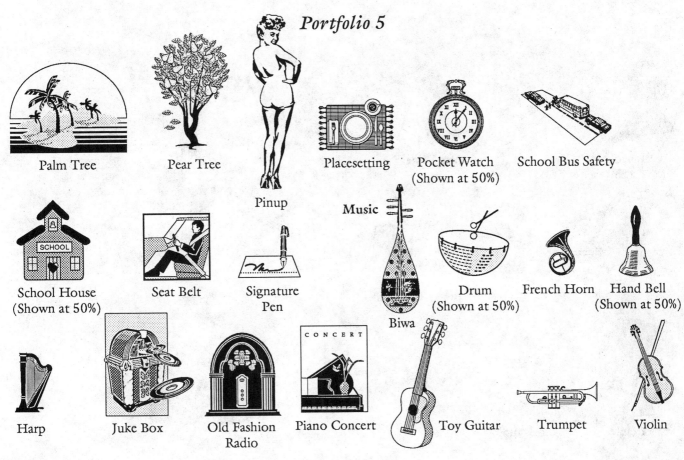

Palm Tree

Pear Tree

Pinup

Placesetting

Pocket Watch
(Shown at 50%)

School Bus Safety

School House
(Shown at 50%)

Seat Belt

Signature
Pen

Music

Biwa

Drum
(Shown at 50%)

French Horn

Hand Bell
(Shown at 50%)

Harp

Juke Box

Old Fashion
Radio

Piano Concert

Toy Guitar

Trumpet

Violin

Portfolio 4

Months

Portfolio 7

Abe Lincoln (Shown at 50%)   Actress   Box Camera   Einstein   Excited People   Family Bike Outing

Fishing   George Washington   Handcrafts   Mermaid   Modern Man 1   Modern Man 2   Modern Woman

Nofretete   Stork/Boy   Stork/Girl   Tap Dancer   Uncle Sam

Portfolio 8

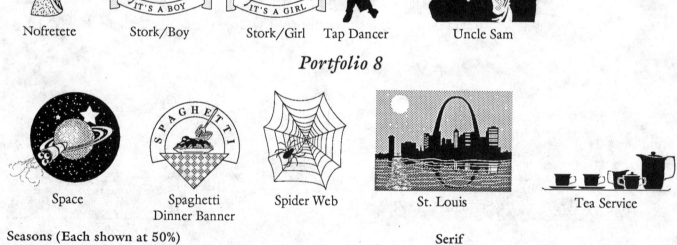

Space   Spaghetti Dinner Banner   Spider Web   St. Louis   Tea Service

Seasons (Each shown at 50%)   Serif

A - Z: Each is a separate image file, the file is also saved in the ABC block seen here.

ABCDE FGHIJK LMNOP QRSTU VWXYZ

Portfolio 9

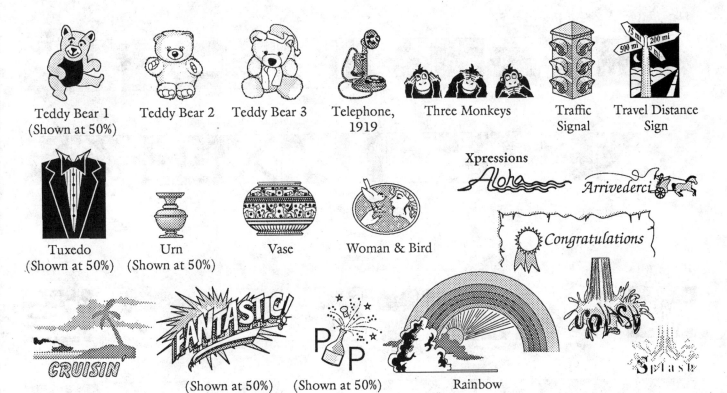

Teddy Bear 1 (Shown at 50%) Teddy Bear 2 Teddy Bear 3 Telephone, 1919 Three Monkeys Traffic Signal Travel Distance Sign

Tuxedo (Shown at 50%) Urn (Shown at 50%) Vase Woman & Bird Xpressions — Aloha Arrivederci Congratulations

CRUISIN' FANTASTIC! (Shown at 50%) (Shown at 50%) Rainbow Splash

Portfolio 10

Flags (Historic): All shown at 50%.

The Flag of 1777 Flag of 1795 The 48-Star Flag The Bear Flag Confederate Flag I Confederate Flag II Confederate Flag III

The Continental Colors Dutch East India Company The French Flag New England Flag I New England Flag IV The Other Flag of 1777 Perry's Flag

Russian American Company Spanish Flag Texas Flag The Viking Flag

Zodiac Symbols

Aquarius Aries Cancer Capricorn Gemini Leo Libra Pisces Sagittarius Scorpio Taurus Virgo

Portfolio 11

Flag Letters A-Z: All shown at 50%.

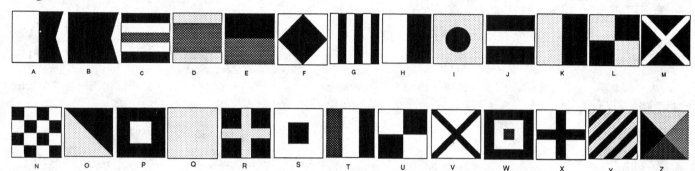

Flags: All shown at 50%.

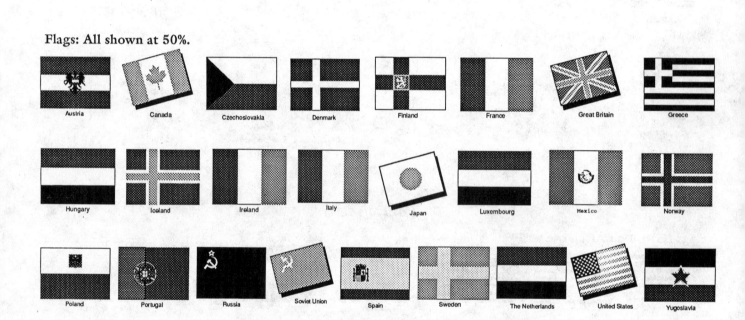

International Numerals: All shown at 50%.

Sports 1

Archery   Athlete w/Flag   Baseball 1   Baseball 2   Basketball   Billiards

Bowling   Boxing   Cricket   Discus

Sports 2

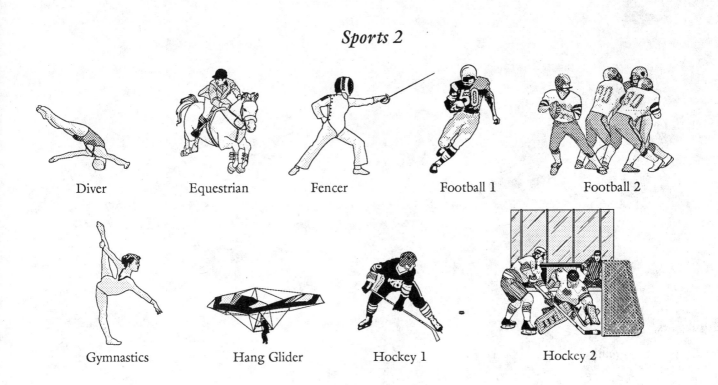

Diver   Equestrian   Fencer   Football 1   Football 2

Gymnastics   Hang Glider   Hockey 1   Hockey 2

Sports 3

Hurdler Ice Skater Jet Skier Kayaker Lay-Up Motorcycler

Putter Rings Runner Sitting Athete Skier 1

Sports 4

Ski Machine Skier 2 Soccer Speed Skater Sprinter Surfer

Swimming Ten Speed Racer Tennis 2 Weight Lifter Windsurfer

Tennis 1

Transportation 1

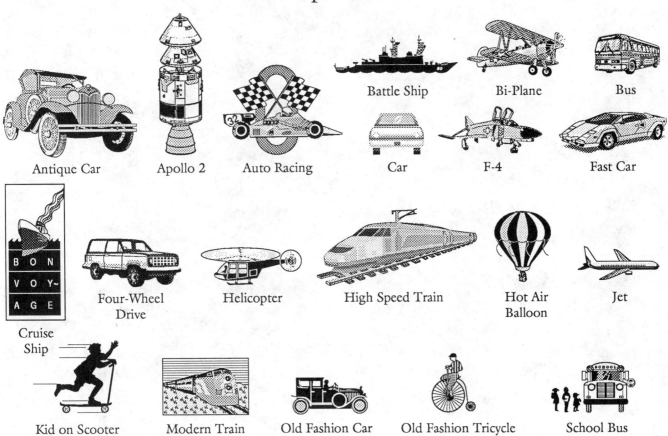

Antique Car

Apollo 2

Auto Racing

Battle Ship

Bi-Plane

Bus

Car

F-4

Fast Car

Cruise Ship

Four-Wheel Drive

Helicopter

High Speed Train

Hot Air Balloon

Jet

Kid on Scooter

Modern Train

Old Fashion Car

Old Fashion Tricycle

School Bus

Transportation 2

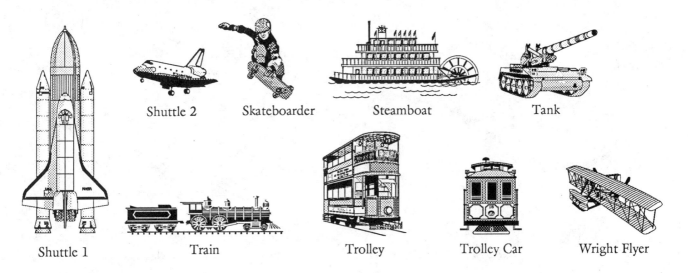

Shuttle 2

Skateboarder

Steamboat

Tank

Shuttle 1

Train

Trolley

Trolley Car

Wright Flyer

Casady & Greene, Inc.

22734 Portola Drive
Salinas, CA 93908-1119
408-484-9228
408-484-9218 fax
800-359-4920 orders only

Collection	Format	No./Size Disks	Price	Computer
Vivid Impressions!:				
Volume 1 Holidays & Festive Events	EPS	7-800K	$ 65.00	Mac/IBM

Notes:

• Sold only as a 7-disk set.
• Disk A is not shown; that disk consists of colorized versions of many of the images found on the other disks in the set.

Vivid Impressions: Disk E-1

Hallowe'en

Jack O'Montage

Owl & Tree

Witch Montage

Black Cat

Cat-Line

Presidents and Independence Day

Lincoln

Washington

Eagle & Stars

Oval Border

Banner

Star

Vivid Impressions: Disk E-2

Valentine

Vivid Impressions: Disk E-3

Carousel

Vivid Impressions: Disk E-4

Easter Montage

Harvest Montage/Acorn Border

Vivid Impressions: Disk E-5

Castle & Ocean

Cookie Bell-grey

Cookie Bell-line

Cookie Deer-grey

Cookie Deer-line

Cookie Heart-grey

Cookie Heart-line

Cookie Tree-grey

Cookie Tree-line

Deer

Santa

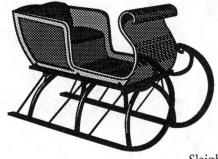

Sleigh

Vivid Impressions: Disk E-6

New Year's Eve

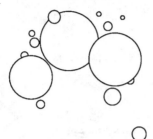

Bubbles

Couple

Xmas Trees

Bare Tree

Decorated Tree

Gifts

Tree & Gifts

Vivid Impressions: Cats Disk

Each letter is a separate file.

Cathay Europa Designs
P.O. Box 310
Sanbornville, NH 03872
207-967-5358
800-533-5504 orders only

◆

Collection	Format	No./Size Disks	Price	Computer
GlobalArt™ Oriental Images	Paint or EPS	2-800K	$125.00	Mac

GlobalArt™ *Oriental Images: Decorative Accents*

Birds & Blossoms

Boats on the River

Butterflies

China Sails

Crane & Pine Tree

Fish & Lily Pads

Fish

Ink Brush Fisherman

Floral Embellishments

Stork in Pines/Swan

Flying Crane

Flying Home

Going Home

Ming Dynasty Horse

Landscape Designs

Mandarin Ducks

Medallions, Yin/Yang

Ming Dynasty Tiger

Moon River

On the Li River

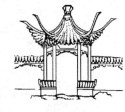
Pagoda Gate

Regal Crane

Rooster, Hen and Eggs

Lovebirds

Fu, Longvity;
Shou, Luck

Stork in Marsh

Flower Vase

GlobalArt™ Oriental Images: Embellishments

Bamboo

Bamboo Designs

Blossom Branch

Chinese Birds

Chinese Opera Mask

Chinese Opera Mask 2

Conversation

Crane Medallion

Daffodil Designs

Dragons

Early Spring

Fish Design

Goose Design

Herons and Cattails

Horse and Wagons

Ink Brush-Load Carrier

Japanese Lady

Leopards

Lily

On the Water

Owl

Plum Blossoms

Pretty Lady

Parrot

Collector Software
1535 West Holt
Pomona, CA 91768
714-620-9014 information only
(No telephone orders please)

———————◆———————

Collection	Format	No./Size Disks	Price	Computer
Christmas Bears	Paint	1-400K	$12.00	Mac
Family Bears	Paint	1-400K	$12.00	Mac
Fantasy Bears	Paint	1-400K	$12.00	Mac
Holiday Bears	Paint	1-400K	$12.00	Mac
Message Bears	Paint	1-400K	$12.00	Mac
Recreation Bears	Paint	1-400K	$12.00	Mac
Romance Bears	Paint	1-400K	$12.00	Mac
Special Day Bears	Paint	1-400K	$12.00	Mac
Working Bears	Paint	1-400K	$12.00	Mac

Notes:

• 9-disk set retails for $99.00.

Christmas Bears

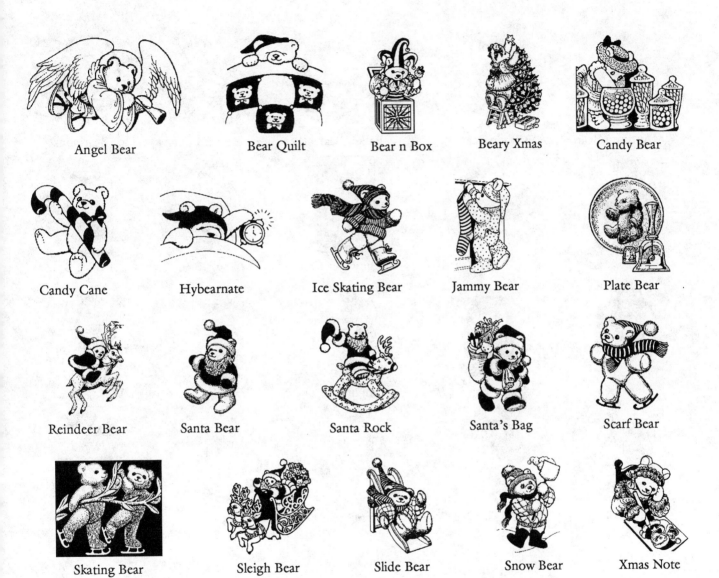

Angel Bear   Bear Quilt   Bear n Box   Beary Xmas   Candy Bear

Candy Cane   Hybearnate   Ice Skating Bear   Jammy Bear   Plate Bear

Reindeer Bear   Santa Bear   Santa Rock   Santa's Bag   Scarf Bear

Skating Bear   Sleigh Bear   Slide Bear   Snow Bear   Xmas Note

Holiday Bears

Autumn Bear	Balloon Bear	Basket Bear	Bear n Bunny	Bearloons
Beartsy Ross	Bearwitched	Bunny Suit Bear	Clown Bear	Coffee Bears
Dracubear	Easter Bearsket	Injun Bear	Liberty Bears	Package Bear
Parasol Bear	Pilgrim Bear	Pumpkin Bear	Turkey Bear	Uncle Sam Bear

Romance Bears

Arrow Bear

Balcony Bears

Bear Hugs

Bear Mine

Bear Vows

Bears' Picnic

Bride Bear

Courtship Bear

Cupid Bear

Dressy Bear

Flowers Bear

Glamour Bear

Heart Bear

Love Letter Bear

Love Mac

Love-u-Bear

Toasting Bears

Valentine Bear

Waltzing Bears

Wedding Bears

Family Bears

Baby Bear	Bear Tub	Beary Carriage	Dolly Bear	Fridge Bear
Gramps Bear	Granny Bear	Guest Bear	Hugging Bear	Lullabear
Mama Bear	Mom Bear	Papa Bear	Quilt Bear	Rocking Bear
Sorry Bear	Spanking Bear	Stork Bear	Tea Bear	Wicker Bear

Special Day Bears

Bear Awards

Bear Bag

Bear Mug

Bearleader

Bearthday Presents

Card Bear

Dear Bear

Gift Bear

Grad Bear

Happy Bearthday

Joyful Bear

Kite Bears

Moving Bears

Olympic Bear

Soda Bear

Swinging Bear

Thank You Bear

Top Hat Bear

Umbearella

Vote Bear

Message Bears

Banner Bear   Bear Cutting   Bear Weight   Bearsiness Card   Border Bears

Box Bear 1   Box Bear 2   Bye Bye Bear   Corner Bear   Crying Bear

Dunce Bear   Note Bear   Pencil Bear   Pledge Bear   Sad Bag Bear

Stamp Bear   T Shirt Bear   Tummy Bear   Upward Bear   Writing Bears

Fantasy Bears

Bear Flight   Bearlerina   Bears' Nest   Bedtime Bear

Castle Bear   Dollar Bear   Harlequin Bear   Jester Bear

Juggler Bear   Knight Bear   Magician Bear   Pirate Bear   Pocket Bear

Rose Bear   Scissors Bear   Ship Bear   Spinning Bear

Time Bear   Toothbeary   Vaudeville Bear

Recreation Bears

Bearball	Bearobics	Book Bear	Checkers Bears	Climbing Bear
Croquet Bear	Dancing Bear	Fishing Bear	Golf Cub	Hula Bear
Hunt Bear	Knitting Bear	Phonobear	Portrait Bear	Roller Bear
Ski Bear	Strong Bear	Surf Bear	Swim Bear	Toy Boat Bear

Working Bears

Air Bear   Artist Bear   Bear Peep   Bearber Pole   Bearforce

Blackboard Bear   Cowbear   Engineer Bear   Libearace

Libearian   Mac-n-Bear   Painter Bear   Paperbear   Printing Bear

Register Bear   Salesbear   Seamstress Bear   Sorting Bear   Tailor Bear

Waiter Bear

Computer A.D.vantage

P.O. Box 2329
Camarillo, CA 93011
805-485-2688

———————◆———————

Collection	Format	No./Size Disks	Price	Computer
A.D.vantage Paint	Paint	1-800K	$34.95	Mac
A.D.vantage Sampler '91	EPS	2-800K	$19.95	Mac
A.D.vantage PostScript Vol. 1.1*	EPS	9-800K	$79.95	Mac

Notes:

*Not shown or indexed in this volume. Contact Computer A.D.vantage for more information.

A.D.vantage Paint

Aliens

Alien 01

Alien 03

Alien 06

Alien 10

Alien 11

Alien 13

Skateboading Spaceman

People

Axe Man

Business Man

Camera Woman

Couch Potatoes

Couple in Love?

Frog Legs

Happy Couple

Head Sketch

Joyful

A.D.vantage Paint (continued)

People (continued)

Lecturing   Mac Attack 1   Mac Attack 2   Neck Problems

New Glasses   Oil Change   Reporter/Female   Waiter   Woman

Recreation

All Am. Sportsman 1   All Am. Sportsman 2   Diving Catch   Entertainment System

Family TV (Small)   Golfer   Line Tackler

A.D.vantage Paint (continued)

Muscle Man   Referee   Runner   Singer/Jazz

Stuffed Animals   The Big Catch   Watching TV   Weight Training Woman

A.D.vantage Sampler '91 Disk 1

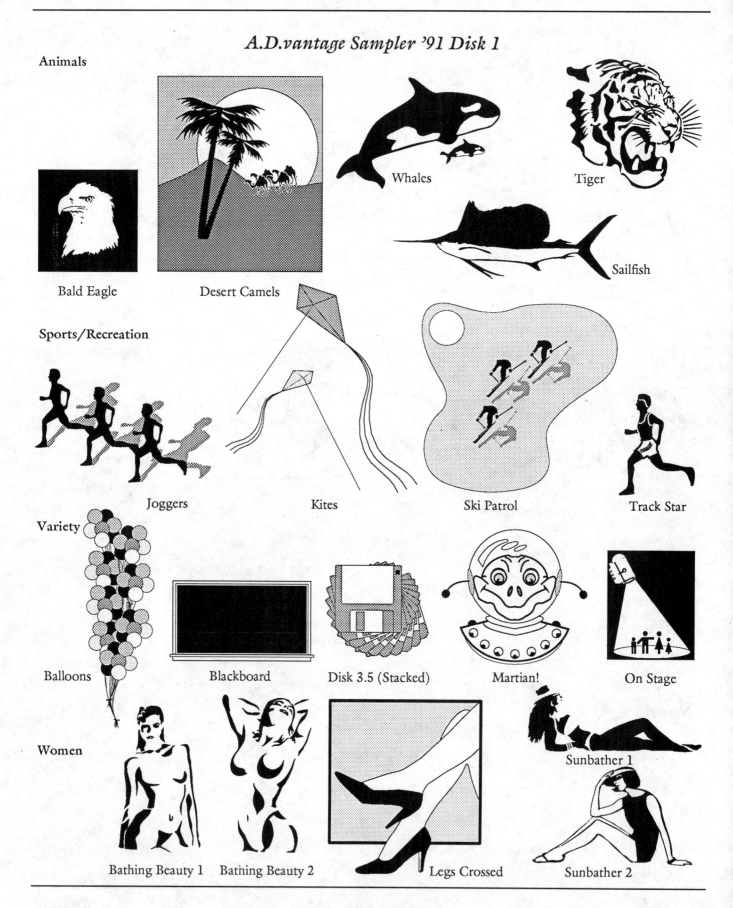

Animals

Bald Eagle

Desert Camels

Whales

Tiger

Sailfish

Sports/Recreation

Joggers

Kites

Ski Patrol

Track Star

Variety

Balloons

Blackboard

Disk 3.5 (Stacked)

Martian!

On Stage

Women

Bathing Beauty 1

Bathing Beauty 2

Legs Crossed

Sunbather 1

Sunbather 2

A.D.vantage Sampler '91 Disk 2

Backgrounds

Bkgrd 06

Bkgrd 09

Bkgrd 10

Borders

Border 01

Border 03d

Border 04

Border 07

Frames

Frame 01

Frame 02

A.D.vantage Sampler '91 Disk 2 (continued)

Frames (continued)

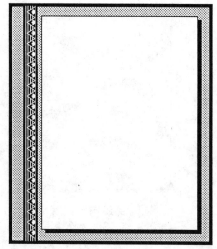

Frame 06

Frame 07

Miscellaneous

Ribbon Medal

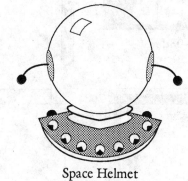

Space Helmet

Visa Card

Davka Corporation
845 N. Michigan Avenue, Suite 843
Chicago, IL 60611
312-944-4070
800-621-8227 orders only

---◆---

Collection	Format	No./Size Disks	Price	Computer
DavkaGraphics I	FullPaint	1-800K	$34.95	Mac
DavkaGraphics II	FullPaint	1-800K	$34.95	Mac
DavkaGraphics III	FullPaint	1-800K	$34.95	Mac
DavkaGraphics EPS: Jewish Holidays	EPS	1-800K	$79.95	Mac
DavkaGraphics EPS: Israel*	EPS	1-800K	$79.95	Mac

Notes:

* Not shown or indexed in this volume. Contact Davka Corporation for more information.

DavkaGraphics I

Bar/Bat Mitzvah

Biblical Figures

People

Sabbath

Signs

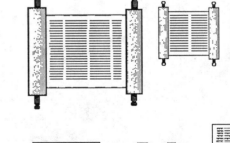

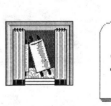

Torah

DavkaGraphics I (continued)

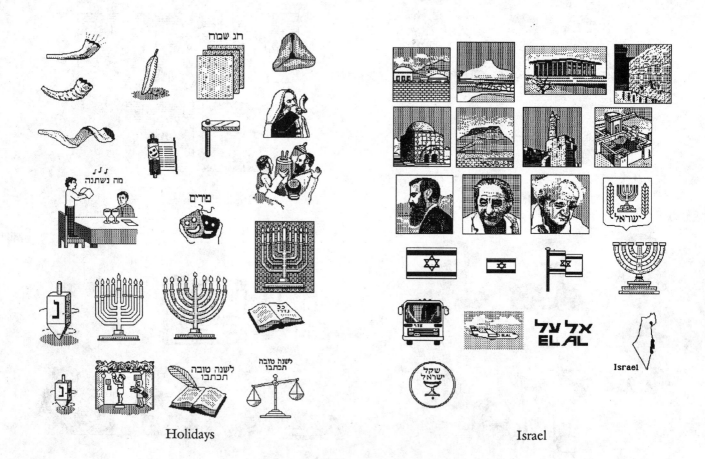

Holidays

Israel

Symbols

DavkaGraphics II

Fonts & Borders

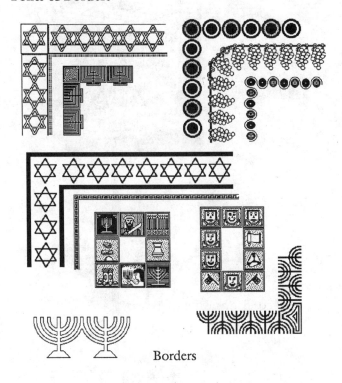

Borders

Shadow Font

Holidays

Hanukah

Menorahs

DavkaGraphics II (continued)

Holidays (continued)

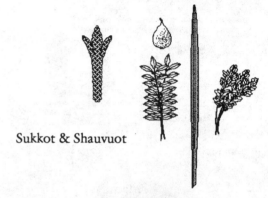

Passover

Sukkot & Shauvuot

Israel

Jerusalem

Kotel

Various Scenes

DavkaGraphics II (continued)

People

People

Studying Talmud

Ritual Objects

Rosh Hashana Plate

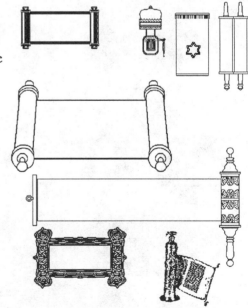

Miscellaneous Objects

Scrolls

DAVKA CORPORATION

DavkaGraphics II (continued)

Symbols

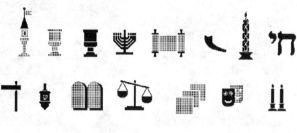

DavkaBats

Seals

Words

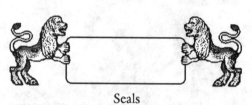

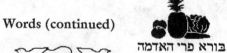

Star of David

Words (continued)

Shalom

Blessings

DavkaGraphics III

Font 1

אבגדהוזח
טיכלמנסע
פצקרשת
רסורץ
0987654321

Font 2

אבגדהוזחטי
כלמנסעפצ
קרשתרסורץ

Font 3

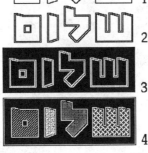

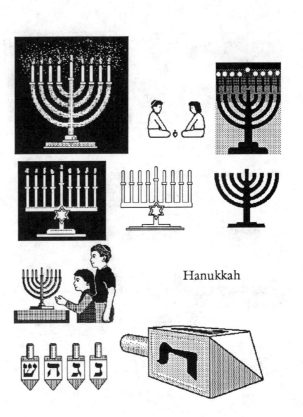

Hanukkah

DavkaGraphics III (continued)

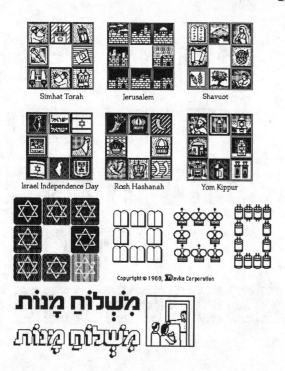

Simhat Torah   Jerusalem   Shavuot

Israel Independence Day   Rosh Hashanah   Yom Kippur

Copyright © 1988, Davka Corporation

Holiday Borders

Rosh Hashanah

Hanukkah

Purim

Holiday Calendars

Holiday Headlines

Lulav

DavkaGraphics III (continued)

Build your own
Sukkah

Use the lasso to drag items
from below. Decorate your
own sukkah!

Moed

Sukkot

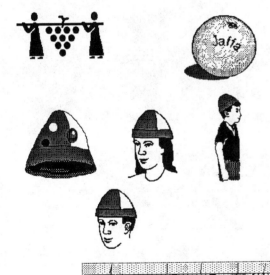

Signs

People, Places, Things

Teaching

DavkaGraphics III (continued)

Activities

Tamuz	Sivan	Iyar	Nisan
תמוז	סיון	אייר	ניסן
Heshvan	Tishri	Elul	Av
חשון	תשרי	אלול	אב
Adar	Shevat	Teveth	Kislev
אדר	שבט	טבת	כסלו

Hebrew Months

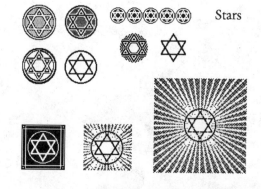

Stars

Mazel Tov

Synagogue

DavkaGraphics.EPS: Holidays

Apple &
Honey

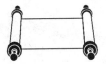

Big Scroll

Blowing the
Shofar

Candles

Challot

Dreidel

Four Cups

Grogger

Hanukkah

Hanukkah
Dingbat

Hanukkah
Menorah

Hanukkah
Script

Happy Purim

Kiddush Cup

Lag B'Omer

Lulav &
Etrog

Matzah

Moed

Next Year

Pesah

Planting a
Tree

Praying
Man

Purim

Purim Masks

Rosh
Hashanah

Shabbat

Shabbat
Shalom

Shanah
Tovah

Shavuot

Shavuot
Hebrew

Simhat Tovah

Simhat Torah
Scroll

Sukkot

Sukkot
Dingbat

Tu B'Shevat

Yom Kippur

Dubl Click

9316 Deering Avenue
Chatsworth, CA 91311
818-700-9525

———————◆———————

Collection	Format	No./Size Disks	Price	Computer
WetPaint™:				
Volume 1: Classic Clip Art*	Paint	3-800K	$89.95	Mac
Volume 2: For Publishing*	Paint	3-800K	$89.95	Mac
Volume 3: Animal Kingdom*	Paint	3-800K	$89.95	Mac
Volume 4: Special Occasions*	Paint	3-800K	$89.95	Mac
Volume 5: Printer's Helper*	Paint	3-800K	$89.95	Mac
Volume 6: Industrial Revolution*	Paint	3-800K	$89.95	Mac
Volume 7: Old Earth Almanac*	Paint	3-800K	$89.95	Mac
Volume 8: Island Life*	Paint	3-800K	$89.95	Mac
Volume 9: All The People*	Paint	3-800K	$89.95	Mac
MacTut With ProGlyph**	Paint	2-800K	$49.95	Mac

Notes:

* Not shown in its entirety in this book. Due to the large amount of electronic clip art available from this company, we are showing only one page of samples from each of the volumes. Dubl Click's volumes have approximately 75–100 paint images in each topical set.

**Not shown in this volume. MacTut is Egyptian-style art, and includes a bitmapped font. Contact Dubl Click for more information.

• CD-ROM available for $349.95.

Volume 1: Classic Clip Art

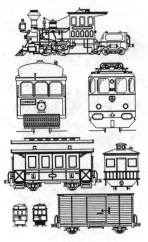

All Aboard #2

Be Mine

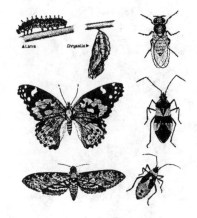

Bug Life

Computers #3

Howdy Pard

Money, Money

Sea & Ski

Travel

Xmas Season

Because of the large amount of clip art available in this volume, we are showing only samples of the artwork.

Animals #1

Volume 2: For Publishing

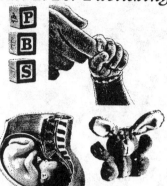

Baby Miracle

Capital Letters #1

Fitness #2

Holy Places

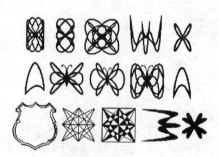

Logo Shapes #2

Scenes #1

T-Shirt Shop

Warm Things

Because of the large amount of clip art available in this volume, we are showing only samples of the artwork.

Volume 3: Animal Kingdom

Burros & Buffalos

Camels

Domestic Dogs

Flitterbies

Giant Panda

Great Cats

In Deep Places #2

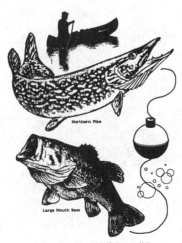

Let's Go Fishing #1

Tortoises

Because of the large amount of clip art available in this volume, we are showing only samples of the artwork.

Volume 4: Special Occasions

Angels #1

Black & White

Children

Jonah & Angel

Kewpie Summer

Lessons

Moses, Bread & Angel

The Cooks

Waltz & Dance Border

Because of the large amount of clip art available in this volume, we are showing only samples of the artwork.

Volume 5: Printer's Helper

Ali & Friends

Banners & Bells

Borders & Frames

Fancy Headers

Flower & Clown Circles

Gargoyle & Farm

N

Oak, Rose, Nouveau

Punch Finis

Because of the large amount of clip art available in this volume, we are showing only samples of the artwork.

Volume 6: Industrial Revolution

Boys & Shopping Signs

2 Bikes

Dance Hall Girl

Dangerous Types

Discussions

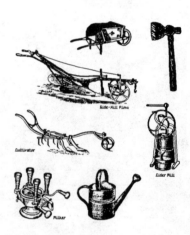

Farm Equipment

Lingerie

Racing Yacht & Longboat

The News

Because of the large amount of clip art available in this volume, we are showing only samples of the artwork.

Volume 7: Old Earth Almanac

Animals

Baby Fun

Corner Flower, Menu

Happy

Lovers

Mother & Babe

Orangutan

Sea Life

Stork & Flamingo

Because of the large amount of clip art available in this volume, we are showing only samples of the artwork.

Volume 8: Island Life

Australian Labels

Bottlenose Dolphins

Hula #1

Island Flora #3

Kangaroo M.C.

Little Grass Shack

Playing Possum #1

Surfing Safari #1

Walrus Pair

Because of the large amount of clip art available in this volume, we are showing only samples of the artwork.

Volume 9: All the People

Albert, Leo & Vincent

At Home #4

Building

Babies

DTP

Hockey

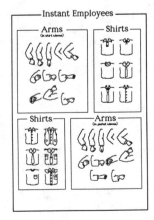

Instant Employees #2

Three Sports

Vacation Family

Because of the large amount of clip art available in this volume, we are showing only samples of the artwork.

Dynamic Graphics

6000 N. Forest Park Drive, P.O. Box 1901
Peoria, IL 61656-1901
800-255-8800 orders only
309-688-5873 fax

———————◆———————

Collection	Format	No./Size Disks	Price	Computer
Designer's Club CD-ROM, Volume 1*	EPS	1 CD-ROM	$594.00	Mac/IBM
Designer's Club CD-ROM, Volume 2*	EPS	1 CD-ROM	$594.00	Mac/IBM
Designer's Club Monthly Subscription*	EPS	2 to 4-800K	$49.50	Mac/IBM
Electronic Clipper Monthly Subscription*	EPS/TIFF	9+ 800K	$67.50/mo	Mac/IBM

Notes:

NOTICE TO ALL USERS:

* Not shown in its entirety in this book. Due to the large amount of electronic clip art available from this company, we are showing only one page of samples from each of the sets.

DYNAMIC GRAPHICS

Designer's Club

CD ROM Volume 1 Samples

Athletics 1   Commerce 1   Commerce 2   Design Elements 1   Humor   Leisure Time 1

People 1   People 2   Sales & Promotions   School Days 1   Seasonal 1   Seasonal 2

CD ROM Volume 2 Samples

Athletics 2   Attention Getters   Borders & Designs   Christmas & Food   Commerce 3

Design Elements 2   Health & Medical 1   People & Commerce   Sales & Leisure   Seasonal 3   Seasonal 4   Spring & Lifestyles

Designer's Club August 1991 Samples

Because of the large amount of clip art available in this volume, we are showing only samples of the artwork.

Electronic Clipper, August 1991

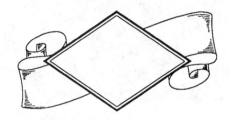

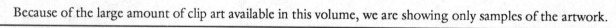

Because of the large amount of clip art available in this volume, we are showing only samples of the artwork.

Electric Beach Computer Products

5538 Pearl Road
Cleveland, OH 44129
216-845-6260
800-837-6260 Orders/FAX

Collection	Format	No./Size Disks	Price	Computer
Coloring Book Volume 1	Paint	1-400K	$12.95	Mac
Coloring Book Volume 2	Paint	1-400K	$12.95	Mac
Coloring Book Volume 3	Paint	1-400K	$12.95	Mac
Coloring Book Volume 4	Paint	1-400K	$12.95	Mac
Coloring Book Volume 5*	Paint	1-400K	$12.95	Mac
Coloring Book Volume 6*	Paint	1-400K	$12.95	Mac
Coloring Book Volume 7*	Paint	1-400K	$12.95	Mac
Christmas Clip Art Volume 1	Paint	1-400K	$14.95	Mac
Christmas Clip Art Volume 2*	Paint	1-400K	$14.95	Mac
Christmas Clip Art Volume 3*	Paint	1-400K	$14.95	Mac
Easter Clip Art Volume 1	Paint	1-400K	$14.95	Mac
Easter Clip Art Volume 2*	Paint	1-400K	$14.95	Mac
Business Clip Art Volume 1	Paint	1-400K	$14.95	Mac
Business Clip Art Volume 2*	Paint	1-400K	$14.95	Mac
Borders Volume 1*	Paint	1-400K	$14.95	Mac
Borders Volume 2*	Paint	1-400K	$14.95	Mac
Borders Volume 3*	Paint	1-400K	$14.95	Mac
Borders Volume 4*	Paint	1-400K	$14.95	Mac
Borders Volume 5*	Paint	1-400K	$14.95	Mac
Borders Volume 6*	Paint	1-400K	$14.95	Mac

Notes:

* Not shown or indexed in this volume. Contact Electric Beach for more information.

• All four Coloring Book volumes $39.95.

• Sampler Coloring Book & Clip Art Disk (not shown in this book) $6.95.

• Note that some of this company's images appear sideways. If you wish to edit and print them in a horizontal format, you'll need a program such as Canvas or SuperPaint that lets you do so.

Business Volume 1

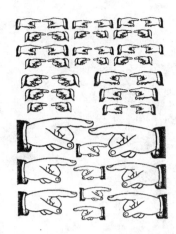

Accents 01

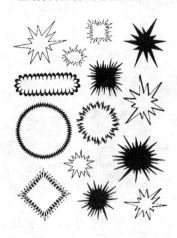

Accents 02

Arrows 01

Arrows 02

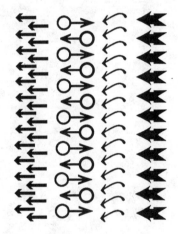

Arrows 03

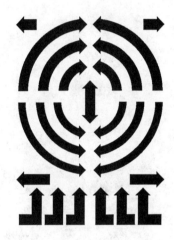

Arrows 04

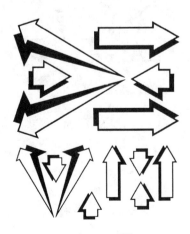

Arrows 05

Banners 01

Office 01

Business Volume 1 (continued)

Office 02

Office 03

Starbursts 01

Starbursts 02

Stars 01

Christmas Clip Art Volume 1

Basket, Snowflake

Bulbs, Wreath

Candles, Santa

Children, Snowman

Father Time, New Year

Flowers, Tree, Decorations

Santas, Candy Cane

Santas, Reindeer

Christmas Clip Art Volume 1 (continued)

Snowman, Santa

Stocking, Candy

Tree, Snow, Wreaths

Easter Clip Art Volume 1

Candles

Christ on Cross

Christ, Prayer

Church Bulletin Cover

Cross & Bible (Large)

Cross, Communion

Crosses

Flowers, Palm Sunday

Flowers, Sunrise

Easter Clip Art Volume 1 (continued)

He is Risen, Christ

Rabbits & Eggs

Rabbits, Child, Dove

The Tomb & Christ

Clip Art and Coloring Book Volume 1

Appaloosa

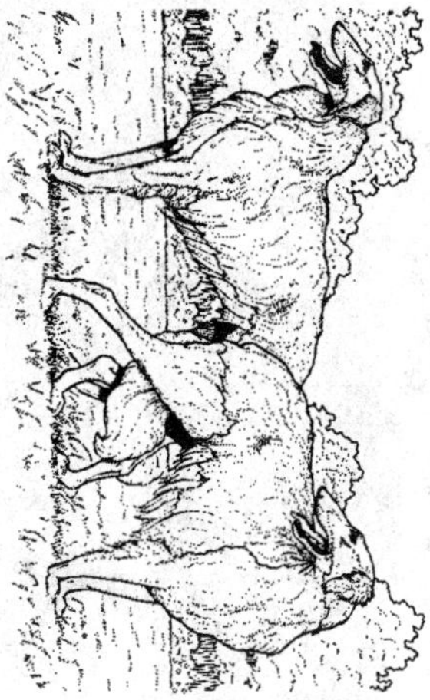

Borzoi

Dalmatian

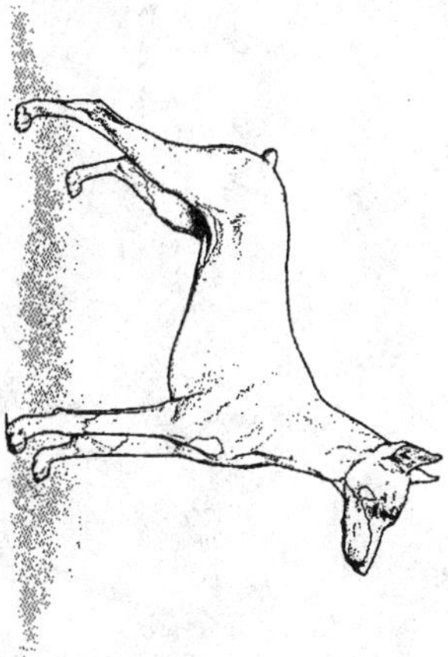

Doberman Pinscher

English Sheepdog

Japanese Bobtail

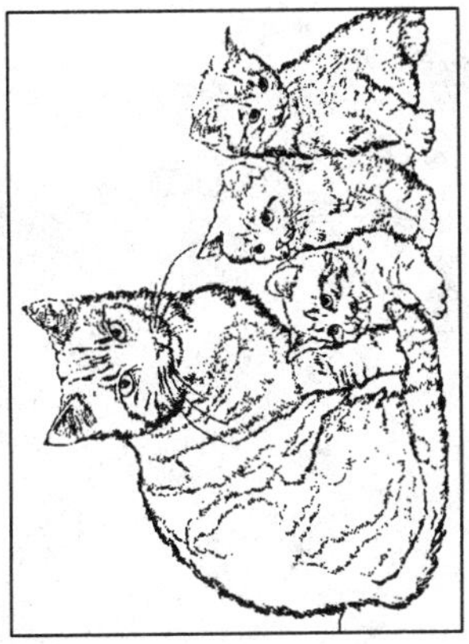

Marmalade Short-tail

Morgan

Persian Kitten

Clip Art and Coloring Book Volume 1 (continued)

Pteranodon

Saddlebred

Shaded Cameo Persian

Shetland Pony

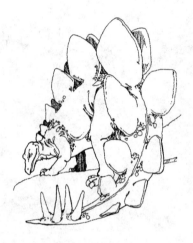

Stegosaurus

Teratosaurus

Triceratops

Clip Art and Coloring Book Volume 2

American Shetland   Ankylosaurus   Arab

Balinese   Beagle   Chow Chow

Collie   Dachshund   Friesian

Clip Art and Coloring Book Volume 2 (continued)

Kittens

Pinto

Plateosaurus

Protoceratops

Ragdoll

Short-Hair

Spinosaurus

Antosaurus

Archelon

Armadillo

Barracuda

Bluebirds

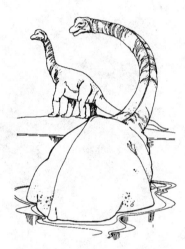

Brachiosaurus

Cardinals

Elasmosaurus

Flounder

Clip Art and Coloring Book Volume 3 (continued)

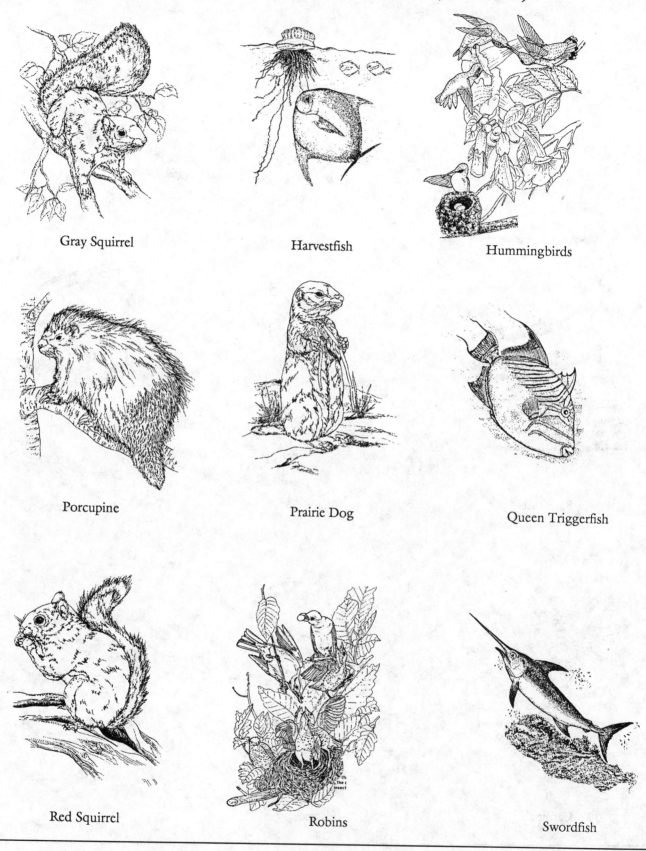

Gray Squirrel

Harvestfish

Hummingbirds

Porcupine

Prairie Dog

Queen Triggerfish

Red Squirrel

Robins

Swordfish

Clip Art and Coloring Book Volume 4

Angel Fish

Asiatic Lady's Slipper

Azalea

Black Eyed Susan

Caribbean Flamingo

Cockatoo

Common Peafowl

Discus

Easter Orchid

Clip Art and Coloring Book Volume 4 (continued)

Jack-in-the-Pulpit

Pearl Gourami

Red Passion Flower

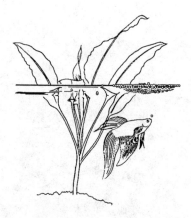

Siamese Fighting Fish

Sunbittern

Tallflower

Water Lily

Electronic Pen Ltd.
4131 Cimarron Drive
Clarkston, GA 30021
404-751-8040
404-296-8623 fax

◆

Collection	Format	No./Size Disks	Price	Computer
Visual Arts Designers Resource*	EPS	3-800K	$125.00	Mac/IBM
Visual Arts Networking Resource*	EPS	2-800K	$125.00	Mac/IBM
Visual Arts Publishers Resource	EPS	6-800K	$195.00	Mac/IBM

Notes:

*Not shown or indexed in this volume. Contact Electronic Pen for more information

• All art has been compressed onto the 800K disks.
• Designers Resource is a collection of EPS backgrounds, gradations, scenes, overlays, and design elements.
• Networking Resource is a set of PostScript fonts and accompanying black-and-white EPS clip art consisting of networking equipment.
• Includes a utility called Phoenix which allows you to lighten or darken as well as rotate any image before placing it into the document.

ELE

TVA Disk One

Food & Leisure

Apple Core   Beer Pump   Cassette   Cherries   Cocktail Splash

Coffee Cup   Hamburger   Instrument Icons   Music

Compact Discs   Sunset   Synth

Records

Strawberry   Sports Icons #1   Sports Icons #2   Sports Icons #3

The Optic   Violin   Wine Bottle   Wine Glasses

TVA Disc One (continued)

Office

Angle Poise Lamp

Filing Cabinet

Pen

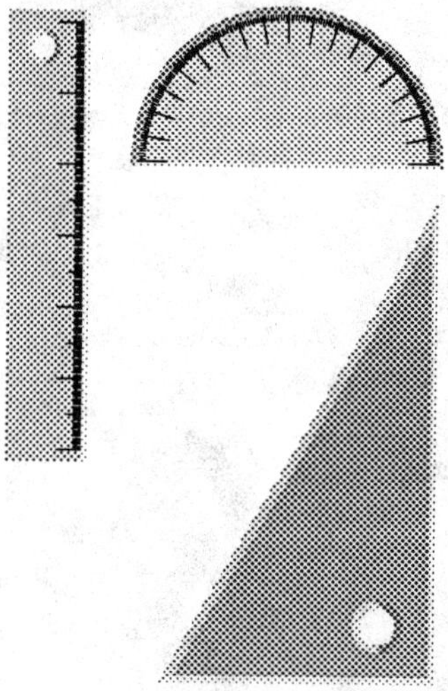

Geometry Set

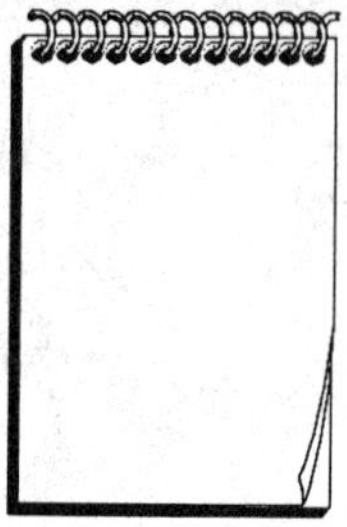

Notepad

Paperclipped Pages

Pencil

Phone

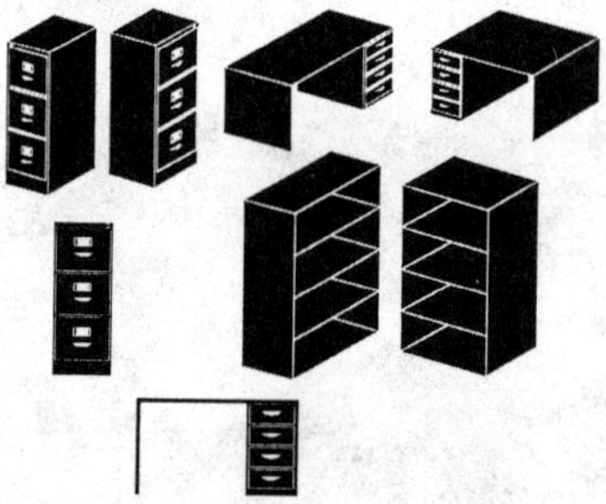

Simple Office Furniture

Swivel Chair

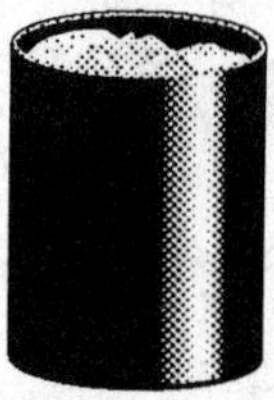

Wastepaper

TVA Disc Two

Modern Caps (Each letter is a separate EPS file.)

ABCDEFGHIJKLM
NOPQRSTUVWXYZ

Artist Ballerina Cook Footballer Happy Guy Lady Jogger Lady Runner Lady Typer

Man at Desk 1 Man at Desk 2 Runner Skier Soccer Swimmers Golfer

Hands Tennis Waiter

Press For Action Man in Suit Mug Shot Lady Face

Rip Caps (Each letter is a separate EPS file.)

ABCDE
FGHIJKLMNO
PQRSTUVWXYZ

TVA Disc Three

Avantec (Each letter is a separate EPS file.)

A B C D E F G H I J K L
M N O P Q R S T U V W X Y Z

General

Analogue Watch

Barred Window

Blank Certificate

Bow Tie

Closed Door

Candle

Closed Book

Dice

Film

Flower

Key

Key Ring

Lock & Key

Screwdriver

Illustrative Map

Pipe

Plant #1

Ringpull

Plant #2

Open Door

Scale

Palm Tree

Quill & Inkpot

Stopwatch

Wall Clock

World Globe

Winter Tree

Watch Hands

Open Book

Watch Example

TVA Disc Four

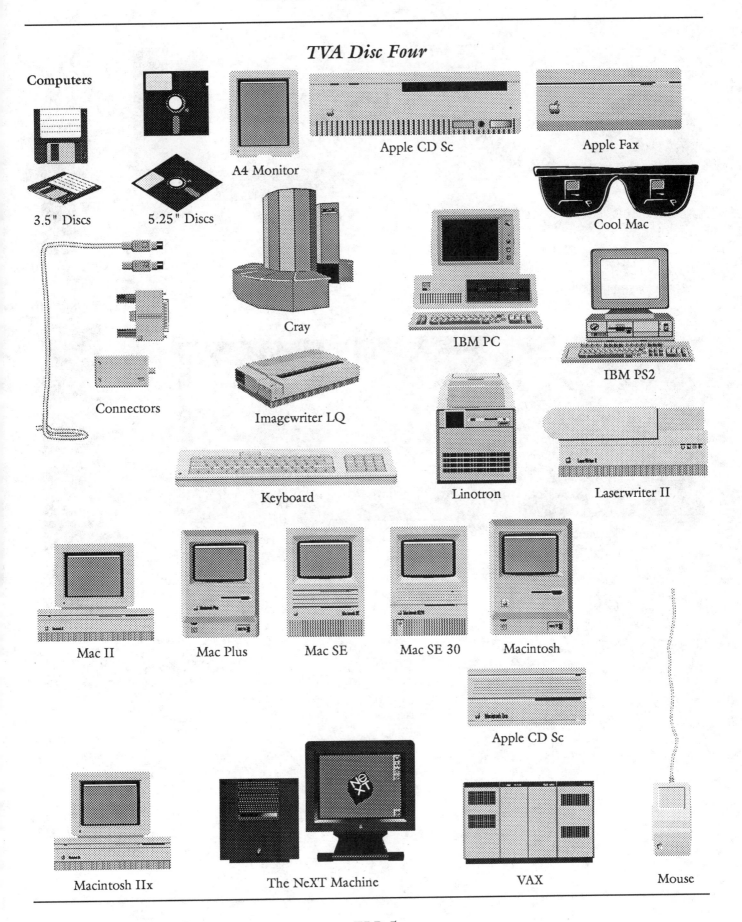

Computers

3.5 " Discs

5.25 " Discs

A4 Monitor

Apple CD Sc

Apple Fax

Cool Mac

Connectors

Cray

Imagewriter LQ

IBM PC

IBM PS2

Keyboard

Linotron

Laserwriter II

Mac II

Mac Plus

Mac SE

Mac SE 30

Macintosh

Apple CD Sc

Macintosh IIx

The NeXT Machine

VAX

Mouse

TVA Disc Four (continued)

Layout Enhancers

Circle BW

Confidential

Grad BW Horiz

Grad WB Horiz

Grad BW Vert   Grad WB Vert

Grad Underline

Page Background #1

Page Background #2

Page Background #3

Grey

Press Release

Swish

Top Secret

TVA Disk Five

Dingbatz

Access

Amex

CD Logo

Eurocard

MasterCard

Visa

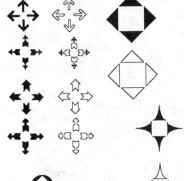

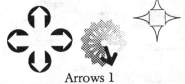
Arrows 1

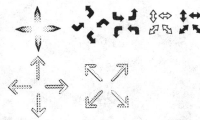
Arrows 2

Computer Dingbatz

Balloons

Litter

Dingbatz 1

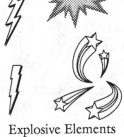
Explosive Elements

Expressions

Weather Dingbatz

Hi-Tech

Plane

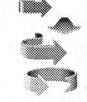
Shaded 3D Arrows

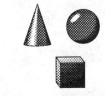
Shaded 3D Shapes

Shiny Dollar

Shiny Pound

Phone Symbols

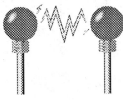
Sparking

Union Jack

United States of Europe

USA Flag

TVA Disc Five (continued)

Layout Enhancers

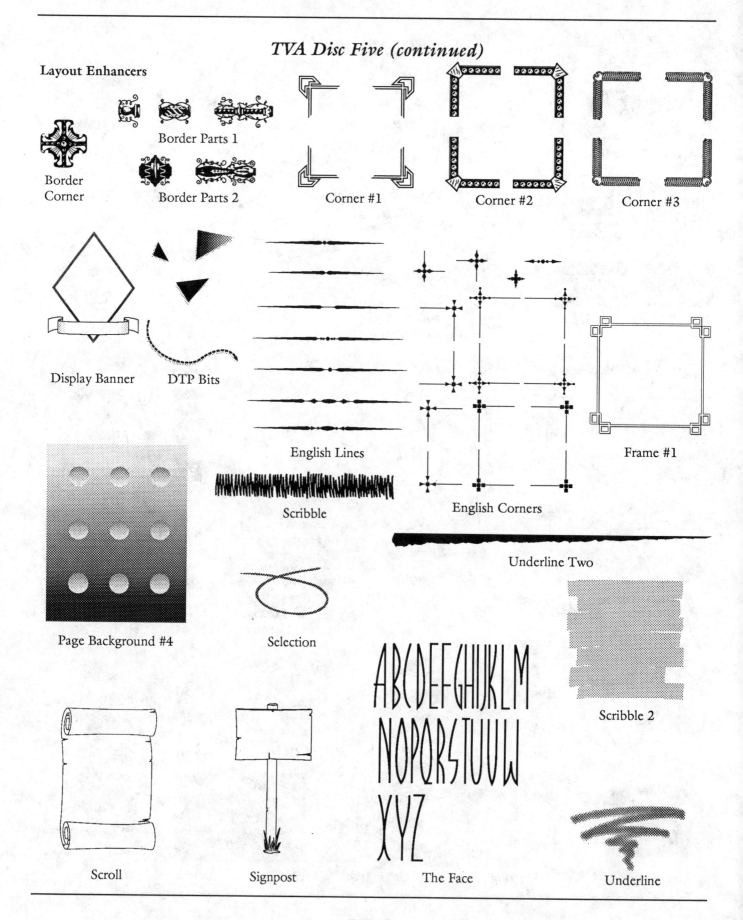

Border Parts 1

Border Corner

Border Parts 2

Corner #1

Corner #2

Corner #3

Display Banner

DTP Bits

English Lines

Scribble

English Corners

Frame #1

Page Background #4

Selection

Underline Two

Scribble 2

Scroll

Signpost

The Face

Underline

TVA Disc Six

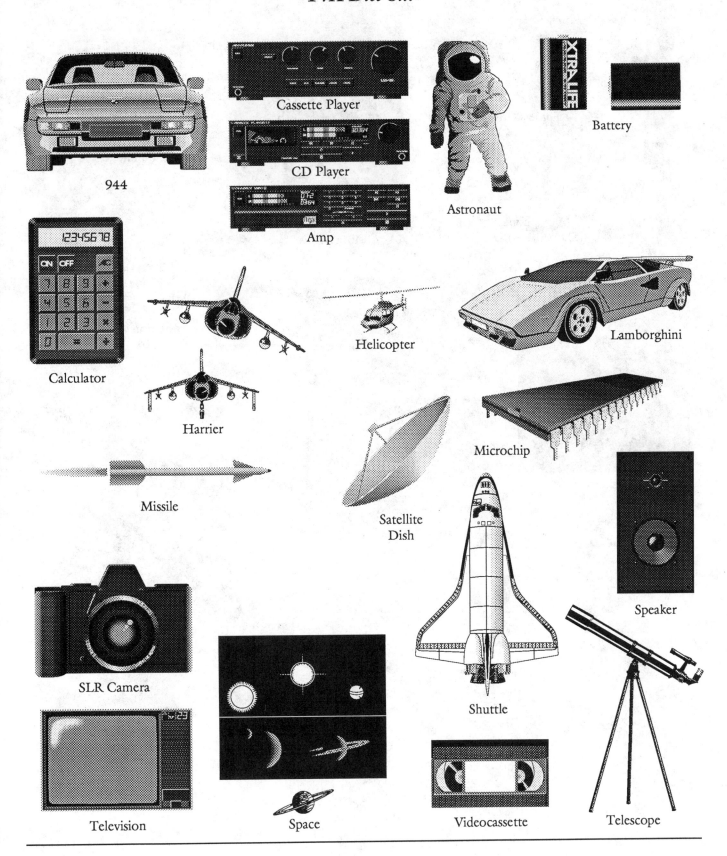

944

Cassette Player

CD Player

Amp

Astronaut

Battery

Calculator

Harrier

Helicopter

Lamborghini

Missile

Microchip

Satellite
Dish

Speaker

SLR Camera

Shuttle

Television

Space

Videocassette

Telescope

TVA Extra Disc

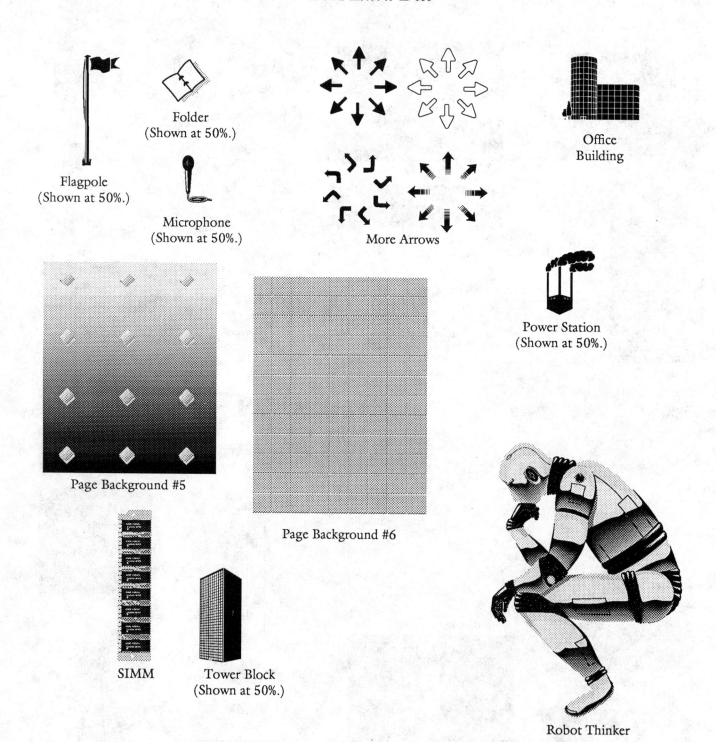

Flagpole
(Shown at 50%.)

Folder
(Shown at 50%.)

Microphone
(Shown at 50%.)

More Arrows

Office
Building

Power Station
(Shown at 50%.)

Page Background #5

Page Background #6

SIMM

Tower Block
(Shown at 50%.)

Robot Thinker

Enzan Hoshigumi
c/o Qualitas Trading Company
6907 Norfolk Road
Berkeley, CA 94705
415-848-8080
415-848-8009 fax

◆

Collection	Format	No./Size Disks	Price	Computer
Borders Scroll	Paint	3-800K	$99.95	Mac
Japanese Clip Art Scroll I: Heaven	Paint	1-800K	$79.95	Mac
Japanese Clip Art Scroll II: Earth	Paint	1-800K	$79.95	Mac
The Year of the Dragon	Paint	1-800K	$29.95	Mac

Scroll 1: Heaven

Characters

Dec Art

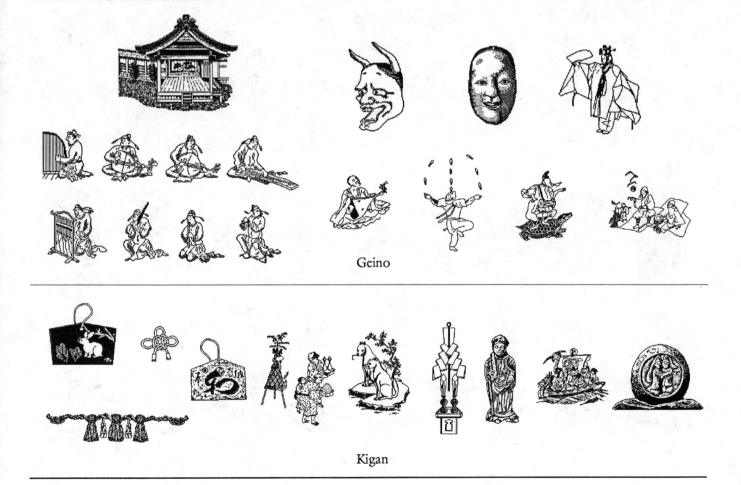

Geino

Kigan

Scroll 1: Heaven (continued)

Mandalas

Matsuri

Pic Chars

Scroll 1: Heaven (continued)

Reiju

Sengai

Scroll 1: Heaven (continued)

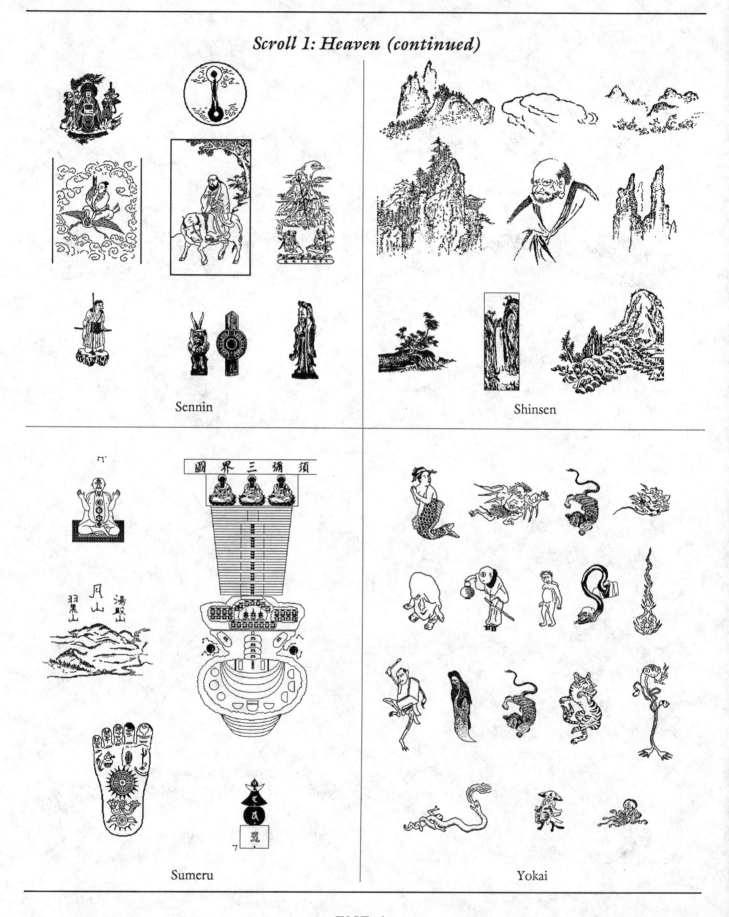

Sennin

Shinsen

Sumeru

Yokai

ENZAN HOSHIGUMI

Scroll 2: Earth

Fuji

Hokusai

誕生気
日月明見
松竹梅秋冬舞存心度
時入学春夏料何礼度
謹賀新年申代慶父母
祈本祝美喜愛引結婚元願二四六九
今築卒業有難越第上幸陣円暑七十

御中先後
大小
正

忌賀賀賀

一三五八
百千万

Ink Brush

Jomon

Scroll 2: Earth (continued)

Kacho

Kankon

Kano

Motifs

Scroll 2: Earth (continued)

Samurai

Symbols

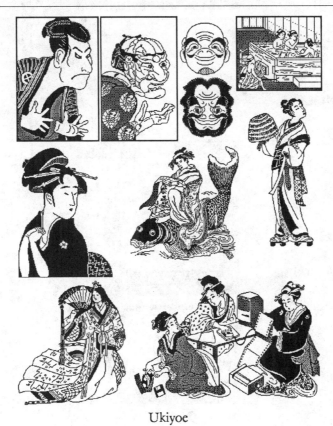

Ukiyoe

Borders Scroll Disk 1

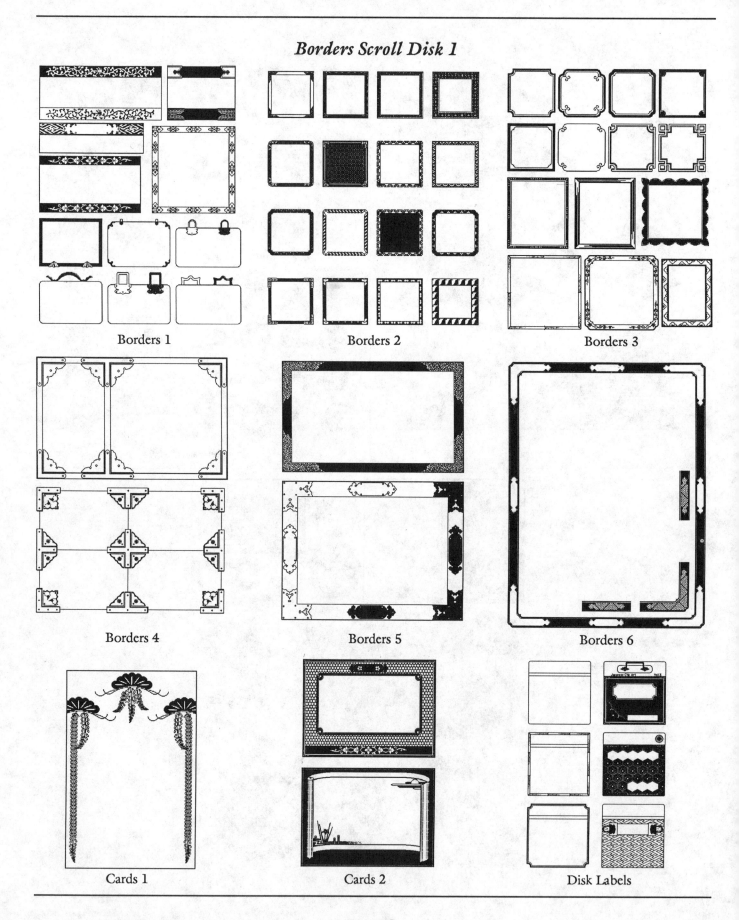

Borders 1

Borders 2

Borders 3

Borders 4

Borders 5

Borders 6

Cards 1

Cards 2

Disk Labels

Borders Scroll Disk 1 (continued)

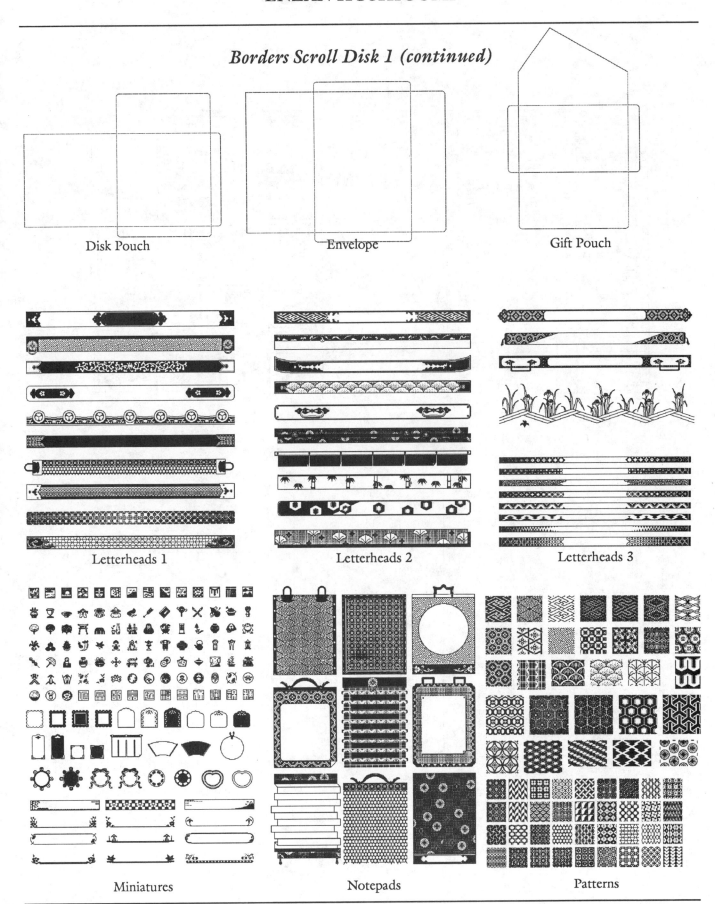

Disk Pouch

Envelope

Gift Pouch

Letterheads 1

Letterheads 2

Letterheads 3

Miniatures

Notepads

Patterns

Borders Scroll Disk 1 (continued)

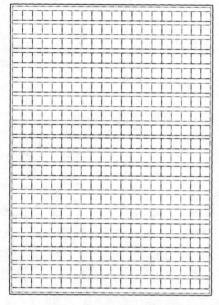

Reportpaper

Scrolls

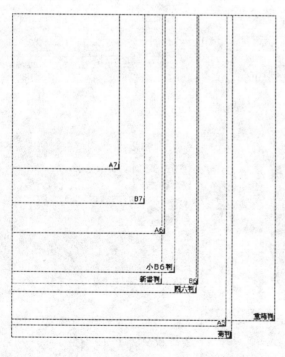

Sizes 1

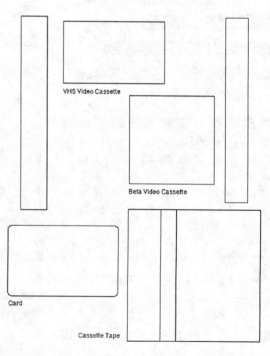

Sizes 2

Borders Scroll Disk 2

Ceramic Art

Doutaku

Inkstone Case

Megascroll

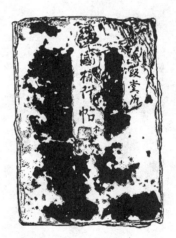

Old Book

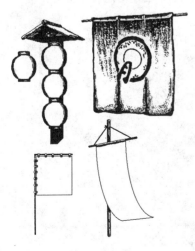

Shop Entries

Signboards 1

Signboards 2

Borders Scroll Disk 2 (continued)

Signboards 3

Signboards 4

Signboards 5

Signboards 6

Signboard 7

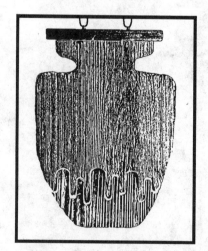

Signboard 8

Borders Scroll Disk 3

Bamboo

Card Border 1

Card Border 2

Card Border 3

Card Border 4

Card Border 5

Card Border 6

Card Border 9

Card Border 10

Wild Geese

Borders Scroll Disk 3 (continued)

Card Border 10

Card Border 11

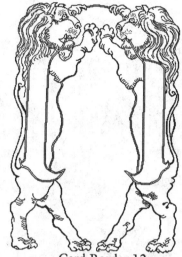

Card Border 12

Card Border 13

Card Border 14

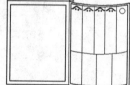

Card Border 15

Hikifuda

Large Border 1

Large Border 2

Large Border 3

Large Border 4

The Year of the Dragon

Dragon 1

Dragon 2

Dragon 3

Dragon 4

Dragon 5

Dragon 6

Dragon 7

Dragon 8

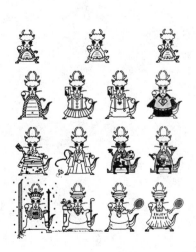

Dragon Club

The Year of the Dragon (continued)

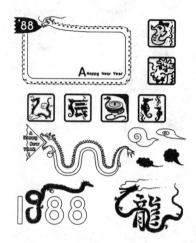

New Year 1

New Year 2

New Year 3

New Year 4

The Characters

FM Waves

70 Derby Alley
San Francisco, CA 94102
415-474-7464
415-474-2820 fax
800-487-1234

Collection	Format	No./Size Disks	Price	Computer
Agenda for the 90's	TIFF	6-800K	$99.00	Mac/IBM
Borders	EPS	6-800K	$99.00	Mac/IBM
Business Cartoons	TIFF	6-800K	$99.00	Mac/IBM
Fantasy	TIFF	7-800K	$99.00	Mac/IBM
Fashion	TIFF	6-800K	$99.00	Mac/IBM
Glamour	TIFF	7-800K	$99.00	Mac/IBM
MacToons	EPS	1-800K	$20.00	Mac/IBM
Arrows*	EPS	3-800K	$49.00	Mac/IBM
Children*	TIFF	6-800K	$99.00	Mac/IBM
Design Elements*	EPS	1-800K	$49.00	Mac/IBM
Education*	TIFF/EPS	6-800K	$99.00	Mac/IBM
Graphic News Network Volume 1*	TIFF/EPS	5-800K	$99.00	Mac/IBM
Health & Fitness*	TIFF/EPS	4-800K	$99.00	Mac/IBM
Icons*	EPS	4-800K	$49.00	Mac/IBM
World Costumes & Flags*	TIFF/EPS	6-800K	$99.00	Mac/IBM

Notes:
*Not shown or indexed in this volume. Contact FM Waves for more information.
• Because TIFF images take up so much disk space, FM Waves has made all of their images fairly small, in order to put more art on each disk. Therefore, we have shown their art in a format that is only a 30% to 50% reduction, compared to a typical 25% reduction. See the introduction of this book for a discussion of percentage sizing.
• All art has been compressed onto the 800K disks.
• Graphic Originals CD-ROM I contains all 6 portfolios shown in this book, plus Animals (100 images) plus demos and bonus images for $279.00.
• Graphic Originals CD-ROM II contains all 8 portfolios not shown for $279.00.
• DTPro CD-ROM contains Arrows, Borders, Design Elements and Icons for $149.00.
• GNN, The Graphic News Network, is a monthly subscription service of 50 current events-related clip art images plus 2 special editions containing 50 bonus images each. Contact FM Waves for more information.

Agenda for the 90's

Drugs & Violence

Armed Kid

Ashtray

Crack Menace

Different Allegiances

Gang Hand

Gun Control

Hoodlum

Kids at War

Loaded Cigarette

Martytr

On Duty

Outlaw

Police Search

Police Woman

Smokehead

Toughs

Under Arrest

Under Fire

Environment

A Close Watch

Butterfly

Chemical Plant

Child Planting Trees

Deer/Factory

Egg World

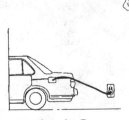
Electric Car

Elephant

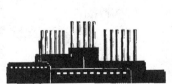
Factory

Futuristic

Hug a Tree

Agenda for the 90's (continued)

Environment (continued)

Hunter   Kids at Play   Lightbulb Globe   Lumberjack   Mountain Lion   Nuclear Plant

O2 Balloon   Ocean Pollution   Oil Drip   Oil Drum   Oil Spill   Recycle

Recycling Bins   Recycling Elf   Storks   Toxic Waste   Trash Can   Water Waste

Miscellaneous

Airplane   Burial Site   Condom   Empty Bowl   Fireman

Grocer   Man in Wheelchair   No Sex   Packed In

Agenda for the 90's (continued)

Politics & Economics

Africa   Bush & Gorby   Chancellor Kohl   Climb to the Top   Communication   Destitute Toddler

**Politics & Economics:
Education Folder**

Books-Horizontal   Books-Vertical   Computer for Baby   Road to Success   Teacher

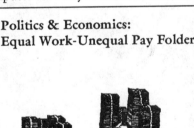

**Politics & Economics:
Equal Work-Unequal Pay Folder**

EEC Barbarians   EEC Cheesecake   Stacks of Money   Success Man   Success Woman

For Democracy

Homeless Sign

**Politics & Economics:
Hands Shaking Folder**

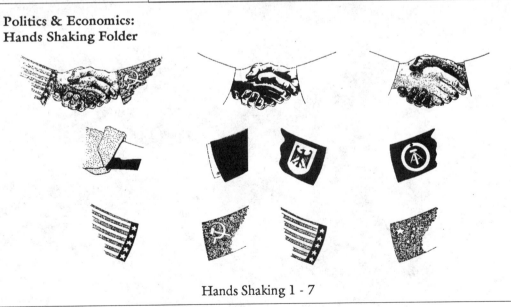

Hands Shaking 1 - 7

Agenda for the 90's (continued)

Politics & Economics (continued)

Kohl Drags B & G

Selling Out

Spare Change

Taxes

Thanks Buddy

Donald Trump

Uncle Sam

Uncle Sam Peel

Politics & Economics: Stretching Dollar Folder

Person Pulling 1 - 9, Person Pulling Outline, Stretching Dollar

Borders

Basic Borders
Each border file includes a completed border as well as a building blocks folder, seen here, to create a custom size.

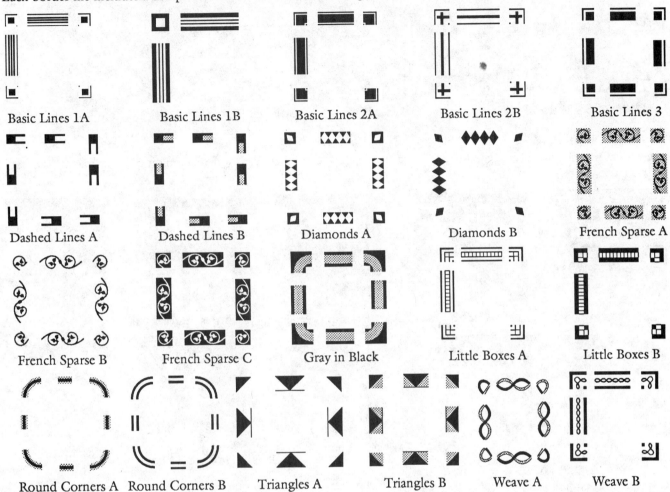

| Basic Lines 1A | Basic Lines 1B | Basic Lines 2A | Basic Lines 2B | Basic Lines 3 |

| Dashed Lines A | Dashed Lines B | Diamonds A | Diamonds B | French Sparse A |

| French Sparse B | French Sparse C | Gray in Black | Little Boxes A | Little Boxes B |

| Round Corners A | Round Corners B | Triangles A | Triangles B | Weave A | Weave B |

Modern Borders
Each border file includes a completed border as well as a building blocks folder, seen here, to create a custom size.

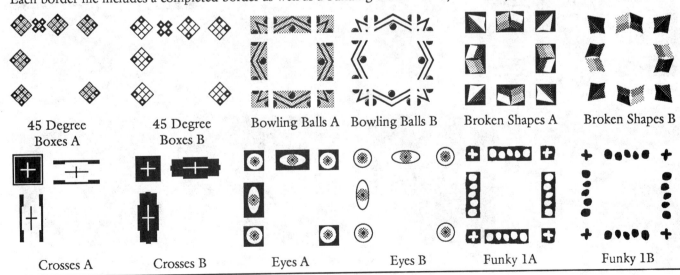

| 45 Degree Boxes A | 45 Degree Boxes B | Bowling Balls A | Bowling Balls B | Broken Shapes A | Broken Shapes B |

| Crosses A | Crosses B | Eyes A | Eyes B | Funky 1A | Funky 1B |

Borders (continued)

Modern Borders (continued)
Each border file includes a completed border as well as a building blocks folder, seen here, to create a custom size.

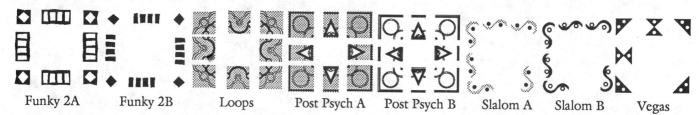

Funky 2A   Funky 2B   Loops   Post Psych A   Post Psych B   Slalom A   Slalom B   Vegas

Old Fashioned Borders
Each border file includes a completed border, a corner of each shown below, as well as a building blocks folder, used to create a custom size.

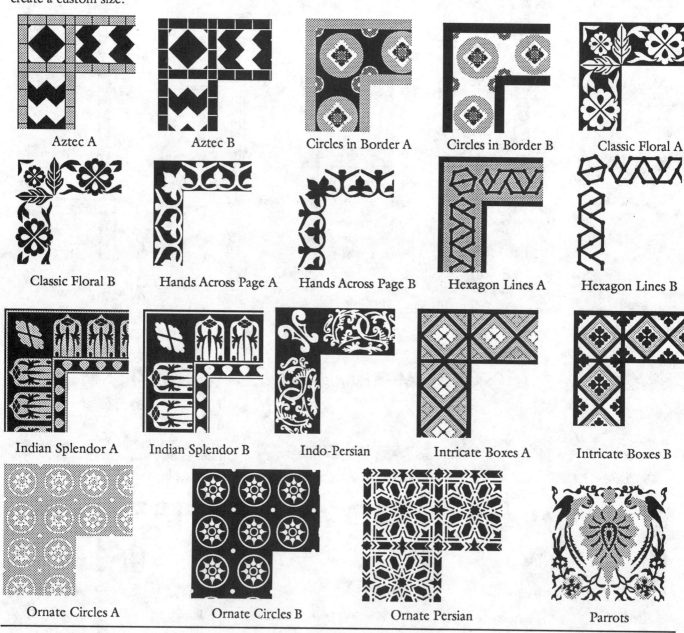

Aztec A   Aztec B   Circles in Border A   Circles in Border B   Classic Floral A

Classic Floral B   Hands Across Page A   Hands Across Page B   Hexagon Lines A   Hexagon Lines B

Indian Splendor A   Indian Splendor B   Indo-Persian   Intricate Boxes A   Intricate Boxes B

Ornate Circles A   Ornate Circles B   Ornate Persian   Parrots

Business Cartoons

Airplane Nap	Alligator Man	Attack	Bad Forecast	Bad Luck
Balancing	Ball & Chain	Balloon	Bored to Death	Brick Man
Buried Hand	Businessmen Fighting	Cape Man	Celebration	Cheers	Computer Friend
Computer Phobia	Crowd of Men	Cut on Dotted Line	Daydreamer	Deadline
Desk Dance	Don't Forget	Drunk Man	Empty Sign	Express

Business Cartoons (continued)

Feeling Small   Fight on Building   Flicking Finger   Frantic   Glutton   Go!

Good Forecast   Great Luck   Guy 1   Guy 2   Hand Holding Little Hand   Hand Sign 1

Hand Sign 2   Happy Boss   Happy Buck   Harshing Down   Hero

Idea Bulb   In Box   Juggling   Killing Your Mac   Look Up!

Looming Deadline   Magic Carpet   Maniac Boss   Money Juggler   Mr. Enthusiasm

Business Cartoons (continued)

Networking   Newspaper   No!   Number 1   Off the Chart

Office Disco   Office Hijinks   Office Prankster   On the Top

Only 8 Arms   Overworked   Paper Airplane   Paperwork   Party Man

Party Talk   Piece of the Puzzle   Playing Cards   Pointer   Posting a Bill

Prepared   Punishment   Ready to Eat   Remember   Running Late

Business Cartoons (continued)

Rx for Success   Sad Sack   Salute   Sharks   Shooting the Phone   Sign with Man

Slacking Off   Slow Meeting   Snooty   Take a Bow   The Boot

Thpbbt!   Throttled   Thumbs Up!

Trash   Trophy   Unenthusiastic   User Friendly

Whoa! Slow Down   Woman 1   ZZZ

Creatures

Fantasy

Aged Troll   Bad Guys   Bigfoot   Brontosaurus   Death's Taker   Dinosaur on Page

Dinosaur with Tracks   Finned Dinosaur   Juggernaut   Mighty Warriors   Monster Funeral

Rex   Theodore Dragon   Thunder Lizard   Zombie

Dwarves & Elves

Balancing Dwarf   Camping Dwarf   Caring for Donkeys   Diver Elf   Dragon with Elf   Dwarf in a Mess

Fantasy (continued)

Dwarves & Elves (continued)

Dwarf Pointing

Dwarf with Flowers

Dynamite Dwarf

Dwarves on a Ladder

Elf at Work

Elf in a Float

Elf Jumping Rope

Elf on Skis

Elf Pulling Left

Elf Pulling Right

Elf Soft Shoe

Elf with Hammer

Elven Brawl

Elves at Play

Endangered Dwarf

Frögryder

Fantasy Head

Gourmet Meal

Hobo Elf

Homeless Elves

Java

Jolly Elf

Juggling Dwarf

La Mort du Mac

Leaf Ride

Naked Dwarf

Smoking Elves

Fantasy (continued)

Folklore & Mythology

Arthur

Big Bad Wolf

Cave Man

Charon

Dark Towers

Don Quixote

Enchantress

Fallen Brother

Giant King

Goblin King

Grendel

Grim Reaper

Jack Climbing
the Stalk

Joan of Arc

Liberty Leading

Macbeth's
Witches

Mermaid

Minotaur

Naked Death

Odysseus

Oh Romeo

Paul Bunyan

Rat King

Fantasy (continued)

Folklore & Mythology (continued)

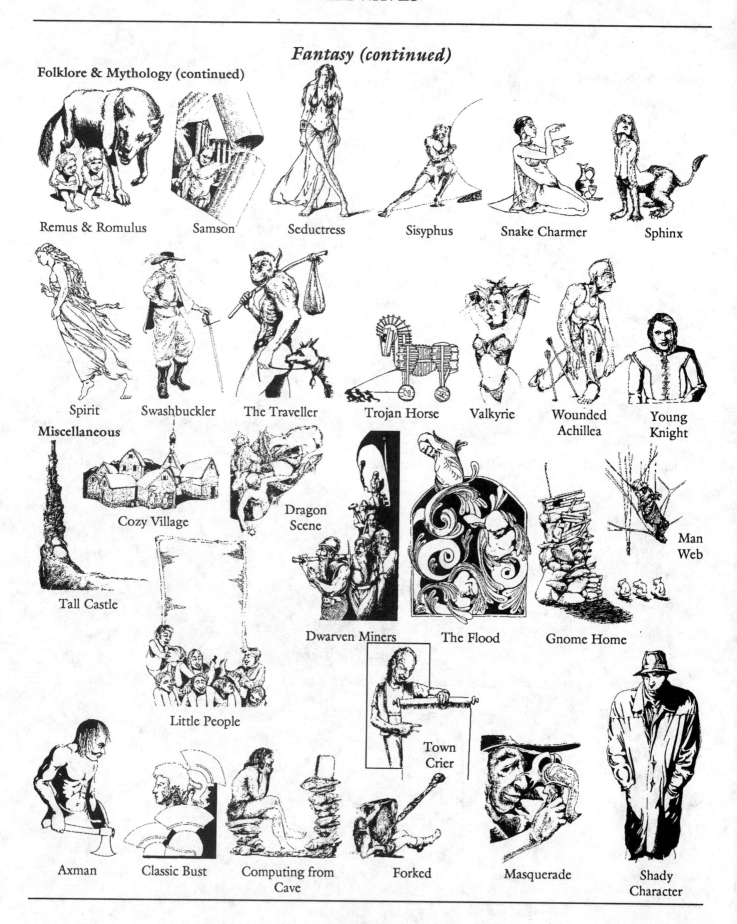

Remus & Romulus

Samson

Seductress

Sisyphus

Snake Charmer

Sphinx

Spirit

Swashbuckler

The Traveller

Trojan Horse

Valkyrie

Wounded Achillea

Young Knight

Miscellaneous

Cozy Village

Dragon Scene

Tall Castle

Little People

Dwarven Miners

The Flood

Gnome Home

Man Web

Town Crier

Axman

Classic Bust

Computing from Cave

Forked

Masquerade

Shady Character

Fashion

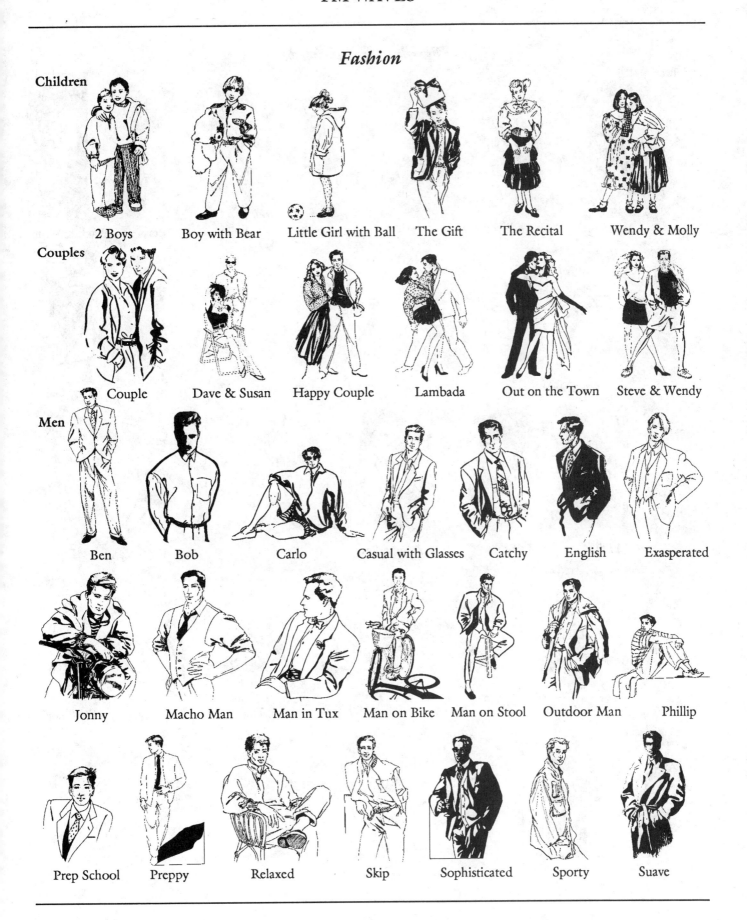

Children

2 Boys   Boy with Bear   Little Girl with Ball   The Gift   The Recital   Wendy & Molly

Couples

Couple   Dave & Susan   Happy Couple   Lambada   Out on the Town   Steve & Wendy

Men

Ben   Bob   Carlo   Casual with Glasses   Catchy   English   Exasperated

Jonny   Macho Man   Man in Tux   Man on Bike   Man on Stool   Outdoor Man   Phillip

Prep School   Preppy   Relaxed   Skip   Sophisticated   Sporty   Suave

Fashion (continued)

Women

Alexandra	At the Club	Barbara	Barbie	Belle	Berta	Black & White
Bold	Cammy	Carla	Carrie	Casual Woman	Cathy	Coy Gal
Cross-Armed Lady	Deborah	Demanding	Denise	Dominique		Erica
Fashion Queen	Gigi	Gloria	Heidi	High Heels	Impression	In the Shadows
Jamie	Jess	Jill	Karen	Lili	Long-legged Lady	Lorna

Fashion (continued)

Women (continued)

Mary · Meg · Melissa · Modern Goddess · Mysterious · Olé · Phone Chat

Safari · Sally · Sarah · Sassy Girls · Scholar · Seducer · Simple Elegance

Slinky · Solemn · Sophisticated · Sultry · Summer Breeze · Sylvia · The Swimmer

Tina · Understated · Watching · Watercolor · Woman in Evening Gown · Woman in Pantsuit

Woman in Peasant Skirt · Woman on the Town · Woman with Dane · Working Mother · Yvette

Glamour

Luxuries

30's Glamour Girl · Alfa · Antique Lady · Candlestick · Car Ride · Cat on Pillow

Champagne · Chilled Champagne · Cigarette Holder · Classic Car · Classic Old Car · Cruisin'

Flower Arrangement · Gull Wing · Iris · Marilyn · Picnic · Whole World in Hands · Woman on Car

Romance

Adored · At the Opera · Birds & Lovers · Kitty · Lady in a Swing · Lounge Lizard

Lovebirds · Lovely Lady · Lovers Dance · Lovers Silhouette · Lusty Lady · Man & Woman · Medieval Delights

Glamour (continued)

Romance (continued)

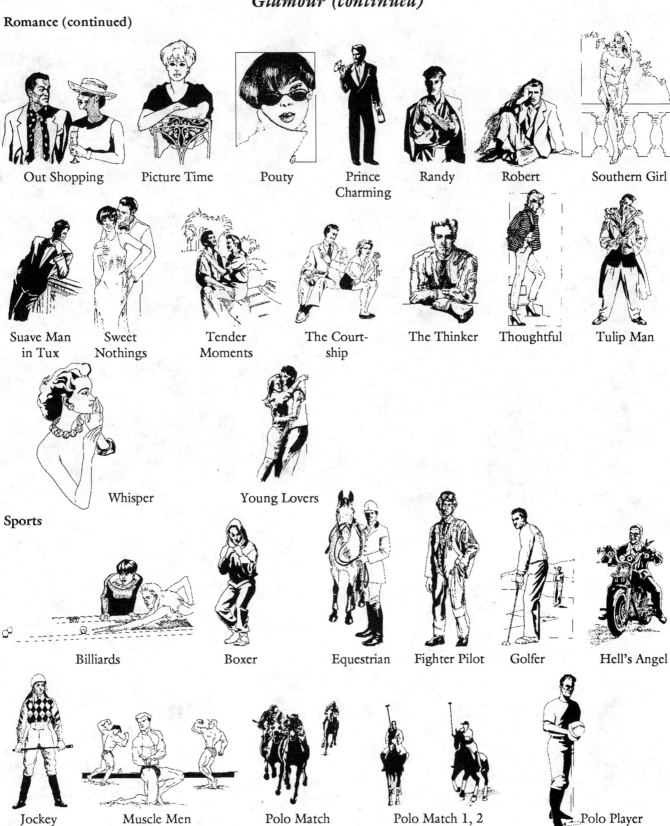

Out Shopping | Picture Time | Pouty | Prince Charming | Randy | Robert | Southern Girl

Suave Man in Tux | Sweet Nothings | Tender Moments | The Court-ship | The Thinker | Thoughtful | Tulip Man

Whisper | Young Lovers

Sports

Billiards | Boxer | Equestrian | Fighter Pilot | Golfer | Hell's Angel

Jockey | Muscle Men | Polo Match | Polo Match 1, 2 | Polo Player

Glamour (continued)

Sports (continued)

Scuba Diver   Tennis Girl   The Chaps   The Squash Player   The Workout   Waterskier   Waterskiing   Woman on Bicycle

Work & Leisure

Bathing Beauty 1   Above the Beach   Bathing Beauty 2   Beach Goddess   Bellhop   Bon Voyage   Cocktail Waitress

Evening Out   Framed Man   Gabbing   Gossip   Man in Chair   Merry Porter   Ocean Liner

On the Phone   Palm Tree Gal   Relaxation   Soothing   Summer's Day   Tanning

The Executive   The Spread   The Stretch   Travel Agent   Tropical Breakfast   Vespa   Woman with Wine

MacToons

Beginner Mac   Cheering Mac   Director Mac   Flying Mac

Graduate Mac   Hatchet Mac   Joker Mac   Lounge Mac

Mac Artist   Mac with Sign   Newspaper Mac   No Question

No!   Sick Mac   Sliding Mac   Using Mac

Grafx Associates

3165 E. 5th Street
Tucson, AZ 85716
602-327-5885

———————◆———————

Collection	Format	No./Size Disks	Price	Computer
Southwest Collection:				
Volume 1: Borders & Elements	EPS	5-800K	$89.95	Mac/IBM
Volume 2: Pottery & Baskets	EPS	7-800K	$89.95	Mac/IBM
Volume 3: Rugs & Blankets	EPS	6-800K	$89.95	Mac/IBM
Volume 5: Kachina Faces & Garments	EPS	5-800K	$89.95	Mac/IBM
Volume 6: Bead Designs	EPS	5-800K	$89.95	Mac/IBM
Volume 7: Custom SW Typefaces	EPS	4-800K	$89.95	Mac/IBM
Volume 8: Miscellaneous SW Graphics	EPS	5-800K	$89.95	Mac/IBM

Notes:

• All disks are in color.
• The entire Southwest Collection is $524.95.

Volume 1: Borders & Elements
Disk 1: Borders (Corners)

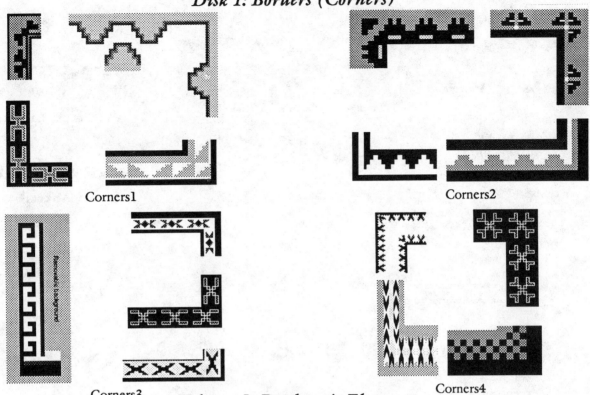

Corners1

Corners2

Corners3

Corners4

Volume 1: Borders & Elements
Disk 2: Borders (Linears)

Hopilinear

Linears1

Linears2

Linears3

Linears4

Volume 1: Borders & Elements
Disk 3: Elements (Accents)

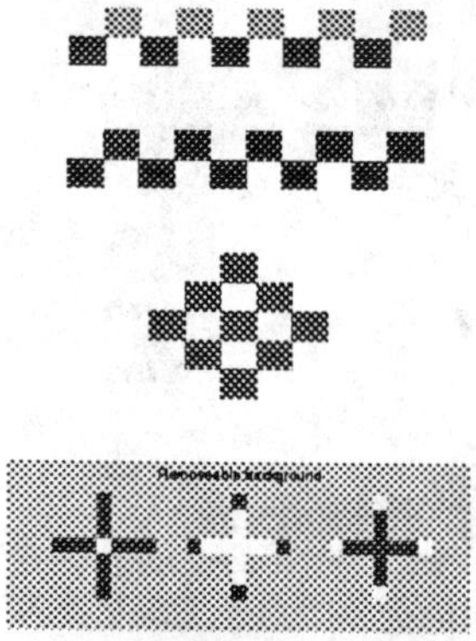

Screen added to expose light elements.

Accents1

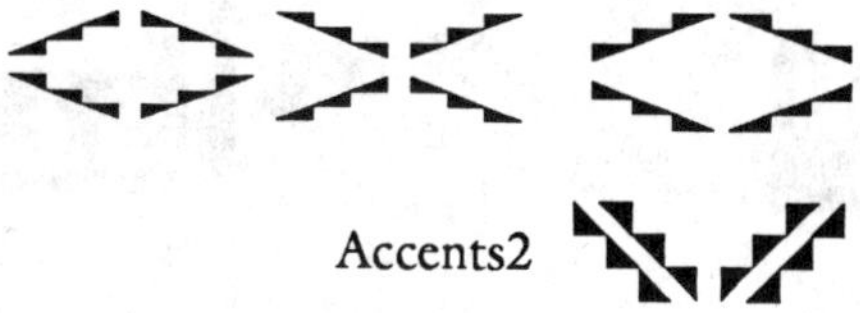

Accents2

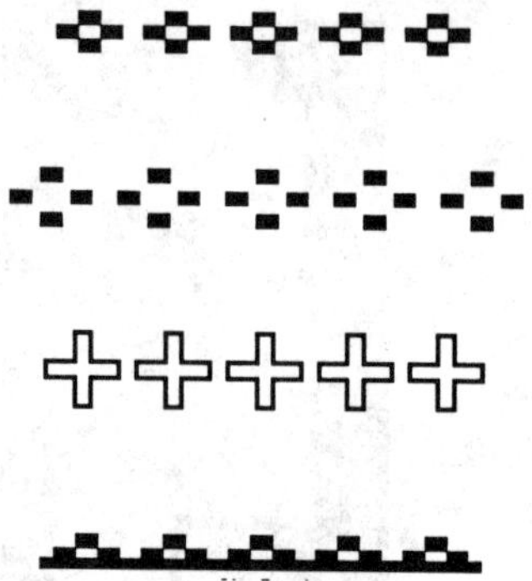

Accents3

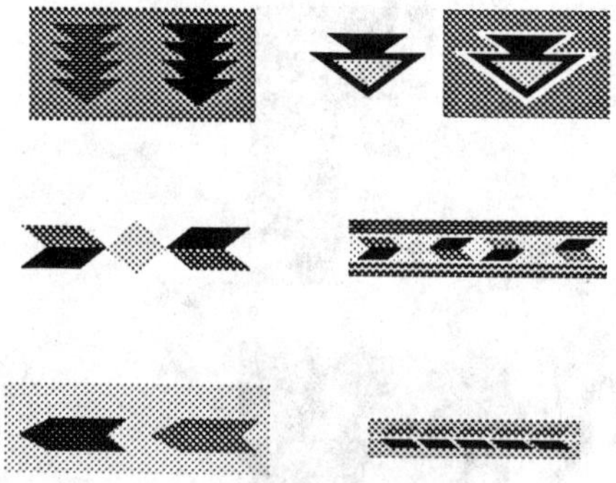

Accents4

Accents5

Accents6

Volume 1: Borders & Elements
Disk 4: Elements 2

Triangles

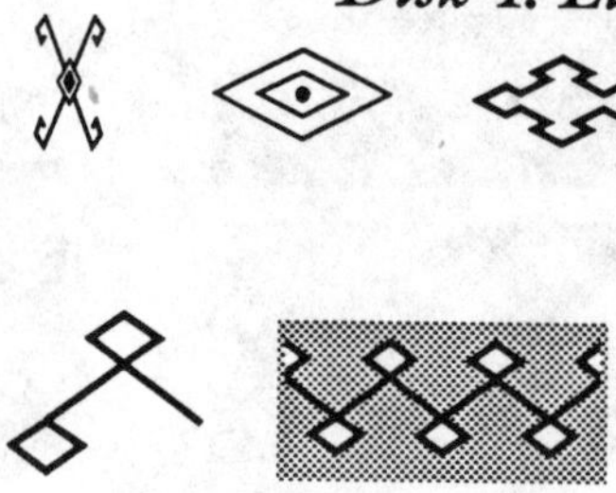

Pueblo

Diamond

Squash Blossom

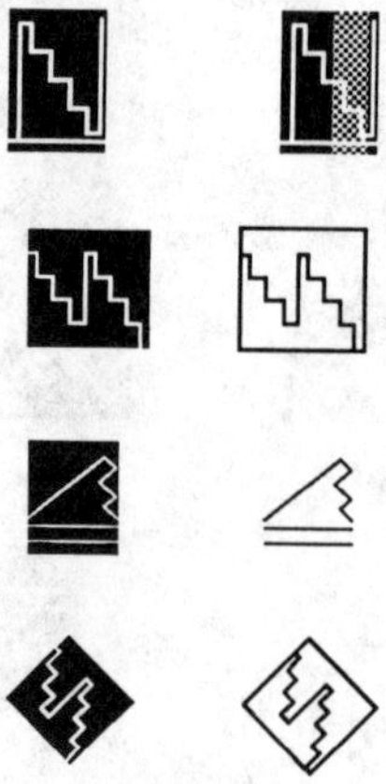

Mountain Silhouette

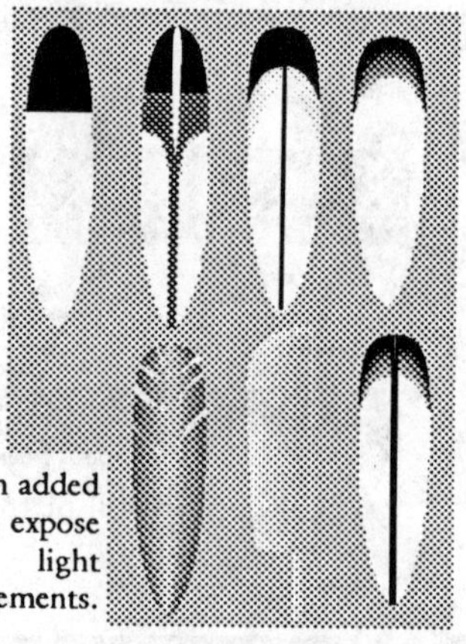

Screen added to expose light elements.

Feathers

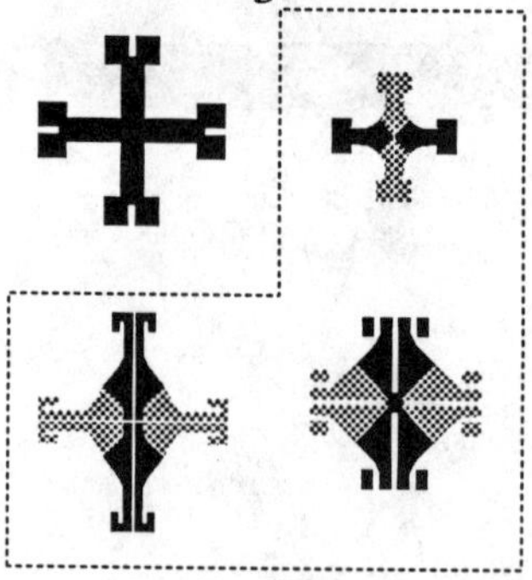

Stepped Mountain

Volume 1: Borders & Elements
Disk 5: Hopi Symbols

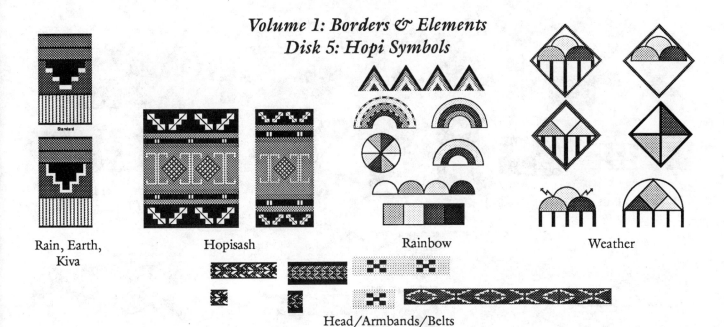

Rain, Earth, Kiva

Hopisash

Rainbow

Weather

Head/Armbands/Belts

Volume 2: Pottery & Baskets
Disk 1: Filled Pots 1

Filled Acoma Pot 2

Filled Acoma Pot 3

Wedding Jar

Volume 2: Pottery & Baskets
Disk 2: Filled Pots 2

Filled Acoma Pot 1

Maricopa Pots

Volume 2: Pottery & Baskets
Disk 3: Decorative Patterns

Acoma Pottery Patterns

Santa Clara Pottery Patterns

Birds1

Flowers1

ZiaPatterns1

ZiaPatterns2

ZiaPatterns3

Volume 2: Pottery & Baskets
Disk 4: Pottery Examples

Acoma1

Acoma3

Ziapot1

Ziapot2

Volume 2: Pottery & Baskets
Disk 5: Baskets 1

Apache1

Apache2

Coyote

Hopi Basket

Volume 2: Pottery & Baskets
Disk 6: Baskets 2

 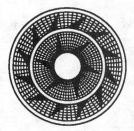   

Navajo Wedding Basket · Papago1 · Pima1 · Pima2 · Pima3

Volume 2: Pottery & Baskets
Disk 7: Additional Graphics

SJPat · Jar/Vase
Screen added to expose light elements. · Acoma2 · Basketweave

Volume 3: Rugs & Blankets
Disk 1: Rugs 1

  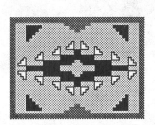 

ChiefRug · Ganado · Two Gray Hills · Wide Ruins

Volume 3: Rugs & Blankets
Disk 2: Rugs 2

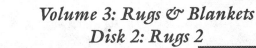    

Chinle · Crystal · NavajoRug · Teec Nos Pas Rug

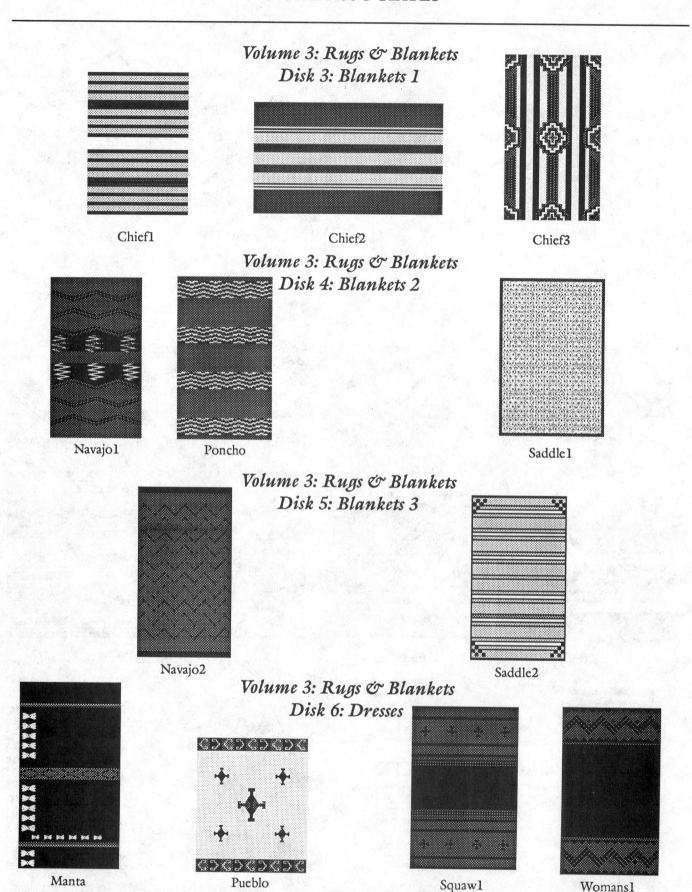

Volume 3: Rugs & Blankets
Disk 3: Blankets 1

Chief1

Chief2

Chief3

Volume 3: Rugs & Blankets
Disk 4: Blankets 2

Navajo1

Poncho

Saddle1

Volume 3: Rugs & Blankets
Disk 5: Blankets 3

Navajo2

Saddle2

Volume 3: Rugs & Blankets
Disk 6: Dresses

Manta

Pueblo

Squaw1

Womans1

Volume 5: Kachina Faces & Garments
Disk 1: Faces 1

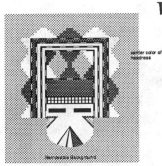

Butterfly Girl

Broad-Faced Kachina

Chief/Guard Faces

Volume 5: Kachina Faces & Garments
Disk 2: Faces 2

Cloud, Snow Kachina

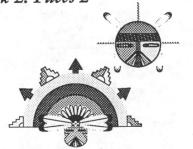

Cloud Man Faces

Volume 5: Kachina Faces & Garments
Disk 3: Faces 3

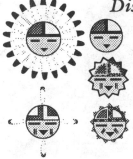

Sun God Faces

Morning Singer Kachina

Volume 5: Kachina Faces & Garments
Disk 4: Garments

Hopi Ceremonial Shawl

Hopi Sash

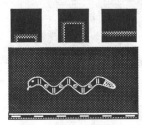

Hopi Ceremonial Kilts

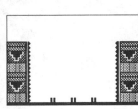

Kachina Kilt

Wedding Belt

Volume 5: Kachina Faces & Garments
Disk 5: Symbols

Rain, Earth, Kiva Pattern

Hopi Sash

Rainbow Symbols

Weather

Volume 6: Bead Designs
Disk 1: Rosettes

  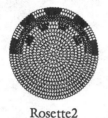

Pueblo, Zuni Rosettes   Rosette2

Volume 6: Bead Designs
Disk 2: Apache Beadwork

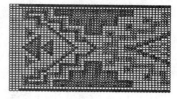

Apache   Miscellaneous

Volume 6: Bead Designs
Disk 3: Sioux Beadwork 1

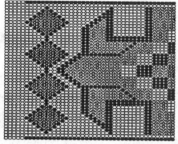

Sioux

Volume 6: Bead Designs
Disk 4: Sioux Beadwork 2

Sioux3

Sioux2

Volume 6: Bead Designs
Disk 4: Ute Beadwork

UteMNTN

Volume 7: Custom Southwest Typefaces
Disk 1: Barbed Wire (A - N)

Volume 7: Custom Southwest Typefaces
Disk 2: Barbed Wire (O - Z)

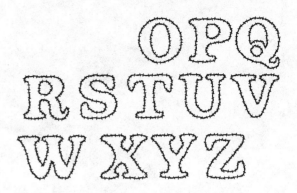

Volume 7: Custom Southwest Typefaces
Disk 3: Barbed Wire (Numbers)

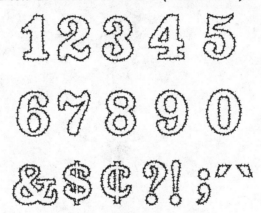

Volume 7: Custom Southwest Typefaces
Disk 4: Cactus

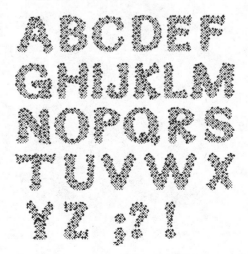

Volume 8: Miscellaneous Southwest Graphics
Disk 1: Miscellaneous 1

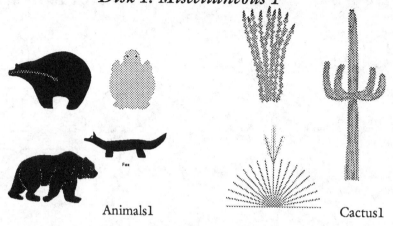

Animals1   Cactus1

Volume 8: Miscellaneous Southwest Graphics
Disk 2: Miscellaneous 2

Chili1   Insects1   Lizards1

Volume 8: Miscellaneous Southwest Graphics
Disk 3: Miscellaneous 3

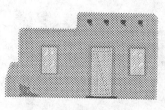

Corn1   House1   Thunderbird1

Volume 8: Miscellaneous Southwest Graphics
Disk 4: Miscellaneous 4

Birds1

Coyotes1

Coyotes2

Flowers1

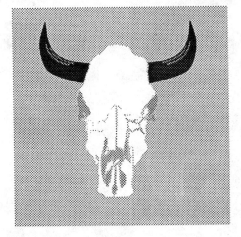

Skull1
Screen placed behind image to expose light object.

Volume 8: Miscellaneous Southwest Graphics
Disk 5: Upgrade 1

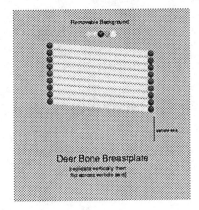

BrstPlt

Hired Hand Design

3608 Faust Avenue
Long Beach, CA 90808
213-429-5653

◆

Collection	Format	No./Size Disks	Price	Computer
Moonlight ArtWorks:				
Disks 1 & 2	EPS	2-800K	$49.00	Mac/IBM
Holiday Set	EPS	2-800K	$49.00	Mac/IBM
Logomaster Set	EPS	2-800K	$49.00	Mac/IBM
Set 4	EPS	2-800K	$49.00	Mac/IBM

Notes:

• Any 3 sets for $99.00; all 4 sets for $129.50.

Moonlight Artworks: Disk 1

Credit Cards

Hands

Rubber Stamps

    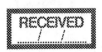

Moonlight Artworks: Disk 1 (continued)

Symbols

Type

Moonlight Artworks: Disk 2

Credit Cards 2

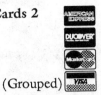

(Grouped)

Hands 2

Diskettes

Diskette 1   Diskette 1 black   Diskette 2   Diskette w/shadow

---

General

A Block   Artichoke   Bowler Hat   Cruise Ship Bow   Desk Phone

Firecracker   George Washington   Medal w/ Ribbon   Medal w/ Ribbons   Palm Tree

Six-Pack   Wine Bottle & Glass   Zebra   Phone w/Cord

Moonlight Artworks: Disk 2 (continued)

Silhouettes

2 Men   2 Women   Man w/Card   Man w/Pointer

Symbols

Cornet   Cornet, Black   Diskette   Flag 1   Flag 2   Flag, Screen

Hammer   IBM   Macintosh   Martini, Black   Saw, Black   Snifter Glass

Snifter Glass, Black   Snowflake on Black   Wine Glass   Wine Glass, Black

Type

Moonlight Artworks: Holiday Set Disk A

Decorations

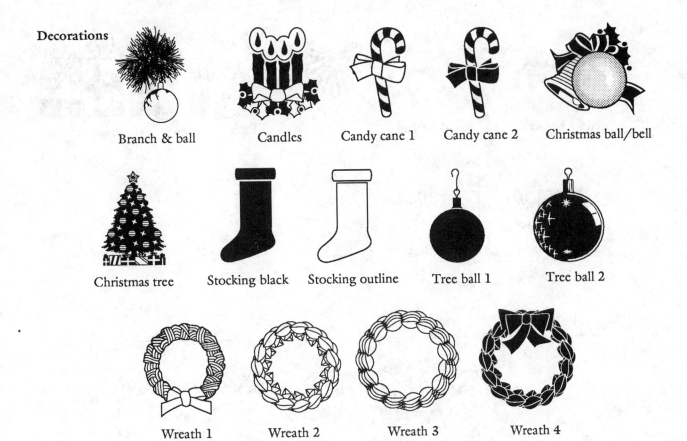

Branch & ball Candles Candy cane 1 Candy cane 2 Christmas ball/bell

Christmas tree Stocking black Stocking outline Tree ball 1 Tree ball 2

Wreath 1 Wreath 2 Wreath 3 Wreath 4

Figures

Angel 1 Angel 2 Cherub 1 Cherub 2 Magi

Christmas shoppers Santa Claus face Santa w/bag Santa w/reindeer

Moonlight Artworks: Holiday Set Disk A (continued)

Gifts

Bow 1 black   Bow 1 outline   Bow 2   Present   Presents

Tag 1 black   Tag 1 outline   Tag 2A   Tag 2B

Holly Border

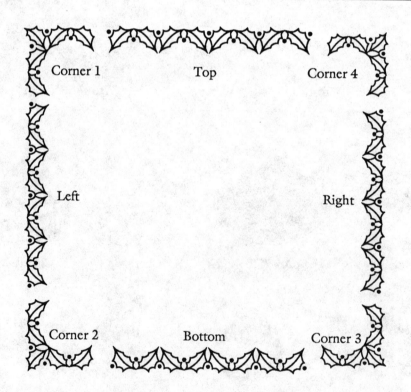

Corner 1   Top   Corner 4

Left   Right

Corner 2   Bottom   Corner 3

Moonlight Artworks: Holiday Set Disk B

Easter

Bunny black

Bunny outline

Crosses & scroll

Easter egg 1

Lily

Easter egg 2

Lettering

Moonlight Artworks: Holiday Set Disk B (continued)

New Year

Confetti field 1

Confetti field 2

Confetti field 3

New Year cherub 1 & 2

Party gal

Party guy

Symbols

Cake 1 candle

Cake 1 candle outline

Cake w/candles

Jack-O-Lantern 1 & 2

Others

Menorah 1

Menorah 2

Mogen (Star of) David

Pumpkin

Shamrock

Shamrock outline

Uncle Sam

US Flag

Valentine heart

Valentines

Thanksgiving

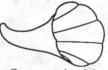
Cornucopia plain

Turkey dinner black

Turkey outline

Moonlight Artworks: Logomaster Disk A

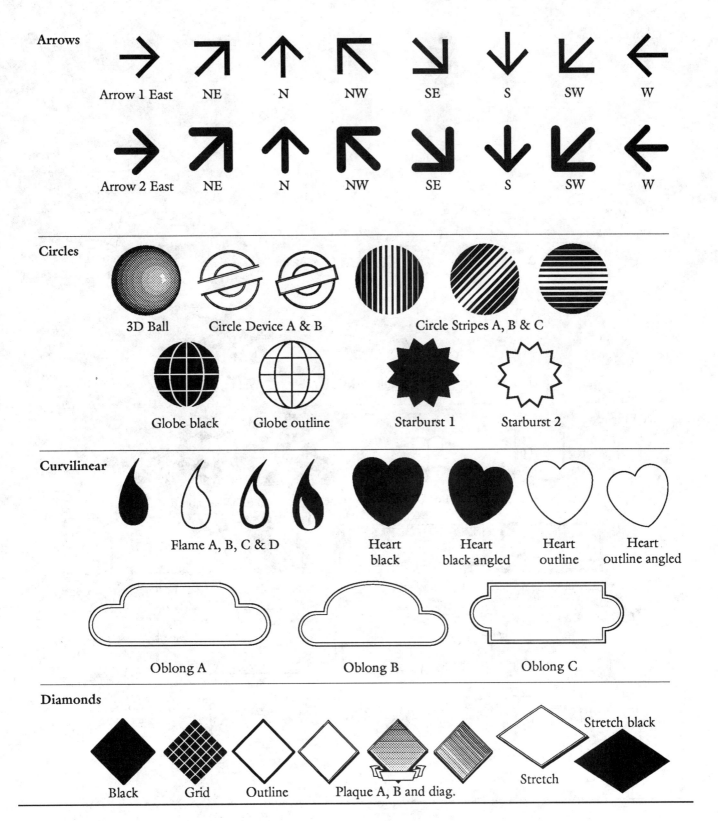

Arrows

Arrow 1 East   NE   N   NW   SE   S   SW   W

Arrow 2 East   NE   N   NW   SE   S   SW   W

Circles

3D Ball   Circle Device A & B   Circle Stripes A, B & C

Globe black   Globe outline   Starburst 1   Starburst 2

Curvilinear

Flame A, B, C & D   Heart black   Heart black angled   Heart outline   Heart outline angled

Oblong A   Oblong B   Oblong C

Diamonds

Stretch black

Black   Grid   Outline   Plaque A, B and diag.   Stretch

Moonlight Artworks: Logomaster Disk A (continued)

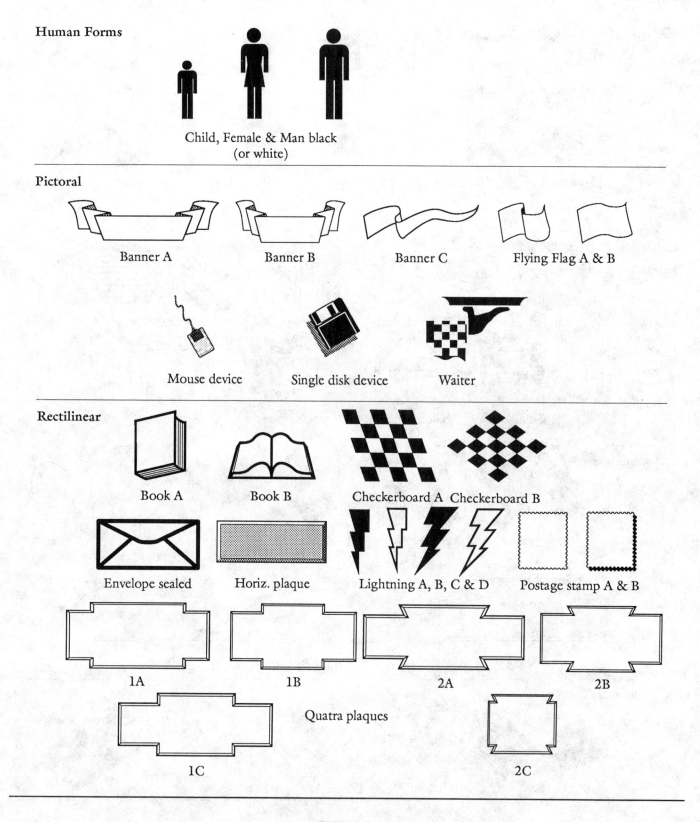

Human Forms

Child, Female & Man black
(or white)

Pictoral

Banner A

Banner B

Banner C

Flying Flag A & B

Mouse device

Single disk device

Waiter

Rectilinear

Book A

Book B

Checkerboard A   Checkerboard B

Envelope sealed

Horiz. plaque

Lightning A, B, C & D

Postage stamp A & B

1A

1B

2A

2B

Quatra plaques

1C

2C

Moonlight Artworks: Logomaster Disk A (continued)

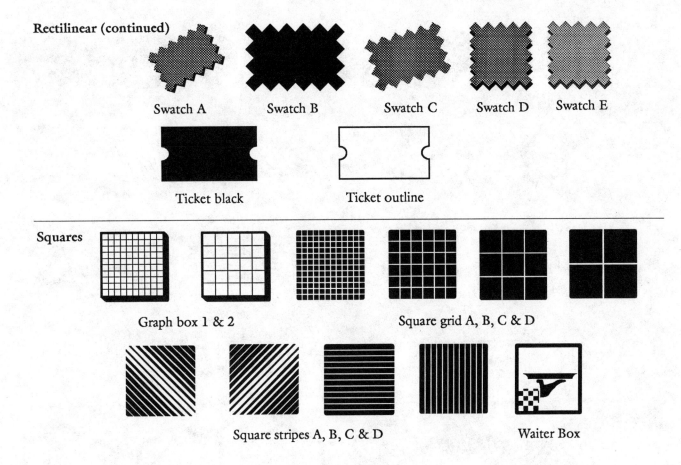

Rectilinear (continued)

Swatch A   Swatch B   Swatch C   Swatch D   Swatch E

Ticket black   Ticket outline

Squares

Graph box 1 & 2   Square grid A, B, C & D

Square stripes A, B, C & D   Waiter Box

Moonlight Artworks: Logomaster Disk B

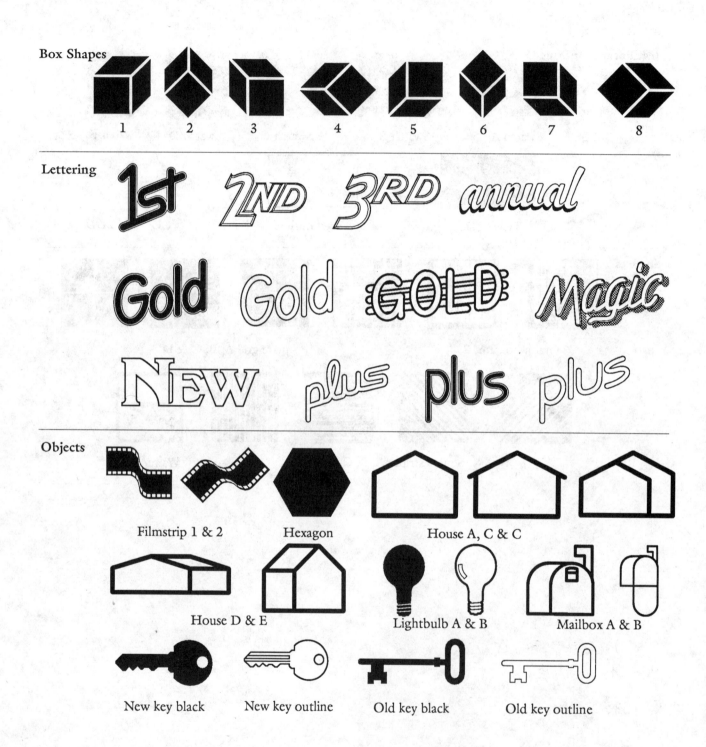

Box Shapes

1 2 3 4 5 6 7 8

Lettering

1st 2ND 3RD annual

Gold Gold GOLD Magic

New plus plus plus

Objects

Filmstrip 1 & 2   Hexagon   House A, C & C

House D & E   Lightbulb A & B   Mailbox A & B

New key black   New key outline   Old key black   Old key outline

Moonlight Artworks: Logomaster Disk B (continued)

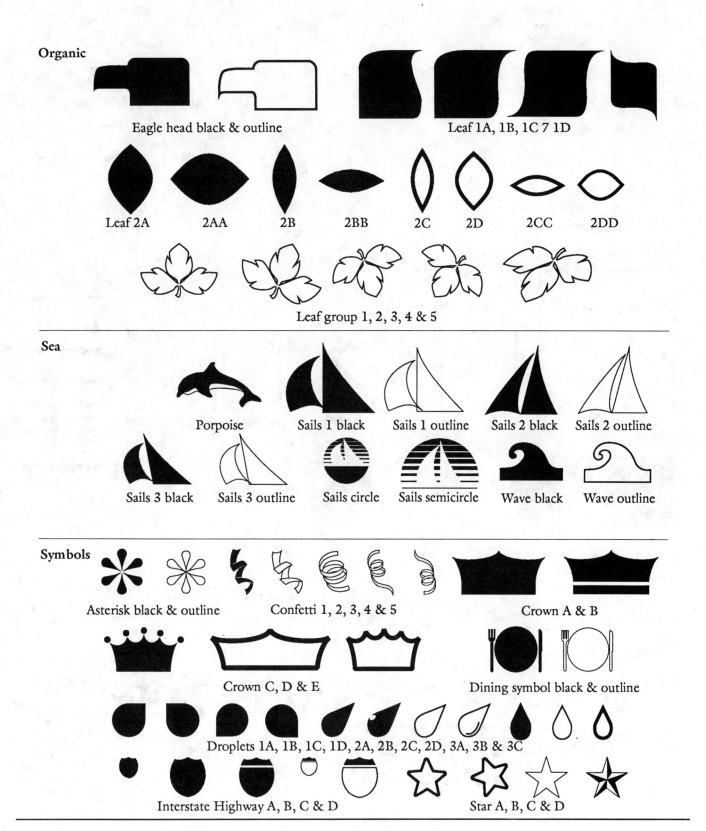

Organic

Eagle head black & outline

Leaf 1A, 1B, 1C 7 1D

Leaf 2A   2AA   2B   2BB   2C   2D   2CC   2DD

Leaf group 1, 2, 3, 4 & 5

Sea

Porpoise   Sails 1 black   Sails 1 outline   Sails 2 black   Sails 2 outline

Sails 3 black   Sails 3 outline   Sails circle   Sails semicircle   Wave black   Wave outline

Symbols

Asterisk black & outline   Confetti 1, 2, 3, 4 & 5   Crown A & B

Crown C, D & E   Dining symbol black & outline

Droplets 1A, 1B, 1C, 1D, 2A, 2B, 2C, 2D, 3A, 3B & 3C

Interstate Highway A, B, C & D   Star A, B, C & D

Set 4, Disk A

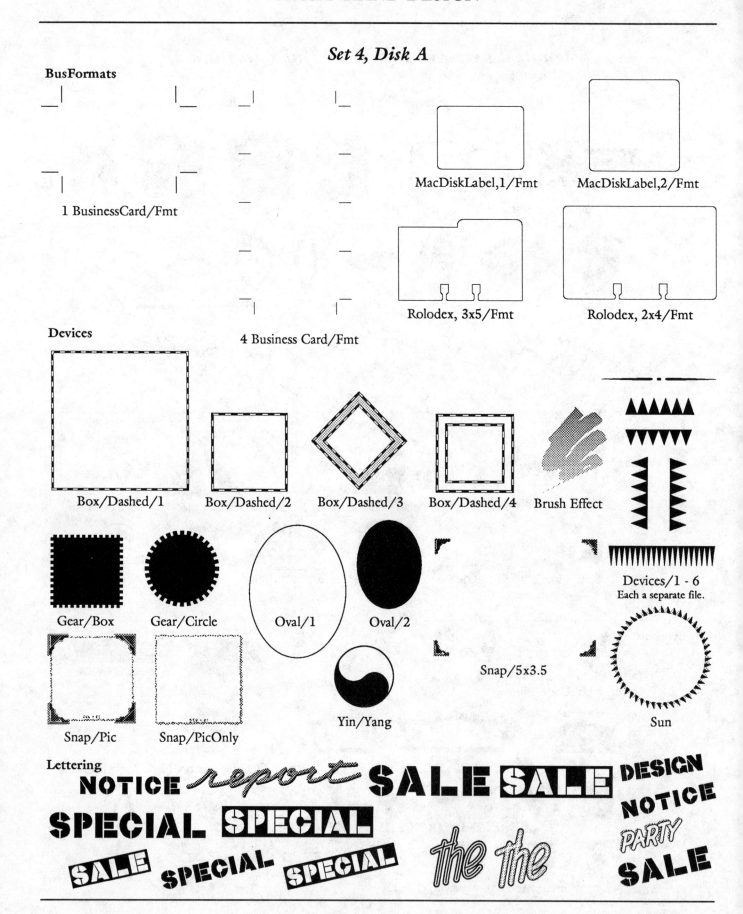

BusFormats

1 BusinessCard/Fmt

4 Business Card/Fmt

MacDiskLabel,1/Fmt

MacDiskLabel,2/Fmt

Rolodex, 3x5/Fmt

Rolodex, 2x4/Fmt

Devices

Box/Dashed/1

Box/Dashed/2

Box/Dashed/3

Box/Dashed/4

Brush Effect

Devices/1 - 6
Each a separate file.

Gear/Box

Gear/Circle

Oval/1

Oval/2

Snap/5x3.5

Sun

Snap/Pic

Snap/PicOnly

Yin/Yang

Lettering

NOTICE report SALE SALE DESIGN

SPECIAL SPECIAL NOTICE

SALE SPECIAL SPECIAL the the PARTY

SALE

Set 4, Disk B

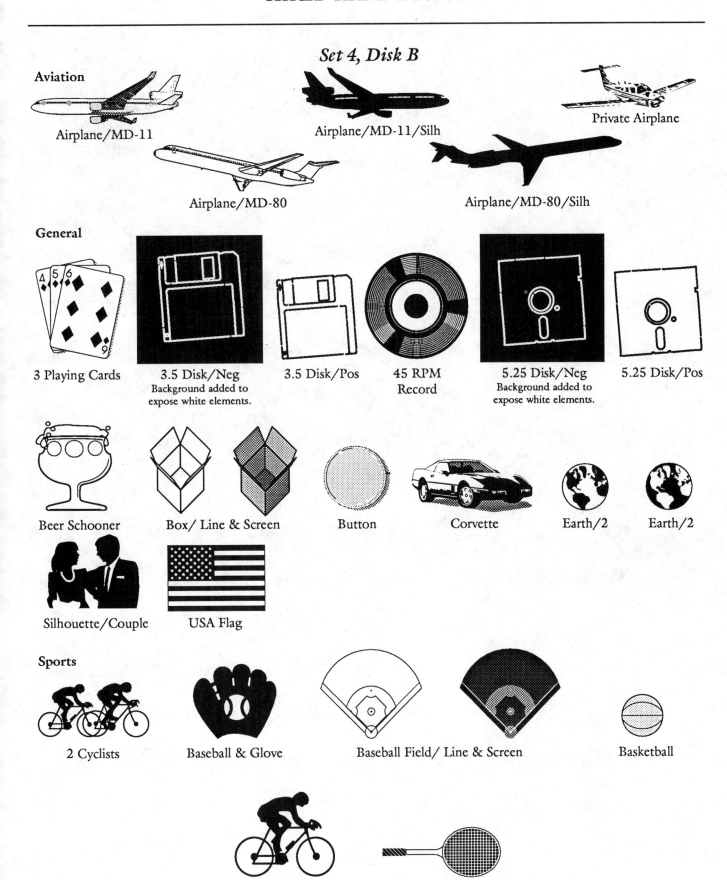

Aviation

Airplane/MD-11

Airplane/MD-11/Silh

Private Airplane

Airplane/MD-80

Airplane/MD-80/Silh

General

3 Playing Cards

3.5 Disk/Neg
Background added to
expose white elements.

3.5 Disk/Pos

45 RPM
Record

5.25 Disk/Neg
Background added to
expose white elements.

5.25 Disk/Pos

Beer Schooner

Box/ Line & Screen

Button

Corvette

Earth/2

Earth/2

Silhouette/Couple

USA Flag

Sports

2 Cyclists

Baseball & Glove

Baseball Field/ Line & Screen

Basketball

Cyclist

Tennis Racket

Image Club Graphics

#5, 1902 - 11th Street SE
Calgary, Alberta
Canada T2G 3G2
403-262-8008
800-661-9410
403-261-7013 fax

❖

Collection	Format	No./Size Disks	Price	Computer
Digit-Art:				
Volume 1: Miscellaneous*	EPS	3-800K	$99.00	Mac/IBM
Volume 2: Miscellaneous*	EPS	4-800K	$99.00	Mac/IBM
Volume 3: Miscellaneous*	EPS	2-800K	$99.00	Mac/IBM
Volume 4: Cartoon People*	EPS	2-800K	$99.00	Mac/IBM
Volume 5: Cartoon People*	EPS	2-800K	$99.00	Mac/IBM
Volume 6: Business & Industry*	EPS	2-800K	$99.00	Mac/IBM
Volume 7: World Maps*	EPS	8-800K	$99.00	Mac/IBM
Volume 8: Miscellaneous*	EPS	3-800K	$99.00	Mac/IBM
Volume 9: Design Elements*	EPS	4-800K	$99.00	Mac/IBM
Volume 10: Design Letters*	EPS	1-800K	$99.00	Mac/IBM
Volume 11: Design Letters*	EPS	1-800K	$99.00	Mac/IBM
Volume 12: Symbols & Headings*	EPS	2-800K	$99.00	Mac/IBM
Volume 13: Food & Entertainment*	EPS	3-800K	$99.00	Mac/IBM
Volume 14: Occasions*	EPS	3-800K	$99.00	Mac/IBM
Volume 15: Lifestyles*	EPS	3-800K	$99.00	Mac/IBM
Volume 16: Office and Education*	EPS	4-800K	$99.00	Mac/IBM
Volume 17: Universal Symbols*	EPS	5-800K	$99.00	Mac/IBM
Volume 18: Celebrity Caricatures*	EPS	6-800K	$99.00	Mac/IBM
Volume 19: Silhouettes*	EPS	2-800K	$99.00	Mac/IBM
Volume 20: Design Backgrounds*	EPS	11-800K	$99.00	Mac/IBM
Volume 21: Fabulous Fifties*	EPS	6-800K	$99.00	Mac/IBM
Volume 22: Business Cartoons*	EPS	7-800K	$99.00	Mac/IBM
Volume 23: Borders & Ornaments*	EPS	11-800K	$99.00	Mac/IBM

Notes:
* Not shown in its entirety in this book. Due to the large amount of electronic clip art available from this company, we are showing and indexing only one page of samples from each of the volumes.
• All disks are compressed and include an auto-unstuffing utility.
• The ArtRoom CD-ROM includes Volumes 1 through 23 for $799.00; includes The Image Retriever application.
• The Darkroom CD-ROM (not shown) is black-and-white clip photography.
• Art & Type Vendor contains their entire clip art and font collection on one pay as you go CD-ROM.

Volume 1: Miscellaneous

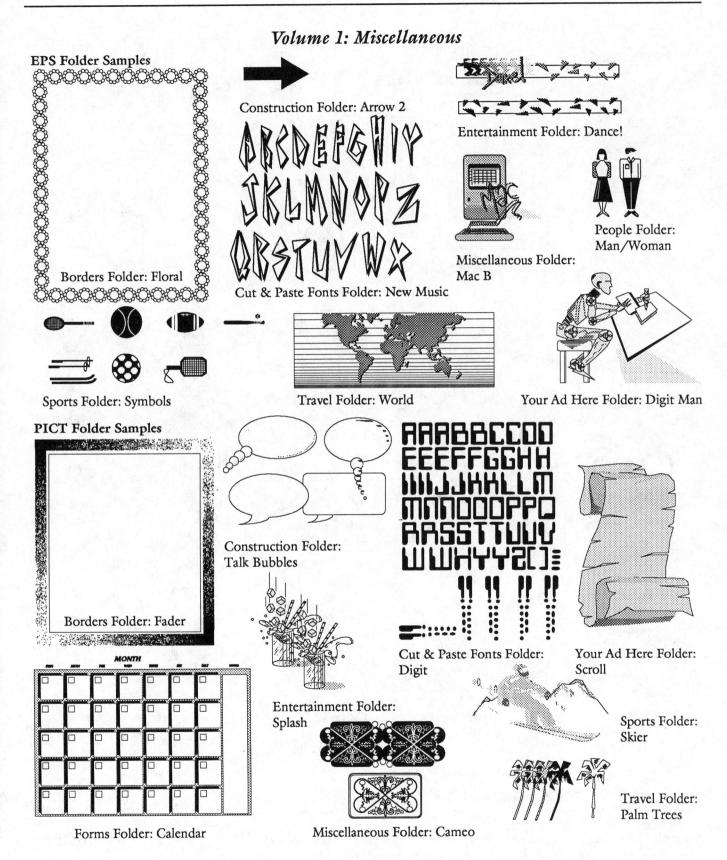

EPS Folder Samples

Borders Folder: Floral

Construction Folder: Arrow 2

Entertainment Folder: Dance!

Cut & Paste Fonts Folder: New Music

Miscellaneous Folder: Mac B

People Folder: Man/Woman

Sports Folder: Symbols

Travel Folder: World

Your Ad Here Folder: Digit Man

PICT Folder Samples

Borders Folder: Fader

Construction Folder: Talk Bubbles

Cut & Paste Fonts Folder: Digit

Your Ad Here Folder: Scroll

Entertainment Folder: Splash

Sports Folder: Skier

Forms Folder: Calendar

Miscellaneous Folder: Cameo

Travel Folder: Palm Trees

MONTH

Because of the large amount of clip art available in this volume, we are showing only samples of the artwork.

Volume 2: Miscellaneous

EPS Folder Samples

Cartoons Folder:
Mr. Handyman

Certificates Folder: Diploma 3

Clip Art Folder: Liberty

Construction Folder:
Quotes

Line Tapes Folder: Corner E

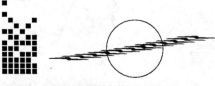

Logos Folder: Logos 1

Your Ad Here Folder: Tag

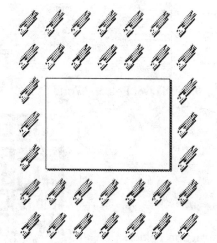

Page Templates: Poster

People Folder: Business Man

Symbols Folder:
Credit Card

PICT Folder Samples

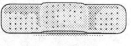

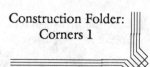

People Folder:
Waiter

Construction Folder:
Corners 1

Cartoons Folder:
Cool Horse

Clip Art Folder:
Bandaid

Line Tapes Folder: Streamer Border

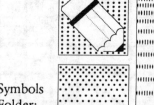
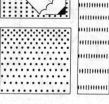

Symbols
Folder:
Pencil

Not shown:
Samples from the PICT Templates Folder & the PICT Your Ad Here Folder

Because of the large amount of clip art available in this volume, we are showing only samples of the artwork.

Volume 3: Miscellaneous

Business Folder Samples

Credit Cards   Graph   Newspaper   Telephone 3

Cartoons Folder Samples   **Cricket Folder Samples**

Happy Guy   Naughty   Clip   Ribbon

Entertainment Folder Samples   **Occassions Folder Samples**

Coffee Cup   Ice Cream   Christmas Tree Bulb   Frankenstein

Miscellaneous Folder Samples

American Eagle   Check Mark   Director's Chair   Toothbrush

Because of the large amount of clip art available in this volume, we are showing only samples of the artwork.

Volume 4: Cartoon People

Animals Folder Samples

Bird   Dog A   Dragon   Shark

Guy & Accessories Folder Samples

Guy   Cap   Floppy Hat   Grimace   Xmas Hat

Miscellaneous Folder Samples

Angel   Beauty Queen   Cave Man   Helicopter Pilot   Surgeon

Not People Folder Samples

Beer   Couch   Good Idea   Mailbox   Popcorn

Sports Folder Samples

Football   Ski   Tennis

Because of the large amount of clip art available in this volume, we are showing only samples of the artwork.

Volume 5: Cartoon People

Animals Folder Samples

Dog C Elephant Fish Parrot

Handyman Folder Samples

Drill Painter Screwdriver Trimmer

Miscellaneous Folder Samples

Paying Customer Pioneer Ad Teacher Man Workman

Not People Folder Samples   **Office Folder Samples**   **Sports Folder Samples**

Rockets The End Business Woman Uptight Golf Surfer

Because of the large amount of clip art available in this volume, we are showing only samples of the artwork.

Volume 6: Business & Industry

Agriculture Folder Samples

Corn

Business Folder Samples

$ Money

Animals

Flowers

Clock

Morning Paper

Entertainment Folder Samples

Compact Disk

Microphone · Take One

Equipment Folder Samples

Bus · Pickup · Wrench

Science Folder Samples

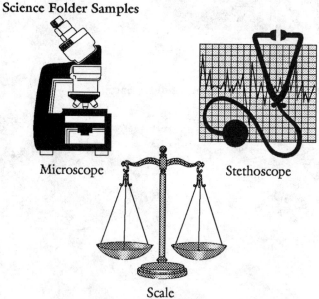

Microscope · Stethoscope

Scale

Trades Folder Samples

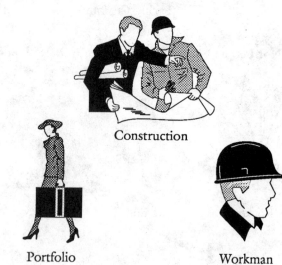

Construction

Portfolio · Workman

Because of the large amount of clip art available in this volume, we are showing only samples of the artwork.

Volume 7: World Maps

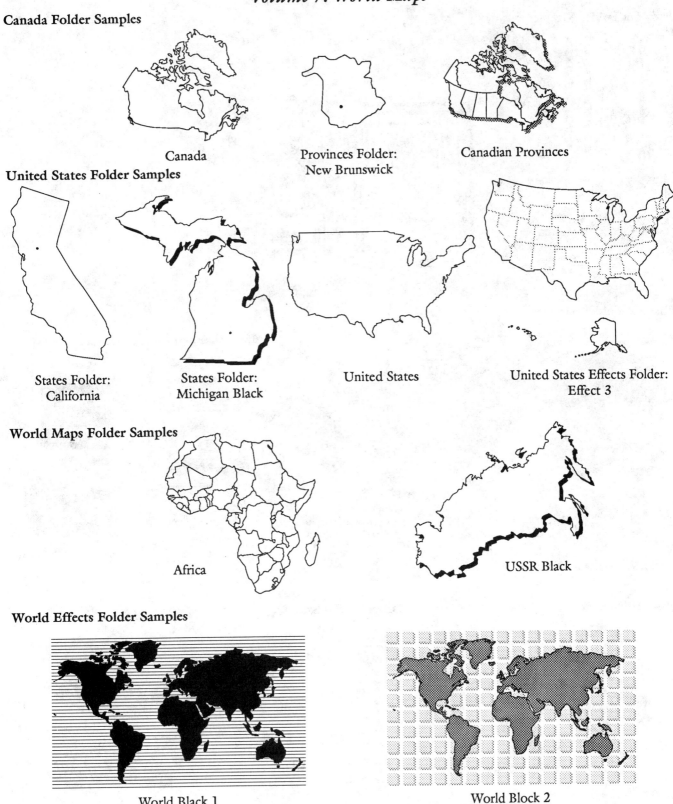

Canada Folder Samples

Canada

Provinces Folder:
New Brunswick

Canadian Provinces

United States Folder Samples

States Folder:
California

States Folder:
Michigan Black

United States

United States Effects Folder:
Effect 3

World Maps Folder Samples

Africa

USSR Black

World Effects Folder Samples

World Black 1

World Block 2

Because of the large amount of clip art available in this volume, we are showing only samples of the artwork.

Volume 8: Miscellaneous

Artroom Folder Samples

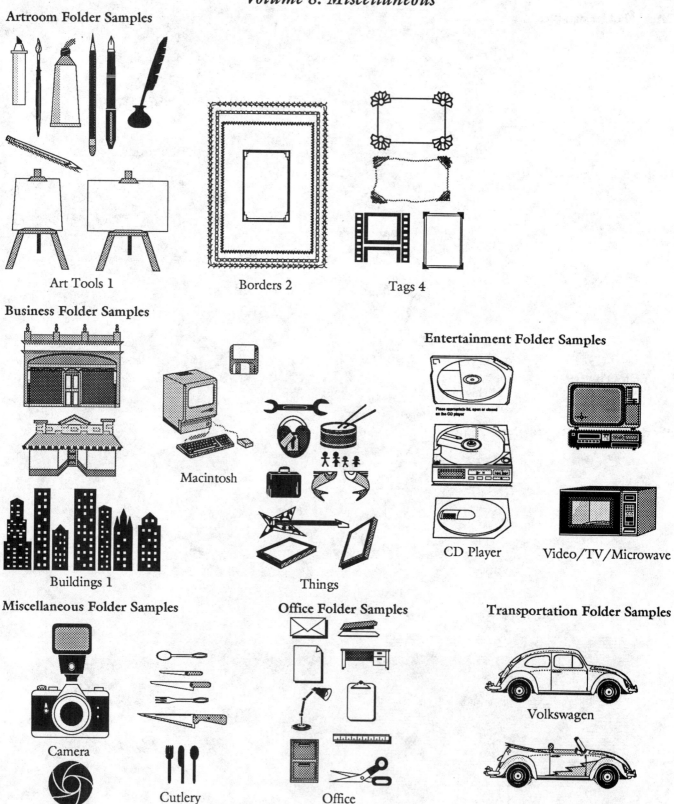

Art Tools 1

Borders 2

Tags 4

Business Folder Samples

Entertainment Folder Samples

Macintosh

Buildings 1

Things

CD Player

Video/TV/Microwave

Miscellaneous Folder Samples

Office Folder Samples

Transportation Folder Samples

Camera

Cutlery

Office

Volkswagen

Because of the large amount of clip art available in this volume, we are showing only samples of the artwork.

Volume 9: Design Elements

Chrome Border Folder

Down Left & Horizontal

Design Elements Folder Samples

1/3 50
OFF

Headings Folder Samples

DESIGN

TIPS

FAST LANE

WET

Letters Folder Samples

License Plate Font   President Font

Mortices Folder Samples

Crumpled Paper

Marble Slab

Venetian Blinds

Because of the large amount of clip art available in this volume, we are showing only samples of the artwork.

Volume 10: Design Letters

Bee Bopp

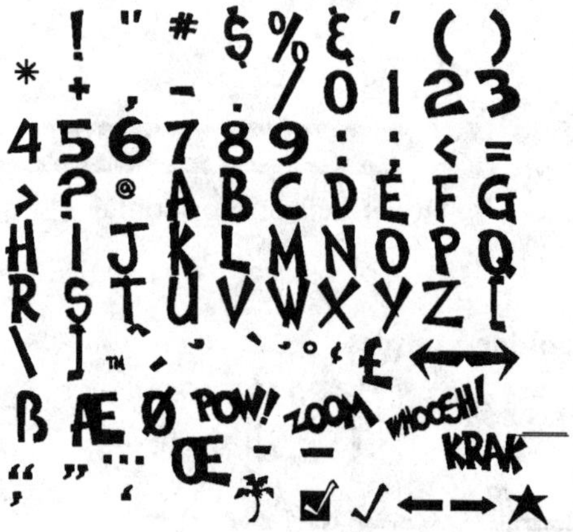

Comic Book 2

Fastlane

Headliner

Savage

Sterling

Because of the large amount of clip art available in this volume, we are showing only samples of the artwork.

Volume 11: Design Letters

! " # $ % & ' ( ) . + , - . / 0 1 2 3
4 5 6 7 8 9 ; ; = ? . A B C D E F G H I
J K L M N O P Q R S T U V W X Y Z [\
] _ a b c d e f g h i j k l m n o p q
r s t u v w x y z { } / A A

Aria

Fina

Liberty

Rubber Stamp

Theater

Because of the large amount of clip art available in this volume, we are showing only samples of the artwork.

Volume 12: Symbols & Headings

Art Folder Samples

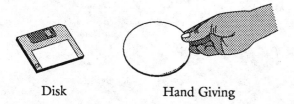
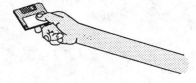

Disk   Hand Giving   Hand with Disk   Record Album

Headings Folder Samples

Mortices Folder Samples

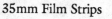

35mm Film Strips   Text Box 4   Tilted Box with Shadow

Symbols Folder Samples

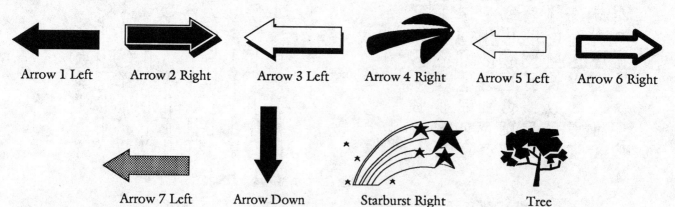

Arrow 1 Left   Arrow 2 Right   Arrow 3 Left   Arrow 4 Right   Arrow 5 Left   Arrow 6 Right

Arrow 7 Left   Arrow Down   Starburst Right   Tree

Because of the large amount of clip art available in this volume, we are showing only samples of the artwork.

Volume 13: Food & Entertainment

Entertainment Folder Samples

Disc Jockey 1

Ballet

Theater

Hollywood

Food Folder Samples

Birthday Cake

Chinese Chef

Dairy

Late Night Dinner

Symbols Folder Samples

Coffee

Hamburger

Smoking

Templates Folder Samples

Art Deco Template

Party Invitations

Because of the large amount of clip art available in this volume, we are showing only samples of the artwork.

Volume 14: Occasions

Borders Folder Samples

Candy Canes 1, 2

Candy Canes Horizontal

Rudolph

Poinsettias

Santa Mast

Christmas & New Year Folder Samples

Blitzen   Elf 1   Happy New Year   Santa Claus   Year's End

Halloween Folder Samples

Haunted House   Pumpkin 2   Trick or Treat

Miscellaneous Folder Samples

Religion Folder Samples

Abe Lincoln

Graduate   Just Married   Star of David   Madonna

Because of the large amount of clip art available in this volume, we are showing only samples of the artwork.

Volume 15: Lifestyles

Cultures Folder Samples

Egypt

Russia

United States

Spain

Leisure Folder Samples
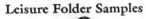

Barbeque

Computer Wiz

Sharp Shopper

Summer Time

Occupation Folder Samples
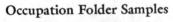

Bad Connection

Clown

Photographer

Scientist

Sports Folder Samples

Bowling

Fitness

Water Skier

Because of the large amount of clip art available in this volume, we are showing only samples of the artwork.

Volume 16: Office & Education

Business Scenes Folder Samples

Businessmen Folder Samples

Authority

Hand Holding
Coffee

Businessman
Running

Man With Chart

Men Shaking
Hands

Businesswomen Folder Samples

Computers Folder Samples

Woman With
Filebox

Woman With
Phone

Laptop

Mac II cx

NeXt Cube

Name Plates Folder Samples

Office Supplies Folder Samples

School Supplies Folder Samples

School Scenes Folder Sample

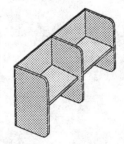

Ballpoint Pen

Tape Dispenser

French Curve
2

Workstation

Cheerleader

Because of the large amount of clip art available in this volume, we are showing only samples of the artwork.

Volume 17: Universal Symbols

Animals Folder Samples

Bear   Giraffe   Seahorse

Arrows Folder Samples

3D Arrow Left   Cursor Down Left   Square Arrow Right

Astrology/Astronomy Folder Samples

Aquarius   Conjunction   Sagittarius   Uranus

Geology Folder Samples

Brackish Water Fossil   Foraminifera   Landslide

Handforms Folder Samples

International Folder Samples

Arrival   Mail   Water Fountain

Mechanical Folder Samples

Anchor   Camper Dump   Wrench

Meteorology Folder Samples

Drizzle   Moderate Rain   Wind 50 Knots

Photography Folder Samples

Bright Sun   Film Thread   Zoom

Shapes Folder Samples

Club   Triangle 3

Sports Folder Samples

Biathlon   Weightlifting

Traffic Control Folder Samples

Bumps in Road   Y Intersection

Because of the large amount of clip art available in this volume, we are showing only samples of the artwork.

Volume 18: Celebrity Caricatures

Arts Folder Samples
                                 Business Folder Samples

Andy Warhol   Mark Twain   Salvatore Dali   Donald Trump   Lee Iacocca   Steve Jobs

Entertainment Folder Samples
                                   History Folder Samples

Arsenio Hall   Bob Hope   Walter Cronkite   Adolph Hitler   Emperor Hirohito   Socrates

Music Folder Samples
                                   Politics Folder Samples

Mick Jagger   Dolly Parton   Madonna   George Bush   Lech Walesa   Saddam Hussein

Religion Folder Samples
                                   Royalty Folder Samples

 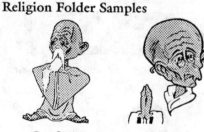   

Confucius   Mahatma Ghandi   Mother Theresa   Jackie Onassis   Princess Diana

Sports Folder Samples

Don King   Jack Nicklaus   Wayne Gretzky

Because of the large amount of clip art available in this volume, we are showing only samples of the artwork.

Volume 18: Silhouettes

At Work Folder Samples

Astronaut   Photographer   Singer

Children Folder Samples

Child Playing   Halloween

Indoor Sports Folder Samples

Chess   Volleyball

Men Folder Samples

Reading Book   Pointing Left   Man on Stool

Summer Sports Folder Samples

Freefall   Sprinter

Team Sports Folder Samples

Football Catch   Slap Shot

Water Sports Folder Samples

Rowing   Waterski

Winter Sports Folder Samples

Speed Skater   Bobsled

Women Folder Samples

Couple Waltzing   Woman With Cane   Woman With Laundry

Because of the large amount of clip art available in this volume, we are showing only samples of the artwork.

Volume 20: Design Backgrounds

High Tech Folder Sample: Brass Buttons

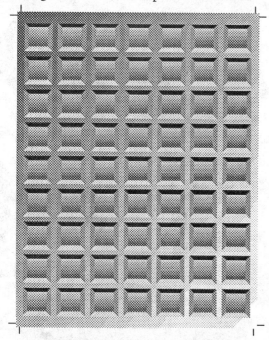

Patterns Folder Sample: Falling Cubes

Scenic & Nature Folder Sample: Starry Sky

Textures Folder: Stone Path

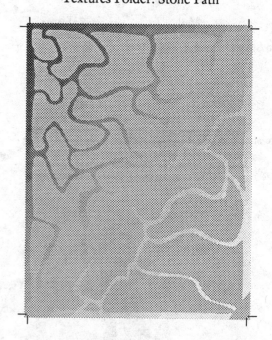

Because of the large amount of clip art available in this volume, we are showing only samples of the artwork.

Volume 21: Fabulous 50's

Bright Future Folder Samples

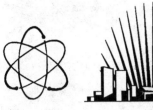  

Atomic   Future City   The Big One

Business & Occupations Folder Samples

Car Hop   Contractor   Woman on Phone

Happy Home Folder Samples

Billy's Homework   Off to Church   Weekend Dad

Headline Helpers Folder Samples

Bad News   Judge   Swell Guy

Mortices Folder Samples

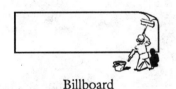 

Billboard   Watch This Space

Nonsense Folder Samples

Road Scare   Dame on a Gun

Pin Ups Folder Samples

Chain Poppin' Hunk   Pin Up   Winking Girl

Sports & Leisure Folder Samples

 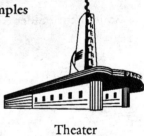

Ballroom Dancing   Theater

Swell Headers Folder Samples

Transportation Folder Samples

Big Car   See Dick Drive

Fighter Plane

Because of the large amount of clip art available in this volume, we are showing only samples of the artwork.

Volume 22: Business Cartoons

Business Life Folder Samples

Bear Market   Creative Door   Real Estate for Sale   Slide Show   Workload

Desk Jobs Folder Samples

Deadly Interview   Out to Lunch   Really Out   Sucker Break   Workaholic Vacation

Funny Money Folder Samples

1040 Time   Gal Stretches a Buck   Mister Bill   Sea of Debt   Time is Money

Office Equipment Folder Samples

Bud Gets E Mail   Family Portrait   Post-Bomb Blues   Typesetter

People Folder Samples   **Words Folder Samples**

Brief Moment   Mad at the World   Yelling Boss   Getting Too Involved   You're Invited

Because of the large amount of clip art available in this volume, we are showing only samples of the artwork.

Volume 23: Borders & Ornaments

Banners Folder Samples

Centerpieces Folder Samples

Electric Eye

Acorn

Floral 1 - Top

Cat Tail 1

Corners Folder Samples

Butterfly & Lily LL

Floral 1 UR

Nouveau LL

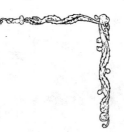

Vine UR

Flourishes & Rules Folder Samples

Engraved Rule

Flourish 4

Twisted Rule

Nouveau Drop Caps Folder Samples

Page Borders Folder Sample

Ornaments Folder Samples

Bouquet 2

Floral 14

Sea Shell

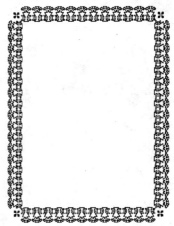

Aztec 2

Because of the large amount of clip art available in this volume, we are showing only samples of the artwork.

Innovation Advertising & Design
41 Mansfield Avenue
Essex Jct., VT 05452
802-879-1164
802-878-1768 fax
800-255-0562

Collection	Format	No./Size Disks	Price	Computer
AdArt:				
Business Symbols Collection*	EPS	4-800K	$99.00	Mac/IBM
Flags of the World**	EPS	5-800K	$99.00	Mac/IBM
International Symbols & Icons Vol. 1	EPS	4-800K	$99.00	Mac/IBM
International Symbols & Icons Vol. 2	EPS	4-800K	$99.00	Mac/IBM
Logos & Trademarks Vol. 1	EPS	2-800K	$99.00	Mac/IBM
Logos & Trademarks Vol. 2	EPS	2-800K	$99.00	Mac/IBM
Logos & Trademarks Vol. 3	EPS	2-800K	$99.00	Mac/IBM
Logos & Trademarks Vol. 4	EPS	2-800K	$99.00	Mac/IBM
Logos & Trademarks Vol. 5*	EPS	2-800K	$99.00	Mac/IBM
Vinyl Cutter's Collection*	EPS	5-800K	$199.00	Mac/IBM

Notes:

*Not shown or indexed in this volume. Contact Innovation for more information.

** Flags of the World is a collection of full-color international flags, of which we have only shown a sampling. The art in this set has been compressed onto the 800K disks.

Flags of the World

Flags of the World is a collection of 175 EPS international flags. Each flag is in full color. We are showing five black-and-white samples from the collection at 100%. Contact Innovation Advertising & Design for more information.

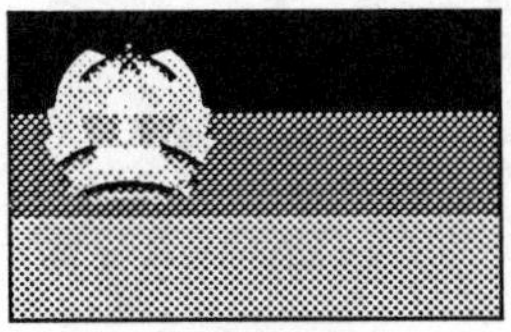
Afghanistan

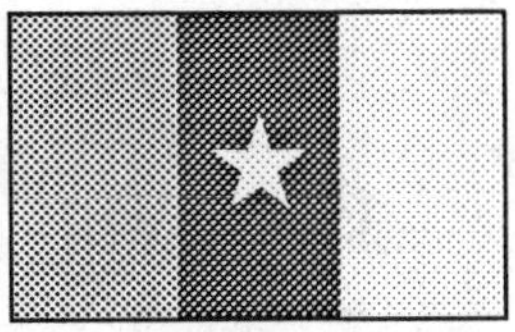
Cameroon

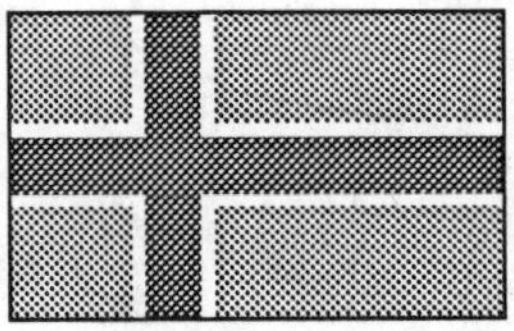
Iceland

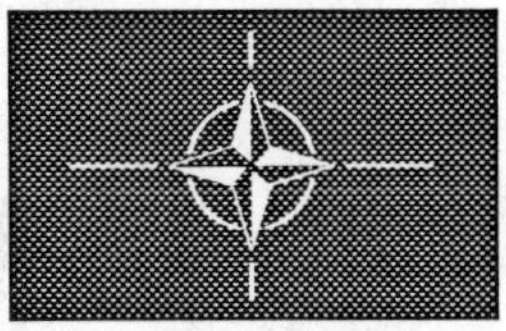
Sri Lanka

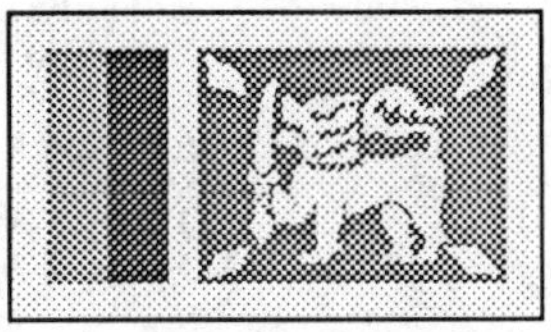
N.A.T.O.

International Symbols & Icons, Volume 1, Disk A

Astrology

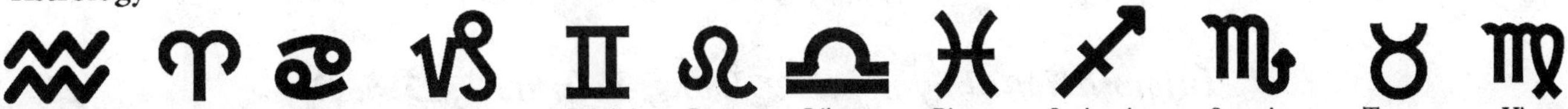
Aquarius, Aries, Cancer, Capricorn, Gemini, Leo, Libra, Pisces, Sagittarius, Scorpio, Taurus, Virgo

Astronomy

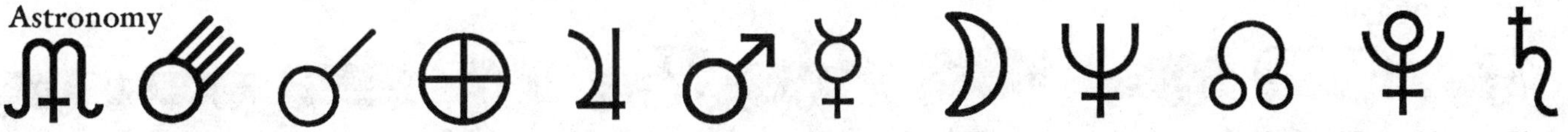
Autumn, Comet, Conjunction, Earth/Creation, Jupiter/Thursday, Mars/Tuesday, Mercury/Wednesday, Moon/Monday, Neptune, Node, Opposition, Pluto

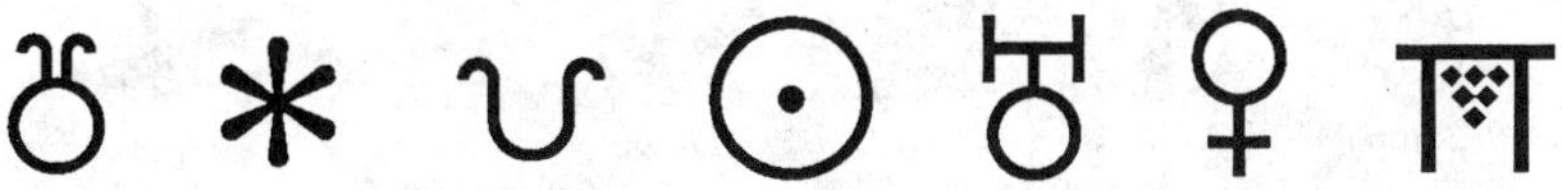
Spring, Star, Summer, Sun/Sunday, Uranus, Venus/Friday, Winter

Business Icons

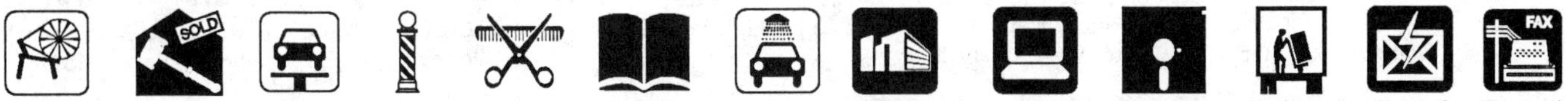

Antiques, Auction, Auto Service, Barber, Beauty Shop, Book Store, Car Wash, Commercial, Computer, Computer Supplies, Delivery, E-Mail, Facsimile

Farm, Florist, Gifts, Grocery, Industrial, Jewelry, Kennel, Lab, Machinery, Marine, Marketing, Medicine, Money

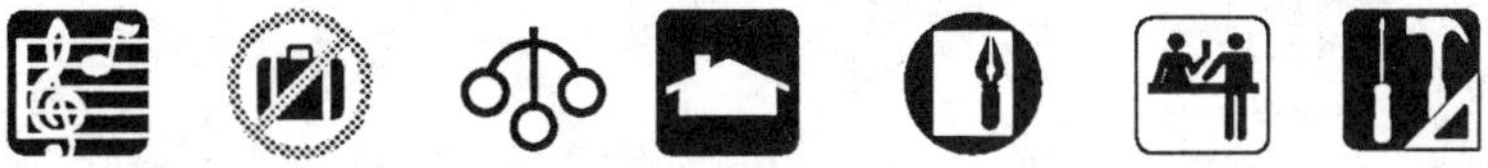
Music, No Soliciting, Pawn Shop, Residential, Stationery, Ticket Purchase, Tools

Religion

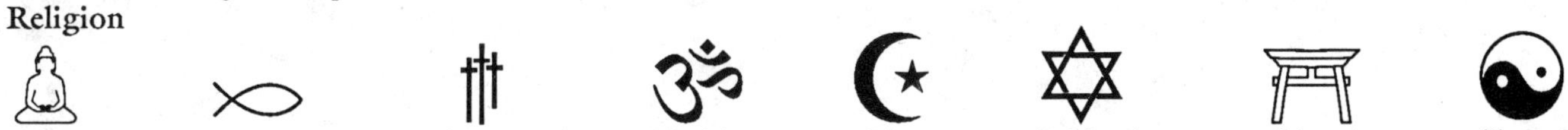
Buddhism, Christianity/The Fish, Christianity/Cross, Hinduism, Islam, Judaism/Star of David, Shinto/Torii, Taoism/Yin & Yang

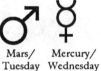

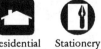

International Symbols & Icons, Volume 1, Disk A (continued)

Weather Maps

Cloudy   Partly Cloudy   Rain   Snow   Sunny   Thunderstorm

Weather Prognostics

Drizzle   Dust Whirls   Freezing Rain   Hail   Hurricane   Moderate Icing   Moderate Turbulence   Sand Storm   Severe Icing   Severe Turbulence   Showers

Snow   Squall   Thunderstorm   Tornado   Tropical Storm

International Symbols & Icons, Volume 1, Disk B

Heavy Equipment

         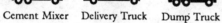

Backhoe   Bus Side   Cement Mixer   Delivery Truck   Dump Truck   Farm Tractor   Fork Lift   Oil Truck   Tractor Trailer   Van

Map Icons

        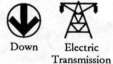

Airport   Boat Access   Cathedral Church   Christian Mission   Coal Mine   Compass   Compass B   Dam   Down   Electric Transmission   Exposed Wreck

Factory   Golf Course   Gravel Pit   Historic Site   Hydroelectric Plant   Left   Lighthouse   Lodging   Lookout Tower   Mine   Mineral Spring   Mohammadan Mosque

Monument   Museum   National Wildlife   Nuclear Power Plant   Oil   Pagoda (Temple)   Picnic Area   Ranger Station   Right   School   Seaport

Synagogue   Telecommunications   Tourist Activities   Up   Windmill

International Symbols & Icons, Volume 1, Disk B (continued)

Miscellaneous

Air, Auto Accidents, Bar, Coffee, Crime, Dancing, Democrat, Family, Fast, Land, Life, Locked, Motion Picture, Noise, Population, Recycle, Republican, Slow, Stable, Time, Unlocked, Water, Wedding

Occupations

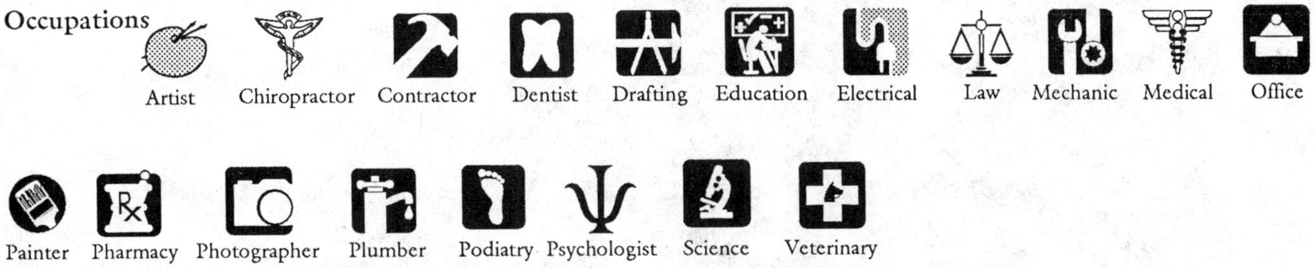

Artist, Chiropractor, Contractor, Dentist, Drafting, Education, Electrical, Law, Mechanic, Medical, Office, Painter, Pharmacy, Photographer, Plumber, Podiatry, Psychologist, Science, Veterinary

International Symbols & Icons, Volume 1, Disk C

Packaging Symbols

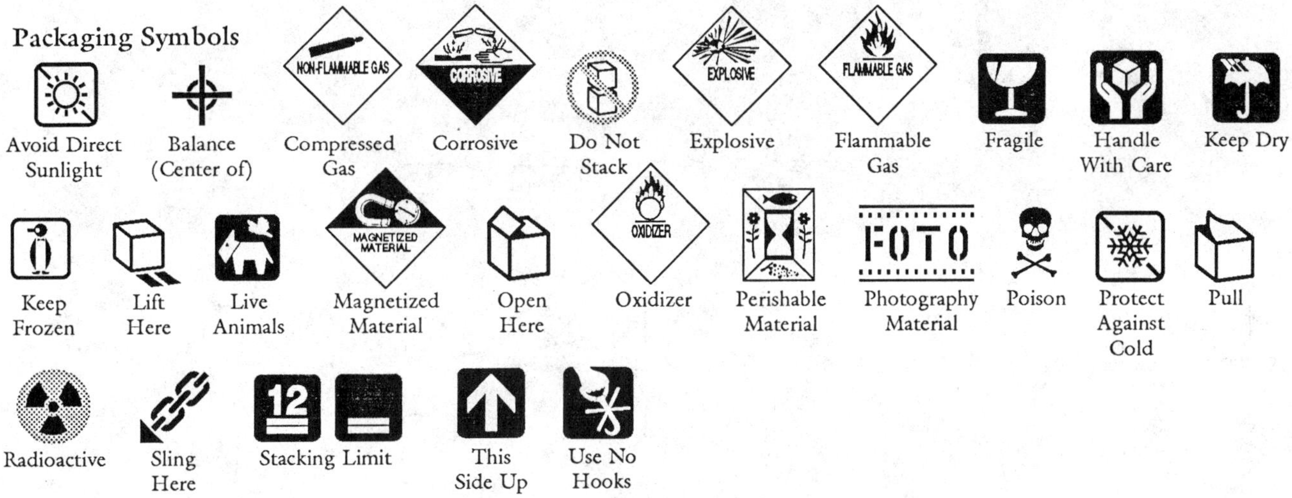

Avoid Direct Sunlight, Balance (Center of), Compressed Gas, Corrosive, Do Not Stack, Explosive, Flammable Gas, Fragile, Handle With Care, Keep Dry, Keep Frozen, Lift Here, Live Animals, Magnetized Material, Open Here, Oxidizer, Perishable Material, Photography Material, Poison, Protect Against Cold, Pull, Radioactive, Sling Here, Stacking Limit, This Side Up, Use No Hooks

Public Services

Ampitheater, Campfire, Car Pool, Dressing Room, Elevator, Food, Fuel, Handicap, Hearing Impaired, Hospital, Info, Library, Lodging, LP Fuel, Mail, Male/Female, Men, Men & Women, No Parking, No Smoking, Parking, Pets on Leash, Shower, Smoking, Telephone, Telephone B, Trailer Sanitary Station, Women

International Symbols & Icons, Volume 1, Disk C (continued)

Safety

Biohazard, Do Not Use Hands, Don't Drink & Drive, Fallout Shelter, Fire Alarm, Fire Extinguisher, High Voltage, Men Working, No Bare Feet, No Bicycles, No Entry, No Open Flame, No Pets, No Trucks, Sharp, Slippery, Stop, Warning, Wear Earmuffs, Wear Goggles, Wear Hardhat, Wear Safety Belts, Yield

Seasons

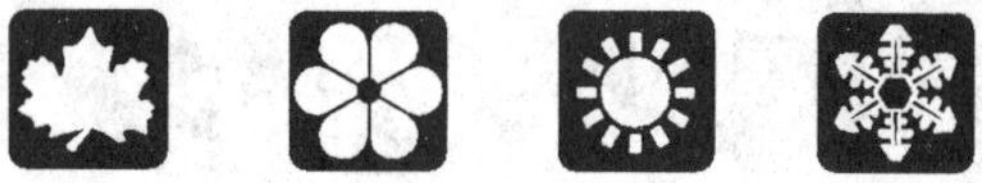

Fall, Spring, Summer, Winter

International Symbols & Icons, Volume 1, Disk D

Bonus Art

Globe 1, Globe 2, Recycle 1, Recycle 2, Recycle 3, World

Emergency

Fire, First Aid, Medic Alert, Poison, Police

Sports & Recreation

Archery, Baseball, Basketball, Bicycling, Billiards, Boating, Bobsleigh, Bowling, Boxing, Campground, Canoeing, Cross Country Skiing, Curling, Diving, Downhill Skiing, Equestrian, Fencing, Field Hockey, Figure Skating, Fishing, Football, Golf, Gymnastics, Hiking, Horse Riding, Hunting, Ice Hockey, Judo, Luge, Ping Pong, Playground, Rowing, Sailing, Scuba Diving, Shuffleboard, Ski Jumping, Slalom Skiing, Sledding, Snowmobiling, Soccer, Softball, Speed Skating, Surfing, Swimming, Tennis, Track & Field, Volleyball, Walking, Water Polo, Water Skiing, Weight Lifting, Wind Surfing, Wrestling

International Symbols & Icons, Volume 1, Disk D (continued)

Travel

Airplane, Auto, Baggage, Bicycle, Bus, Camper Trailer, Car Rental, Customs, Heliport, Immigration, Motor Scooter

Motor Cycle, Railway Station, Recreational Vehicle, Ship, Street Car, Taxi, Train, Tramway, Truck

International Symbols & Icons, Volume 2, Disk A

Animals

Ant, Bird, Buffalo, Bull, Cat, Chicken, Cow, Deer, Dog, Dolphin, Donkey, Elephant

Fish, Fish Bowl, Horse 1, Horse 2, Insect, Kangaroo, Longhorn, Loon, Paw Print, Pig, Poodle, Seagulls, Seal, Sheep

Medical

Admissions, Ambulance, Blood Donor, Caduceus, Cardiology, Child Care, Dermatology, Dressing Room, Drug Store, Emergency, General Medicine

House Calls, Infant, Maternity, Neurosurgery, Nursery, Nurses, Opthamology, Orthopedics, Pathology, Pediatric Clinic, Pediatrics

Red Crescent, Red Lion & Sun, Vaccination, Visitors, X-Ray

Safety

Cancer Hazard, Danger, Emergency Exit, Fire Alarm, Fire Escape, High Voltage 2, Hot, Inhalation Hazard, Laser Beam, Magnetic Fields

No Eating Or Drinking, Peligro, Seat Belts, Slow Moving, Static Sensitive 1, Static Sensitive 2, Watch Your Hands, Wet Paint

International Symbols & Icons, Volume 2, Disk A (continued)

Traffic

Danger/ Avalanches | Drawbridge | Expressway | Falling Rocks | Highway Shield | Pedestrians Only | Railroad Crossing | Riverbank | Route Shield | School Crossing

Slippery Road | Tow Away Zone | Traffic Signal | Youth Hostel

International Symbols & Icons, Volume 2, Disk B

Business

Accountant | Appointments | Audio Cassette | Ballet | Broadcasting | Camera Store | Candy Store | Capitol Building | CD-ROM | Chemical

Cigarettes | Commerce | Construction | Cosmetics | Currency Exchange | Diskette 3.5 | Dry Cleaning | Emission Controls | Entertainment | Exercise Equipment | Farmer

Fax | Fire Department 1 | Fire Department 2 | Furniture | Gift Shop | Glassware | Grocery Store | Handshake | Health Spa/ Sauna | Insurance | Janitor

Jeweler | Labels | Language | Lumber | Lumber Wood | Management | Masonry | Mechanic | Movies | Natural Gas | Oil Well

Open 24 Hours | Paper | Pawn Shop | Perfume | Photographer | Pick & Shovel | Printing 1 | Printing 2 | Radio | Rain Gear | Real Estate | Registration

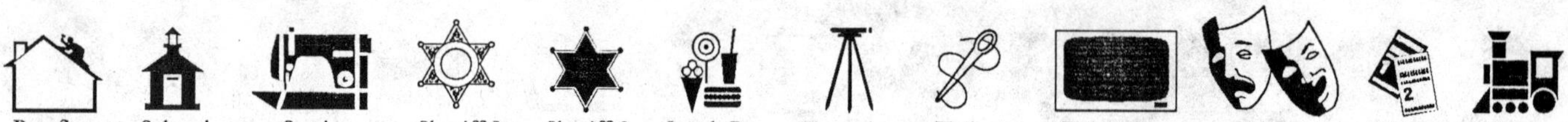

Roofing | School House | Sewing Machines | Sheriff 1 | Sheriff 2 | Snack Bar | Surveying | Tailor | Television | Theater | Tickets | Toys

Transmission Auto | Transmission Standard | Typography | Vending Machines | Video Cassette | Video Store | Waiting Room | Watch

International Symbols & Icons, Volume 2, Disk C

Recreation
Clubs · Diamonds · Dreydle-Gimmel · Dreydle-He · Dreydle-Noon · Dreydle-Pe · Dreydle-Shin · Hearts · Spades

Recycle
Can Receptacle · Earth Matters · Environmental Choice · Glass Receptacle · Oil Recycling · Paper Receptacle · Pitch In! · Read Then Recycle · Recyclable 1

Recyclable 2 · Recyclable 3 · Recyclable HDPE · Recyclable LDPE · Recyclable Other · Recyclable PETE · Recyclable PP · Recyclable PS · Recyclable V · Recycle 1

Recycle 2 · Recycle 3 · Recycle 4 · Recycle 5 · Recycle 6 · Recycle 7 · Recycle 8 · Recycle Corrugated · Recycled · Recycled Paper · Trash Receptacle

Religion
Bible · Chi Rho · Christ Victorious · Christianity/Fish 2 · Church · Confucianism · Cross 2 · Cross 3 · Cross 4 · Cross 5 · Cross 6

Episcopal Church · Irish Cross · Judaism (Life) · Kirpan · Mandala · Menorah · Methodist · Orthodox Cross · Prayer · Sacred Fire · St. Clement · Taoism

Ten Commandments · Triquetra · Vatican · Zen

International Symbols & Icons, Volume 2, Disk D

Misc.

 4-Leaf Clover
 Apple
 Auto Racing
 Blue Ribbon
 Broken Heart
 Check Mark
 Cherries
 Cigarette Lighter
 Confederate Flag
 Cornucopia
 Crown 1

 Crown 2
 Crystal Ball
 Dark
 Eagle of Saladin's
 Escalator
 Finish Flags
 Fluer-de-lis
 Globe 1
 Globe 2
 Golf 2
 Hammer & Sickle
 Happy

 Hearing
 Horn
 Hour Glass
 Lamp
 Liberty Bell
 Light
 Light Bulb
 Lost & Found
 Luggage Locker
 Maple Leaf
 Memory
 No Tropical Oils
 Oranges

 Peace
 Rampant Lion
 Rose
 Sad
 Shamrock
 Soccer Ball
 Stairs
 Star
 Strawberry
 Sun 1
 Sun 2
 Target
 Telephone 3

 Telephone 4
 Telephone 5
 Temperature
 Tree
 Trident
 Unisex
 US Eagle
 US Flag
 US Map
 Volume
 Wheel of Law
 Wine
 World

Transportation

 Bulldozer
 Camper
 Car Ferry
 Dump Truck
 Fire Truck
 Gondola
 Monorail

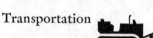 Pulp Truck
 Sailboat
 Schooner
 Sports Car
 Tow Truck

Logos & Trademarks, Volume 1, Disk A

Logos & Trademarks, Volume 1, Disk B

Logos & Trademarks, Volume 2, Disk A

Logos & Trademarks, Volume 2, Disk B

Logos & Trademarks, Volume 3, Disk A

 Admiral. AGWAY *Amana.*  AVIA BASF

American Heart Association

American Lung Association

 BLACK & DECKER® BROOKS. *brother.* BURGER KING

 CANTEEN  CASIO.  CONVERSE  DOMINO'S PIZZA DP Fit for Life *Dr Pepper.* DUNKIN' DONUTS®

 Elks Club  *Emerson*™ EPSON® EUREKA Find Us Fast In The Yellow Pages FORMICA Glidden

 GoldStar Good Housekeeping Heineken  Hotpoint Find Us in the Yellow Pages  I.O.O.F.

 JENN·AIR JENSEN® JVC Kenmore. KENWOOD

 Kiwanis Club Kmart  Knights of Columbus THE BOLD LOOK OF KOHLER. Konica KRAFT  *L.A. GEAR*

LA-Z-BOY® Levi's Litton

Logos & Trademarks, Volume 3, Disk B

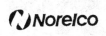 7UP MADE IN U.S.A. Magic Chef® *Makita* Masons McDonald's MEMOREX

MICHELOB. *Lite* MINOLTA *mita* MITSUBISHI *Nikon.* LOYAL ORDER OF MOOSE NABISCO

 Norelco Olin. OFFICIAL OLYMPIC SPONSOR OLYMPUS® PENTAX Pizza Hut. PPG INDUSTRIES

Quasar. Ocean Pacific *Radio Shack* *Ray·Ban* REDKEN *Reebok*

ROTARY RUSSELL ATHLETIC SANYO savin *SEARS* *Sealy.* *Serta* SIMMONS SKIL

STANLEY Steel *Sunbeam* *TAPPAN.* TARGET TDK. Technics

TIMEX® TOSHIBA U.S. GRADE A VUARNET FRANCE WAL-MART WANG XEROX YASHICA *Zenith*

Logos & Trademarks, Volume 4, Disk A

Logos & Trademarks, Volume 4, Disk B

Letterspace

100 Wooster Street 2 fl
New York, NY 10012-3845
212-226-8766

———————◆———————

Collection	Format	No./Size Disks	Price	Computer
DesignClips Natural Environment Series:				
Birds	EPS	1-800K	$49.95	Mac/IBM
Fish	EPS	1-800K	$49.95	Mac/IBM
Flowers	EPS	1-800K	$49.95	Mac/IBM
Fruit	EPS	1-800K	$49.95	Mac/IBM
Insects	EPS	1-800K	$49.95	Mac/IBM
Invertebrates	EPS	1-800K	$49.95	Mac/IBM
Mammals	EPS	1-800K	$49.95	Mac/IBM
Reptiles & Amphibians	EPS	1-800K	$49.95	Mac/IBM
Trees, Leaves & Plants	EPS	1-800K	$49.95	Mac/IBM
Vegetables	EPS	1-800K	$49.95	Mac/IBM

Notes:

• The identical artwork shown for this company is also arranged on disks called The Habitat Collection, a selection of animals and plants packaged together according to the natural environment they share. Each set contains 50 of the same images found in the Natural Environment Series inhabiting the following locales: The Desert, The Lakes, The Mountains, The Rain Forest, The Ocean, and The Sky.

• All art has been compressed onto the 800K disks.

DesignClips Natural Environment Series: Birds

Albatross

Bird of
Paradise

Bittern

Blackbird

Bluebird

Canary

Cardinal

Chicken

Cockatoo

Crane

Crow

Cuckoo

Curlew

Dodo

Dove

Eagle

Duck

Falcon

Finch

Flamingo

Goose

Heron

Hummingbird

Kiwi

Macaw

Mockingbird

DesignClips Natural Environment Series: Birds (continued)

Mynah	Ostrich	Owl	Parrot	Peacock
Pelican	Penguin	Pheasant	Pigeon	Quail
Roadrunner	Robin	Rooster	Sandpiper	Seagull
Skylark	Sparrow	Stork	Swallow	Swan
Toucan	Turkey	Woodpecker	Wren	

DesignClips Natural Environment Series: Fish

Albacore

Anchovy

Angelfish

Bandtail Puffer

Barracuda

Bluefin Tuna

Blue Marlin

Bonito

Butterfly Fish

Cod

Dolphin

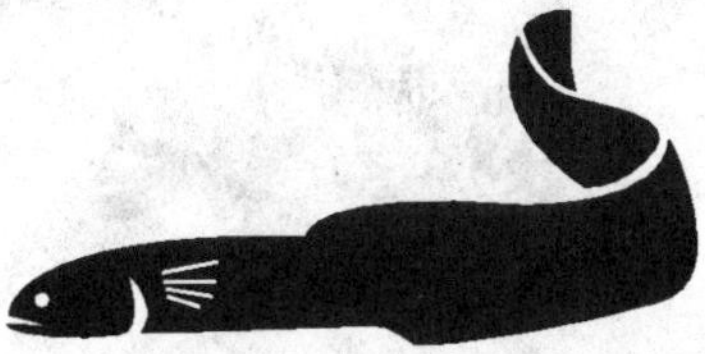

Electric Eel

Flounder

Flyingfish

Globe

Goldfish

Great White Shark

Grouper

Grunion

Herring

Mackerel

Mahi Mahi

Mako Shark

Manta Ray

Neon Goby

DesignClips Natural Environment Series: Fish (continued)

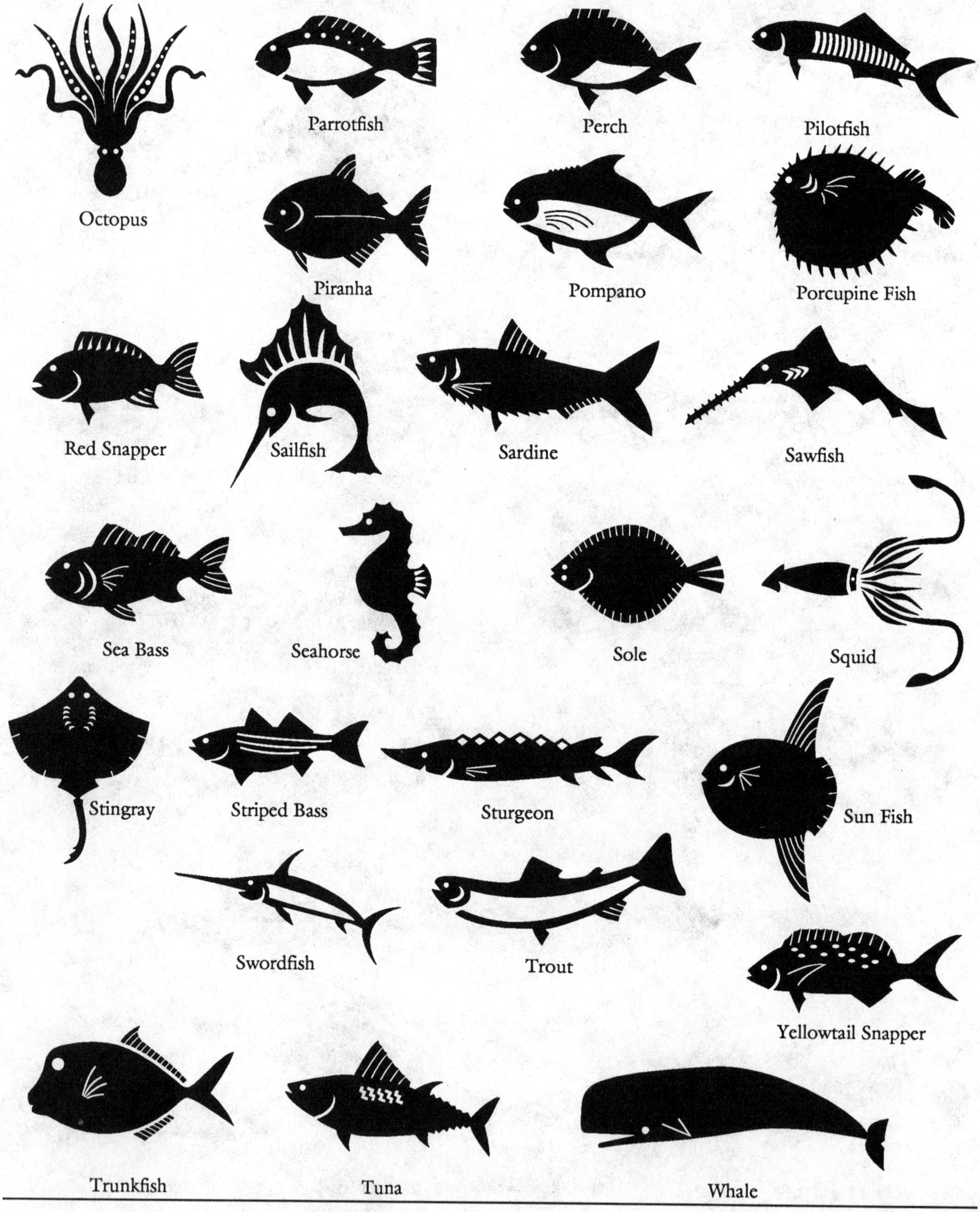

Octopus

Parrotfish

Perch

Pilotfish

Piranha

Pompano

Porcupine Fish

Red Snapper

Sailfish

Sardine

Sawfish

Sea Bass

Seahorse

Sole

Squid

Stingray

Striped Bass

Sturgeon

Sun Fish

Swordfish

Trout

Yellowtail Snapper

Trunkfish

Tuna

Whale

DesignClips Natural Environment Series: Flowers

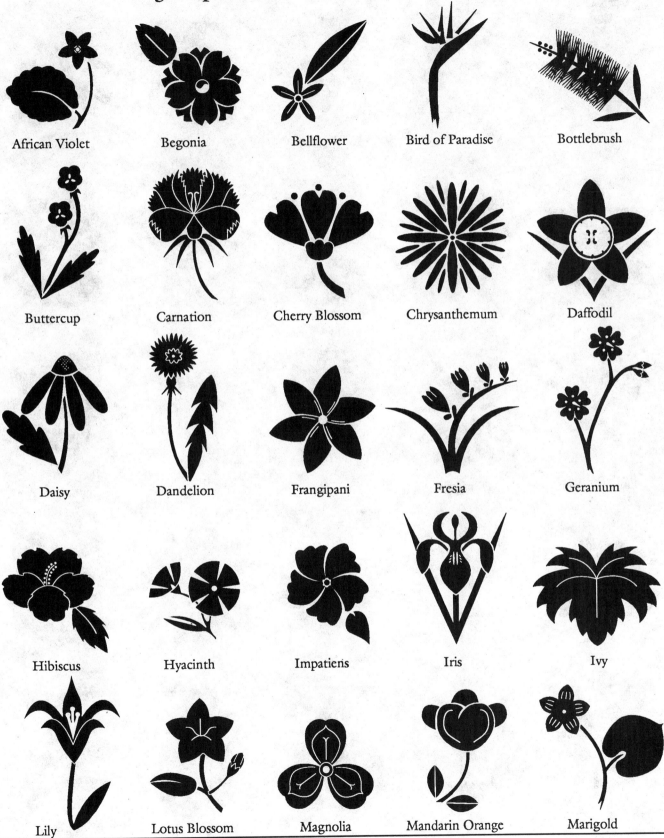

African Violet	Begonia	Bellflower	Bird of Paradise	Bottlebrush
Buttercup	Carnation	Cherry Blossom	Chrysanthemum	Daffodil
Daisy	Dandelion	Frangipani	Fresia	Geranium
Hibiscus	Hyacinth	Impatiens	Iris	Ivy
Lily	Lotus Blossom	Magnolia	Mandarin Orange	Marigold

DesignClips Natural Environment Series: Flowers (continued)

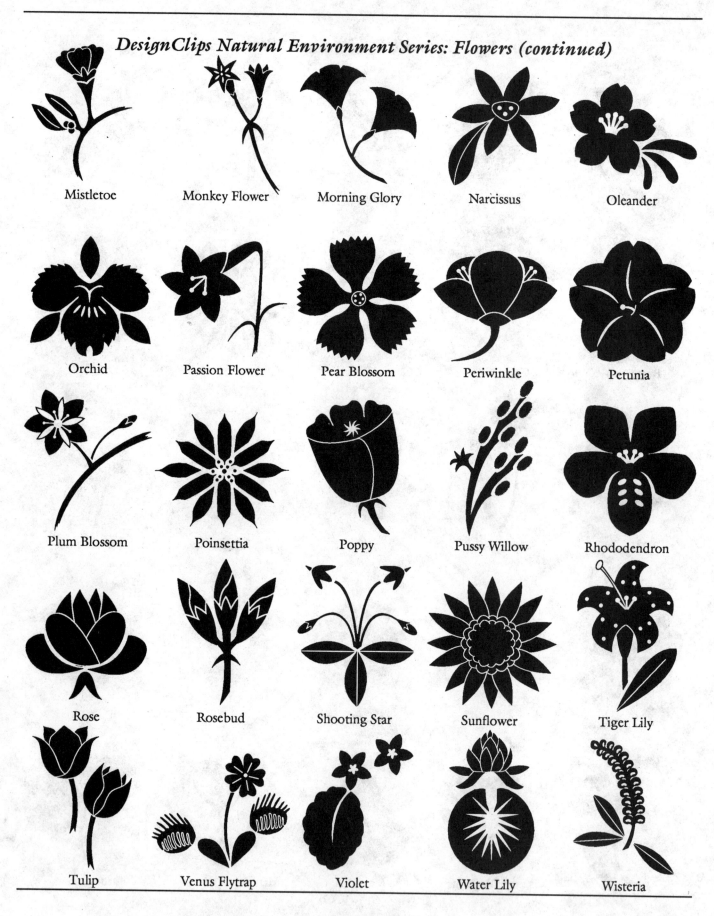

Mistletoe	Monkey Flower	Morning Glory	Narcissus	Oleander
Orchid	Passion Flower	Pear Blossom	Periwinkle	Petunia
Plum Blossom	Poinsettia	Poppy	Pussy Willow	Rhododendron
Rose	Rosebud	Shooting Star	Sunflower	Tiger Lily
Tulip	Venus Flytrap	Violet	Water Lily	Wisteria

DesignClips Natural Environment Series: Fruit

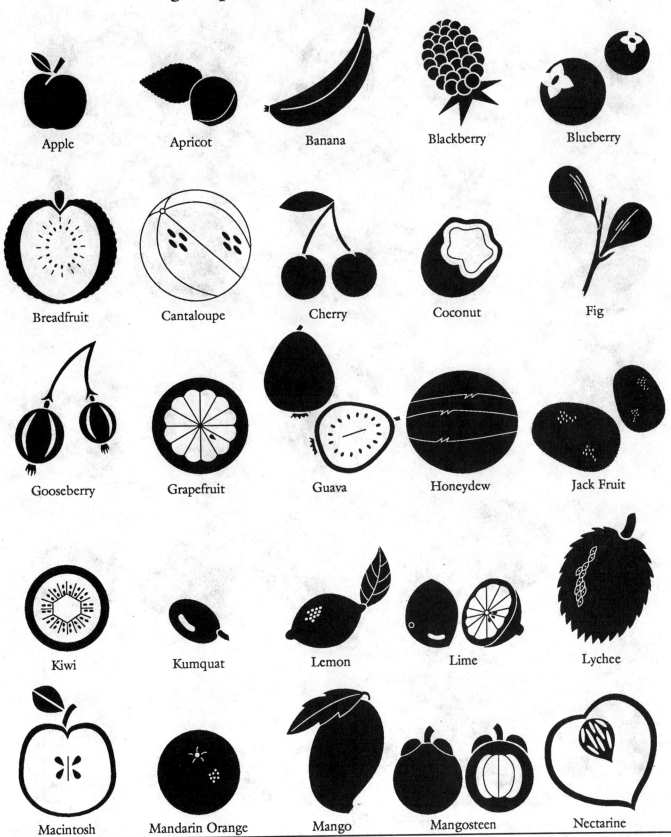

Apple   Apricot   Banana   Blackberry   Blueberry

Breadfruit   Cantaloupe   Cherry   Coconut   Fig

Gooseberry   Grapefruit   Guava   Honeydew   Jack Fruit

Kiwi   Kumquat   Lemon   Lime   Lychee

Macintosh   Mandarin Orange   Mango   Mangosteen   Nectarine

DesignClips Natural Environment Series: Fruit (continued)

Orange   Papaya   Passion Fruit   Peach   Pear

Persimmon   Pineapple   Plantain   Plum   Pomegranate

Poppy   Prickly Pear   Prune   Rambutan   Raspberry

Red Grapes   Sapodilla   Sorrel   Starfruit   Strawberry

Tamarind   Tangerine   Ugli   Watermelon   White Grapes

DesignClips Natural Environment Series: Insects

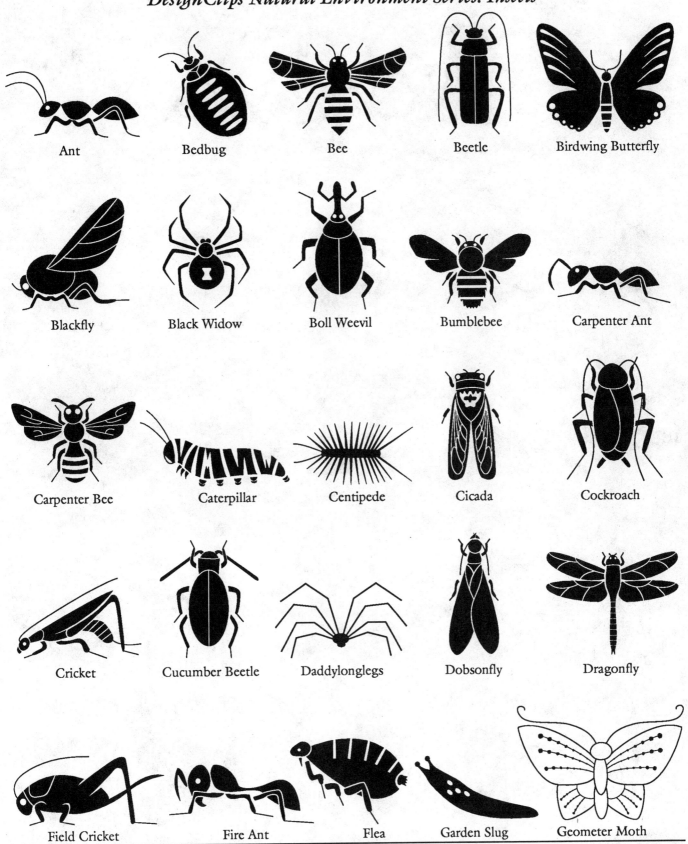

Ant	Bedbug	Bee	Beetle	Birdwing Butterfly
Blackfly	Black Widow	Boll Weevil	Bumblebee	Carpenter Ant
Carpenter Bee	Caterpillar	Centipede	Cicada	Cockroach
Cricket	Cucumber Beetle	Daddylonglegs	Dobsonfly	Dragonfly
Field Cricket	Fire Ant	Flea	Garden Slug	Geometer Moth

DesignClips Natural Environment Series: Insects (continued)

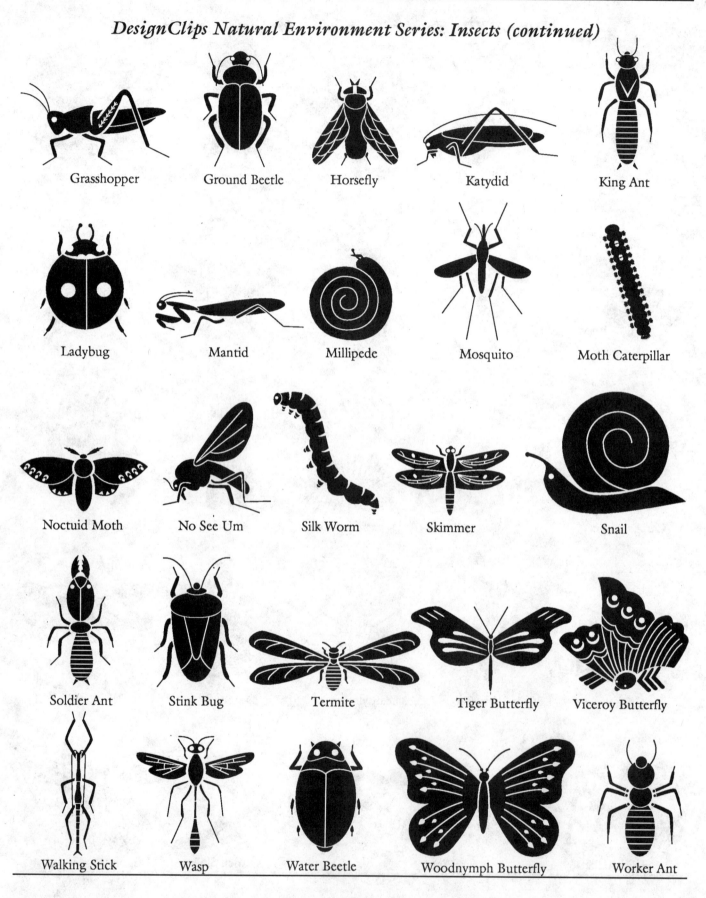

Grasshopper Ground Beetle Horsefly Katydid King Ant

Ladybug Mantid Millipede Mosquito Moth Caterpillar

Noctuid Moth No See Um Silk Worm Skimmer Snail

Soldier Ant Stink Bug Termite Tiger Butterfly Viceroy Butterfly

Walking Stick Wasp Water Beetle Woodnymph Butterfly Worker Ant

DesignClips Natural Environment Series: Invertebrates

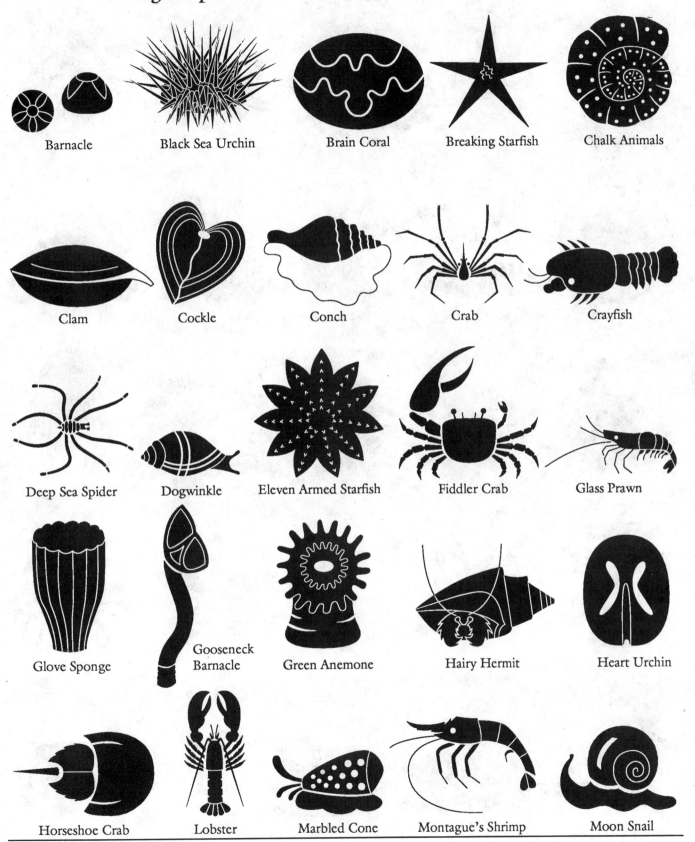

Barnacle

Black Sea Urchin

Brain Coral

Breaking Starfish

Chalk Animals

Clam

Cockle

Conch

Crab

Crayfish

Deep Sea Spider

Dogwinkle

Eleven Armed Starfish

Fiddler Crab

Glass Prawn

Glove Sponge

Gooseneck Barnacle

Green Anemone

Hairy Hermit

Heart Urchin

Horseshoe Crab

Lobster

Marbled Cone

Montague's Shrimp

Moon Snail

DesignClips Natural Environment Series: Insects (continued)

Mussel	Nautilus	Oyster	Prawn	Rock Boring Sea Urchin
Sand Dollar	Scale Worm	Scallop	Sea Anemone	Sea Cucumber
Sea Snail	Sea Urchin	Shrimp	Small Headed Worm	Speckled Jellyfish
Spiny Lobster	Staghorn Coral	Star Coral	Starfish	Stone Crab
Trumpet Worm	Tulip Snail	Whelk	White Anemone	Zebra Flatworm

DesignClips Natural Environment Series: Mammals

Aardvark   Armadillo   Bear   Beaver   Buffalo

Camel   Cat   Cattle   Cheetah   Chimpanzee

Chipmunk   Coati   Cow   Deer   Dog

Donkey   Elephant   Fox   Giraffe   Gorilla

Hare   Hippopotamus   Horse   Kangaroo   Koala Bear

DesignClips Natural Environment Series: Mammals (continued)

Leopard   Lion   Mink   Monkey   Moose

Mouse   Panda   Panther   Pig   Platypus

Porcupine   Rabbit   Raccoon   Rat   Reindeer

Rhinoceros   Seal   Sheep   Skunk   Squirrel

Tiger   Walrus   Water Buffalo   Wild Boar   Zebra

DesignClips Natural Environment Series: Reptiles & Amphibians

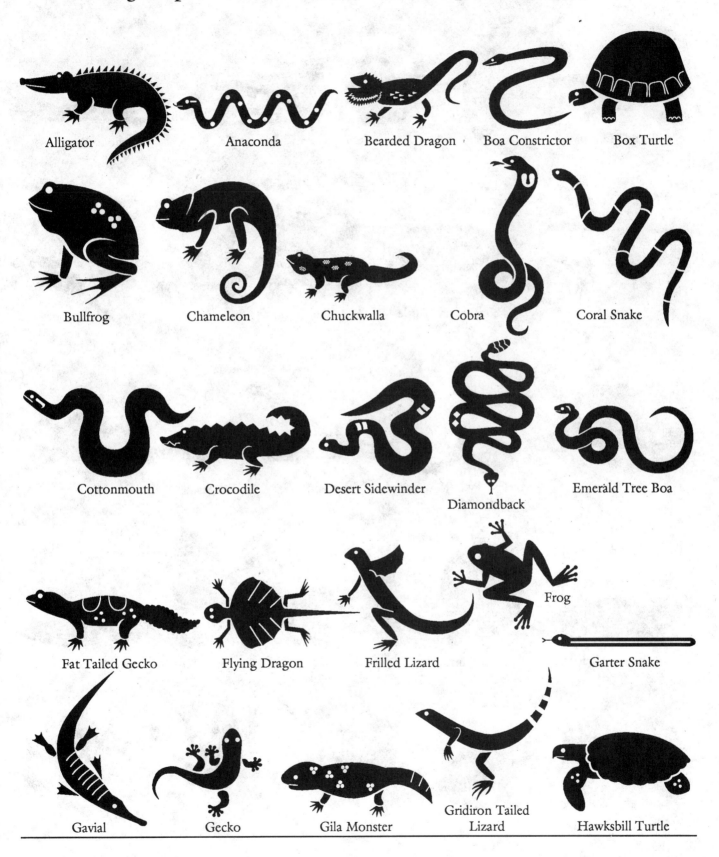

Alligator

Anaconda

Bearded Dragon

Boa Constrictor

Box Turtle

Bullfrog

Chameleon

Chuckwalla

Cobra

Coral Snake

Cottonmouth

Crocodile

Desert Sidewinder

Diamondback

Emerald Tree Boa

Fat Tailed Gecko

Flying Dragon

Frilled Lizard

Frog

Garter Snake

Gavial

Gecko

Gila Monster

Gridiron Tailed
Lizard

Hawksbill Turtle

DesignClips Natural Environment Series: Reptiles & Amphibians (continued)

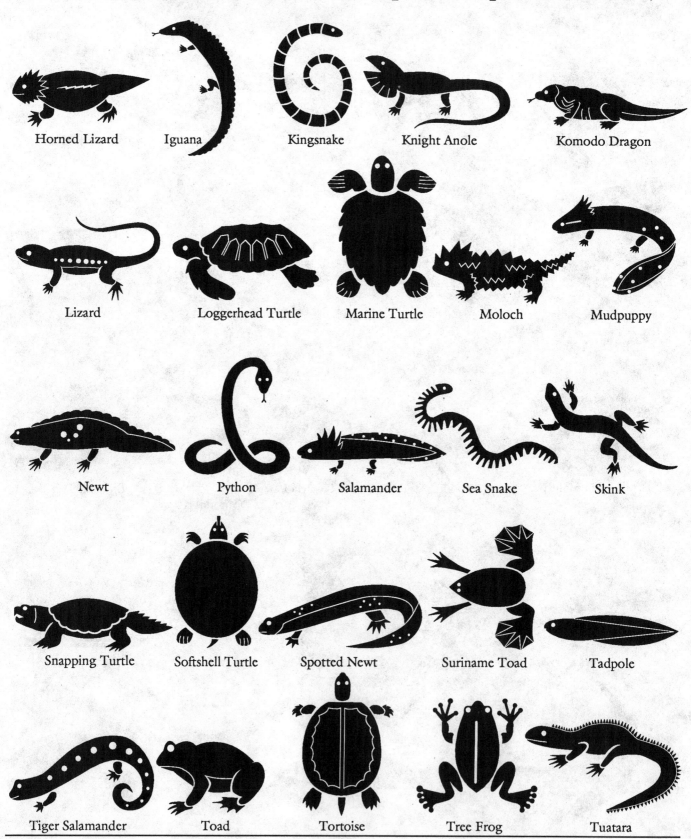

Horned Lizard Iguana Kingsnake Knight Anole Komodo Dragon

Lizard Loggerhead Turtle Marine Turtle Moloch Mudpuppy

Newt Python Salamander Sea Snake Skink

Snapping Turtle Softshell Turtle Spotted Newt Suriname Toad Tadpole

Tiger Salamander Toad Tortoise Tree Frog Tuatara

DesignClips Natural Environment Series: Trees, Leaves & Plants

Acacia	Aloe Yucca	Ash	Bamboo	Banana Leaf
Basswood	Beech	Birch	Butternut	Cactus
Caper	Cedar	Cherry	Chestnut	Cotton
Dogwood	Douglas Fir	Echeveria	Elder	Elm
Eucalyptus	Fern	Fig	Hickory	Joshua Tree

DesignClips Natural Environment Series: Trees, Leaves & Plants (continued)

Magnolia	Mahogany	Mangrove	Maple Leaf	Mesquite
Mint Leaf	Mulberry	Nutmeg	Oak	Palm
Palmetto	Pecan	Pine	Plantain Leaf	Pussy Willow
Redwood	Reeds	Rubber Plant	Saguaro	Sugar Cane
Sycamore	Walnut	Washingtonia Palm	Walnut	Witch Hazel

DesignClips Natural Environment Series: Vegetables

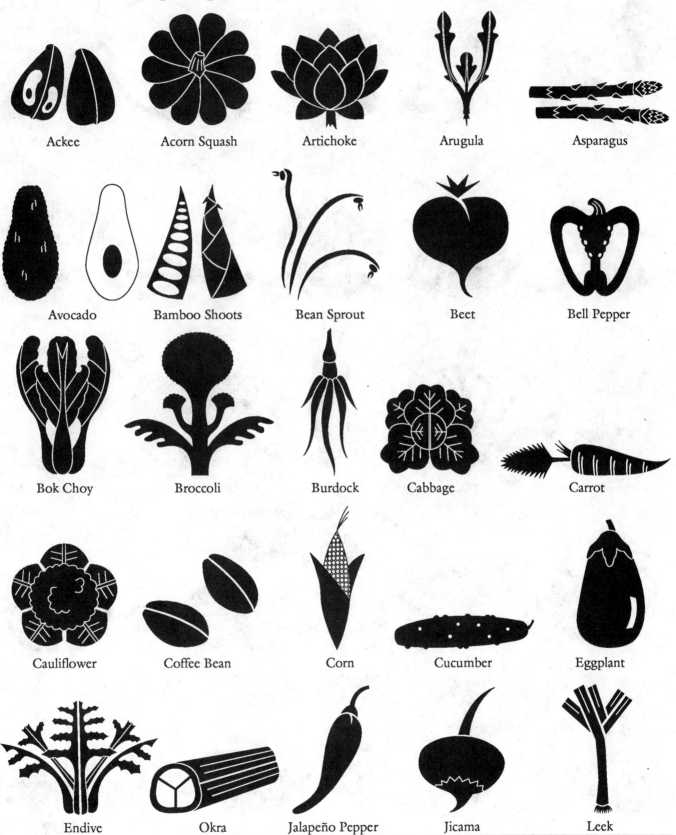

Ackee	Acorn Squash	Artichoke	Arugula	Asparagus
Avocado	Bamboo Shoots	Bean Sprout	Beet	Bell Pepper
Bok Choy	Broccoli	Burdock	Cabbage	Carrot
Cauliflower	Coffee Bean	Corn	Cucumber	Eggplant
Endive	Okra	Jalapeño Pepper	Jicama	Leek

DesignClips Natural Environment Series: Vegetables (continued)

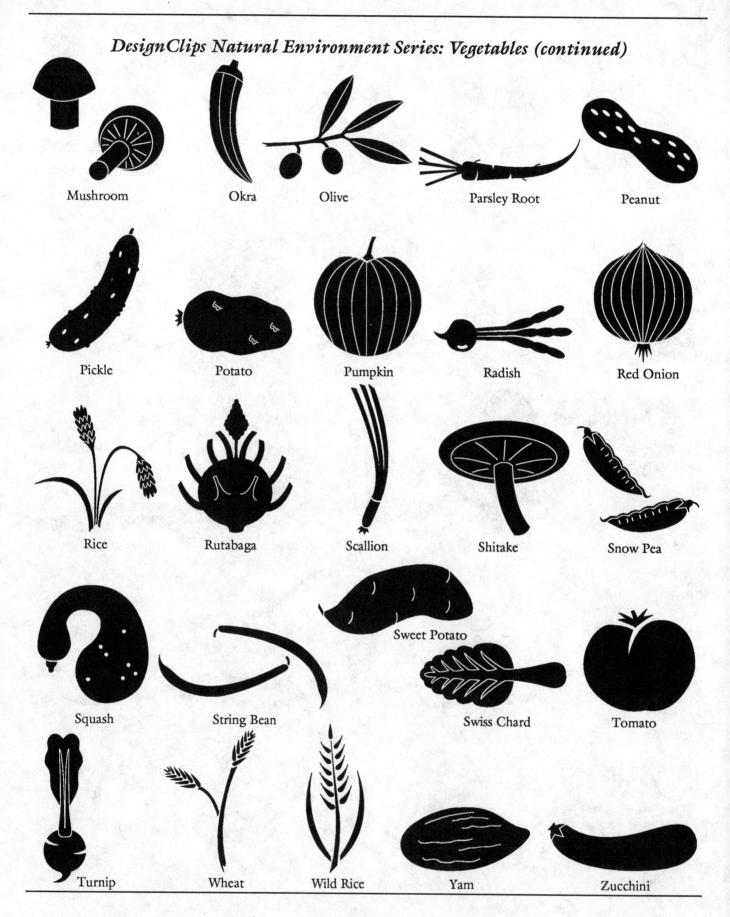

Mushroom   Okra   Olive   Parsley Root   Peanut

Pickle   Potato   Pumpkin   Radish   Red Onion

Rice   Rutabaga   Scallion   Shitake   Snow Pea

Sweet Potato

Squash   String Bean   Swiss Chard   Tomato

Turnip   Wheat   Wild Rice   Yam   Zucchini

Magnum Software
21115 Devonshire Street, Suite 337
Chatsworth, CA 91311
818-700-0510

◆

Collection	Format	No./Size Disks	Price	Computer
McPic! Volume 1	Paint	1-400K	$49.95	Mac
McPic! Volume 2	Paint	1-400K	$49.95	Mac

McPic! Volume 1

Animals

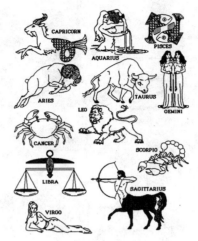

Astrology

Business 1

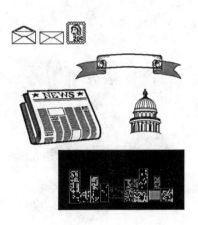

Business 2

Fun 1

Fun 2

Holiday 1

Holiday 2

Home

McPic! Volume 1 (continued)

Misc 1 Misc 2 Misc 3

Money Nature People 1

People 2 Sports Symbols Transportation

McPic! Volume 2

Animals

Communications

Exotica 1

Exotica 2

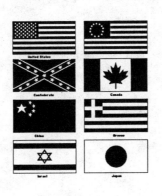

Flags 1

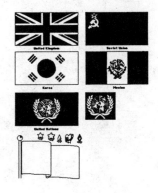

Flags 2

Food

Home

Maps 1

McPic! Volume 2 (continued)

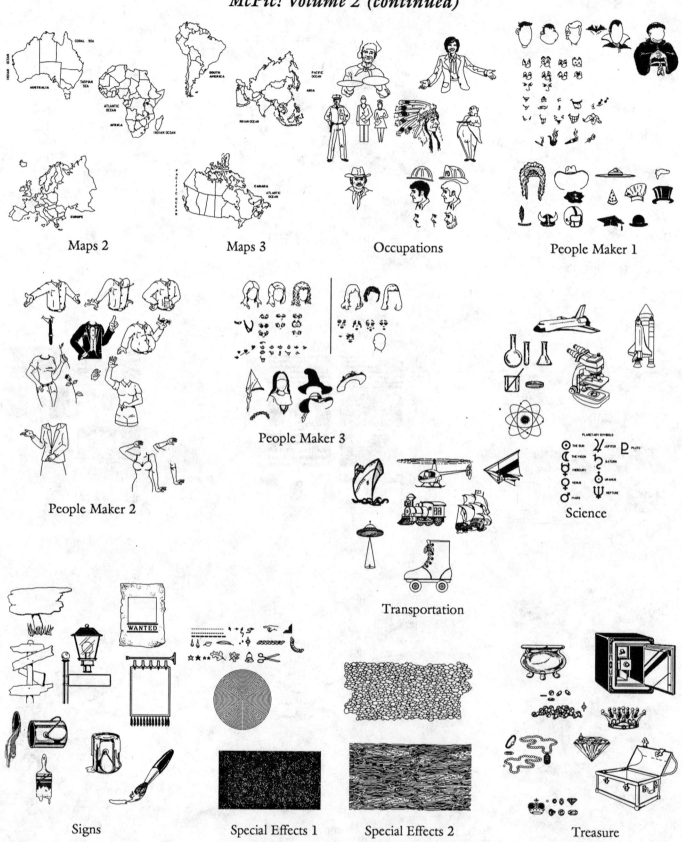

Maps 2   Maps 3   Occupations   People Maker 1

People Maker 2   People Maker 3   Science

Transportation

Signs   Special Effects 1   Special Effects 2   Treasure

Medina Software

P.O. Box 521917
Longwood, FL 32752-1917
407-260-1676

―――――――――◆―――――――――

Collection	Format	No./Size Disks	Price	Computer
Religious Art Portfolio 1	Paint	1-800K	$24.95	Mac
ElectroBits	Paint	1-800K	$24.95	Mac

Borders

Religious Art Portfolio

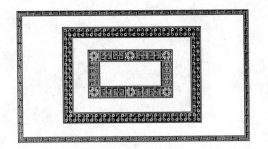

Borders

Illustrated Border

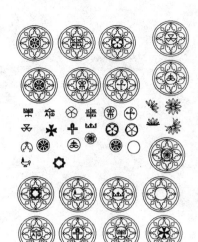

Ornament Kit

Christian Symbols

ANDREW

BARTHOLOMEW

CHRIST

CHRIST

JESUS CHRIST

JAMES THE GREATER

JAMES THE LESSER

THE APOSTLE PAUL

PHILIP

JUDAS

THE APOSTLE PETER

THADDAEUS: (Jude).
A missionary with Simon.

Apostolic Symbols

ACT OF GRACE COMPLETE: "Abide in me, and I in you." (John)

RED ROSE: Martyrdom

CHRISTMAS ROSE: Christ's nativity

ARK OF THE COVENANT: Old Testament symbol of Christ.

NOAH'S ARK: Symbolic of the Church.

FLEUR-DE-LIS: The human and divine Christ. (Phil)

GOD: Omnipresent and omniscient. (Heb)

GOD REACHES DOWN with gift of salvation. (John)

THE TRINITY

EARTH: Waste and void. (Gen)

FAMILY: Y, woman; Λ, man; o o, children

THE TRINITY

EYE OF FIRE: "...God is a consuming fire..." (Deut.)

CREATION COMPLETE: "... and man became a living soul." (Gen.)

OLIVE OIL: Holy Spirit, Grace, Salvation. (Heb.)

MAN SEEKS SALVATION: Ask, Seek, Knock. (Mat.)

DEATH: "...and so death passed upon all men..." (Rom.)

Ark, Creation, Etc.

Religious Art Portfolio (continued)

Bibles, Brimstones........

Crosses, Ornaments & Gideon

Christian Symbols

Light of the World......

Greeting Card Folder

Greeting Card Template   Greeting Card #1

MEDINA SOFTWARE

Religious Art Portfolio (continued)

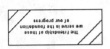

Greeting Card #2

Luke 22:50

Religious Images #1

Religious Images #2

Religious Images #3

Religious Images #4

Religious Art Portfolio (continued)

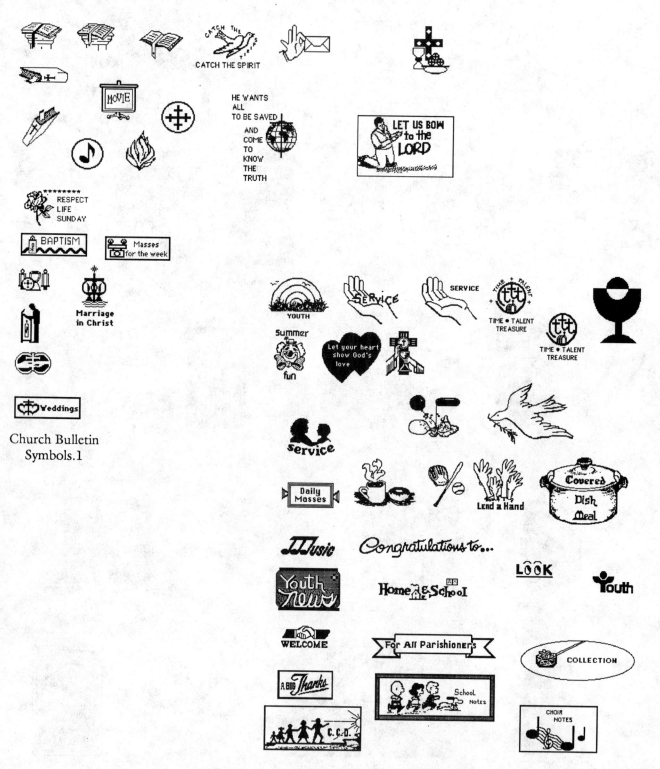

Church Bulletin Symbols.1

Church Bulletin Symbols.2

ElectroBits

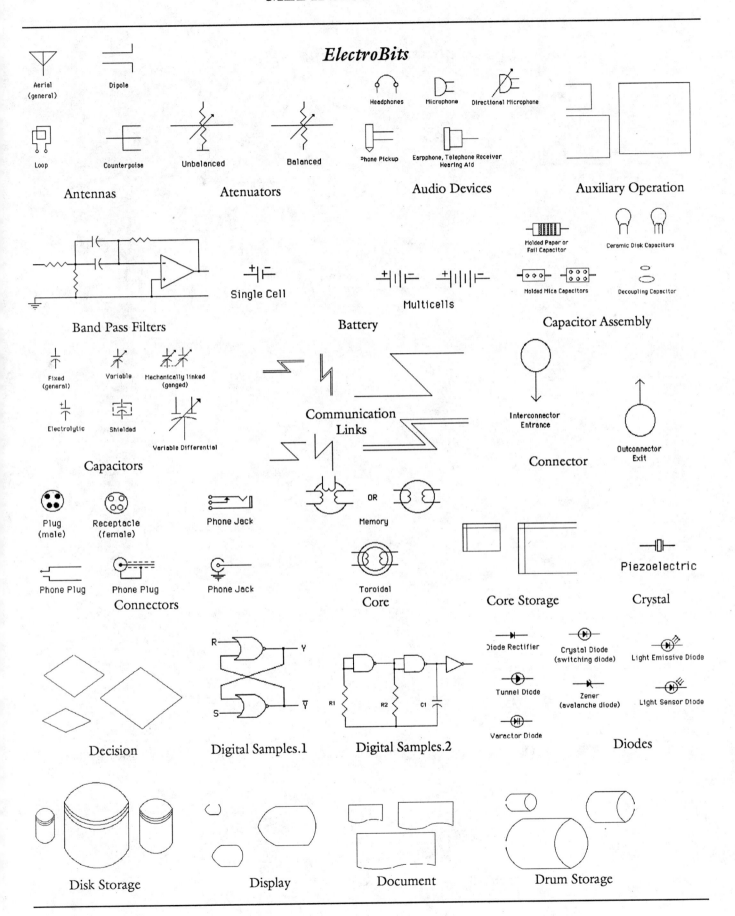

Aerial (general)

Dipole

Loop

Counterpoise

Unbalanced

Balanced

Antennas

Atenuators

Headphones

Microphone

Directional Microphone

Phone Pickup

Earpphone, Telephone Receiver Hearing Aid

Audio Devices

Auxiliary Operation

Band Pass Filters

Single Cell

Battery

Multicells

Molded Paper or Foil Capacitor

Ceramic Disk Capacitors

Molded Mica Capacitors

Decoupling Capacitor

Capacitor Assembly

Fixed (general)

Variable

Mechanically linked (ganged)

Electrolytic

Shielded

Variable Differential

Capacitors

Communication Links

Interconnector Entrance

Outconnector Exit

Connector

Plug (male)

Receptacle (female)

Phone Jack

Memory

Phone Plug

Phone Plug

Phone Jack

Toroidal Core

Core Storage

Piezoelectric

Crystal

Connectors

Decision

R

Y

S

Ȳ

Digital Samples.1

R1

R2

C1

Digital Samples.2

Diode Rectifier

Crystal Diode (switching diode)

Light Emissive Diode

Tunnel Diode

Zener (avalanche diode)

Light Sensor Diode

Varactor Diode

Diodes

Disk Storage

Display

Document

Drum Storage

ElectroBits (continued)

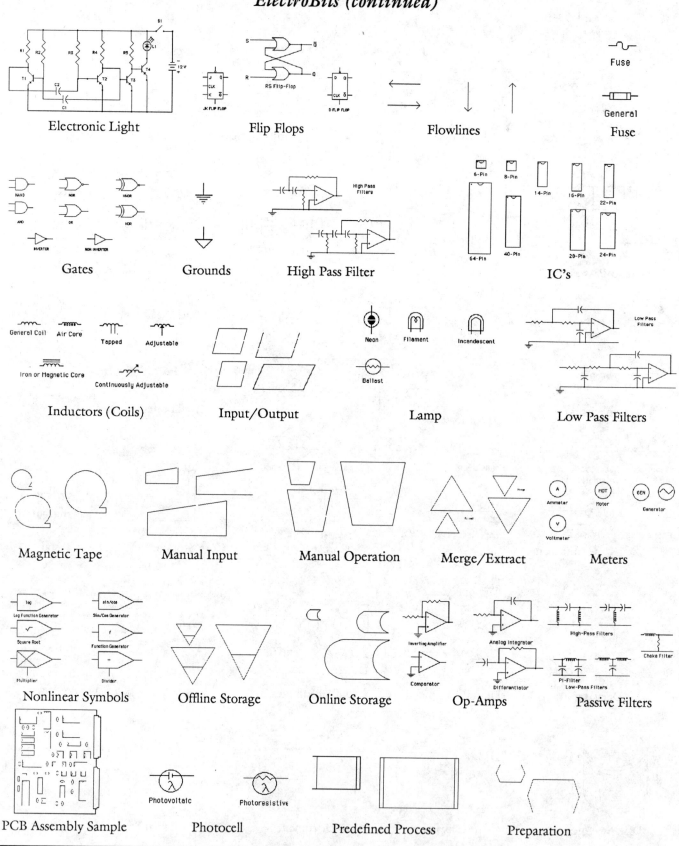

Electronic Light   Flip Flops   Flowlines   Fuse / General Fuse

Gates   Grounds   High Pass Filter   IC's

Inductors (Coils)   Input/Output   Lamp   Low Pass Filters

Magnetic Tape   Manual Input   Manual Operation   Merge/Extract   Meters

Nonlinear Symbols   Offline Storage   Online Storage   Op-Amps   Passive Filters

PCB Assembly Sample   Photocell   Predefined Process   Preparation

ElectroBits (continued)

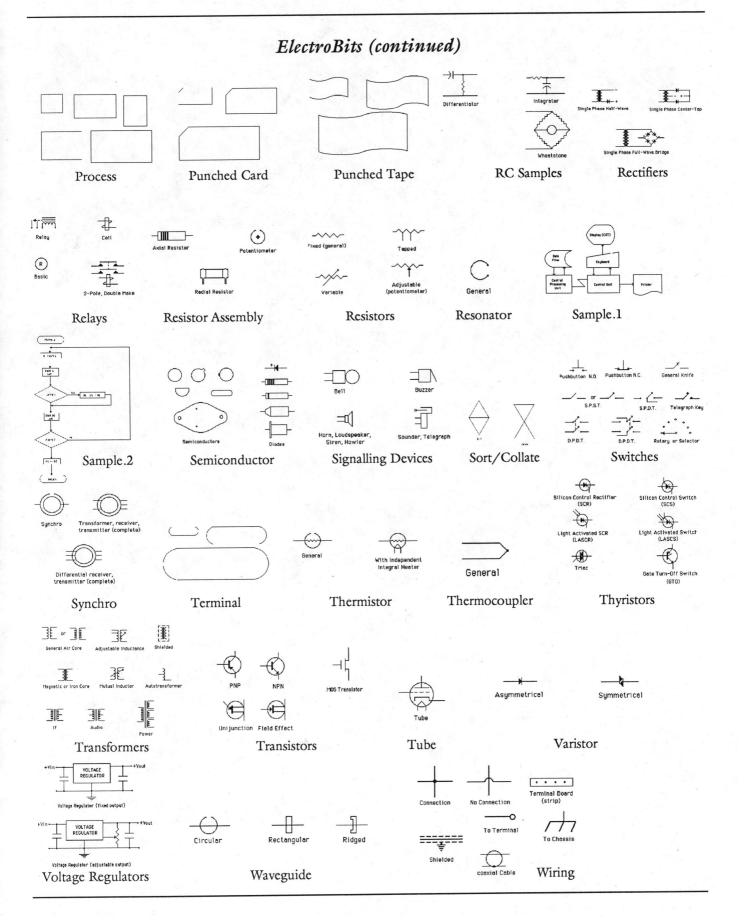

Process   Punched Card   Punched Tape   RC Samples   Rectifiers

Relays   Resistor Assembly   Resistors   Resonator   Sample.1

Sample.2   Semiconductor   Signalling Devices   Sort/Collate   Switches

Synchro   Terminal   Thermistor   Thermocoupler   Thyristors

Transformers   Transistors   Tube   Varistor

Voltage Regulators   Waveguide   Wiring

Metro ImageBase, Inc.

18623 Ventura Boulevard
Tarzana, CA 91356
818-881-1997
800-525-1552
818-881-4557 fax

◆

Collection	Format	No./Size Disks	Price	Computer
Alphabets***	EPS	5-800K	$145.00	Mac/IBM
Art Deco*	TIFF	6-800K	$145.00	Mac/IBM
Borders & Boxes*	TIFF	4-800K	$145.00	Mac/IBM
Business Graphics*	TIFF	6-800K	$145.00	Mac/IBM
Computers & Technology*	TIFF	5-800K	$145.00	Mac/IBM
Exercise & Fitness*	TIFF	4-800K	$145.00	Mac/IBM
Food*	TIFF	6-800K	$145.00	Mac/IBM
The Four Seasons*	TIFF	5-800K	$145.00	Mac/IBM
Headings****	EPS	3-800K	$145.00	Mac/IBM
Health Care*	TIFF	5-800K	$145.00	Mac/IBM
Holiday Basics**	TIFF	3-800K	$ 59.95	Mac/IBM
Image Basics*****	TIFF	3-800K	$ 59.95	Mac/IBM
Newsletter Maker*	TIFF	4-800K	$145.00	Mac/IBM
Nine to Five*	TIFF	5-800K	$145.00	Mac/IBM
People*	TIFF	6-800K	$145.00	Mac/IBM
Religion*	TIFF	5-800K	$145.00	Mac/IBM
Report Maker*	TIFF	5-800K	$145.00	Mac/IBM
Team Sports*	TIFF	4-800K	$145.00	Mac/IBM
Travel*	TIFF	5-800K	$145.00	Mac/IBM
Weekend Sports*	TIFF	5-800K	$145.00	Mac/IBM

Notes:
* Not shown in its entirety in this book. Due to the large amount of electronic clip art available from this company, we are showing only one page of samples from each of the volumes.
** Not shown or indexed in this volume. Contact Metro ImageBase for more information.
*** 12 alphabets and 460 images.   **** 150 images   *****42 images
• All art has been compressed onto the 800K disks. There are 100 images per package except as noted.
• Because of their size and detail, images are shown slightly larger than 25%.

Alphabets

Note: There are no numbers or punctuation marks in this alphabet.

Note: These are the only punctuation marks in this alphabet.

Note: These are the only punctuation marks in this alphabet.

Note: There are no numbers or punctuation marks in this alphabet.

Because of the large amount of clip art in this volume, we are showing only samples of the artwork.

Art Deco

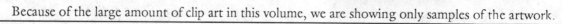

Because of the large amount of clip art in this volume, we are showing only samples of the artwork.

Borders & Boxes

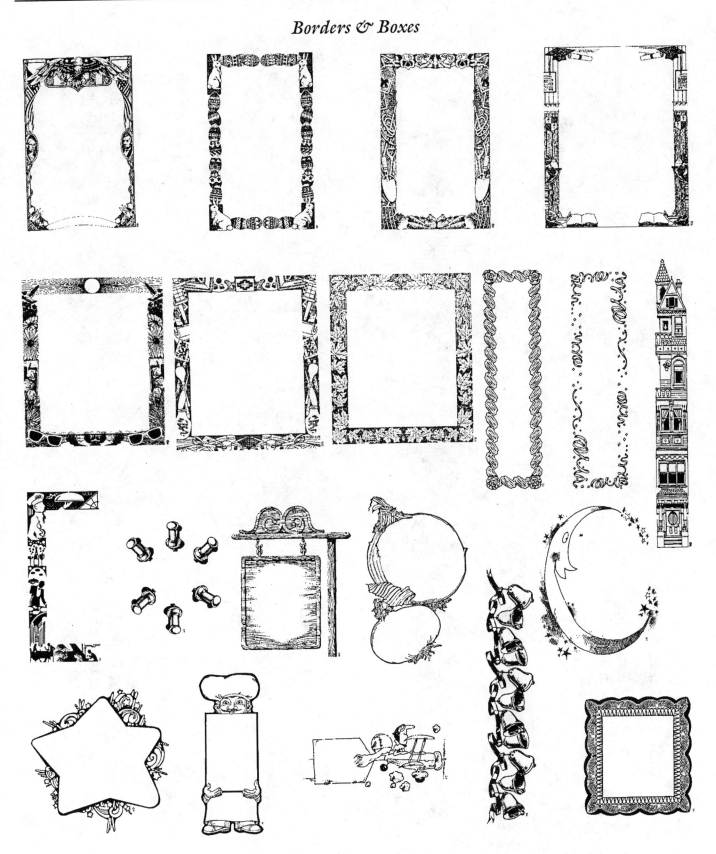

Because of the large amount of clip art in this volume, we are showing only samples of the artwork.

Business Graphics

Because of the large amount of clip art in this volume, we are showing only samples of the artwork.

Computers & Technology

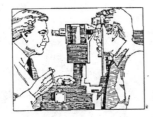

Because of the large amount of clip art in this volume, we are showing only samples of the artwork.

Exercise & Fitness

Because of the large amount of clip art in this volume, we are showing only samples of the artwork.

MET-6

Food

Because of the large amount of clip art in this volume, we are showing only samples of the artwork.

The Four Seasons

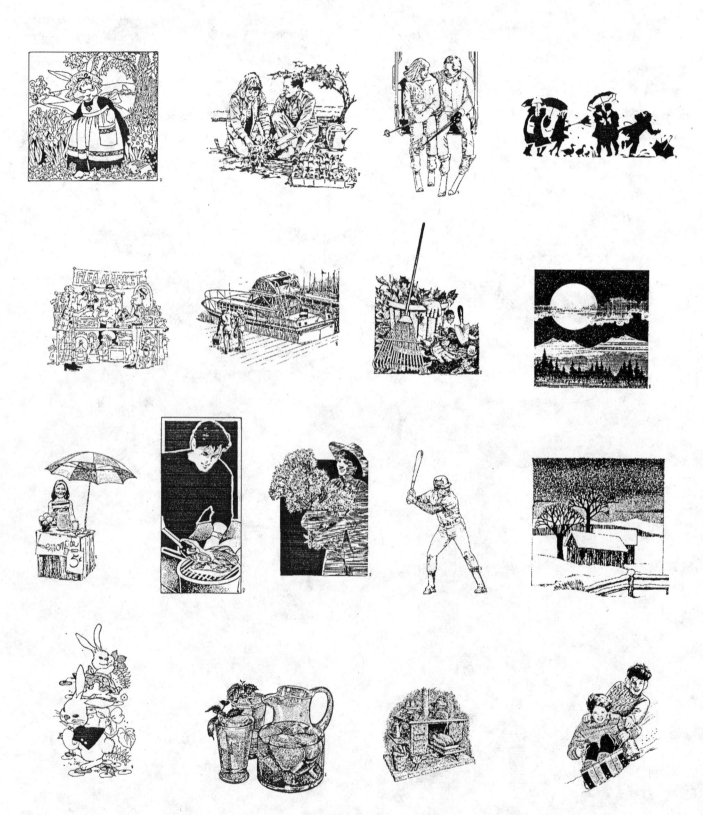

Because of the large amount of clip art in this volume, we are showing only samples of the artwork.

Headings

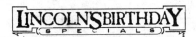

Because of the large amount of clip art in this volume, we are showing only samples of the artwork.

Health Care

Because of the large amount of clip art in this volume, we are showing only samples of the artwork.

Image Basics

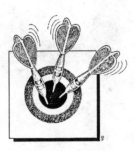

Because of the large amount of clip art in this volume, we are showing only samples of the artwork.

METRO IMAGEBASE, INC.

Newsletter Maker

Because of the large amount of clip art in this volume, we are showing only samples of the artwork.

Nine to Five

Because of the large amount of clip art in this volume, we are showing only samples of the artwork.

People

Because of the large amount of clip art in this volume, we are showing only samples of the artwork.

Religion

Because of the large amount of clip art in this volume, we are showing only samples of the artwork.

Report Maker

Because of the large amount of clip art in this volume, we are showing only samples of the artwork.

Team Sports

Because of the large amount of clip art in this volume, we are showing only samples of the artwork.

MET-17

Travel

Because of the large amount of clip art in this volume, we are showing only samples of the artwork.

Weekend Sports

Because of the large amount of clip art in this volume, we are showing only samples of the artwork.

MicroMaps Software

P.O. Box 757

Lambertville, NJ 08530

609-397-1611

800-334-4291

◆

Collection	Format	No./Size Disks	Price	Computer
MapArt EPS*	EPS	8-800K	$179.00	Mac/IBM
MapArt PICT*	PICT	5-800K	$179.00	Mac
MapArt Paint*	Paint	1-800K	$79.00	Mac
MapArt PCX*	PC Paint	1-720K or 2-360K	$79.00	IBM
MapPacks*:				
World Regions*:				
Africa*	EPS	2-H.D.**	$49.00	Mac/IBM
Antarctica*	EPS	1-H.D.	$49.00	Mac/IBM
Asia*	EPS	3-H.D.	$49.00	Mac/IBM
Australia & New Zealand*	EPS	1-H.D.	$49.00	Mac/IBM
Central America*	EPS	1-H.D.	$49.00	Mac/IBM
Europe*	EPS	3-H.D.	$49.00	Mac/IBM
Mediterranean*	EPS	2-H.D.	$49.00	Mac/IBM
Middle East*	EPS	1-H.D.	$49.00	Mac/IBM
North America*	EPS	2-H.D.	$49.00	Mac/IBM
Pacific Islands*	EPS	1-H.D.	$49.00	Mac/IBM
South America*	EPS	2-H.D.	$49.00	Mac/IBM
U.S.S.R.*	EPS	2-H.D.	$49.00	Mac/IBM
USA: 50 States by County*	EPS or PICT	3-800K	$49.00	Mac/IBM
Global Perspective Images*	EPS or PICT	2-800K	$49.00	Mac/IBM

Notes:

* Not shown in its entirety in this book. Due to the large amount of electronic clip art available from this company, we are showing only a few samples from each of the volumes. Contact MicroMaps for more information.

**H.D. (High Density) Disks have a 1.4 meg capacity.

• MapArt includes 4 world maps (2 with continent outlines, 2 with country outlines), 12 regional maps (Africa, Antarctica, Central America, East Asia, Europe, Mediterranean, Middle East, North America, North Pole, South America, SouthAsia, and South Pacific), and 25 country maps (Australia, Brazil, Canada, China, Finland, France, Germany, India, Ireland, Israel, Italy, Japan, Mexico, Mongolia, Northern Ireland, New Zealand, Norway, South Africa, Spain & Portugal, Sweden, Switzerland, U.S.A., U.S.S.R., and the United Kingdom).

• All 12 World Regions MapPacks can be purchased as a set for $299.00.

MapArt

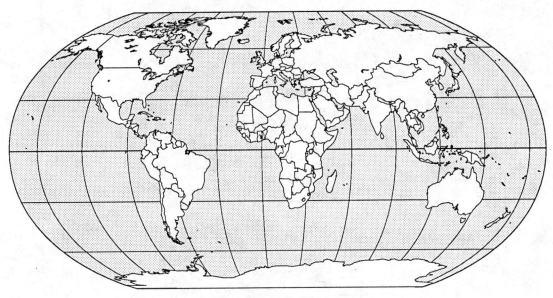

Robinson World Map

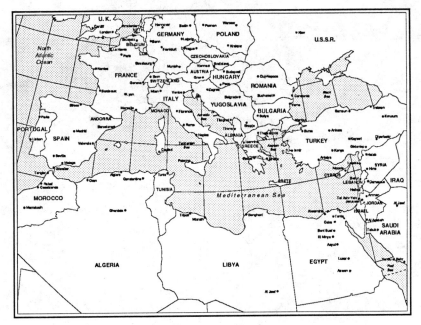

Mediterranean Region

Because of the large amount of clip art in this volume, we are showing only samples of the artwork.

MapArt (continued)

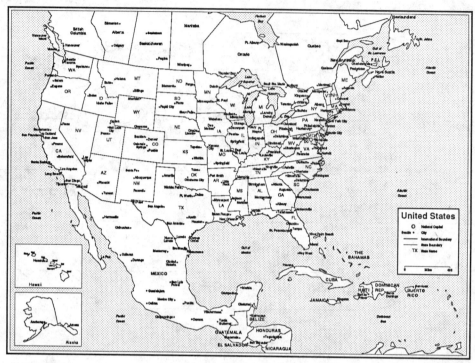

USA

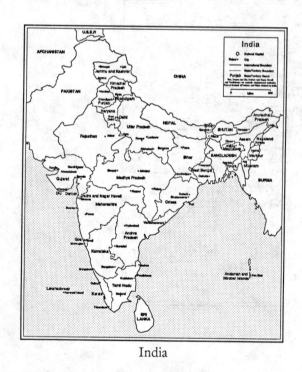

India

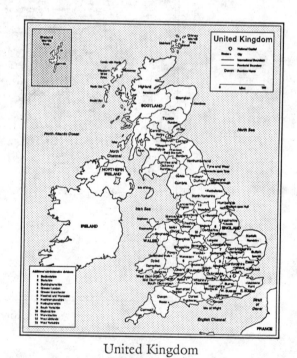

United Kingdom

Because of the large amount of clip art in this volume, we are showing only samples of the artwork.

MapPacks

Global Perspectives: North Pole

Global Perspectives: Europe

States by County: East North Central

States by County: Michigan

Because of the large amount of clip art in this volume, we are showing only samples of the artwork.

MapPacks (continued)

High Detail Country Maps: Ireland

High Detail Country Maps: Italy

High Detail Country Maps: Cuba

Because of the large amount of clip art in this volume, we are showing only samples of the artwork.

Multi-Ad Services

1720 W. Detweiller Drive
Peoria, IL 61615
309-692-1530
800-447-1950 orders and information

Collection	Format	No./Size Disks	Price	Computer
ProArt Professional Art Library:				
Borders/Headings	EPS	6-800K	$139.00	Mac/IBM
Business	EPS	5-800K	$139.00	Mac/IBM
Business 2	EPS	5-800K	$139.00	Mac/IBM
Christmas*	EPS	5-800K	$139.00	Mac/IBM
Education	EPS	5-800K	$139.00	Mac/IBM
Food	EPS	11-800K	$139.00	Mac/IBM
Generic Products*	EPS	5-800K	$139.00	Mac/IBM
Health/Medical	EPS	5-800K	$139.00	Mac/IBM
Holidays	EPS	7-800K	$139.00	Mac/IBM
People	EPS	13-800K	$139.00	Mac/IBM
Religious Images*	EPS	5-800K	$139.00	Mac/IBM
Sports	EPS	7-800K	$139.00	Mac/IBM
ProArt Professional Library Portfolio**	EPS	CD-ROM	$595.00	Mac/IBM

Notes:

* Not shown or indexed in this book. Contact Multi-Ad Services for more information.
** Not shown or indexed in this book. This CD contains over 3,000 pieces of art covering more than 50 categories, and includes a run-time version of Multi-Ad Search and a time-saving catalog of all the art, complete with keywords. Contact Multi-Ad Services for more information.
• Any three sets for $375.00.
• ProArt on CD:
   Trilogy 1: Business, Sports, & Holidays
   Trilogy 2: Borders & Headings, Food, & People
   Trilogy 3: Christmas, Generic Products & Religious Images
   Trilogy 4: Education, Business 2 & Health/Medical

Borders & Headings

General Borders Folder Samples

  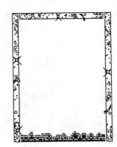 

Barbed Wire Border • Dog Bone Border • Progress Border • Restaurant Border

General Headings Folder Samples

Moonlight Madness • Sale 2 • Chalk Up Savings • Grand Opening

Mortices Folder Samples

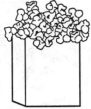 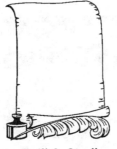  

Box of Popcorn • Quill & Scroll • Western • Snowflake

Seasonal Borders Folder Samples

Christmas • Hearts • Spring • Witch

Seasonal Headings Folder Samples

Autumn Sale • Ring in the New • Summertime Sale • Winter Clearance

Because of the large amount of clip art available in this volume, we are showing only samples of the artwork.

Business

Computers Folder Samples

CD Disk   Mac II   PS/2

Finance Folder Samples

Dollar   Tax Time

General Folder Samples

Film   Handshake

Headings Folder Samples

Buildings   Office Supplies

Merchandise   Tractor

Logos Folder Samples

Objects Folder Samples

Conference Table   Toolbox

Occupations Folder Samples

People Folder Samples

Chef   Executive Woman   Teacher   Couple #2   Man #7   Women #1

Places Folder Samples

Symbols Folder Samples

Capitol Building Washington   Airplane   Currency Exchange   Hotel   No Entry   Woman

Because of the large amount of clip art available in this volume, we are showing only samples of the artwork.

Business 2

Businessmen Folder Samples

Taking Notes

Businesswomen Folder Samples

Auctioneer   Man on Phone   Businesswoman #3   Thinking   Working Mother

Frames Folder Samples

Headings Folder Samples

Coins Frame   Wavy Dollar Sign Frame   Businesswomen's Week   Made in the USA

Meetings Folder Samples

Miscellaneous Folder Samples

Business Meeting   Tax Couple   Briefcase   Newspaper

Money Folder Samples

Office Equipment Folder Samples

Cascading Coins   Tax Refund   Car Phone   Typewriter

Office Supplies Folder Samples

Workers Folder Samples

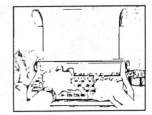

Notepad   Rolodex   Profit   Typing Hands

Because of the large amount of clip art available in this volume, we are showing only samples of the artwork.

Education

Books Folder Samples

Books on Desk

Stack of Books 2

Frames/Mortices Folder Samples

Class of Mortice

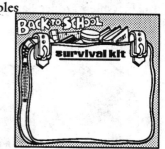

Survival Kit Mortice

Graduates Folder Samples

Female Grad 1

Male Grad 3

Graduation Folder Samples

Diploma, Hat & Mug

Receiving Diploma

Headings Folder Samples

Back to Class 1

Teacher's Day

Miscellaneous Folder Samples

Chalk Board

Lunch Box & Thermos

School Folder Samples

Study Time Folder Samples

ABC Kids

Boy at Computer

Children Raising Hands

Supplies Folder Samples

Apple, Notebook & Ruler

Geometry Tools

Paintbrush

School Supplies

Because of the large amount of clip art available in this volume, we are showing only samples of the artwork.

Food

Baked Goods Sample

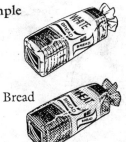

Bread

Dairy Folder Samples

Butter

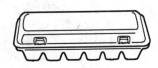

Eggs

Ice Cream Sundae

Food Groups Folder Samples

Cereal & Grains, Fruit, Vegetables

Food Headings Folder Samples

Bakery

Frozen Food

Fruit Folder Samples

Apples in Basket

Oranges

Meat Folder Samples

Chicken Fried

Hamburger

Prepared Foods Folder Samples

Pizza

Strawberry Shortcake

Submarine Sandwich

Vegetables Folder Samples

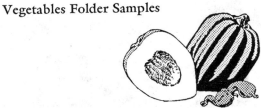

Acorn Squash

Indian Corn

Onions

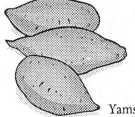

Yams

Because of the large amount of clip art available in this volume, we are showing only samples of the artwork.

Health & Medical

Dental Folder Samples

Doctors Folder Samples

First Aid Folder Sample

 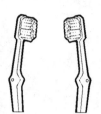   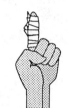

Dental Collage   Toothbrush   Doctor & Patient   Mother & Child w/ Doctor   Bandaged Finger

Hospital Care Folder Samples

Medical Diagrams Folder Samples

Hospital & Friends   Vital Signs   Eye Profile   Heart & Lungs

Medical Equipment Folder Samples

Medical Supplies Folder Samples

 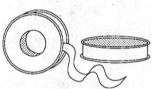 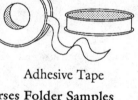 

Blood Pressure Cuff   Stethoscope Mortice   Adhesive Tape   Pill Bottles

Miscellaneous Folder Samples

Nurses Folder Samples

Doctor's Office   Stork   Maternity Nurse   Wheelchair & IV

Professionals Folder Samples

Symbols Folder Samples

Lab Tech   Woman Doctor   No Smoking   Symbol of Access

Because of the large amount of clip art available in this volume, we are showing only samples of the artwork.

Holidays

Birthdays Folder Sample

Happy Birthday

Christmas Folder Samples

Angel

Candy Canes

Santa w/Toys

Columbus Day Folder Sample

Columbus

Easter Folder Samples

Bunny Lifting Egg

Easter Basket

Fall Folder Sample

Leaves & Acorns

Father's Day Folder Sample

Father Bear

Halloween Folder Samples

Cat 1

Ghost

Hanukkah Folder Samples

Happy Hanukkah

Shalom Dove

Independence Day Folder Sample

Fireworks

Memorial Day Folder Sample

Memorial Day 1

Misc. Holidays Folder Sample

Sadie Hawkins Day

Mother's Day Folder Sample

Mother's Day

Samples not shown from the following folders: New Year's Day, New Year's Eve, Presidents' Day, Rev. King's Birthday, Spring, St. Patrick's Day, Summer, Thanksgiving, Valentine's Day, Veteran's Day, and Winter.

Because of the large amount of clip art available in this volume, we are showing only samples of the artwork.

People

Children Folder Samples

Flower Girl

Kids in Raincoats

Couples Folder Samples

Couple Celebrating

Western Couple

Entertainment Folder Samples

Band Leader

Magician

Families Folder Samples

Family Eating

Mother & Son

Leisure Folder Samples

Cross-Country Skier

Girl Biking

Ski Woman

Sunbathers

Men Folder Samples

Casual Man

Grandfather

Man on Bike

Man Wearing Tuxedo

Women Folder Samples

Working Folder Sample

Bride

Oriental Model

Pediatrician & Baby

Because of the large amount of clip art available in this volume, we are showing only samples of the artwork.

Sports

Baseball Folder Samples

Baseball Card

Batter 2

Basketball Folder Samples

Basketball 4

Women's Basketball

Football Folder Samples

Cheerleader

Football Player 2

Golf Folder Samples

Golf 2

Golfer 2

Hockey Folder Samples

Hockey 1

Hockey 4

Olympic Sports Folder Samples

Diver 1

Track 2

Recreational Sports Folder Samples

Horse Race

Runner

Soccer Folder Samples

Soccer 2

Soccer 6

Sports Logos Folder Samples

Cycling

Luge

Yachting

Tennis Folder Sample

Tennis 1

Tennis 5

Because of the large amount of clip art available in this volume, we are showing only samples of the artwork.

Studio Advertising Art

P.O. Box 43912
Las Vegas, NV 89116
702-641-7041
800-453-1860 Ext. R-641 orders only
702-641-7001 fax

◆

Collection	Format	No./Size Disks	Price	Computer
Borders	EPS	4-800K	$79.00	Mac/IBM
Business*	EPS	5-800K	$149.00	Mac/IBM
Christmas*	EPS	1-800K	$19.95	Mac/IBM
Click & Clip 500	EPS	15-800K	$395.00	Mac/IBM
Click & Clip 500 II*	EPS	18-800K	$395.00	Mac/IBM
Food*	EPS	3-800K	$99.00	Mac/IBM
International Symbols	EPS	2-800K	$99.99	Mac/IBM
International Symbols II*	EPS	1-800K	$49.99	Mac/IBM
Medical/Health*	EPS	3-800K	$149.00	Mac/IBM
Military Art	EPS	4-800K	$149.00	Mac/IBM
Real Estate Art*	EPS	3-800K	$95.00	Mac/IBM
Road & Warning Signs	EPS	2-800K	$99.00	Mac/IBM
Seasonal*	EPS	1-800K	$19.95	Mac/IBM
Trademarks & Logos*	EPS	23-800K	$249.00	Mac/IBM

Notes:

*Not shown or indexed in this volume. Due to the large amount of electronic clip art available from this company, we are showing only 5 of the available volumes. Contact Studio Advertising Art for more information.

• Studio also has a quarterly subscription service. Quarterly issues beginning in Winter 1987 contain 50 images each (1200K) and sell for $39.95. Any four back issues $125.00, and a one-year subscription is also $125.00.

Borders Disk 1: Horizontal

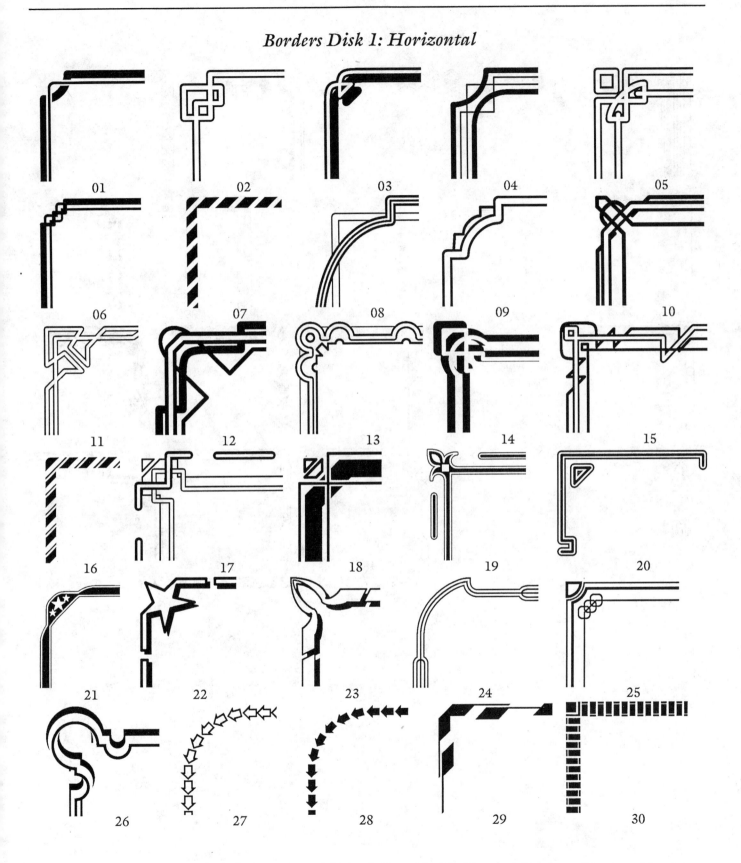

Shown are 100% representations of the corners of the borders on this disk. They are all horizontally oriented borders.

Borders Disk 2: Horizontal

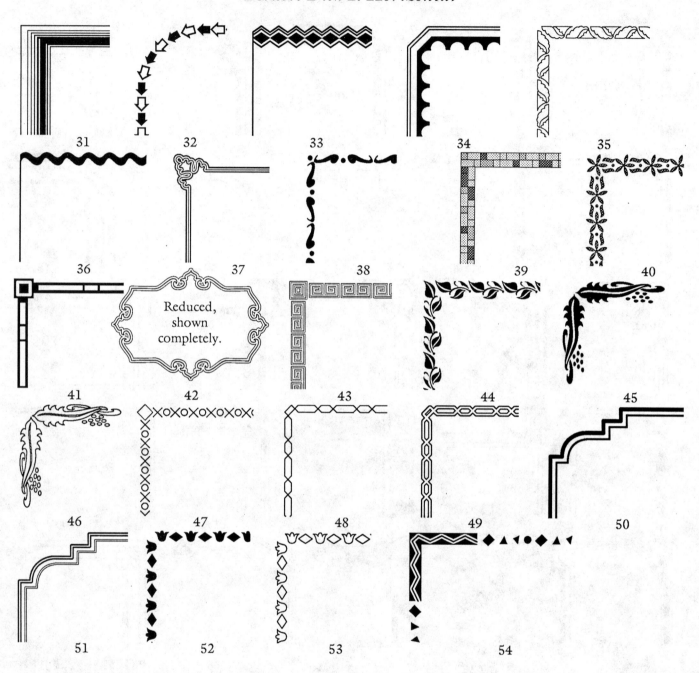

Reduced, shown completely.

31   32   33   34   35

36   37   38   39   40

41   42   43   44   45

46   47   48   49   50

51   52   53   54

Shown are 100% representations of the corners of the borders on this disk. They are all horizontally oriented borders.

Borders Disk 3: Horizontal

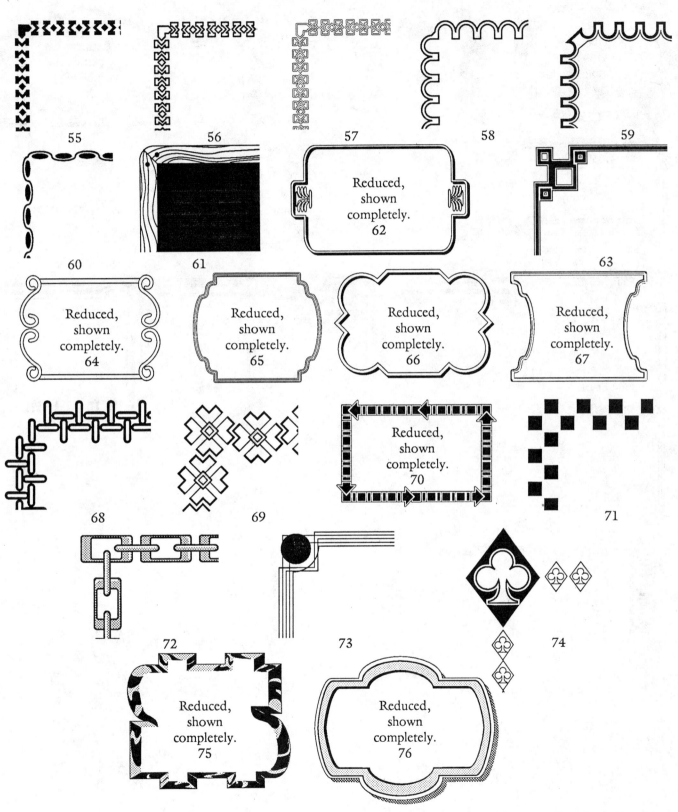

55

56

57

58

59

60

61

Reduced,
shown
completely.
62

63

Reduced,
shown
completely.
64

Reduced,
shown
completely.
65

Reduced,
shown
completely.
66

Reduced,
shown
completely.
67

68

69

Reduced,
shown
completely.
70

71

72

73

74

Reduced,
shown
completely.
75

Reduced,
shown
completely.
76

Shown are 100% representations of the corners of the borders on this disk. They are all horizontally oriented borders.

Borders Disk 4: Horizontal

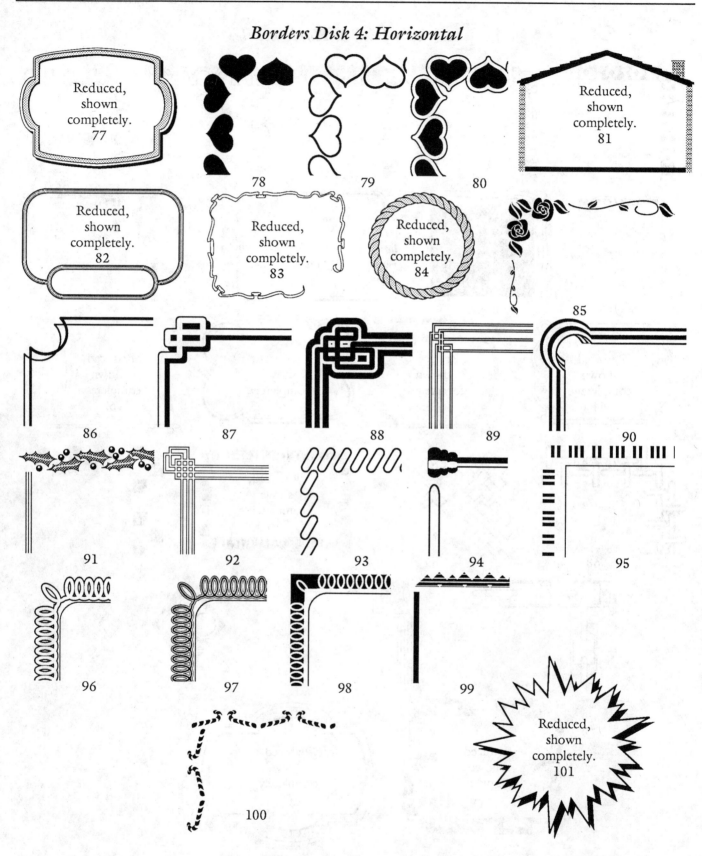

Reduced, shown completely.
77

78

79

80

Reduced, shown completely.
81

Reduced, shown completely.
82

Reduced, shown completely.
83

Reduced, shown completely.
84

85

86

87

88

89

90

91

92

93

94

95

96

97

98

99

100

Reduced, shown completely.
101

Shown are 100% representations of the corners of the borders on this disk. They are all horizontally oriented borders.

Click and Clip 500 Disk #1

100 Dollar Bill

3-1/2 Disk

500 Dollar Bill

Abraham Lincoln

Aircraft Carrier

Alabama

Alarm Clock

Alaska

Anchor

Arkansas

Astronaut

Atom

Awards Medal

Aztec

Baby Buggy

Back to School

Balloon, Hot Air

Banner

Banner Space

Bar-B-Que

Barrel

Baseball Catcher

Basket

Basketball & Basket

Bear A

Bear B

Bee

Beehive

Bell, Liberty

Bicycle A

Bicycle B

Bird Design A

Bird Design C

Blocks

Blowing Bubbles

Click and Clip 500 Disk #2

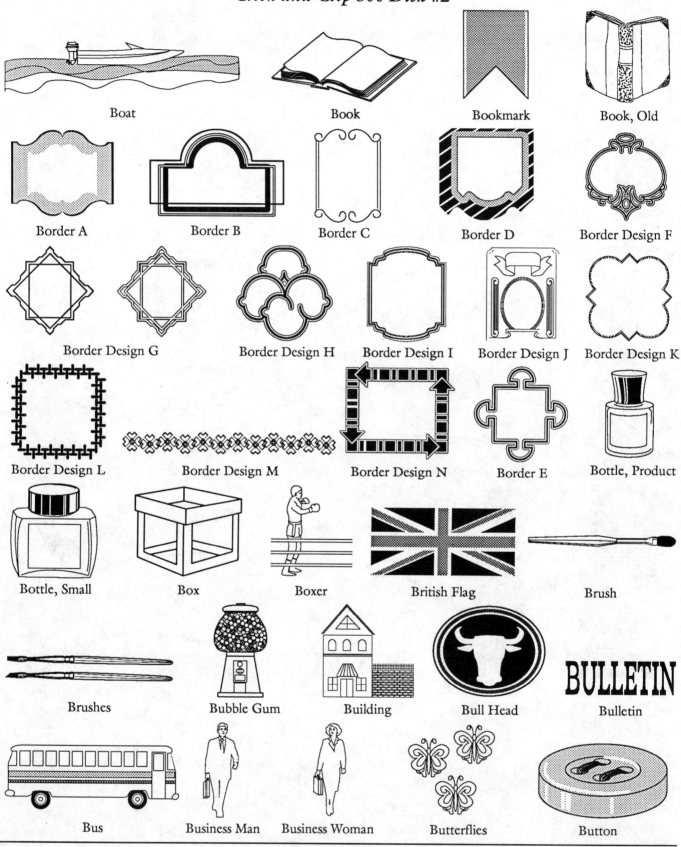

Boat

Book

Bookmark

Book, Old

Border A

Border B

Border C

Border D

Border Design F

Border Design G

Border Design H

Border Design I

Border Design J

Border Design K

Border Design L

Border Design M

Border Design N

Border E

Bottle, Product

Bottle, Small

Box

Boxer

British Flag

Brush

Brushes

Bubble Gum

Building

Bull Head

Bulletin

Bus

Business Man

Business Woman

Butterflies

Button

Click and Clip 500 Disk #3

Calculator California Cameo Can Canadian Maple Leaf Cancelled Stamp

Candle Holder Candles Candy Cane Canning Jar Cannon

Card File Cash Register Castle Chain Border

Chainsaw Check-Marked Boxes Checkered Flag Cheese Chef

Chef's Hat Chick Christmas Ornament Christmas Stocking Christmas Tree City Clipboard

Clock A Clock B Clouds Clover Coin

Colorado

Click and Clip 500 Disk #4

Company News   Computer A   Computer B   Computer C   Connecticut

Cool   Copier   Corkscrew   Corn   Cosmetics A

Cosmetics B   Coupon   Covered Wagon A   Covered Wagon B   Crayons

Credit Cards   Credit Cards Line Art   Cross A   Cross B   Cross D

Crown A   Crown B   Cup   Cupid   Curved Road Sign   Deadbolt Lock

Delaware   Dept News   Derringer (Hand Gun)   Design A   Design B

Design C

Click and Clip 500 Disk #5

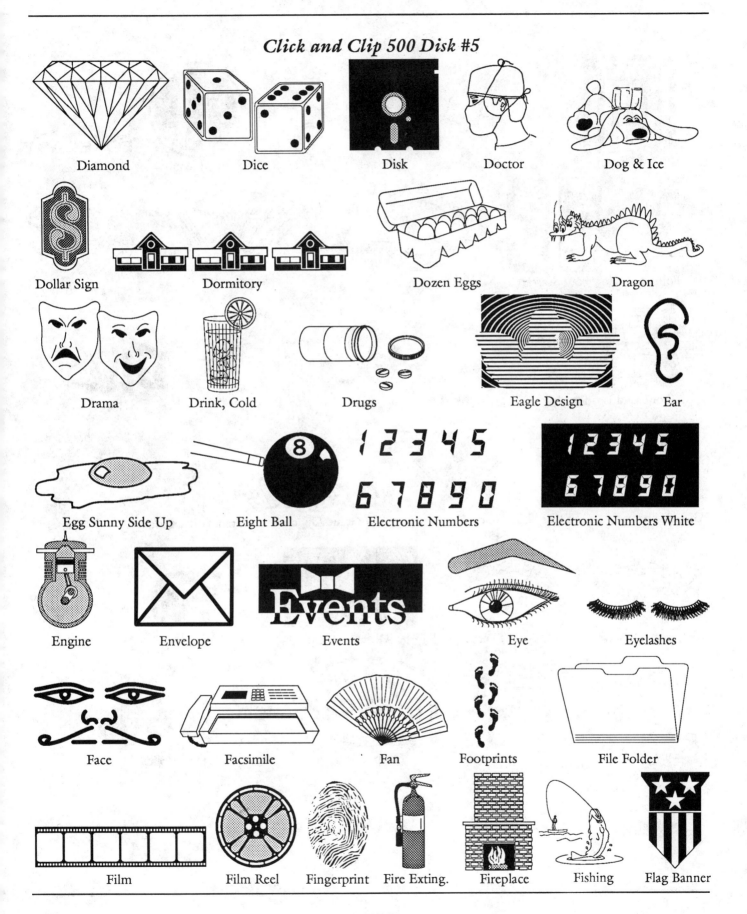

Diamond

Dice

Disk

Doctor

Dog & Ice

Dollar Sign

Dormitory

Dozen Eggs

Dragon

Drama

Drink, Cold

Drugs

Eagle Design

Ear

Egg Sunny Side Up

Eight Ball

Electronic Numbers

Electronic Numbers White

Engine

Envelope

Events

Eye

Eyelashes

Face

Facsimile

Fan

Footprints

File Folder

Film

Film Reel

Fingerprint

Fire Exting.

Fireplace

Fishing

Flag Banner

Click and Clip 500 Disk #6

Flag Design Florida Flower Food Cart Food Symbol Forecast

Fountain Four Seasons Frame Free Frog

Front-End Loader Garbage Can Gears Georgia Gifts

Girl/Swimwear Golf Ball Graduation Zone Grand Opening Grandfather Clock Grapes

Grapes and Cheese Group of People Growth Chart Hand Pointing Handprints

Hand Saw Handgun Happy Birthday Happy Holiday

Click and Clip 500 Disk #7

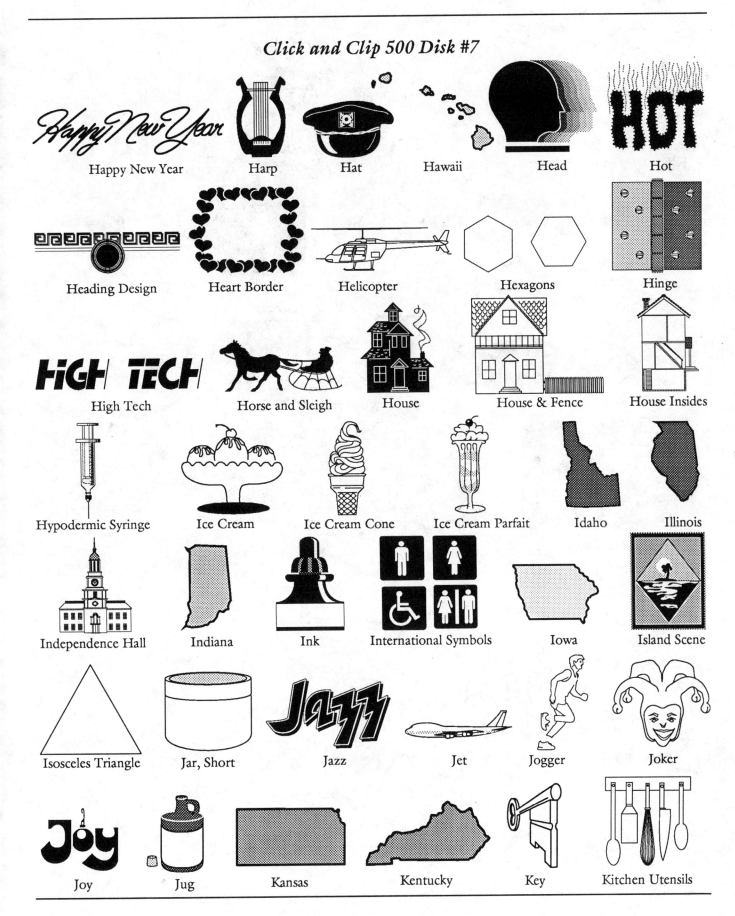

Happy New Year	Harp	Hat	Hawaii	Head	Hot
Heading Design	Heart Border	Helicopter	Hexagons	Hinge
High Tech	Horse and Sleigh	House	House & Fence	House Insides
Hypodermic Syringe	Ice Cream	Ice Cream Cone	Ice Cream Parfait	Idaho	Illinois
Independence Hall	Indiana	Ink	International Symbols	Iowa	Island Scene
Isosceles Triangle	Jar, Short	Jazz	Jet	Jogger	Joker
Joy	Jug	Kansas	Kentucky	Key	Kitchen Utensils

Click and Clip 500 Disk #8

| Knight | Laboratory Equipment | Lady | Lamp A | Lamp B | Lamp C | Lantern |

| Laser Printer | Leaves Falling | Life Preserver | Lightbulb | Lighthouse |

| Lion Head | Lips | Louisiana | Luggage | Magic Lamp |

| Magnifier | Mailbox | Maine | Man | Man & Desk | Map, Old |

| Marker | Maryland | Massachusetts | Match | Medical Emblem | Menu |

| Menu Breaks | Merry Christmas | Michigan | Microphone | Microscope |

Click and Clip 500 Disk #9

Minnestoa	Mississippi	Missouri	Money Clip	Montana	Moon, Man in the
Mortar and Pestle	Motorcycle	Motorcycle Rider	Mountain	Mousetrap	Mug	Muscle Man
Mushrooms	Music A	Music B	Nebraska	Neighborhood	New Hampshire
New Jersey	New Mexico	New York	News	No Parking	Noel
North Carolina	North Dakota	Notebook	Nurse	Observatory	Paris
Octagon	Parrot	Ohio	Oil Derrick	Oklahoma	Orange Slices	Oregon
Owl	Padlock	Paint Brush	Paint Brush Splatter	Paint Sprayer	Painter's Palette	Palm Trees

Click and Clip 500 Disk #10

 Peace & Dove
 Peacock
 Pelican
 Pencil Holder
 Pencil Sharpener
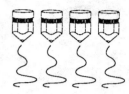 Pencils

 Pennsylvania
 Pentagon
 People Symbols
 Photo Slide
 Piano Keyboard

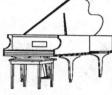 Piano, Grand
 Pie
 Piggy Bank
 Pilgrim
 Pipe Valve A
 Pipe Valve B

 Pizza
 Plant
 Pot of Gold
 Presentation
 Pretzel
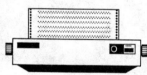 Printer

 Professor
 Profit
 Promotions
Public Notice
 Pyramid

 Quail
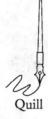 Quill
 Rabbit
 Race Car
 Radio

 Radio Old

Click and Clip 500 Disk #11

Raining	Razor Blade	Recycle	Reindeer	Retirement	Rhode Island
Riverboat	Rocking Horse	Roman Soldier Design	Roof & Chimney	Rooster	Rope Border
Route 1 Sign	Rubber Stamp	Ruler		Rush	Saddle
Safety Pin	Sailboat	Salt & Pepper Mill	Santa	Save	Savings
Scale	Schoolyard	Scope	Screw	Scroll	Scroll Border
Sea & Palm	Seagulls	Seasons Greetings	Service Award		

Click and Clip 500 Disk #12

Shield & Spears

Shields

Ship

Ship's Wheel

Shirt

Shore Design

Ski Boat

Skull & Crossbones

Skyline

Sleigh

Slide Mounts

Smoke Out

Snowman

Soccer Ball

South Carolina

South Dakota

Spark Plug

Sphere

Spiral Border Design

Sports Balls

Sports Out of Focus

Stamps

Staple Remover

Stapler

Star Design

Stars & Stripes A

Stars & Stripes B

Stars & Stripes Banner

State Capitol

Statue of Liberty

Stop Sign

Stork

Strawberry

Street Surfer A

Street Surfer B

Summer Fun

Sun

Sun Design

Click and Clip 500 Disk #13

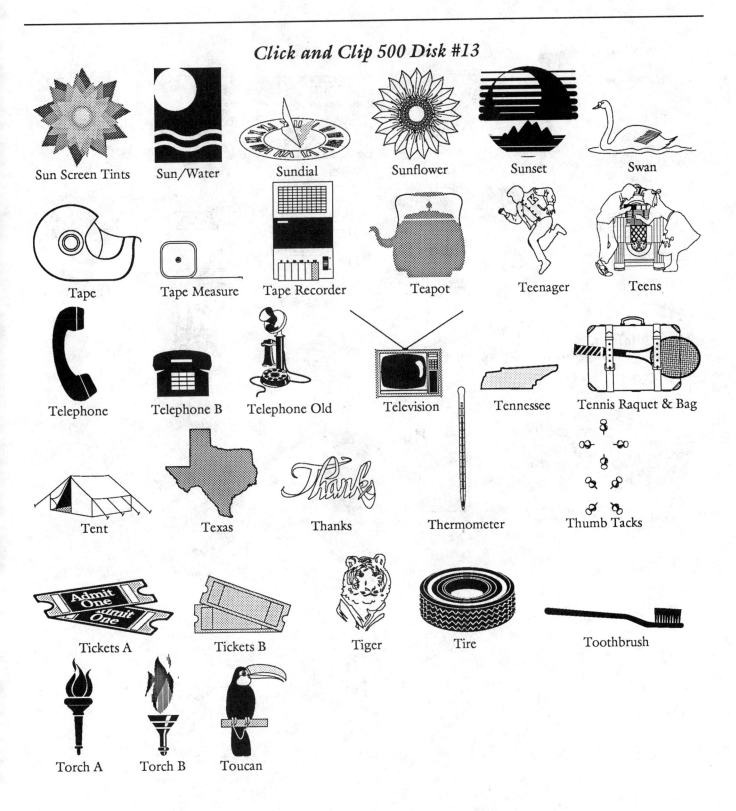

Sun Screen Tints	Sun/Water	Sundial	Sunflower	Sunset	Swan
Tape	Tape Measure	Tape Recorder	Teapot	Teenager	Teens
Telephone	Telephone B	Telephone Old	Television	Tennessee	Tennis Raquet & Bag
Tent	Texas	Thanks	Thermometer		Thumb Tacks
Tickets A	Tickets B	Tiger	Tire	Toothbrush	
Torch A	Torch B	Toucan			

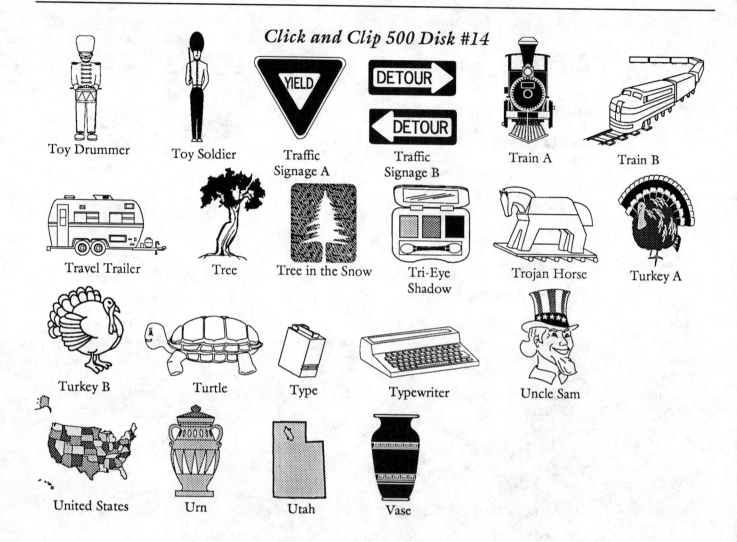

Click and Clip 500 Disk #14

Toy Drummer　　Toy Soldier　　Traffic Signage A　　Traffic Signage B　　Train A　　Train B

Travel Trailer　　Tree　　Tree in the Snow　　Tri-Eye Shadow　　Trojan Horse　　Turkey A

Turkey B　　Turtle　　Type　　Typewriter　　Uncle Sam

United States　　Urn　　Utah　　Vase

Click and Clip 500 Disk #15

Vault   VCR   Vermont   Video Recorder   Violin

Virginia   Washington   Water Cooler   Watermelon   Weather Vane

Welcome   West Virginia   Western Town   William McKinley

Windmill   Wine Bottle   Wisconsin   Witch   Witch Flying   Wizard

World   Wyoming   Zipper

International Symbols I, Disk 1

 Airport Ampitheater Bandaid Bar Bike Route Blood Pressure Bus Service Campfire Permitted Camping Church

 Civil Defense Shelter Coffee Shop Computer Area Computer Area 2 Crosswalk Dam Danger Deer Crossing Dental Directional Arrow, Up

 Directional Arrow, Down Directional Arrow, Left Directional Arrow, Right Do Not Enter Drinking Water Drugs Escalator Down Escalator Up Exercise   Falling Rocks

 Fast Food Feet Fire Extinguisher First Aid Fishing Area Food Services Food/ Cafeteria Fragile Garbage Disposal Gasoline

 Groundwater Drain Handicap Harbor Heart Hiking Area Horseback Riding Hospital Housing Human Brain Information

 Injection

International Symbols I, Disk 2

 Joints/ Bones
 Keep Cool
 Keep Dry
 Kennel
 Key Required to Enter
 Laundry
 Lighthouse
 Lockers
 Lodging
 Mail Area

 Mail/ Postal Service
 Mechanic
 Medical Symbol
 Men
 Microscope
 No
 No Magnetic Fields
 No Swimming
 Observation Point
 Off-Road Permitted

 Parking
 Pharmacy
 Phone
 Photography
 Picnic Area
 Picnic Area Sheltered
 Pier
 Playground
 Police
 Prospecting

 Radiology
 Ranger Station
 Rest Rooms
 Rifle Range
 Rounded Square
 Sailing
 Shelter Area
 Sheltered Camping
 Showers
 Ski Lift

 Snow
 Stairs
 Swimming Permitted
 This Side Up
 Traffic Light Ahead
 Travel Trailers
 Water
 Water/ Drinking
 Women

Military Art 1.1 Disk 1

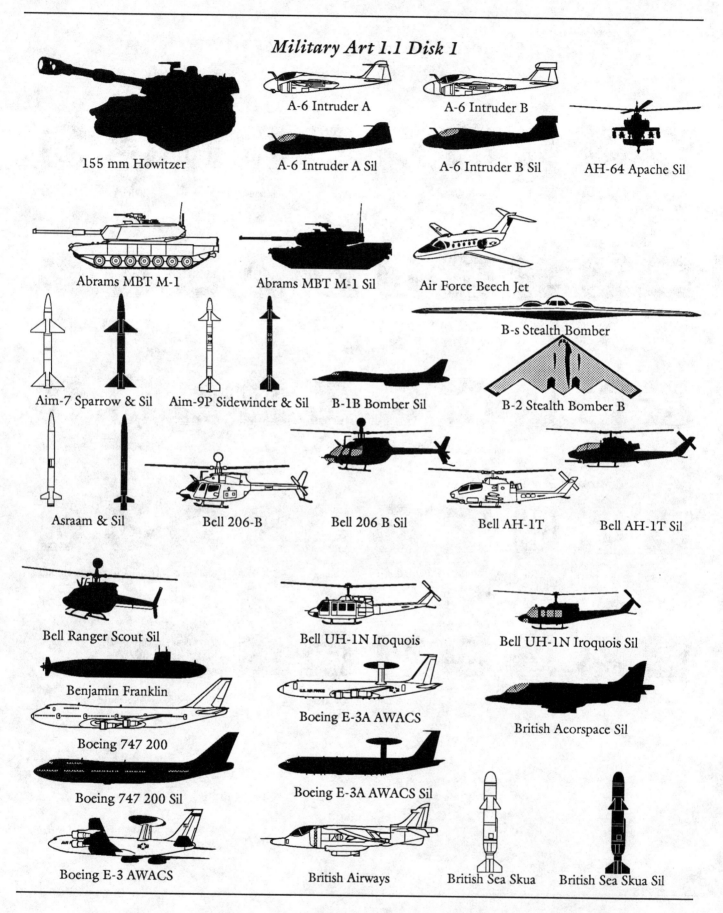

155 mm Howitzer

A-6 Intruder A

A-6 Intruder B

A-6 Intruder A Sil

A-6 Intruder B Sil

AH-64 Apache Sil

Abrams MBT M-1

Abrams MBT M-1 Sil

Air Force Beech Jet

B-s Stealth Bomber

Aim-7 Sparrow & Sil

Aim-9P Sidewinder & Sil

B-1B Bomber Sil

B-2 Stealth Bomber B

Asraam & Sil

Bell 206-B

Bell 206 B Sil

Bell AH-1T

Bell AH-1T Sil

Bell Ranger Scout Sil

Bell UH-1N Iroquois

Bell UH-1N Iroquois Sil

Benjamin Franklin

Boeing E-3A AWACS

British Aeorspace Sil

Boeing 747 200

Boeing 747 200 Sil

Boeing E-3A AWACS Sil

Boeing E-3 AWACS

British Airways

British Sea Skua

British Sea Skua Sil

Military Art 1.1 Disk 2

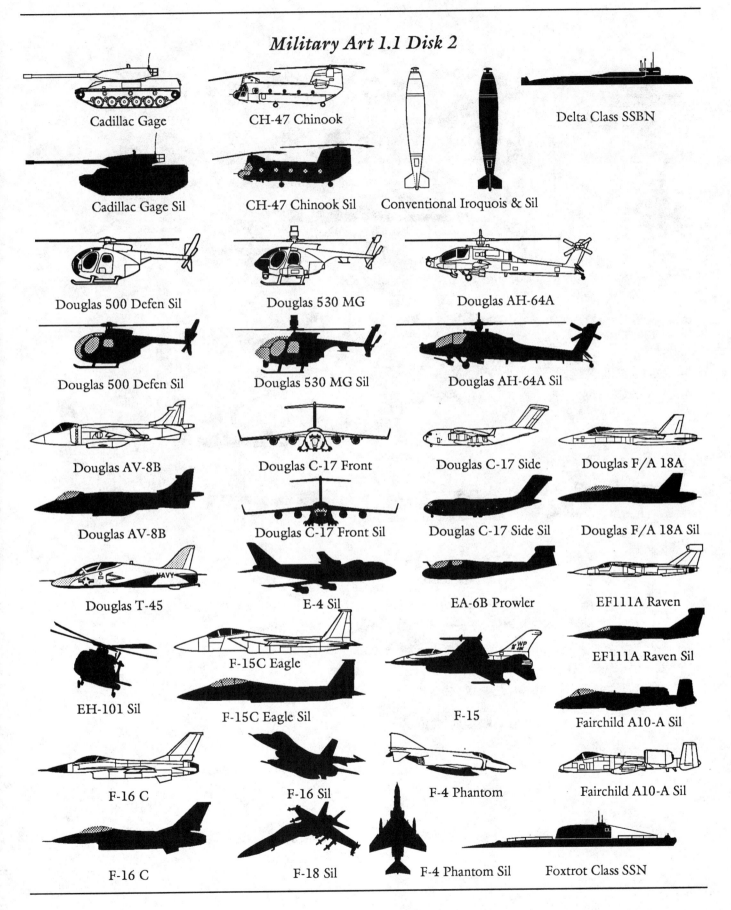

Cadillac Gage

CH-47 Chinook

Delta Class SSBN

Cadillac Gage Sil

CH-47 Chinook Sil

Conventional Iroquois & Sil

Douglas 500 Defen Sil

Douglas 530 MG

Douglas AH-64A

Douglas 500 Defen Sil

Douglas 530 MG Sil

Douglas AH-64A Sil

Douglas AV-8B

Douglas C-17 Front

Douglas C-17 Side

Douglas F/A 18A

Douglas AV-8B

Douglas C-17 Front Sil

Douglas C-17 Side Sil

Douglas F/A 18A Sil

Douglas T-45

E-4 Sil

EA-6B Prowler

EF111A Raven

EH-101 Sil

F-15C Eagle

EF111A Raven Sil

F-15C Eagle Sil

F-15

Fairchild A10-A Sil

F-16 C

F-16 Sil

F-4 Phantom

Fairchild A10-A Sil

F-16 C

F-18 Sil

F-4 Phantom Sil

Foxtrot Class SSN

Military Art 1.1 Disk 3

French Made MBT

Futuristic

Grumman E-2C

Grumman F-14A

Grumman E-2C Sil

Grumman F-14A Sil

Harrier E-2 Sil

Hellfire & Sil

Hotel II Class SSBN

Kashin Class Sil

Israel M-48

KCE-3J

Kiey Class Sil

Knox Class Frigate

Kilo Class SSN

Lockheed C-138H

Learjet

LGM-30 & Sil

Lockheed C-5B

Lockheed C-138H Sil

Los Angeles Class SSBN

Lockheed C-5B Sil

Lockheed P-C3

Lockheed P-C3 Sil

Maverick & Sil

MGM-118 Peacekeeper & Sil

MGOA1-MBT

MGOA1-MBTSil

Mirage 2000

Mirage III

Oberon Sub

Ohio Class SSBN

Military Art 1.1 Disk 4

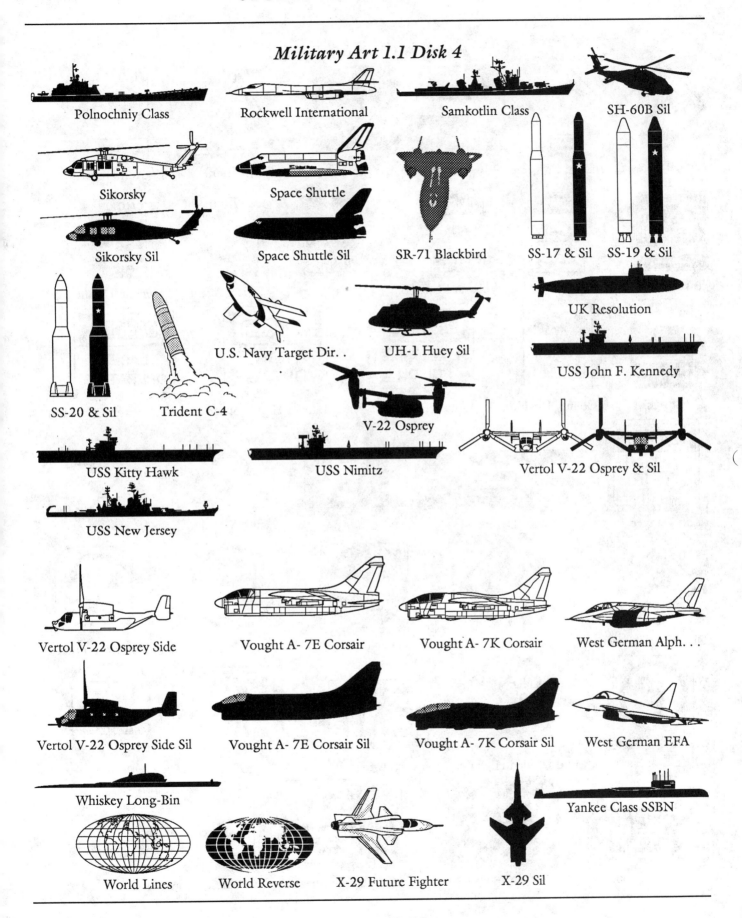

Polnochniy Class

Rockwell International

Samkotlin Class

SH-60B Sil

Sikorsky

Space Shuttle

Sikorsky Sil

Space Shuttle Sil

SR-71 Blackbird

SS-17 & Sil

SS-19 & Sil

SS-20 & Sil

Trident C-4

U.S. Navy Target Dir. . .

UH-1 Huey Sil

UK Resolution

USS John F. Kennedy

V-22 Osprey

USS Kitty Hawk

USS Nimitz

Vertol V-22 Osprey & Sil

USS New Jersey

Vertol V-22 Osprey Side

Vought A- 7E Corsair

Vought A- 7K Corsair

West German Alph. . .

Vertol V-22 Osprey Side Sil

Vought A- 7E Corsair Sil

Vought A- 7K Corsair Sil

West German EFA

Whiskey Long-Bin

Yankee Class SSBN

World Lines

World Reverse

X-29 Future Fighter

X-29 Sil

Road & Warning Signs 1

Animal Crossing, Deer

Animal Crossing, Kangaroo

Arrow

Atomic

Attention

Authorized

Bike Route

Biohazard

Biohazard Isolation

Camping

Cancer Agent

Chemical Storage

Corrosive

County Landfill

Danger Flammable

Danger High Voltage

Danger Laser Operation

Danger Watch Your. . .

Detour

Diesel Fuel Available

Directional Arrow 1 — 2

Directional Arrow 3

Divided Highway

Do Not Enter

Drinking Water

Ear Protection Req.

Electrical Hazard

End Divided Highway

Exit 1

Exit 2

Eye Protection Req.

Film Developing

Fire Extinguisher 1

Fire Extinguisher 2

Fire Extinguisher 3

Road & Warning Signs 1 (continued)

Fire Hose

First Aid

Flammable

Flammable 2

Food

Fork Lifts

Fragile

Gas

Handicap Parking

Handicap Ramp

Handicapped 1

Handicapped 2

Hard Hat Area

Hard Hat Area 2

High Noise Area

Highway 225

Road & Warning Signs 2

Infectious Waste

Information

Intersection, 3 Way

Intersection, 4 Way

Interstate Hwy

Lane Closed

Laser Light

Lodging

Medical Symbol

Men Working

Merging Traffic

Microwave in Use

No Frok Lifts

No Left Turn

No Smoking

No Trucks

No U Turn

No Unauthorized Dumping

Not an Exit

One Way

Ped Xing

Pitch In!

Poison

Radioactive

Restroom Mens

Restroom Womens

Restrooms

Right Lane Ends

Road Hazard

RR Crossing

Safety Shower

Sensitive

Slippery When Wet

Slow

Speed Limit

Static Sensitive Devices

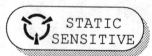
Static Sensitive Device 2

Road & Warning Signs 2 (continued)

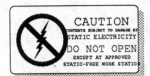

Static Sensitive Devices 3

Static Sensitive Devices 4

Steep Downgrade

Stop Sign

Stretch Before Exercise

Telephone 1

Telephone 2

Traffic Signal Ahead

Truck Route

Two Way Traffic

US 101

US 99

Wash Your Hands

Watch Your Step

Wet Floor

Yield

SunShine

P.O. Box 4351
Austin, TX 78765
512-453-2334

Collection	Format	No./Size Disks	Price	Computer
Visual Delights Collection:	TIFF	4-800K (Mac)	$39.00	Mac/IBM
Abstract and Object Borders		6-720K (IBM)		
Abstract and Object Designs				
Africa				
American West**				
Angels				
Animal Borders	(continued)		(continued)	
Animals for Children	Flower Designs		Panoramic Landscapes***	
Assorted Borders	Flowering Plants		People Borders	
Assorted Cartouches	Friezes and Scrolls		People with Animals	
Bird Designs	Greek and Roman Life		Plant Borders	
Catholic Pictures	Human Interaction		Plant Designs	
Children's Stories	Humor		Reading and Writing	
Chinese and Japanese Pictures	Jewish Pictures		Realistic Birds**	
Christian Scenes	Knighthood		Realistic Insects and Arachnids**	
Christian Symbols	Leaves and Trees		Realistic Landscapes***	
Christmas	Lower Animal Designs		Realistic Mammals**	
Classical Mythology	Mammal Designs		Realistic Reptiles & Amphibians**	
Dance	Mayan Pictures		Realistic Sea Life**	
Death	Men		Sexuality	
Decorative Letters	Middle Eastern Pictures		Shaped Borders	
Easter	Monsters		Silhouettes	
Fantasy	Music		Tree Borders	
Female Nudes	Native Americans		Tree Designs	
Flower and Plant Cartouches	Objets d'Art**		Valentine's Day	
Flower Borders	Optical Illusions and Math		Women	

Notes:

• Due to the large amount of electronic clip art available from this company, we are showing only one page of samples from each of the volumes.

• A Macintosh CD-ROM of the entire Visual Delights collection, over 5800 black and white graphics, is available for $333.00. Included on the CD are desk accessory and application versions of Zedcor's DeskPaint™, which can be used to browse folders of images as if in a slide show. It can also alter, flip, crop, rotate, print, make negatives of, and change the resolution of all the pictures. It can edit scanned images and convert to and from TIFF, compressed TIFF, and PICT formats. Also included on the CD are the user versions of Multi-Ad WordSearch™ and a 10 megabyte Search™ catalog containing thumbnail views, keywords and other information about all the images. Using this application, actual images can be opened, viewed in various sizes, printed, or exported to other programs. Contact SunShine for more information on their art products.

**Consist primarily of halftones, which should not be reduced; only line art samples from this set have been shown.

*** Consist entirely of halftones, which should not be reduced; no samples of these two sets have been shown.

Abstract & Object Borders

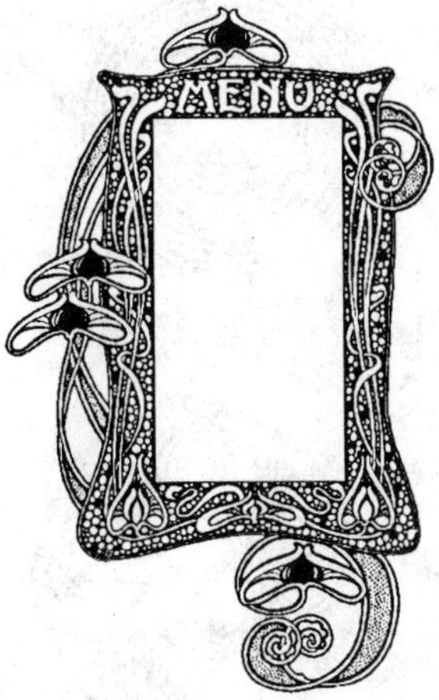

Art Nouveau Menu Border

Columns & Faces Border

Celtic Abstract Border

Filigree Full Border 1

Jagged Border Large A

Oval Border

Square Tableaux Border

Swirly Designs Border

Vanity Border (Shown at 50%)

Because of the large amount of clip art available in this volume, we are showing only samples of the artwork.

Abstract & Object Designs

Arcs in Square Design
(Shown at 50%)

Labyrinth at St. Etienne

Circular Cutout Design 4

Art Nouveau Flourish 1
(Shown at 50%)

Abstract Nordic Design

Egyptian Circles Design

Interwoven Celtic Circle

Irish Knot 1

Scandinavian Knotted Rope

Striped Circle Design
(Shown at 100%)

Overlapping Suns Pattern

Small Art Nouveau Design
(Shown at 50%)

Tiny Flourish
(Shown at 100%)

Because of the large amount of clip art available in this volume, we are showing only samples of the artwork.

Africa

African Couple Masks

African Mother & Child

Benin Chief

Benin Figure
(Shown at 50%)

Bushongo Mask

Decorative African Comb (Shown at 50%)

Cheetah

Nigerian Dancing Mask

Nigerian Figures

Two Stylized African Fish

Because of the large amount of clip art available in this volume, we are showing only samples of the artwork.

American West

Calligraphic Horse
(Shown at 50%)

Charging Bull Silhouette

Horse's Head 3
(Shown at 50%)

Cowboy in Corral
(Shown at 50%)

Cowboy Off Bucking Bronco

Cowboy Roping

Natives & Colonists
(Shown at 50%)

Wilderness Scout

Because of the large amount of clip art available in this volume, we are showing only samples of the artwork.

Angels

Angel Head with Rays
(Shown at 50%)

Angel in Starry
Circle

Angel Repelling
Lightning

Angel Trefoil 2

Angel with Little Child

Angel with Olive Branches

Angel with
Sceptre

Angelic Sunrise

Cherub Flying
(Shown at 50%)

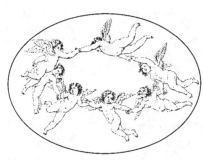

Cherubic Oval
Dance

Male Angel by Pond
(Shown at 50%)

Because of the large amount of clip art available in this volume, we are showing only samples of the artwork.

Animal Borders

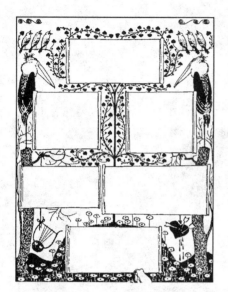

Animal Fantasy Border

Butterflies & Flowers Border

Eagle Mountains Border

Fox & Geese Border
(Shown at 50%)

Rabbit Border

Trees & Animals Border

Serpent & Frog Border

Because of the large amount of clip art available in this volume, we are showing only samples of the artwork.

Animals for Children

Animals Laughing at Fox

Crowned Lion

Donkey in Lion's Skin

Frog Toppling into Water

Goose & Golden Egg

Happy Monkeys
Woodcut

Pumpkinhead

Boy Doll with Bunny

Child on Flying Horse

Tortoise & Hare

Because of the large amount of clip art available in this volume, we are showing only samples of the artwork.

Assorted Borders

Angel Swirls Pastoral Border

Fancy Calligraphic Border

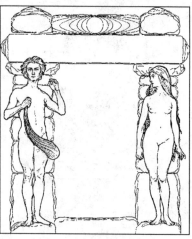

Male & Female Nudes Border

Peacock & Leafy Men Border

Filigree Border

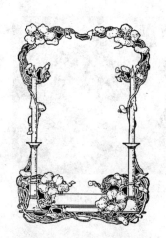

Candles & Flowers Border

Suburban Border

Early Car Border

Plant–Bird Swirls Border 4

Because of the large amount of clip art available in this volume, we are showing only samples of the artwork.

Assorted Cartouches

Alternating Birds
Cartouche

Butterfly Cartouche

Lions & Tongues Cartouche

Peacock Triangle Cartouche

Raven in Snow Cartouche

Two Fish Cartouche

Baroque Cartouche 01
(Shown at 50%)

Baroque Cartouche 04
(Shown at 50%)

Baroque Cartouche 06
(Shown at 50%)

Laughing Satyrs Cartouche

Baroque Cartouche 08
(Shown at 50%)

Zodiac Ring

Persian Cartouche 3

Simple Calligraphic Oval

Because of the large amount of clip art available in this volume, we are showing only samples of the artwork.

Bird Designs

Small Birds & Flowers
(Shown at 50%)

Birds on Rooster Vase
(Shown at 50%)

Displaying Swan

Duckling
(Shown at 50%)

Fowl Tree Cutout

Roosters Silhouette
(Shown at 50%)

Stylized Parrot & Duck
(Shown at 50%)

Twin Hens Cutout
(Shown at 50%)

Two Hens Pecking Silhouette

Wave Design with Water
(Shown at 50%)

Wild Geese Flying
(Shown at 50%)

Peacock Display Cutout

Because of the large amount of clip art available in this volume, we are showing only samples of the artwork.

Catholic Pictures

Altar Tray & Chalice
(Shown at 50%)

Bishop & Clergy
(Shown at 50%)

Bishop with Staff
(Shown at 50%)

Holy Family 2

Madonna & Child 4

Martyrdom of St. Sebastian
(Shown at 50%)

Nun Praying

Nuns in Cloister
(Shown at 50%)

Our Lady of the
Flowers

St. Martin
(Shown at 50%)

Saxon Saint

Because of the large amount of clip art available in this volume, we are showing only samples of the artwork.

Children's Stories

Boy with Girl Mermaid

Cinderella's Coach Silhouette

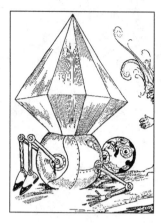

Diamond on Tik-Tok Man

Dorothy with Oz Friends

Fairy Tale Woods

Fancy Dreams

Jack and the
Beanstalk

Pied Piper 1
(Shown at 50%)

Small Pixie
(Shown at 50%)

Rumpelstiltskin
Silhouette

Vegetable Head People

Because of the large amount of clip art available in this volume, we are showing only samples of the artwork.

Chinese & Japanese Pictures

Chinese Bells

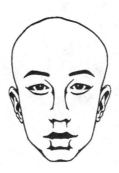

Chinese Emperor's Face

Chinese Oval Border

Chinese Man & Tiger
(Shown at 50%)

Geisha Border

Chinese Sage
(Shown at 50%)

Confucius
(Shown at 50%)

Japanese Maiden

Japanese Mother & Child

Two Japanese Women 2

Oriental Sage Smoking

Because of the large amount of clip art available in this volume, we are showing only samples of the artwork.

Christian Scenes

Blessed Are the Pure

Heavenly Judgment

Plowman Praying

Ascension Woodcut
(Shown at 50%)

Christ in Sepulcher

Crucifixion Woodcut

Jesus Performing Miracles

Manifestation to John

Transfiguration

Because of the large amount of clip art available in this volume, we are showing only samples of the artwork.

Christian Symbols

Celtic Cross Design

Circular Cross Design A

Bird on Rosy Cross

Circular AD 2
(Shown at 50%)

Geometric Cross

INRI Cross
(Shown at 50%)

Circular Alpha Omega 1

Foliated Cross Circle

Cross with Stairs

Small Square Cross
(Shown at 50%)

Tree of Life with Cross
(Shown at 50%)

Ornamental Cross 1
(Shown at 50%)

Ornamental Cross 2

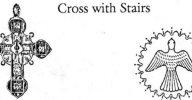

Dove of Peace
Ascending
(Shown at 50%)

Christ Panel

Intertwined ANNO

Intertwined Circular XPC
(Shown at 50%)

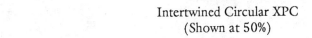

Because of the large amount of clip art available in this volume, we are showing only samples of the artwork.

Christmas

Christmas Carol Ornament

Christmas Stocking Silhouette
(Shown at 100%)

Christmas Travelers

Christmas Tree Border
(Shown at 50%)

Christmas Tree
Ornaments

Peace on Earth

Victorian Carolers Border

Christmas Adoration Border

German Santa Claus

Santa Claus Silhouette
(Shown at 100%)

Because of the large amount of clip art available in this volume, we are showing only samples of the artwork.

Classical Mythology

Adonis & Aphrodite
(Shown at 50%)

Athena

Baby Hercules

Boating on the River Styx

Centaur Woodcut
(Shown at 50%)

Classical Sleep

Cyclops

Goddesses of the Morning
(Shown at 50%)

Sisyphus Rolling Stone

Pegasus on Promontory
(Shown at 50%)

Iris
(Shown at 50%)

Pentagonal Gorgon
(Shown at 50%)

Greek Centaurs Frieze

Because of the large amount of clip art available in this volume, we are showing only samples of the artwork.

Dance

Ballerina & Swirls

Black Dancer

Comic Male Dancer

Exotic Woman Dancer
(Shown at 50%)

Dancer in Motion Frieze

Firebird Ballet Scene

Happy Dancing Satyr 1

Harem Dancer

Siamese Woman Dancer

Harlequin & Columbine

Sylphides Ballet Scene 1

Woman Swirl Dancer

Because of the large amount of clip art available in this volume, we are showing only samples of the artwork.

Death

Bird on Flowering Skull
(Shown at 50%)

Cemetary Diptych
(Shown at 50%)

Cherubs with Dandelions

Death Comes Calling

Death Resting Woodcut

Cobwebbed Skulls
(Shown at 50%)

Grief at Night

Nude with Dead Man

Winged Angel of Death

Woman with Dying Man
(Shown at 50%)

Because of the large amount of clip art available in this volume, we are showing only samples of the artwork.

Decorative Letters

All art on this page shown at 50%.

Because of the large amount of clip art available in this volume, we are showing only samples of the artwork.

Easter

Angelic Easter Child

Easter Basket with Eggs

Easter Bunny Cross
Silhouette

Easter Chicks & Eggs

Easter Eggs 1

Easter Eggs & Birds

Easter Eggs & Plant

Easter Eggs Border

Easter Flowers &
Thorns

Easter Flowers
Circle 3

Girls with Easter Angel

Easter Lilies Design

Flowered Eastern Cross

Easter Flowers Design

Because of the large amount of clip art available in this volume, we are showing only samples of the artwork.

Fantasy

Animate Tree
(Shown at 50%)

Blind Justice & Man
(Shown at 50%)

Cosmic Hands

Sun and Cosmic Hand

Fairy Princess

Magic Logic Man

Faun with Flowers

Creatures Emerging

Time as Old Men

Sphinx with Cosmic Eyes

Maiden Flying Aloft

Because of the large amount of clip art available in this volume, we are showing only samples of the artwork.

Female Nudes

Dancing Nudes Scroll

Miniature Nude on Flowers

Heartsick Nude by Pond

Nude on Bed 2

Vertical Nude Nymphette

Svelte Nude

Nudes with Giant Fish

Daphnis & Chloe Woodcut
(Shown at 50%)

Nude by Pond

Because of the large amount of clip art available in this volume, we are showing only samples of the artwork.

Flower & Plant Cartouches

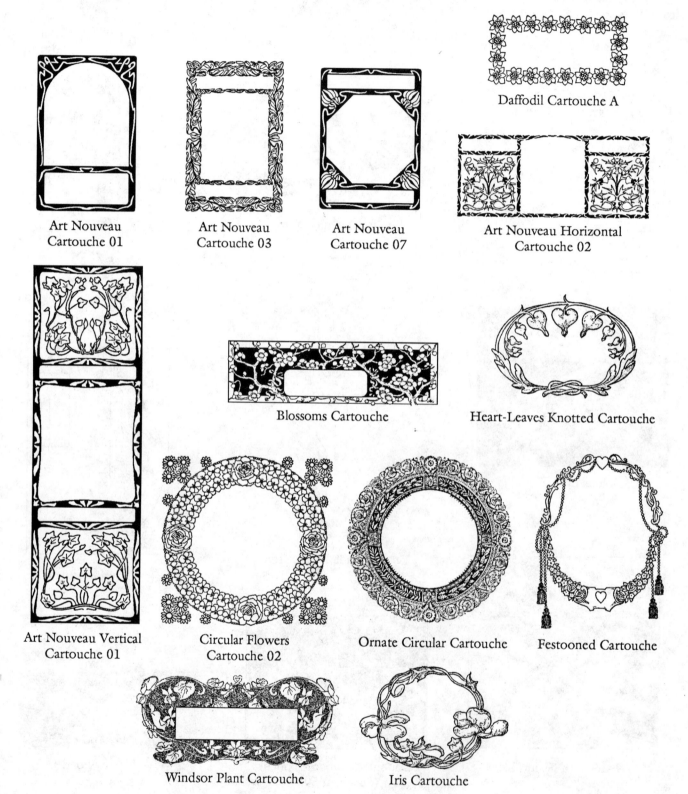

Daffodil Cartouche A

Art Nouveau
Cartouche 01

Art Nouveau
Cartouche 03

Art Nouveau
Cartouche 07

Art Nouveau Horizontal
Cartouche 02

Blossoms Cartouche

Heart-Leaves Knotted Cartouche

Art Nouveau Vertical
Cartouche 01

Circular Flowers
Cartouche 02

Ornate Circular Cartouche

Festooned Cartouche

Windsor Plant Cartouche

Iris Cartouche

All art on this page shown at 50%.

Because of the large amount of clip art available in this volume, we are showing only samples of the artwork.

Flower Borders

Art Nouveau Flower Border

Entwined Flowers Border

Floral Oval Border 2

Floral Two-Panel Border

Lilies & Shells Border

Malindy Floral Border 1B

Malindy Floral Border 3A

Oval Mirror Rose Border

Round-Cornered Floral Border

Sunflowers Border 1

Because of the large amount of clip art available in this volume, we are showing only samples of the artwork.

Flower Designs

Art Nouveau Flowers 1

Beardsley Flower Design 3
(Shown at 50%)

Bellflowers Group

Bouquet in Wicker Basket
(Shown at 50%)

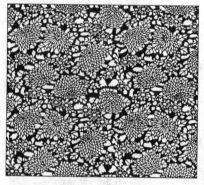

Japanese Flower Design

Paisley Flower Design 1

Large Floral Ornament

Circular Lilies Design
(Shown at 50%)

Flower Vase Circle
(Shown at 50%)

Korean Flower Design
(Shown at 50%)

Octagonal Flowers Design
(Shown at 50%)

Small Art Nouveau
Flower Design
(Shown at 50%)

Small Flower Design 2
(Shown at 50%)

Stylized Lily 1
(Shown at 50%)

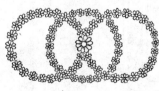

Three Circular Wreaths
(Shown at 50%)

Two Flowers Design
(Shown at 50%)

Vase with Flowers
(Shown at 50%)

Because of the large amount of clip art available in this volume, we are showing only samples of the artwork.

Flowering Plants

American Brooklime

American Rhododendron

Buttercups

Carnations 3

Hellebore 1

Orange Lily

Parrot Tulip
(Shown at 50%)

Pink Azalea

Rose Mallow

Showy Orchis

Turk's Cap Lily

White Lily 1

Wood Lily

Because of the large amount of clip art available in this volume, we are showing only samples of the artwork.

Friezes & Scrolls

Birds & Flowers

Birds & Waves

Curves Frieze 3

Dancer in Motion Frieze

Egyptian Mythology Frieze

Four Crabs Frieze

Hohokam Men Frieze

Thoughtful Man Frieze

Birds & Nest Scroll

Bluebeard Scroll

Double Swirls Scroll

Goddess of Liberty Scroll

Old-Time Printer
Scroll

Sleeping Man
Scroll

Tree Scroll
(Shown at 50%)

Woodpeckers
Scroll

Because of the large amount of clip art available in this volume, we are showing only samples of the artwork.

Greek & Roman Life

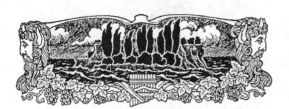

Ancient Greek Island

Antique Roman Ring

Etruscan Vase

Expressive Greek Heads
(Shown at 50%)

Gladiators
(Shown at 50%)

Greek Chariot 1

Greek Man's Profile
(Shown at 50%)

Greek Men with
Canes

Greek Woman on Swing
(Shown at 50%)

Greek Youths Bathing
(Shown at 50%)

Man in Tunic
(Shown at 50%)

Roman Carriage

Roman Woman
Dancing

Stylized Greek
Warriors

Alexander the Great

Running to Babylon
(Shown at 50%)

Because of the large amount of clip art available in this volume, we are showing only samples of the artwork.

Human Interaction

Antique Couple with Wreath
(Shown at 50%)

Couple and New Baby
(Shown at 50%)

Cider Feast
(Shown at 50%)

Couple on Bough Silhouette

Egyptian Lovers

Father and Daughter
(Shown at 50%)

Forest Merrymaking
Silhouette

Harvesters
(Shown at 50%)

Man with Dream Lover

Mother and Child
(Shown at 50%)

Swordfight
Silhouette

Young Carnival Couple

Transfixed Gazes

Young Couple on Horseback

Because of the large amount of clip art available in this volume, we are showing only samples of the artwork.

Humor

Bird Pooping on Skull
on Book

Buffoon

Carpe Diem
(Shown at 50%)

Cockroach Frightening
Old Man

Comet Satire

Comic Grape-Beard Face

Dinosaur Slide Silhouette

Earth and Geese on Wires

Egyptianesque Shoemaker

Firecracker Explosion
(Shown at 50%)

Frozen Man

Mona Lisa Parody
(Shown at 50%)

Man Being Boiled

Because of the large amount of clip art available in this volume, we are showing only samples of the artwork.

Jewish Pictures

Circumcision Tray

Etrog Holder

Jewish Altar B

Jewish Candles Border

Jewish Animal Ornament 3

Jewish Cartouche
(Shown at 50%)

Menorah

Menorah with Curtains

Jewish Man with
Yarmulke

Spiderwebs &
Jewish Ironer

Mogen David Border
2F

Oval Ceremonial Plate

Because of the large amount of clip art available in this volume, we are showing only samples of the artwork.

Knighthood

Chivalry Scenes Border

Determined Knight with Sword
(Shown at 50%)

Flowered Turret

Jousting

King & Reluctant Knight

Knight with Seated Maiden
(Shown at 50%)

Knight with Dead Man

Knights in Combat

Maiden in Tower & Knight

Upsidedown Squire

Because of the large amount of clip art available in this volume, we are showing only samples of the artwork.

Leaves & Trees

Acanthus Leaf

Apple Leaf
(Shown at 50%)

Bay-Leafed Willow Leaf
(Shown at 50%)

Bird Cherry Leaf
(Shown at 50%)

Blossoming Tree Branch

Ceiba Tree

Evergreens

Foliage

Guaiacum

Guelder Rose Leaf

Hazel Leaf
(Shown at 50%)

Hornbeam Leaves

Horse Chestnut Leaf 2

Oak Leaf 1
(Shown at 50%)

Plane Tree Leaf 1

Sycamore Leaf

Scotch Fir Tree
(Shown at 50%)

Because of the large amount of clip art available in this volume, we are showing only samples of the artwork.

Lower Animal Designs

Alligator Design

Butterfly & Plants Design
(Shown at 50%)

Butterfly & Torch
(Shown at 50%)

Butterfly 2

Butterfly Design

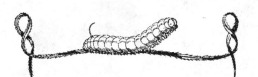

Caterpillar Design

Fish Cutout

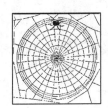

Geometric Spider & Web

Narrow Fish
with Fins

Fish Ornament
(Shown at 50%)

Nigerian Fish
Design

Seahorses Design

Stylized Butterflies

Two Bees Head to Head
(Shown at 50%)

Because of the large amount of clip art available in this volume, we are showing only samples of the artwork.

Mammal Designs

Animals Running
Silhouette

Calligraphic
Elephant

Calligraphic
Twin Whales

Cat
(Shown at 100%)

Cat Silhouette
(Shown at 50%)

Cattle Grazing
(Shown at 50%)

Charging Bull Silhouette
(Shown at 50%)

Deer Ornament

Giraffes

Lion & Sun
(Shown at 50%)

Monkey & Child Design

Panda Cubs Cutout

Stylized Anteater

White Wolf
Triptych

Wolves in Snow

Because of the large amount of clip art available in this volume, we are showing only samples of the artwork.

Mayan Pictures

Capture of Jeweled Skull

Dancer with Animal
Headdress

Gobernador Mask at Uxmal

Mayan Chief

Mayan Hieroglyphic Panel
(Shown at 50%)

Mayan Priest

God of Zero

Offering to Sun God

Ticul Vase
(Shown at 50%)

Winged Man Mayan Plate

Because of the large amount of clip art available in this volume, we are showing only samples of the artwork.

Men

Admiral at the Helm
(Shown at 50%)

Anguished Man

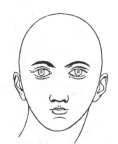

Bald Man's Head
(Shown at 50%)

Cave Man with Club
(Shown at 50%)

Determined Man
(Shown at 50%)

European Man with Flag
(Shown at 50%)

Fat Man Fishing

Frowning Moustached Man

Hunter in Victorian Bed

Magician with Hat

Man Bathing In River
(Shown at 50%)

Man Bearing
Flower Basket

Man Peering Over Wall
(Shown at 50%)

Stylized Man Design
(Shown at 50%)

Upraised-Arms Man
(Shown at 100%)

Wealthy Horseman
(Shown at 50%)

Because of the large amount of clip art available in this volume, we are showing only samples of the artwork.

Middle Eastern Pictures

Ali Baba

Dervish & Boy
(Shown at 50%)

East Meets West

Exotic Veiled Woman
(Shown at 50%)

Harem Eunuch

Kalifs in Bagdad
(Shown at 50%)

Middle Eastern
Farewell

Middle Eastern Horseman 1
(Shown at 50%)

Mosque by Water
(Shown at 50%)

Persian Cartouche 6

Wizard

Sultan with Sword

Turkish Man

Because of the large amount of clip art available in this volume, we are showing only samples of the artwork.

Monsters

Avian Monster Head

Basilisk of Grevinus

Big-Eyed Creature

Chinese Sea Creature 1

Chinese Dragon Growling

Chink & Crevice Bogie

Dragon Devouring Prey

Creature with
Spade Tail

Fuzzy Creature with Skulls
(Shown at 25%)

Gargoyle

Man-Bird

Rukh Lifting Elephants

Spouting Whale Creature

Seven-Headed Beast

All art on this page shown at 50% except as noted.

Because of the large amount of clip art available in this volume, we are showing only samples of the artwork.

Music

Angel Playing Bass
(Shown at 50%)

Bagpipe

Beethoven
(Shown at 50%)

Brahms' Silhouette

Café Singer

Chamber Musicians Silhouette

Cherubic Musicians
(Shown at 50%)

Harp Ornament
(Shown at 50%)

Harpist & Trees
(Shown at 50%)

Musical Conductor
Silhouette 1

Piper Resting
(Shown at 50%)

Young Woman
Cellist

Youth Playing Pipe Circle
(Shown at 50%)

Because of the large amount of clip art available in this volume, we are showing only samples of the artwork.

Native Americans

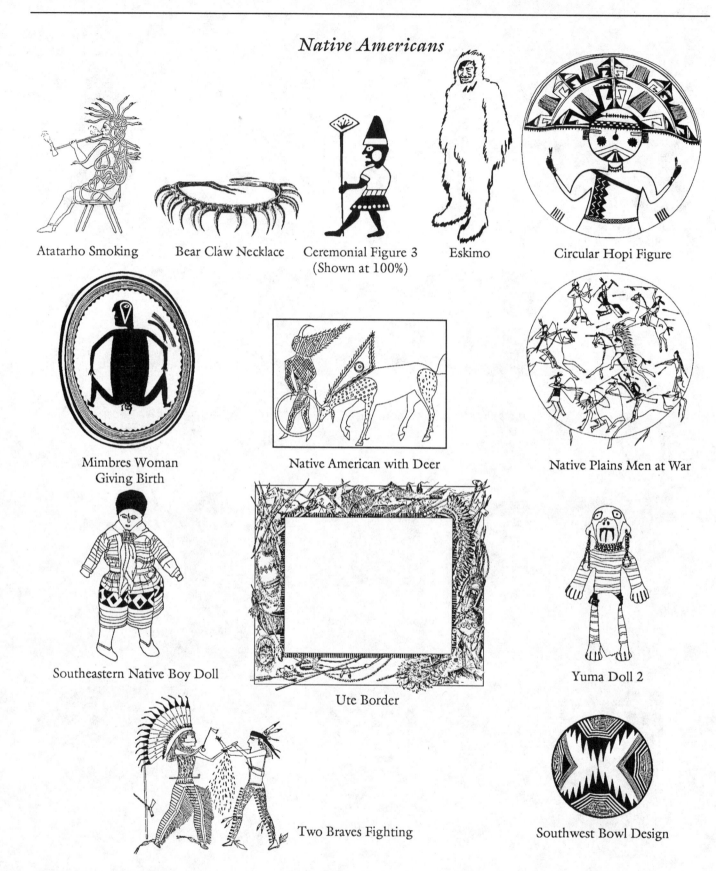

Atatarho Smoking

Bear Claw Necklace

Ceremonial Figure 3
(Shown at 100%)

Eskimo

Circular Hopi Figure

Mimbres Woman
Giving Birth

Native American with Deer

Native Plains Men at War

Southeastern Native Boy Doll

Ute Border

Yuma Doll 2

Two Braves Fighting

Southwest Bowl Design

Because of the large amount of clip art available in this volume, we are showing only samples of the artwork.

Objets d'Art

Biberon

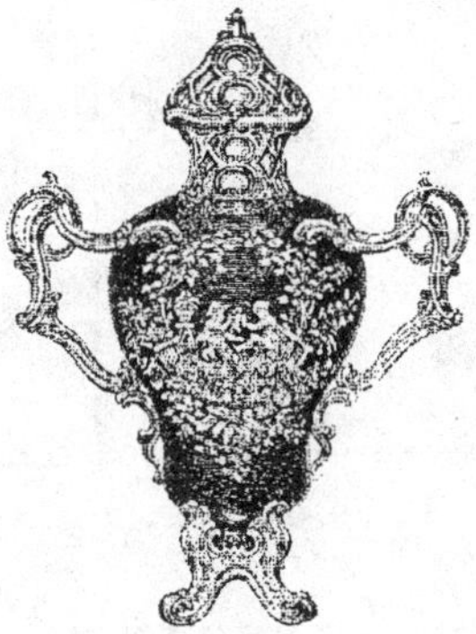

Chelsea Vase

Copper Chalice

Decorative Bird Vase

Foliated Plate

Heron Plate

Indian Plate

Kang Hsi Vase

Old Chair
(Shown at 50%)

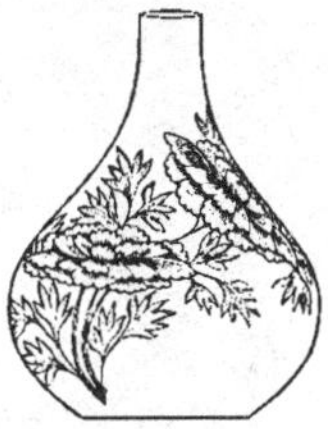

Peony Porcelain Vase

Vases 2

Wrought Iron Door Knocker

Because of the large amount of clip art available in this volume, we are showing only samples of the artwork.

Optical Illusions & Math

Both Circles Are Equal

Circle Seems
Distorted

Frame is Rectilinear

Inner Circles Are Equal 1

Inner Squares Are
Equal

Parallel Lines Bending in 2
(Shown at 50%)

Rear Block Seems Tallest
(Shown at 50%)

Reversing Steps

Obliques Meet on Left Vertical

Reversing Cubes
in Circle

Find the Cat
(Shown at 50%)

Find the Landlord
(Shown at 50%)

Donkey/Doctor
Reversible
(Shown at 50%)

Magic Number Explosion
(Shown at 50%)

Number Symphonies B

Mathematical Woman

Because of the large amount of clip art available in this volume, we are showing only samples of the artwork.

People Borders

Admiral & Mermaids

Banquet

Knight & Maiden

Woman Among Reeds
(Shown at 50%)

Comic Sausage

Hands Reaching

Priestess

Carnival

Lilies & Lyre Players

Woman with Cockatoo

Because of the large amount of clip art available in this volume, we are showing only samples of the artwork.

People & Animals

Bearded Man with
Ravens

Circus Silhouette

Boy Riding Flamingo

Man & Sacred Cow

Elephant Pulls
Tree Silhouette

Animate Celtic Circle

Early Photography

Penguin to Man
Transformation

Riding a Beast
Silhouette

Peaceful Kingdom
Woodcut

Rosenkavalier
with Butterflies

Woman Curve
Design

Woman Bather with Dog

Woman with Coiled Snake
(Shown at 50%)

Woman–Butterfly Metamorphosis
(Shown at 50%)

Because of the large amount of clip art available in this volume, we are showing only samples of the artwork.

Plant Borders

Acanthus Border

Art Nouveau Border 2

Grapes & Leaves Border 1

Octagonal Plant Frame

Small Leaves with Bees

Thistle Border

Vegetable Leaves Border

Vines Border

Wavy Plant Border

Winter Plants Border

Wreathed Pendants Border

Because of the large amount of clip art available in this volume, we are showing only samples of the artwork.

Plant Designs

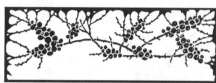

Berry Clusters Design

Abstract Plant
Pattern

Dark & Light Leaves
(Shown at 50%)

Circular Plant Design 3

Fleuron Design

Flowers & Snowflakes
(Shown at 50%)

Fruit Ornament 2

Grape Design

Grapevine Plate

Horizontal Plant Design 1
(Shown at 50%)

Intarsia Plant Design 1

Leafy Corner

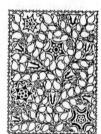

Leaves & Stars

Lotus Design 1
(Shown at 50%)

Simple Plant
(Shown at 50%)

Because of the large amount of clip art available in this volume, we are showing only samples of the artwork.

Reading & Writing

Armchair Reader

Book at Dawn

Book Sunrise

Boy Reading Under Tree

Girl Reading in Forest

Flower & Book

King Writing

Library at Night

Old Books Border
(Shown at 25%)

Pensive Woman Reader A

Renaissance Scholar

Woman Reading in Armchair
(Shown at 25%)

Women Reading
(Shown at 25%)

Writer Silhouette

All artwork on this page shown at 50% except as noted.

Because of the large amount of clip art available in this volume, we are showing only samples of the artwork.

Realistic Birds

Birds & Branch
(Shown at 50%)

Marsh Birds
(Shown at 50%)

Pelican Head
(Shown at 50%)

The volume *Realistic Birds* consists mainly of halftones, which do not reduce well.
The halftones were all too large to show at 100% , and we are therefore showing only line art to represent this set.

Realistic Insects & Arachnids

Ant Feeding
(Shown at 50%)

Black Beetle
(Shown at 50%)

Looper Caterpillar
(Shown at 50%)

Moth
(Shown at 50%)

Wide-Winged Bee
(Shown at 50%)

The volume *Realistic Insects & Arachnids* consists mainly of halftones, which do not reduce well.
The halftones were all too large to show at 100% , and we are therefore showing only line art to represent this set.

Panoramic Landscapes & Realistic Landscapes

The volumes *Panoramic Landscapes* and *Realistic Landscapes* consist entirely of halftones, which do not reduce well.
The halftones were all too large to show at 100% , and we are therefore unable to represent these sets here.

Realistic Mammals

Bear Growling

Caribou on Cliff

Chipmunk

Fierce Lynx
(Shown at 50%)

Giraffe About to Lie
Down

The volume *Realistic Mammals* consists mainly of halftones, which do not reduce well.
The halftones were all too large to show at 100%, and we are therefore showing only line art to represent this set.

Realistic Reptiles & Amphibians

Chameleon
(Shown at 50%)

Coiled Rattlesnake
(Shown at 50%)

Poisonous Snake Head
(Shown at 50%)(Shown
at 50%)

Terrapin Turtle
(Shown at 50%)

The volume *Realistic Reptiles & Amphibians* consists mainly of halftones, which do not reduce well.
The halftones were all too large to show at 100%, and we are therefore showing only line art to represent this set.

Realistic Sea Life

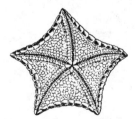

Asterias Tessellata
(Shown at 50%)

Blowfish

Branching Lower Life Form
(Shown at 50%)

Eel 1
(Shown at 50%)

The volume *Realistic Reptiles & Amphibians* consists mainly of halftones, which do not reduce well.
The halftones were all too large to show at 100%, and we are therefore showing only line art to represent this set.

Sexuality

Androgynous
Courtship

Couple in Tub

Devil Pursuing Nude
(Shown at 50%)

Hidden Lechery
(Shown at 50%)

Kama Sutra

Lysistrata

Man Suckling

Man with Nude in Oval
(Shown at 50%)

Naughty Santa Claus

Sexual Pursuit 2

Song of Solomon

Whipping

Reclining Satyr and Woman

Because of the large amount of clip art available in this volume, we are showing only samples of the artwork.

Shaped Borders

Apollo & Companion L-Border   Bonnet L-Border   Daisy T-Border   Floral I-Border

L-Scroll Border   Pilgrims L-Border   Robed Woman U-Border   Sniffing Blossoms L-Border

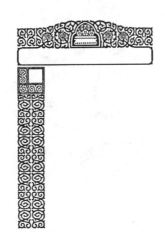

Sunrise U-Border (Shown at 50%)   Symmetric Blocks L-Border   Women & Palm T-Border

Because of the large amount of clip art available in this volume, we are showing only samples of the artwork.

Silhouettes

Acorns & Leaves
Silhouette

Angelic Statue
Silhouette

Animals Running
Silhouette

Arabesque
Silhouette

Artist's Studio
Silhouette

Begging Flowergirl
Silhouette

Birds Crest
Silhouette

Building & Birds
Silhouette

Candle & Smoke
Silhouette

Celebrating Nude
Silhouette

Charging Bull
Silhouette

Cinderella's Coach
Silhouette

Crab Riding Crane
Silhouette

Dancing Devils
Silhouette

Doily Plant Pattern 1

Forest Merrymaking
Silhouette

Hen Cutout 2

Japanese Woman
Silhouette

Tree & Hens
Cutout

Serenading a Woman
Silhouette

Rumpelstiltskin
Silhouette

Because of the large amount of clip art available in this volume, we are showing only samples of the artwork.

Tree Borders

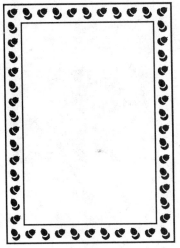

Acorns Border B

Empty Circles Tree Border

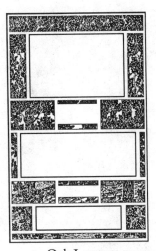

Oak Leaves–
Many Panels Border

Pruned Trees Border

Reflected Trees Border

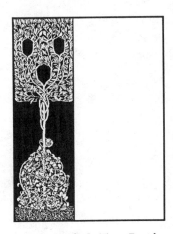

Rose Bush & Tree Border

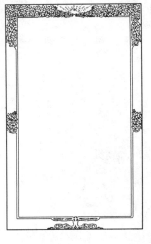

Sunrise & Trees Border

Trees Oval Border

Twin Trees Border Wide

Trees Border

Because of the large amount of clip art available in this volume, we are showing only samples of the artwork.

Tree Designs

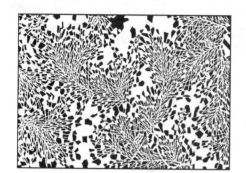

Abstract Pine Design

Arbor Vitae 2
(Shown at 50%)

Chinese Willow Design
(Shown at 50%)

Fruit Design
(Shown at 50%)

Fruited Tree Scene

Ilex Opaca Circle Design
(Shown at 100%)

Japanese Pine Cones

Little Ravenna Trees
(Shown at 50%)

Ornamental Tree Cutout 1
(Shown at 50%)

Oval Tree Silhouette B
(Shown at 50%)

Pine Cone 1
(Shown at 50%)

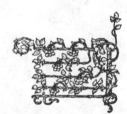

Pruned Tree Design 1

Sculpted Trees Horizontal
(Shown at 50%)

Spiral Branches Design
(Shown at 50%)

Stylized Indian Tree
(Shown at 50%)

Three Trees Design

Because of the large amount of clip art available in this volume, we are showing only samples of the artwork.

Valentine's Day

Antique Couple with Wreath
(Shown at 50%)

Cherub Aiming Arrow
(Shown at 50%)

Cherubs on Sofa
(Shown at 50%)

Couple Embracing
(Shown at 50%)

Couple Boating Silhouette

Elegant Couple Silhouette

Heart & Flowers Design
(Shown at 50%)

Imprisoned Love Emblem
(Shown at 50%)

Heart Chick

Little Heart Border

Revolutionary Valentine

Twin Hearts Cutout

Valentine Cherub
(Shown at 50%)

Valentine Hearts Border

Young Lovers
(Shown at 50%)

Because of the large amount of clip art available in this volume, we are showing only samples of the artwork.

Women

Actress on Stage

Art Nouveau Maiden
(Shown at 50%)

Beautiful Garlanded Woman
(Shown at 50%)

Circle of Women

Garlanded Woman

Maiden in Garden
(Shown at 50%)

Pregnant Woman in
Garden

Two Women with
Peacock

Woman Among Reeds
(Shown at 50%)

Woman in Vineyard

Young Woman's
Silhouette

Woman with Blowing Scarf
(Shown at 50%)

Wreathed Woman
(Shown at 50%)

(Image of Woman Kissing a Flower, Shown at 50%)

Woman Kissing a Flower
(Shown at 50%)

Because of the large amount of clip art available in this volume, we are showing only samples of the artwork.

Tactic Software

11925 SW 128 Street
Miami, FL 33186
305-378-4110
800-344-4818 orders only
305-232-7467 fax

◆

Collection	Format	No./Size Disks	Price	Computer
ArtClips Graphics & Symbols	EPS	4-800K	$99.00	Mac
ArtClips Business Images	EPS	4-800K	$129.00	Mac

Notes:

• Also available from Tactic is a Multi-Media Compact Disk, which retails for $299.00. It includes 160 24-bit color TIFF images, 250 EPS images (the art shown here as well as some other pieces), 500 sound effects, 21 PostScript Type 1 typefaces, and 41 MIDI files. Contact Tactic Software for more information.

Art Clips Graphics & Symbols Disk 1

Boeing 747

Building

Car

Chair

Chinese Boat

Car

Columbia

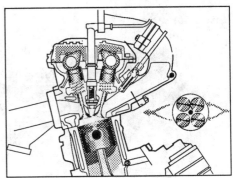

Engine

Formula 3

Locomotive

Old Bicycle

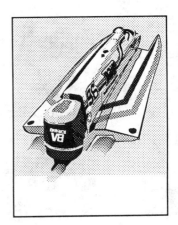

Speedboat

Art Clips Graphics & Symbols Disk 2

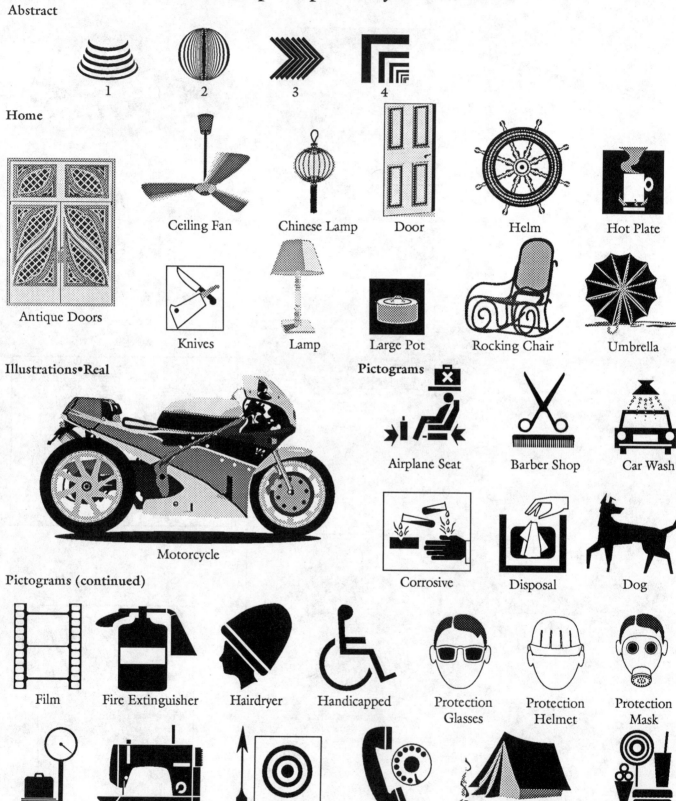

Abstract

1 2 3 4

Home

Antique Doors Ceiling Fan Chinese Lamp Door Helm Hot Plate

Knives Lamp Large Pot Rocking Chair Umbrella

Illustrations•Real

Motorcycle

Pictograms

Airplane Seat Barber Shop Car Wash

Corrosive Disposal Dog

Pictograms (continued)

Film Fire Extinguisher Hairdryer Handicapped Protection Glasses Protection Helmet Protection Mask

Scale Sewing Machine Target Telephone Tent Tidbits

Art Clips Graphics & Symbols Disk 3

Dinosaur

Femme

Giraffe

Horses

Hurdle

Idol

Polo

Roman Bath

Turkish

Zebra

Art Clips Graphics & Symbols Disk 4

Food

Banana   Bread   Cake   Cheese   Cherries   Coffee   Fried Eggs   Lemon

Milk   Peach   Pear

Sports

Ball   Basketball   Bowling   Fish   Golf

Race Flag   Sailboat   Soccer   Swords   Tennis

Miscellaneous

Batteries   Horn   Lens   Racket

Olympics

Basket   Boxing   Cycling   Diving   Fencing   Gymnastics

Handball   Hockey   Karate   Riding   Rowing   Shooting

Skiing   Soccer   Swimming   Track & Field   Volleyball   Weight Lifting

Professions

Bellhop   Nurse   Waiter   Wrestling

TACTIC SOFTWARE

Art Clips Business Images Disk 1

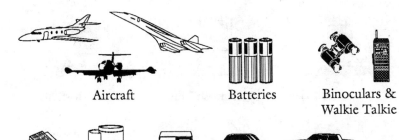
Aircraft

Batteries

Binoculars &
Walkie Talkie

Business
Graphics

Business Machines 1

Business Machines 2

Cars

Cassette & CDs & LP

Clocks & Watches

Compaq portable

Credit cards & Federal Express

Disk 5.25

Disks 3.5

Disks 3.5 w/box

Don't Smoke

Drafting Table

Fire Extinguisher

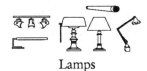
Framers

Helicopters

Imagewriters

Keys

Lamps

TAC-5

Art Clips Business Images Disk 2

Laptop

Laser Printers

Macintosh II

Macintosh Plus

Macintosh SE

Mail

Microcassette
& Recorder

Miscellaneous

Modem

Money 1

Money 2

Money 3

Monitors

Office Furniture

Art Clips Business Images Disk 3

(This image is shown at 100%.)

People

Personal Computer

Phrases 1

Phrases 2

PS/2

Satellite &
Parabolic Antenna

Scanner

Ships & Boat

Stationery 1

Stationery 2

Stationery 3

Stationery 4

Stereo Headphones

Suitcases

Tape Backup & Cartridge

Telephones

Televisions

Truck

Van

Video Cassette & Video Disk

Art Clips Business Images Disk 4

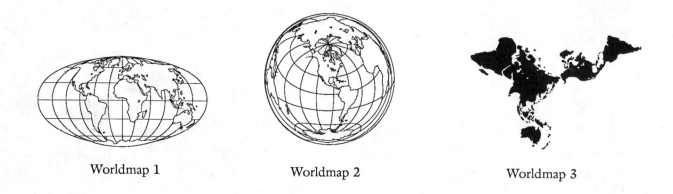

Worldmap 1   Worldmap 2   Worldmap 3

(These images are shown at 100%.)

3G Graphics
11410 N.E. 124th Street Suite 6155
Kirkland, WA 98034
206-367-9321
800-456-0234

Collection	Format	No./Size Disks	Price	Computer
Images With Impact:				
Accents & Borders 1	EPS	5-800K	$129.95	Mac/IBM
Business 1	EPS	4-800K	$129.95	Mac/IBM
Graphics & Symbols 1	EPS	2-800K	$99.95	Mac/IBM
People 1*	EPS	7-800K	$189.95	Mac/IBM

Notes:

*The art in this set has been compressed onto the 800K disks.
• One 800K disk of color art will be sent to all registered owners of the Accents & Borders 1 set. It is shown and indexed in this volume, but it is not counted in the 5 disks listed above for Accents & Borders.
• Prices for the IBM versions may vary. Contact 3G Graphics for more information.

Images With Impact!: Accents & Borders 1 Disk A

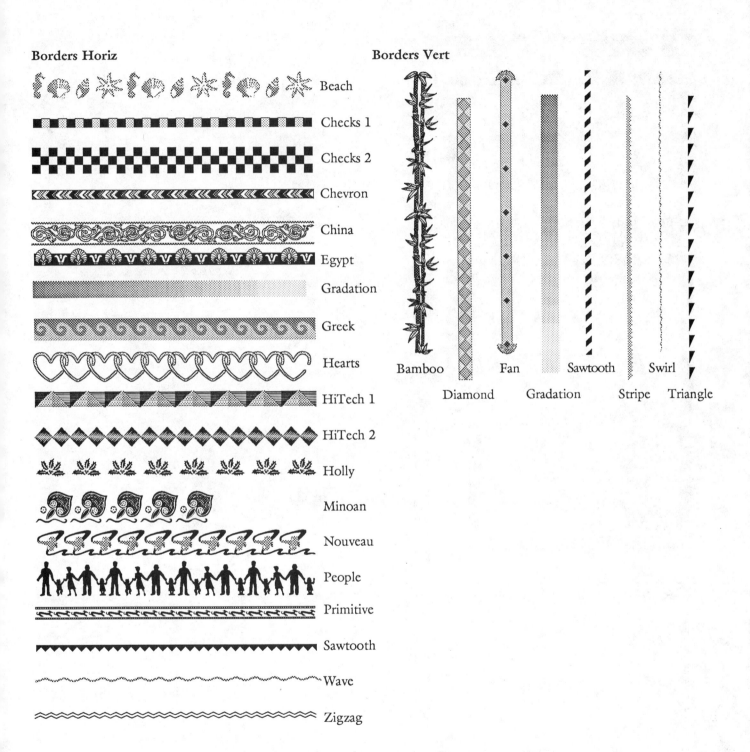

Borders Horiz

Beach
Checks 1
Checks 2
Chevron
China
Egypt
Gradation
Greek
Hearts
HiTech 1
HiTech 2
Holly
Minoan
Nouveau
People
Primitive
Sawtooth
Wave
Zigzag

Borders Vert

Bamboo
Diamond
Fan
Gradation
Sawtooth
Stripe
Swirl
Triangle

Images With Impact!: Accents & Borders 1 Disk B

Designer Sets

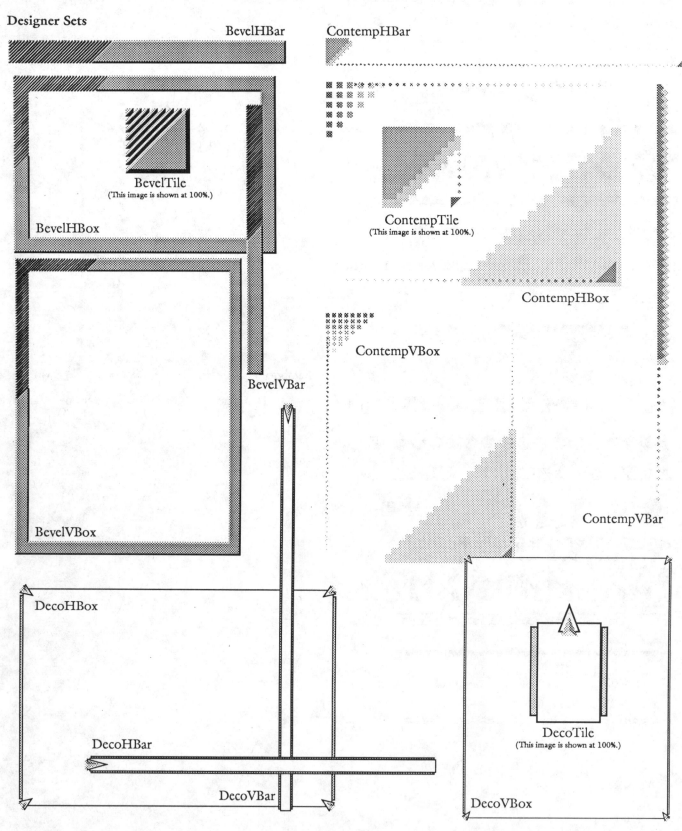

BevelHBar

ContempHBar

BevelTile
(This image is shown at 100%.)

BevelHBox

ContempTile
(This image is shown at 100%.)

ContempHBox

ContempVBox

BevelVBar

BevelVBox

ContempVBar

DecoHBox

DecoTile
(This image is shown at 100%.)

DecoHBar

DecoVBar

DecoVBox

Images With Impact!: Accents & Borders 1 Disk B (continued)

Designer Sets (continued)

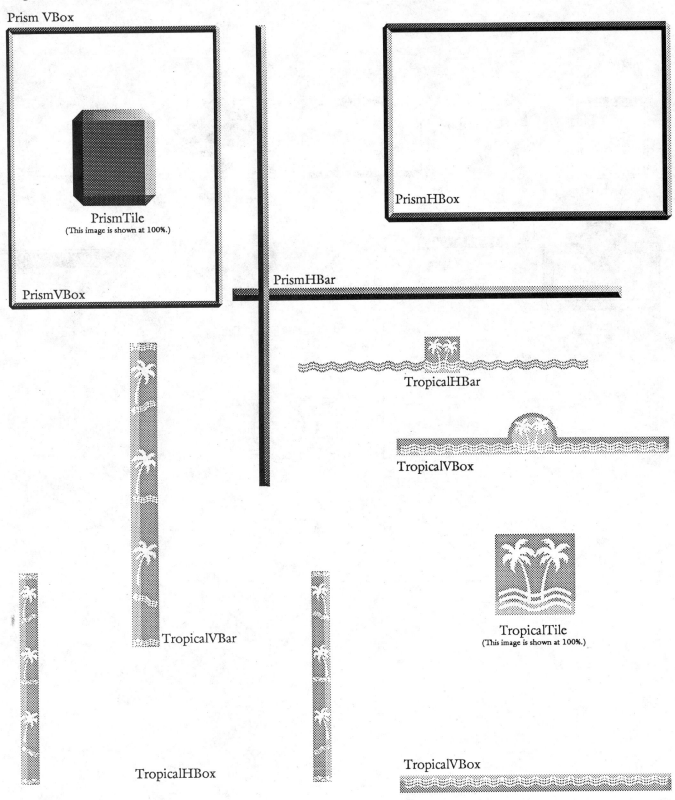

Prism VBox

PrismTile
(This image is shown at 100%.)

PrismVBox

PrismHBox

PrismHBar

TropicalHBar

TropicalVBox

TropicalVBar

TropicalTile
(This image is shown at 100%.)

TropicalHBox

TropicalVBox

Images With Impact!: Accents & Borders 1 Disk B (continued)

Labels

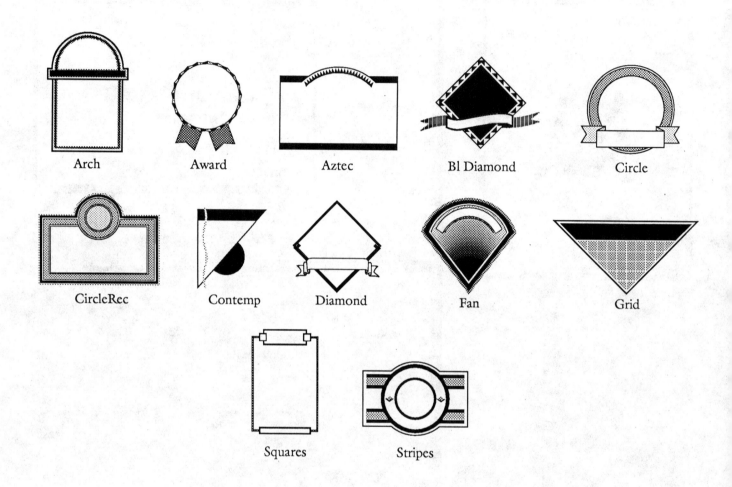

Arch	Award	Aztec	Bl Diamond	Circle
CircleRec	Contemp	Diamond	Fan	Grid
Squares	Stripes			

Images With Impact!: Accents & Borders 1 Disk C

Frames Horiz

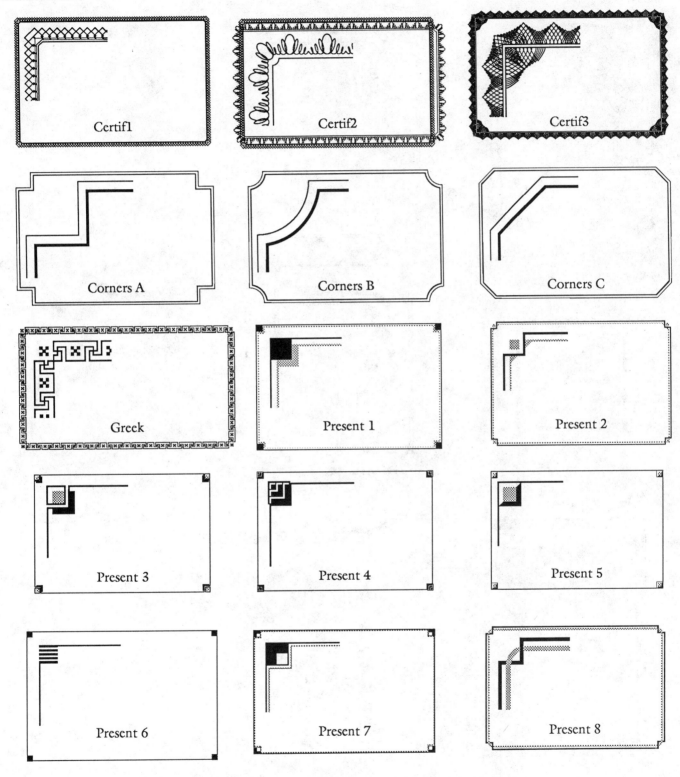

Certif1

Certif2

Certif3

Corners A

Corners B

Corners C

Greek

Present 1

Present 2

Present 3

Present 4

Present 5

Present 6

Present 7

Present 8

Images With Impact!: Accents & Borders 1 Disk C (continued)

Frames Vert

Celtic

China

Contemp

Deco

NouvCurls

NouvFlow

Images With Impact!: Accents & Borders 1 Disk D

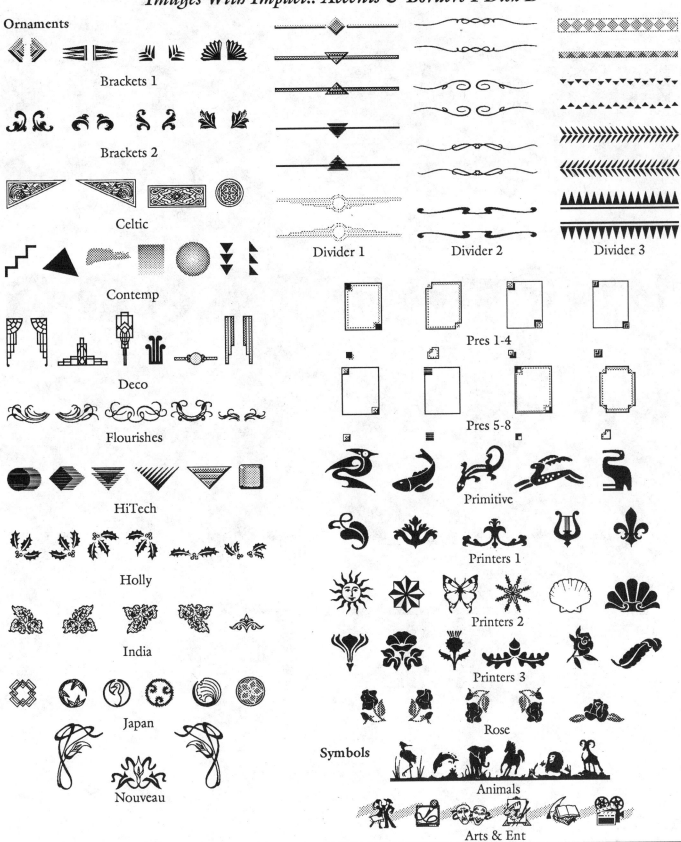

Ornaments

Brackets 1

Brackets 2

Celtic

Contemp

Deco

Flourishes

HiTech

Holly

India

Japan

Nouveau

Divider 1

Divider 2

Divider 3

Pres 1-4

Pres 5-8

Primitive

Printers 1

Printers 2

Printers 3

Rose

Symbols

Animals

Arts & Ent

3G GRAPHICS

Images With Impact!: Accents & Borders 1 Disk E

Symbols

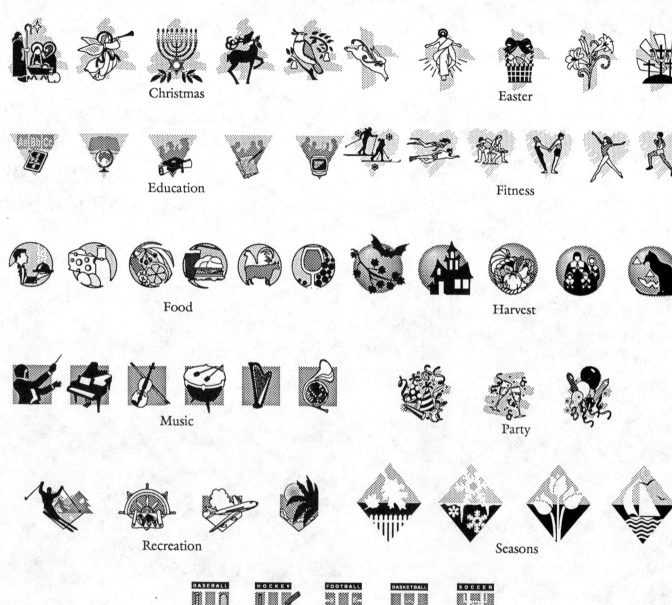

Christmas   Easter

Education   Fitness

Food   Harvest

Music   Party

Recreation   Seasons

Sports

Images With Impact!: Accents & Borders 1 Bonus Color Disk

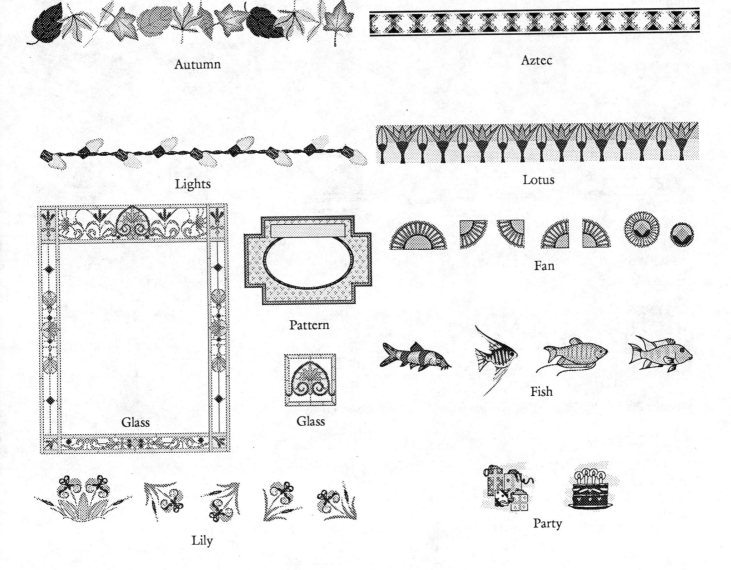

Autumn

Aztec

Lights

Lotus

Pattern

Fan

Glass

Glass

Fish

Lily

Party

3G GRAPHICS

Images With Impact!: Business 1 Disk A

Equipment

3.5 Disk

5.25 Disk

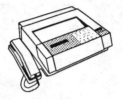

Fax Machine

IBM PC

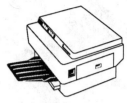

LaserJet

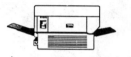

LaserWriter +

LaserWriter II

Mac II

Mac Plus

Mac SE

Modern Phone

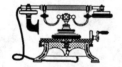

Old Style Phone

PS2 Model 50

Working Hands

Clicking Mouse

Holding Tickets

Inserting Disk

On Folder

Passing Card

Saving

Serving

Shaking

Typing

Voting

Writing

Images With Impact!: Business 1 Disk B

Financial/Success

3D Dollar
Sign

Bear
Market

Bull
Market

Democrat

George
Wash

GOP

Man/
Dollar

Merit

Money Chart

Stacking Bills

Stopwatch

Tickertape

White House

People

Audience

Banker

Computer
Training

Conference

Const
Workers

F Exec
Phone

F Exec Side

F Stylish

F Walking

F & M Agree

Finish Line

Foreman

M Leaning/
Phone

M on the Run

M With Folder

M Youth

Older M
Walking

Overworked

Physician

Images With Impact!: Business 1 Disk C (Symbols)

Communication

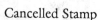

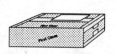

| Cancelled Stamp | Mail | Overnight Letter | Package | Phone | Power Lines | Satellite/Dish |

Computer Networks

CPU's   DEC/VAX

Peripherals   Printers

Dingbats

| 1st Place | Briefcase | Check Mark | Dollar Sign | Idea Light | Bomb Lit | Note Pad | Paper Clip |

| Pencils | Pointing Hand | Push Pin | Question | Stacking Cube | Star |

Occupations

| Accountant | Artist | Auto Mech | Construction | Drafting | Education | Gavel | Horticulture | Media |

| Medical | Medicine | Office | Painter | Pharmacy | Plumber | Real Estate | Scales | Sports |

Public Service

| Baggage | Credit Cards | Male/Female | No Drunk Driving | No Smoking | Restaurant | Wheelchair |

Images With Impact!: Business 1 Disk D

Aerospace

Astronaut   Atomic Energy   F16 Squadron   Shuttle Landing   Shuttle Prelaunch

Framers

Clipboard   Notebook   Open Briefcase   Pencil   Phone Receiver   Presentation

More Symbols: Desktop Publishing

DTP Stages   Graphics & Text   Output   Training

Phrases

Agenda   **CONFIDENTIAL**   *F.Y.I.*   *Goals & Objectives*

Highlights   *Introduction*   *memo*   *Projections*

Q. & A.   *Sales & Expenses*   *Schedule*   *Thank You*

Travel

Big Rig   Continents   Corp Jet   Globe   New Car   Train

Images With Impact!: Graphics & Symbols 1 Disk A

Display Framers

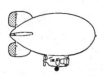

Blimp

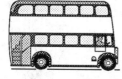

Dbl Decker Bus

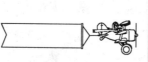

Flying Ace

Notepad

Sandwich Brd Mouse

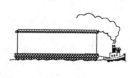

Tug Boat

Graphic Series: Bears

Editor Bear

News Bear

Signing Bear

Graphic Series: Carrier Pigeons

Delivering

Flying Front View

Flying Side View

Graphic Series: Fireworks

Boom 1

Boom 2

Boom 3

Boom 4

Boom 5

Boom 6

Graphic Series: Mimes

Squatting

Standing   Leaping

MultiGraphics

Everyday People

Food Collage

Travel Collage

Images With Impact!: Graphics & Symbols 1 Disk B

Portfolio

Aerobics · Balloons · Cityscape · Dining in Style · Director's Chair · Eagle · Flag

Home · Hot Air Balloon · Mail · Orcas · Penguin · Piggy Bank

Road Scene · Runners · Statue of Liberty · Windsurfer · Woman Leaning

Symbols: Going Places

Bridge · Bus · Campground

City · Country · Fishing

Government · Lighthouse · Plane

Taxi · Train · Residential

Symbols: Things

Coffee Break · Compass · Globe · Money Bag

Motor Cross Flags · Picnic Basket · Present

Scissors · Take a Note · Target · Telephone

People

Boy · Family · Girl · Graduate · Man · Woman

Images With Impact!: People 1 Disk A

Arts & Entertainment

Artist Ballet Conductor Dancers Jazz Modular Arts 1

Modular Arts 2 Movies Occ Arts Violinist

Business 1

At Desk 1 At Desk 2 At Desk 3 At Desk 4 At Desk 5

Car Phone Cash Machine Conference Fencing Harrassed

Images With Impact!: People 1 Disk B

Business 2

Hour Glass
Shown at 50%

Jungle Office
Shown at 50%

Laptop

Lunch Meeting

Mrkt Japan

Modular Business

Mrkt China

Mrkt Europe

Mrkt 1 Flags

Mrkt 2 Flags

Mrkt Russia

Mrkt USA

Reading

Receptionist

Task Juggler F

Task Juggler M

Travel

Working Mother

Images With Impact!: People 1 Disk C

Fitness

Bowling

Cycling

Exercise Bike

Football Teens

Golf

Good Food

Hiking

Modular Fitness 1

Modular Fitness 2

Skiing X-Country

Spa

Tennis

Workout

Images With Impact!: People 1 Disk D

Health Care

Admitting

Checkup

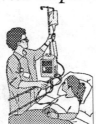
Child IV

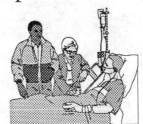
Critically Ill

Dental Office

Modular Health 1

Emergency

Family Visit

M.D. Notebook

Modular Health 2

Newborn

Occs Health

Pediatrician

Physical Therapy

Recovery

Surgeon 1
(Shown at 50%)

Surgeon 2
(Shown at 50%)

Surgeon 3
(Shown at 50%)

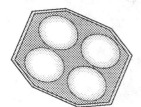
Surgery Light
(Shown at 50%)

Ultrasound

X-Rays

Images With Impact!: People 1 Disk E

Industry

CAD

Chess Board, Chess Pieces 1, Chess Pieces 2

Communication

Construction

Military

Modular Industry 1

Modular Industry 2

Tree Planter

Utility Workers

Occs A

Occs B–C

Occs C

Occs D–F

Occs F–H

Occs I–L

Occs M–O

Occs P–R

Occs S–W

Politician

Scientists

Images With Impact!: People 1 Disk F

Sports

Auto Race   Baseball   Basketball   Bike Race   Cheerleader   Football

Horse Race   Ice Skaters   Karate   Modular Sports 1

Modular Sports 2   Runners   Skier   Soccer

Swimmer   Track

T/Maker® Company

1390 Villa Street
Mountain View, CA 94041
415-962-0195
415-962-0201 fax

Collection	Format	No./Size Disks	Price	Computer
ClickArt® EPS:				
Animals & Nature	EPS	5-800K	$129.95	Mac/IBM
Business Art	EPS	4-800K	$129.95	Mac/IBM
Illustrations	EPS	4-800K	$129.95	Mac/IBM
Sports & Games	EPS	5-800K	$129.95	Mac/IBM
Symbols & Industry	EPS	4-800K	$129.95	Mac/IBM
ClickArt®:				
Business Images*	Paint	1-800K	$49.95	Mac/IBM
Business Cartoons	Paint	1-800K	$49.95	Mac/IBM
Christian Images*	Paint	1-800K	$59.95	Mac/IBM
Events & Holiday Cartoons	Paint	1-800K	$49.95	Mac/IBM
Holidays*	Paint	1-800K	$49.95	Mac/IBM
Personal Graphics*	Paint	1-800K	$49.95	Mac/IBM
Publications*	Paint	1-800K	$49.95	Mac/IBM

Notes:

* Not shown in this book. Due to the large amount of electronic clip art available from this company, we are showing only seven on the available volumes. Contact T/Maker® for more information.
• Because of their original small size, the bitmapped images from T/Maker® are shown at 50%.
• Prices for IBM versions may vary. Contact T/Maker® for details.
• Also available from T/Maker® is ClickArt Color Graphics for Presentations, a collection of more than 250 full-color clip art images; available in PICT2 format for the Macintosh and in Windows Metafile for IBM, at a price of $169.95. In addition, ClickArt Color Graphics for Presentations is available in EPS format for high quality printouts or color separations.
• Contact T/Maker® for information about ClickArt® Newsletter Cartoons by Phil Frank. 100 publication-oriented cartoons in Paint format for Mac and IBM.

TMK

Animals & Nature Disk A

Barley   Bear   Butterfly

Cat 1   Cat 2   Cheetah

Chicken

Border 1
(Shown at 25%)

Border 2
(Shown at 25%)

Cow   Deer

Border 3
(Shown at 25%)

Border 4
(Shown at 25%)

Coast (Shown at 100%)   Desert (Shown at 100%)

Dingbats 1

Due to their original small size, the pictures on this page have been shown at 50% of their original size except as noted.

T/MAKER® COMPANY

Animals & Nature Disk B

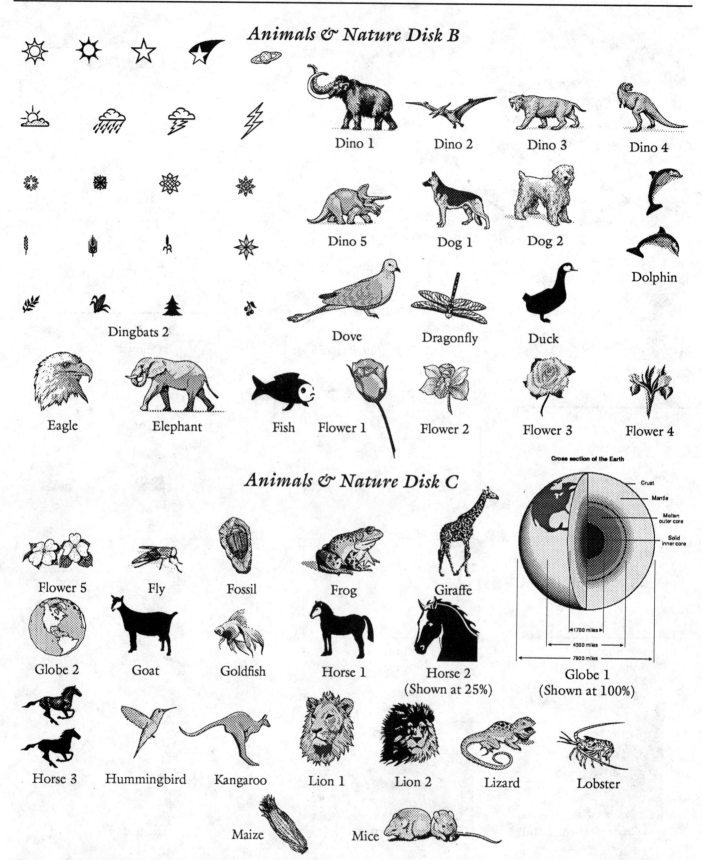

Dino 1   Dino 2   Dino 3   Dino 4

Dino 5   Dog 1   Dog 2   Dolphin

Dingbats 2   Dove   Dragonfly   Duck

Eagle   Elephant   Fish   Flower 1   Flower 2   Flower 3   Flower 4

Animals & Nature Disk C

Flower 5   Fly   Fossil   Frog   Giraffe

Globe 2   Goat   Goldfish   Horse 1   Horse 2 (Shown at 25%)   Globe 1 (Shown at 100%)

Horse 3   Hummingbird   Kangaroo   Lion 1   Lion 2   Lizard   Lobster

Maize   Mice

Cross section of the Earth

Crust
Mantle
Molten outer core
Solid inner core

◄1700 miles►
4300 miles
7900 miles

Due to their original small size, the pictures on this page have been shown at 50% of their original size except as noted.

Animals & Nature Disk D

Monkey

Moons

Mountain (Shown at 100%)

Mushrooms

Oats

Owl

Panda

Penguin

Pheasant

Pig

Pinecone

Plant 1

Plant 2

Plant 3

Plant 4

Plant 5

Puffin

Puppy

Rabbit

Ram

Rice

Rye

Animals & Nature Disk E

Seal

Season 1

Season 2

Season 3

Season 4

Shark

Sheep

Solar System (Shown at 100%)

Shell 1

Shell 2

Shell 3

Shell 4

Snail

Snake

Spider

Symbols

Tree 1

Tree 2

Tree 3

Tree 4

Tree 5

Tree 6

Trout

Turtle

Whale

Wheat

Due to their original small size, the pictures on this page have been shown at 50% of their original size except as noted.

T/MAKER® COMPANY

EPS Business Art Disk A

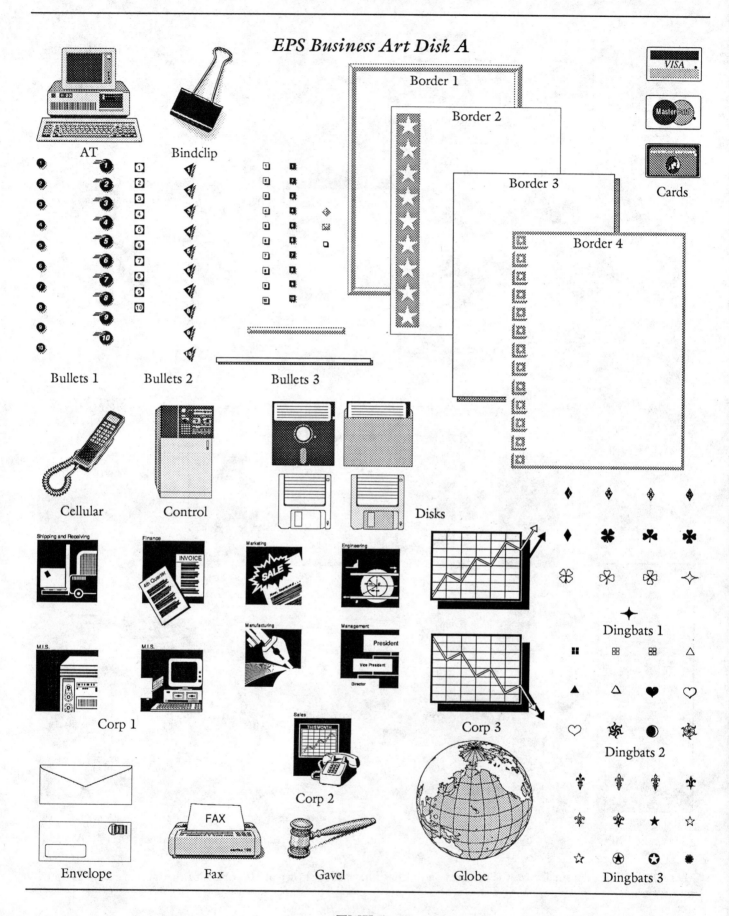

AT · Bindclip · Border 1 · Border 2 · Border 3 · Border 4 · Cards

Bullets 1 · Bullets 2 · Bullets 3

Cellular · Control · Disks · Dingbats 1

Corp 1 · Corp 3 · Dingbats 2

Corp 2

Envelope · Fax · Gavel · Globe · Dingbats 3

TMK-4

EPS Business Art Disk B

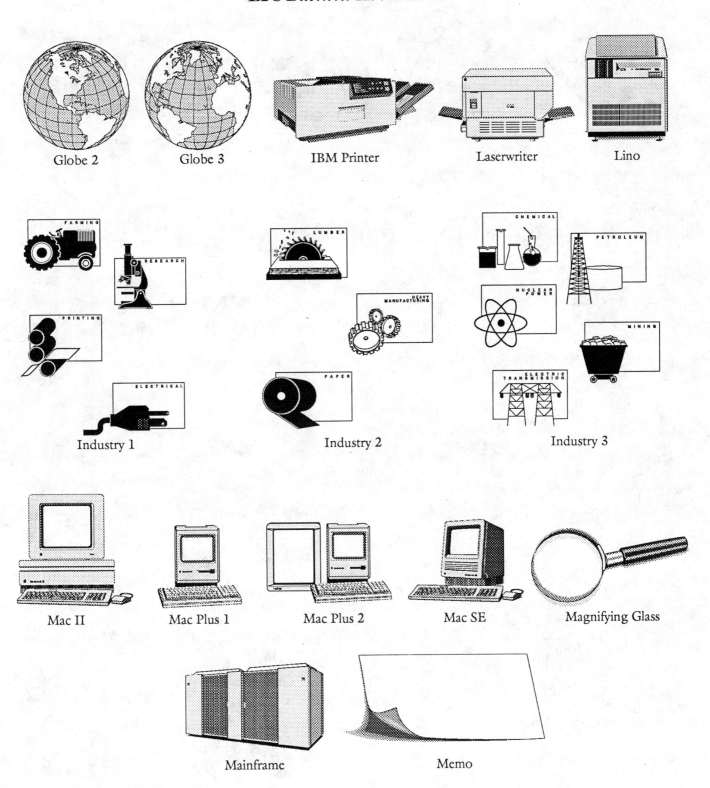

| Globe 2 | Globe 3 | IBM Printer | Laserwriter | Lino |

Industry 1

Industry 2

Industry 3

| Mac II | Mac Plus 1 | Mac Plus 2 | Mac SE | Magnifying Glass |

Mainframe

Memo

EPS Business Art Disk C

Merlin

Movie

NeXT

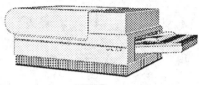

NXT

Occupations 1

Occupations 2

Occupations 3

Occupations 4

 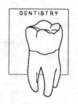   

Occupations 5

Occupations 6

Occupations 7

Overhead

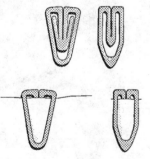 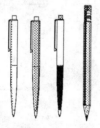  

Paperclips

Pens & Pencil

People 1

People 2

EPS Business Art Disk D

People 3

People 4

Post-it

PS/2

Pushbutton

Rolodex

Scissor 1

Scissor 2

Slide

Stapler

Sun

Tape

Tape Recorder

Tandem

Transportation 1

Transportation 2

Transportation 3

Transportation 4

Vax

EPS Illustrations Disk A

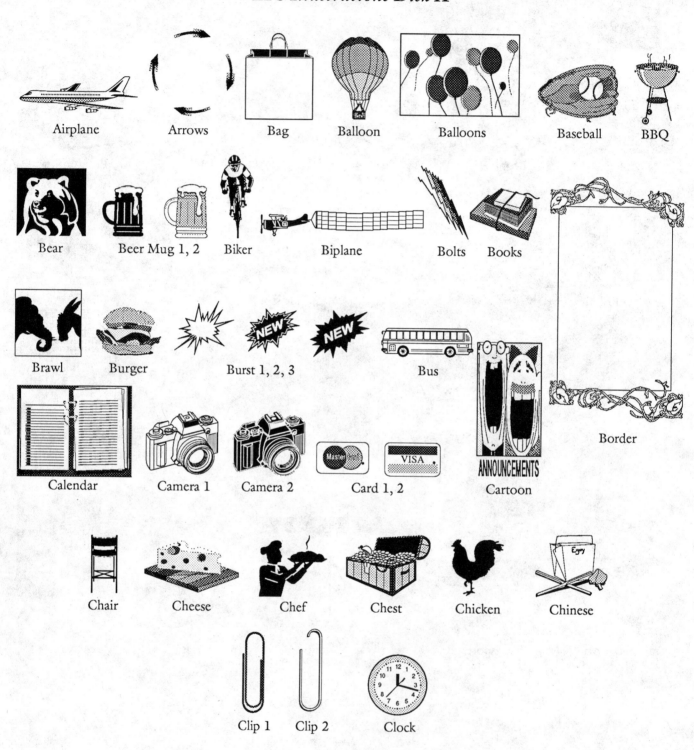

Airplane   Arrows   Bag   Balloon   Balloons   Baseball   BBQ

Bear   Beer Mug 1, 2   Biker   Biplane   Bolts   Books   Border

Brawl   Burger   Burst 1, 2, 3   Bus   Cartoon

Calendar   Camera 1   Camera 2   Card 1, 2

Chair   Cheese   Chef   Chest   Chicken   Chinese

Clip 1   Clip 2   Clock

EPS Illustrations Disk B

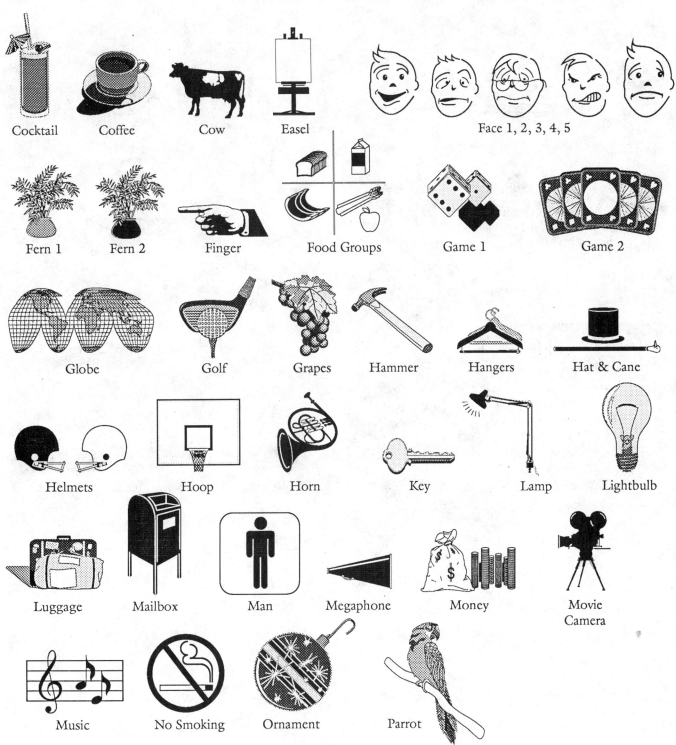

Cocktail   Coffee   Cow   Easel   Face 1, 2, 3, 4, 5

Fern 1   Fern 2   Finger   Food Groups   Game 1   Game 2

Globe   Golf   Grapes   Hammer   Hangers   Hat & Cane

Helmets   Hoop   Horn   Key   Lamp   Lightbulb

Luggage   Mailbox   Man   Megaphone   Money   Movie Camera

Music   No Smoking   Ornament   Parrot

EPS Illustrations Disk C

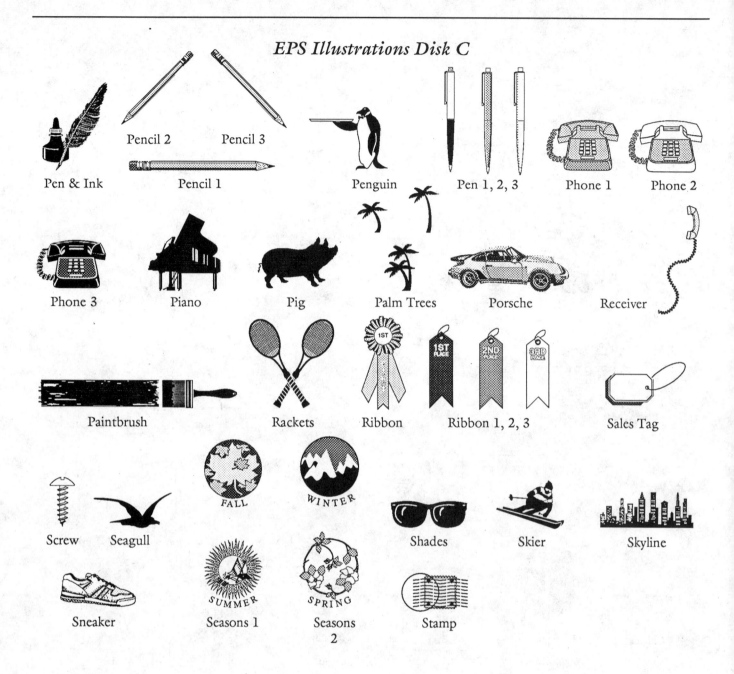

Pen & Ink Pencil 2 Pencil 3 Pencil 1 Penguin Pen 1, 2, 3 Phone 1 Phone 2

Phone 3 Piano Pig Palm Trees Porsche Receiver

Paintbrush Rackets Ribbon Ribbon 1, 2, 3 Sales Tag

Screw Seagull FALL WINTER Shades Skier Skyline

Sneaker Seasons 1 Seasons 2 Stamp

EPS Illustrations Disk D

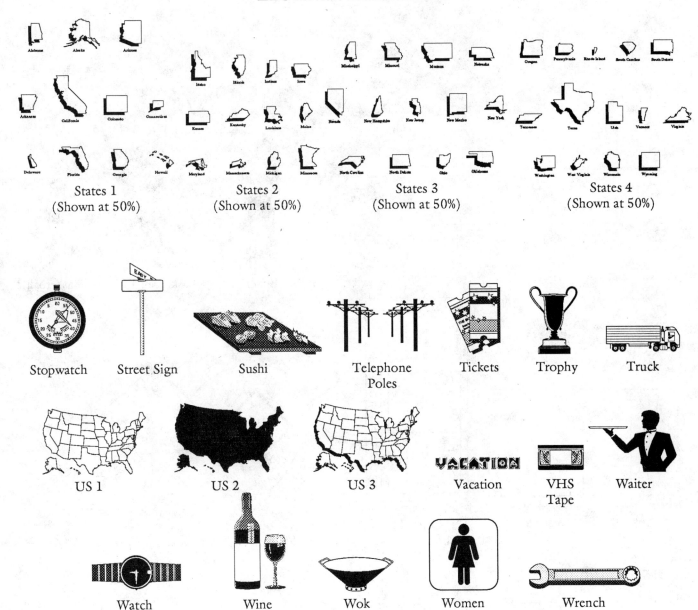

States 1
(Shown at 50%)

States 2
(Shown at 50%)

States 3
(Shown at 50%)

States 4
(Shown at 50%)

Stopwatch Street Sign Sushi Telephone Poles Tickets Trophy Truck

US 1 US 2 US 3 Vacation VHS Tape Waiter

Watch Wine Wok Women Wrench

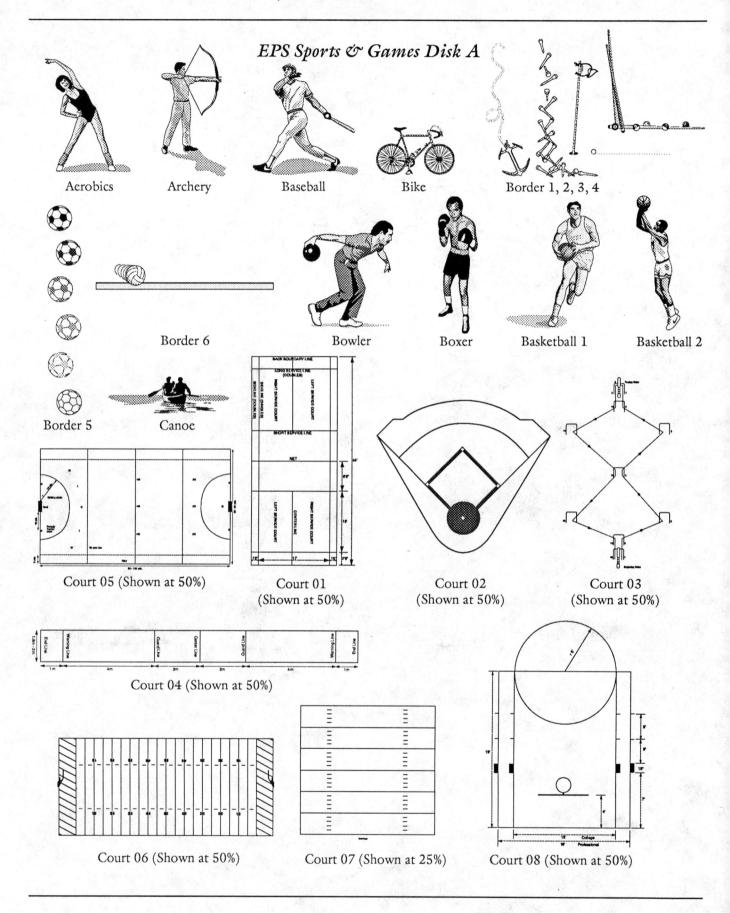

EPS Sports & Games Disk A

Aerobics

Archery

Baseball

Bike

Border 1, 2, 3, 4

Border 6

Bowler

Boxer

Basketball 1

Basketball 2

Border 5

Canoe

Court 05 (Shown at 50%)

Court 01
(Shown at 50%)

Court 02
(Shown at 50%)

Court 03
(Shown at 50%)

Court 04 (Shown at 50%)

Court 06 (Shown at 50%)

Court 07 (Shown at 25%)

Court 08 (Shown at 50%)

T/MAKER® COMPANY

EPS Sports & Games Disk B

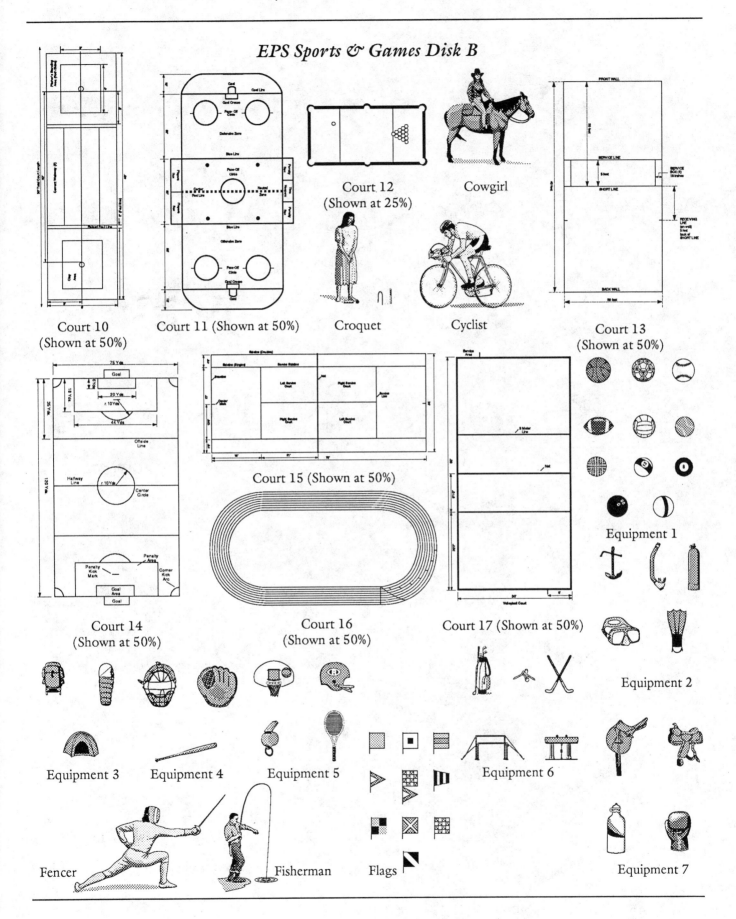

Court 10
(Shown at 50%)

Court 11 (Shown at 50%)

Court 12
(Shown at 25%)

Cowgirl

Croquet

Cyclist

Court 13
(Shown at 50%)

Court 14
(Shown at 50%)

Court 15 (Shown at 50%)

Court 16
(Shown at 50%)

Court 17 (Shown at 50%)

Equipment 1

Equipment 2

Equipment 3

Equipment 4

Equipment 5

Equipment 6

Equipment 7

Fencer

Fisherman

Flags

EPS Sports & Games Disk C

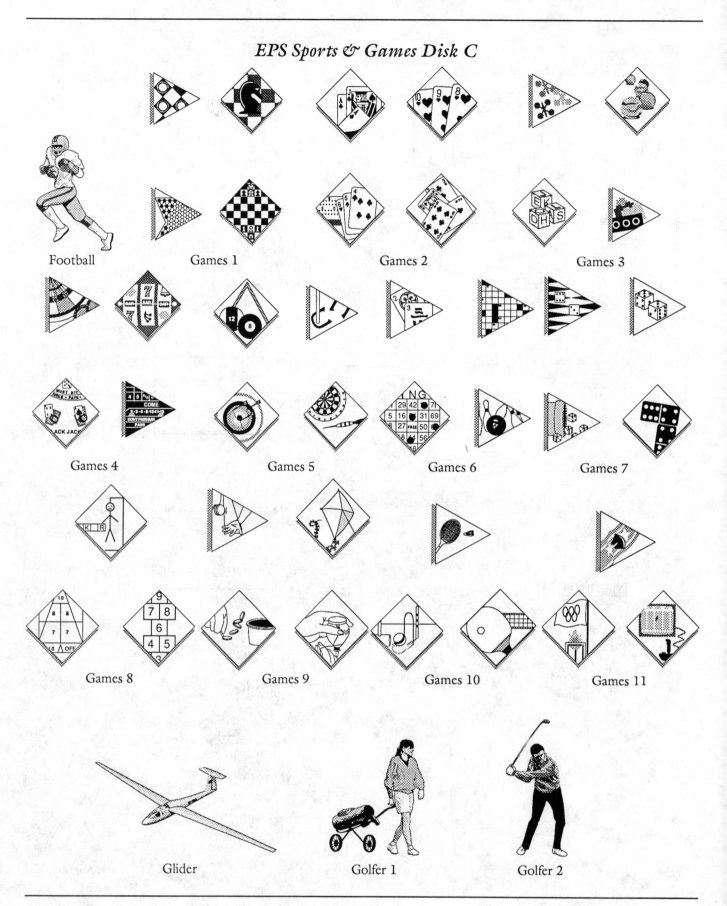

Football

Games 1

Games 2

Games 3

Games 4

Games 5

Games 6

Games 7

Games 8

Games 9

Games 10

Games 11

Glider

Golfer 1

Golfer 2

EPS Sports & Games Disk D

Gymnast Hang Glider Hiker Hockey Horse Jumping Hurdler

Ice Climber Ice Skate Karate Polo

Race Car

Racketball Rifleman Rollerblade Rower

Runner 1 Runner 2 Runner 3 Sailboat

EPS Sports & Games Disk E

Scuba Skateboard Skier 1 Skier 2 Skier 3

Soccer Stadium Surfer Swimmer Symbols 1

Symbols 2 Symbols 3 Symbols 4 Symbols 5

Symbols 6 Tennis Volleyball Waterski Weightlift

Windsurf

EPS Symbols & Industry Volume 1 Disk A

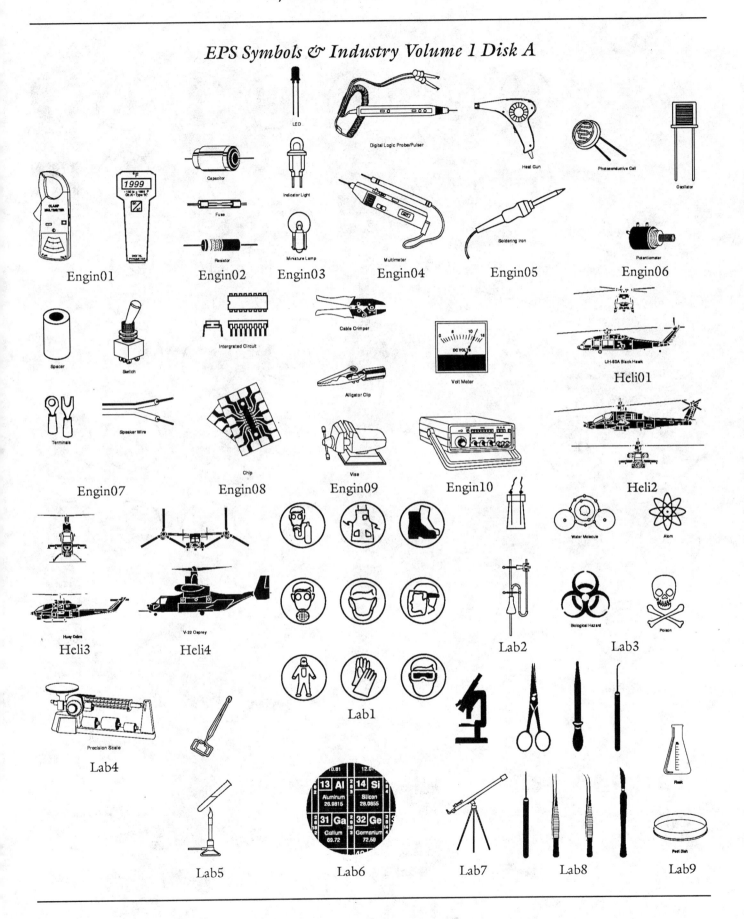

Engin01

Engin02

Engin03

Engin04

Engin05

Engin06

Engin07

Engin08

Engin09

Engin10

Heli01

Heli2

Heli3

Heli4

Lab1

Lab2

Lab3

Lab4

Lab5

Lab6

Lab7

Lab8

Lab9

T/MAKER® COMPANY

EPS Symbols & Industry Volume 1 Disk B

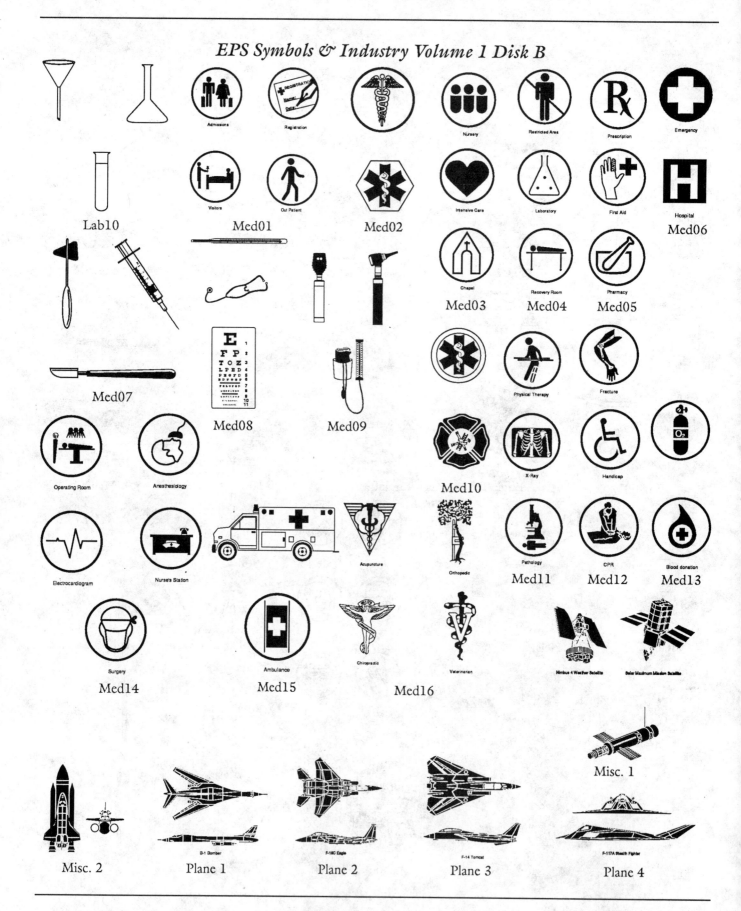

Lab10

Med01

Med02

Med06

Med03 Med04 Med05

Med07

Med08 Med09

Med10

Med11 Med12 Med13

Med14 Med15 Med16

Misc. 1

Misc. 2 Plane 1 Plane 2 Plane 3 Plane 4

EPS Symbols & Industry Volume 1 Disk C

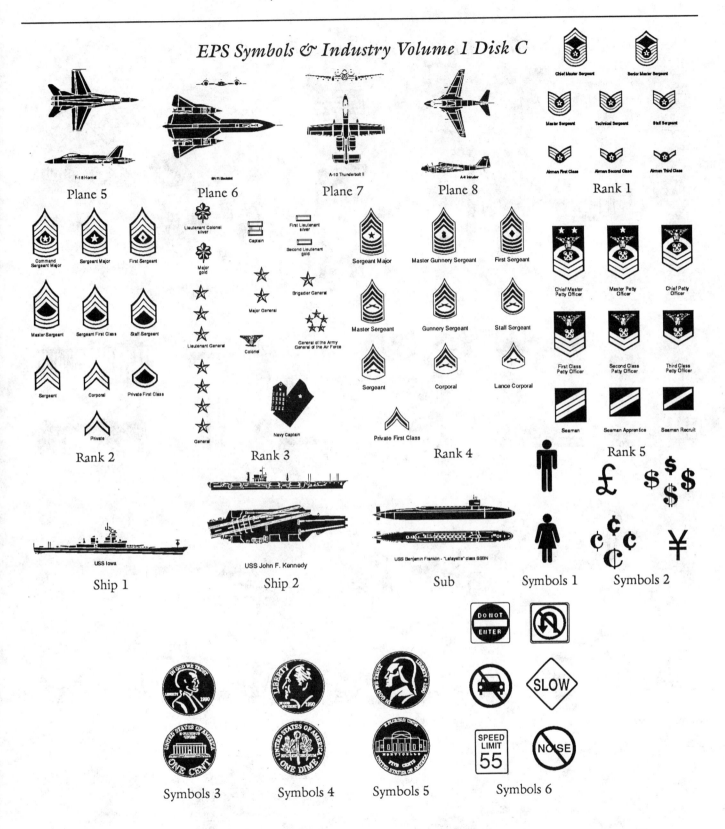

Plane 5

Plane 6

Plane 7

Plane 8

Rank 1

Rank 2

Rank 3

Rank 4

Rank 5

Ship 1

Ship 2

Sub

Symbols 1

Symbols 2

Symbols 3

Symbols 4

Symbols 5

Symbols 6

EPS Symbols & Industry Volume 1 Disk D

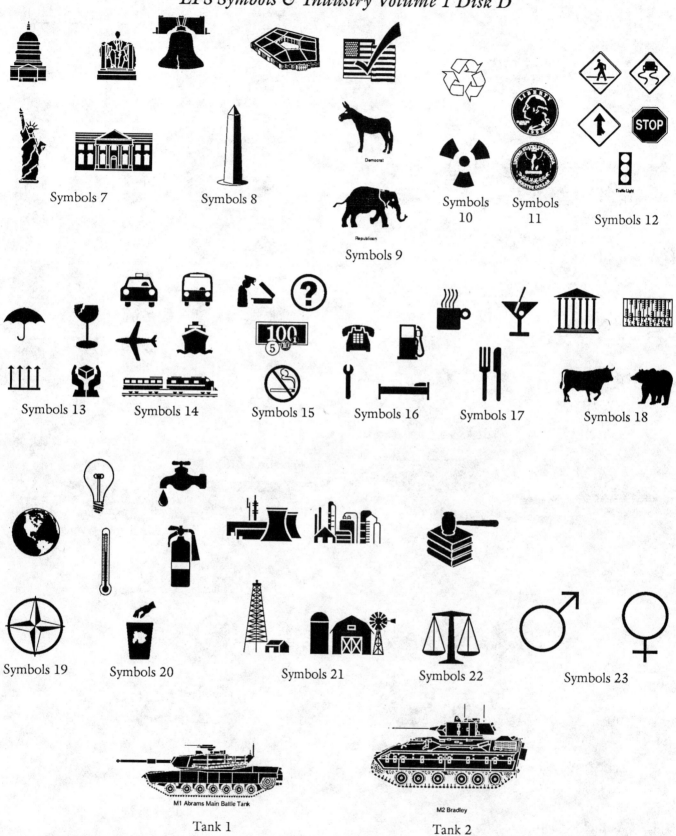

Symbols 7

Symbols 8

Symbols 9

Symbols 10

Symbols 11

Symbols 12

Symbols 13

Symbols 14

Symbols 15

Symbols 16

Symbols 17

Symbols 18

Symbols 19

Symbols 20

Symbols 21

Symbols 22

Symbols 23

Tank 1

Tank 2

Business Cartoons

Computers   Employment   Events 1   Events 2

Finance 1   Finance 2   Finance 3   Framers 1

Framers 2   Headers 1   Headers 2   Headers 3

Business Cartoons (continued)

Health

Hijinks 1

Hijinks 2

Money

Monsters 1

Monsters 2

Overwork 1

Overwork 2

People 1

People 2

People 3

T/MAKER® COMPANY

Business Cartoons (continued)

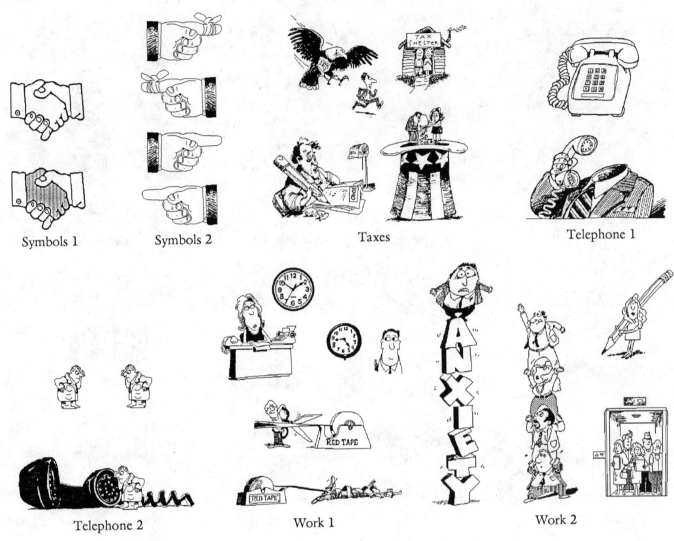

Symbols 1 Symbols 2 Taxes Telephone 1

Telephone 2 Work 1 Work 2

Work 3

Events & Holiday Cartoons

Announcement

Birthday

Christmas 1

Christmas 2

Preeeesenting...

Christmas 3

Circus

Easter

Fourth of July

Graduation

Halloween 1

Halloween 2

Events & Holiday Cartoons (continued)

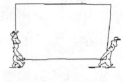

Hanukkah   Headlines 1   Headlines 2   Memos

Merit   New Year's   Parents   Party 1

Party 2   Politics   Reminder

Events & Holiday Cartoons (continued)

Sports   St. Patrick   Summer 1   Summer 2

Thanksgiving   Vacation 1   Vacation 2   Valentines

Work

The Underground Grammarian

Post Office Box 203
Glassboro, NJ 08028
609-589-6477

Collection	Format	No./Size Disks	Price	Computer
Typographers' Ornaments:				
Volume One	EPS	1-800K	$49.50	Mac/IBM
Volume Two	EPS	1-800K	$49.50	Mac/IBM
Volume Three	EPS	1-800K	$49.50	Mac/IBM
Volume Four	EPS	1-800K	$49.50	Mac/IBM
Volume Five	EPS	1-800K	$49.50	Mac/IBM
Volume Six	EPS	1-800K	$49.50	Mac/IBM
Volume Seven	EPS	1-800K	$49.50	Mac/IBM
Volume Eight	EPS	1-800K	$49.50	Mac/IBM
Volume Nine	EPS	1-800K	$49.50	Mac/IBM
Volume Ten	EPS	1-800K	$49.50	Mac/IBM
Birds & Beasts	TIFF	1-800K	$25.00	Mac/IBM
Books & Music	TIFF	1-800K	$25.00	Mac/IBM
Flowers, Etc.	TIFF	1-800K	$25.00	Mac/IBM
Miscellany	TIFF	1-800K	$25.00	Mac/IBM
Ornaments	TIFF	1-800K	$25.00	Mac/IBM
People	TIFF	1-800K	$25.00	Mac/IBM
Whimsies	TIFF	1-800K	$25.00	Mac/IBM
Will Bradley	TIFF	1-800K	$25.00	Mac/IBM
Toujours l'amour	TIFF	1-800K	$25.00	Mac/IBM
Pastoral Scenes*	TIFF	1-800K	$25.00	Mac/IBM
Special Ornaments:				
Bernhard Cursive Flourishes*	EPS	1-800K	$35.00	Mac/IBM
Printers' Devices*	EPS	1-800K	$35.00	Mac/IBM

Notes:

* Not shown or indexed in this volume. Contact The Underground Grammarian for more information.

• The Underground Grammarian also has an ornamental Postscript font, the Troyer Font, which retails for $75.00.

Typographers' Ornaments Volume One

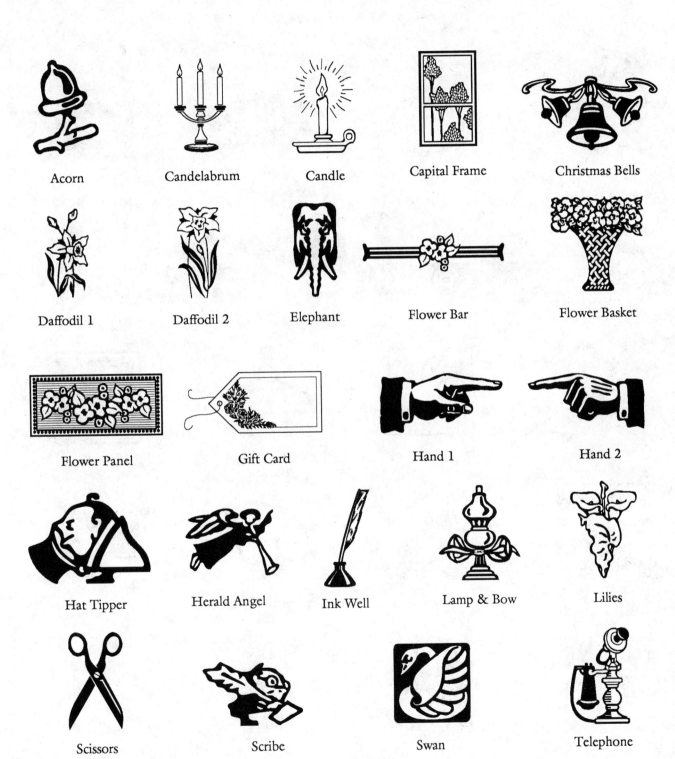

Acorn Candelabrum Candle Capital Frame Christmas Bells

Daffodil 1 Daffodil 2 Elephant Flower Bar Flower Basket

Flower Panel Gift Card Hand 1 Hand 2

Hat Tipper Herald Angel Ink Well Lamp & Bow Lilies

Scissors Scribe Swan Telephone

Typographers' Ornaments Volume Two

Assassin	Bag	Bookshelf	Castle
Cat	Coupe	Couple	Dragon	Elf
Fern	Jackass	Lantern	Le Vin
Locomotive	Longship	Philodendron Leaf	Rose
Sage	Waiter	Windmill	Winter

Typographers' Ornaments Volume Three

Brigand

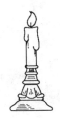

Candle 2

Condor

Fatso

Fly

Flying Fish

Girl with Candle

Hand 3

Horse on Wheels

Horseman

Hound

Kitten

Leaf

Lizard

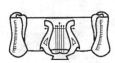

Lyre Scroll

Mushrooms

Oil Lamp

Peacock Fountain

Scholar

Seahorse

Thinker

Unicorn

Typographers' Ornaments Volume Four

Typographers' Ornaments Volume Five

Big Fish

Big Horn Player

Chapbook Directors

Chatting Gents

Cornucopiae

Greek

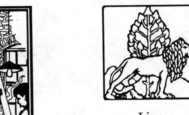

Laborer

Lion

M

Pig Rider

Puppy

Reindeer

Square One

T

Tall Candle

Telephone

Town Crier

Turkey

Typographers' Ornaments Volume Six

Bell

Birds Under Bush

Butterfly

Candle & Pine 2

Candle & Wreath

Candle & Pine 1

Candle

Christmas Tree

Cottage

Creche

Face

Holly Sprig

Little Church

Pansy

Pine Cone

S Claus 2

S Claus

Serpent

Singing Bird

Snow Flake

Snowman

Stocking

Sunrise

Three Candles

Volume Seven: The Troyer Ornaments

Alpha & Omega	Anchor	Apple	Balance	Bell	Bird	Book	Candle & Pine
Candle	Celtic Cross	Cherries	Crane	Crown	Dove	Dragonfly	Eagle
Fish	Flower #1	Flower #2	Flower Panel	Fruit Basket	Globe	Grapes	Harp
Hearts	Hourglass	Jug	Lamp	Laurel Leaves	Medical Symbol	Menora	Mortar & Pestle
Pear	Pine Cone	Rings	Shield	Snake	Star of David	Sun	Venus

Volume Eight: Including More Troyer Ornaments

ANC Left	ANC Right	ANF Left	ANF Right	Apollo	Bells	Berry Corner	Bow & Arrow
Chalice	Cross	Earth Symbol	Feather #1	Feather #2	Flower #3	Flower #4	Flower Spot
Fruit Bunch #1	Fruit Bunch #2	Ink Balls	Key	Lamp	Meeting House	Memorial Flame	Moon
Owl	Prancing Horses	Ribbon & Bow	Sailing Ship	Scallop Shell	Successful Bear	Three Acorns	Tiger

Torch

Typographers' Ornaments Volume Nine

Caryatid

Cloister Tailpiece

Dog

Edging Piece

Floral Spot 1

Floral Spot 2

Floral Spot 3

Floral Spot 4

Floral Spot 5

Floral Spot 6

Floral Spot 7

Laughing Bear

Leaf and Berry Tailpiece

Long Bookshelf

Prancing Creatures

Sunset

Tiny Candle

Wing Left

Wing Right

Typographers' Ornaments Volume Ten

Another Piper

Bagpiper

Barn Owl

Bell Left

Bell Right

Bradley Figure

Candle Bearers

Cupid's Bow

Duck

Face and Rose

Famous Printer

Fiddler

Goat

Horse

Kissing Couple

Leaping Reindeer Left

Leaping Reindeer Right

Little Owl

Palm Tree

Piper with
Drum

Lady with
Rake

Birds and Beasts

Another Turkey

Ass

Aztec Bull

Crow & Urn

Dancing Bear

Dove with Olive Branch

Dove

Duck

Eagle and Books Spot

Elegant Lion

Elephants

Family Picnic

Fancy Rooster

Field Mouse

Giraffe

Goose in Flight

Goose

Hen

Heron and Moon

Horse Head

Hyena

Birds and Beasts (continued)

Lion	Lovebirds	Nasty Animal	Owl in Wood
Owl	Pale Horse	Peacock	Pig
Pigeon	Polar Bear	Prancing Dragon	Rooster
Running Horse	Thoughtful Owl	Tiger	Tiny Owl — Tough Dog
Turkey	Two Strange Cats	Wild Goose	Wolf — Wood Duck

Books & Music

Beethoven

Books Enwreathed

Books in Love

Bookshelf

Candle & Books

Concertinist

Double Pipes

Duo

Dusty Old Books

Girl with Lyre

Homework

Hornbook

Horn Player

Hourglass & Books

Illuminated Manuscript

Instruments of Music

Instruments

Lady Reading

Laughing Books

Limp Book

Books & Music (continued)

Lone Fiddler

Mandolinist

Organist

Original Manuscript

Pipes & Drum

Quartet

Saucy Accordionist

Schoolboy

Serious Reader

Solo Trumpet

Syrinx Tailpiece

Venerable Tomes

Walking Books

Flowers, Etc.

Apple Blossom Corner

Basket & Birds

Bouquet

Carnation

Daisy Tailpiece

Dianthus

Fanciful Tree

Floral Cap Frame 1

Floral Cap Frame 2

Floral Cap Frame 3

Floral Corner

Floral Frame 1

Floral Frame 2

Floral Frame 3

Floral Frame 4

Floral Spot 1

Floral Spot 2

Floral Spot 3

Floral Spot 4

Floral Spot 5

Floral Spot 6

Floral Spot 7

Flowers, Etc. (continued)

Flower Basket

Grape Cluster

Holly Initial Frame

Japanese Blossom 1

Japanese Blossom 2

Japanese Blossom 3

Japanese Blossom 4

Little Lily

Little Wreath

Lily with Frogs

Lily

Potted Rose

Potted Tree

Rose Spot

Rose

Thorny
Rose

Rosebud Bouquet

Rosebud Tailpiece

Rudbeckia

THE UNDERGROUND GRAMMARIAN

Miscellany

Alphabet Border

Ancient FIsh 2

Ancient Fish

Animal Procession

Automobile

Christmas Street Scene

Commerce

Demeter Tailpiece

Departure

Dismayed Clown

Elephant & Castle

Frame 2

Garden Bridge

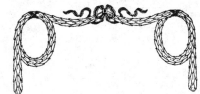

Headpiece 1

Initial Border

Insect

Mermaid Tailpiece

Picnic

Sleigh

Staff of Life

Miscellany (continued)

Steaming Bird   Tall Candle   Tiny House   Tyrant's Foe

Unicorn Rampant   Vain Cherub

Tree Talk

Ornaments

Alpha Aquarius

Alpha Aries

Alpha Cancer

Alpha Capricorn

Alpha Gemini

Alpha Leo

Alpha Libra

Alpha Pisces

Alpha Sagittarius

Alpha Scorpio

Alpha Taurus

Alpha Virgo

Anchor

Bird & Lizard

Cartouche

Chipmunk Tailpiece

Elegant Oil Lamp

Fish Cameo

Five Bats Seal

Four Birds Tailpiece

Ornaments (continued)

Front Path

Gazebo Medallion

Grape Cluster Tailpiece

Herbalist Medallion

Hourglass Cameo

Industry.H

Industry.V

Initial Border 1

Initial Border 2

Initial Border 3

Initial Border 4

Initial Border 5

Lily Tailpiece

Little Cornucopia

Little Ribbon

Lute and Pipes

Palette and Brushes

Proteus Tailpiece

Ribbon Tailpiece

Sailboats

Ornaments (continued)

Small Panel

T

Tailpiece

The End

Two Dolphins Tailpiece

Two Fishes

Vignette 1

Vignette 2

Vignette 3

Watering Can Tailpiece

People

Broody Clown

Children

Damsel Reading

Dancing Children

Dancing Children

Fall

Farm Life

Fisher

Girl Stitching

Girl Feeding Seabirds

Girl with Blooms

Haying

High Meadow

Girl in Orchard

Jaunty Rider

Little Dancer

Mother & Child

Ploughman

Picking Grapes

People (continued)

Potato Diggers

Scoundrels

Slogging Home

Spring

Sturdy Woodsmen

Summer

Typesetter

Vanity, Vanity

Weary Hunter

Window Shoppers

Winter

Whimsies

Astronomer

Big Carrot

Bootfisher

Charlatan

Confused Jockeys

Committee Meeting

Cupid Spot 1

Cupid Spot 2

Dervish

Drunken Coachmen

Devil & Geese

Diver

Elopement

Equestrian

Famous Printer

Goatbump

Ivory Tower

Kiteflying

Lady & Lapdog

Lady with Dogs

Longbow

Lowdown Hornplaying

Mad Motorists

Whimsies (continued)

Mad Poet   Mad Tourist   Man with Gun   Marching Band   Naughty Trombonist

Peepshow Drummer   Prelate   Private Lessons   Proposal   Showgirl

Simpering Clown   Slight Mishap   Specimen   Spooky Figures

Street Astronomy   Slender Chap   Stuffed   Tractarian   Twofaced Orator

Wading Alligator

Wild Dancers

Will Bradley

A Duck

Another Piper

Assasin

Bird & Ribbon

Bouquet 1

Bouquet 2

Bouquet 3

Bradley Figure

Candle Bearers

Chapbook Director 1

Chapbook Director 2

Chapbook Director 3

Chapbook Director 4

Crossed Quills

Cupid's Bow

Fiddler

Flowerpot Twins

Flowerpot

Goat

Grande Dame

Will Bradley (continued)

Horse   Hound   Jester   Kissing Couple

Miscreant   Owl   Peacock 2   Peacock

Puppy   Piper & Pig   Piper & Drum   Snooty Face   Spinning Wheel

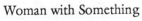

Viol

Woman with Something   Street Peddler   Strange Face   Waiter   Woman with Rake

Toujours l'amour

Adam and Eve

Another Cupid

Bench Tryst

Blind Love

CallowYearning

Courtly Lovers-1

Courtly Lovers-2

Courtly Lovers-3

Cupid-1

Cupid-2

Dancers

Dove Love

Kitty Couple

Goose Herd

Heart Garden

Lap Lovers

Long, Long Kiss

Maillol-1

Maillol-2

Maillol-3

Maillol-4

Moon Spooners

Mounted Lovers

Pucker Up,
Old Sport

Pure Devotion

Shy Suitor

Skating Bunnies

Skinny Smoochers

Spooning Spoons

Visatex
1745 Dell Avenue
Campbell, CA 95008
408-866-6562
800-722-3729

◆

Collection	Format	No./Size Disks	Price	Computer
US Presidents	Paint	1-400K	$35.00	Mac/IBM

U.S. Presidents

1-George Washington   2-John Adams   6-John Quincy Adams   3-Thomas Jefferson

4-James Madison   5-James Monroe   7-Andrew Jackson   8-Martin VanBuren

9-William Henry Harrison   23-Benjamin Harrison   10-Zachary Taylor   23-John Tyler

11-James K. Polk   13-Millard Fillmore   14-Franklin Pierce   15-James Buchanan

U.S. Presidents (continued)

16-Abraham Lincoln

17-Andrew Johnson

18-Ulysses S. Grant

19-Rutherford B. Hayes

20- James A. Garfield

21-Chester Allen Arthur

22 & 24-Grover Cleveland

25-William McKinley

26-Teddy Roosevelt

27-William H. Taft

28-Woodrow Wilson

29-Warren G. Harding

30-Calvin Coolidge

31-Herbert Hoover

32-Franklin D. Roosevelt

33-Harry S. Truman

U.S. Presidents (continued)

34-Dwight D. Eisenhower

35-John F. Kennedy

36-Lyndon B. Johnson

37-Richard M. Nixon

38-Gerald R. Ford

39-Jimmy Carter

40-Ronald Reagan

41-George Bush

41-George Bush

Zondervan Publishing House
800-727-7759

———————◆———————

Collection	Format	No./Size Disks	Price	Computer
ArtSource:				
Volume 1: Fantastic Activities	TIFF	3-800K	$49.95	Mac/IBM
Volume 2: Borders, Symbols, Holidays,				
& Attention-Getters	TIFF	5-800K	$49.95	Mac/IBM
Volume 3: Sports	TIFF	2-800K	$49.95	Mac/IBM
Volume 4: Phrases & Verses	TIFF	2-800K	$49.95	Mac/IBM
Volume 5: Amazing Oddities &				
Appalling Images*				
Volume 6: Spiritual Topics*				

Notes:

*Not shown or indexed in this volume. Contact Zondervan for more information.

• Because TIFF images take up so much disk space, Zondervan has made all of their images fairly small, in order to put more art on each disk. Therefore, we have shown their art in a format that is only a 30% to 50% reduction, compared to a typical 25% reduction. See the introduction of this book for a discussion of percentage sizing.

———

Volume 1: Fantastic Activities Disk 1

aquapar	arcade	atomic	backpack	band	beachpty	bikegang	bowling

bowlnite	brngsnak	btldrive	burbash 1, 2	campfire	campgal	campguy

campsarg	canoe	caroling	carrally	carwash	chillout	chlifeed	cndysale

concert	crbsocr	dategame	dinauct	dinthtr	drama	dramatm

dudes	fair	fallevnt	fastfood	floattrp	fooddrv

foodfare	foodfite

Volume 1: Fantastic Activities Disk 2

frinite

frisbee 1, 2

ULTIMATE FRISBEE

fundrsr

funrun

gagnite

garsale

grad

gradget

guitjam

hayride

highpnt

hikers

hockey

hotchili

hotdog

icecrm

iceskate

lastwave

livngend

lockout

meltdown

minigolf

movie

mtnbike

musicbar

musicrev

nacho

opengym

panbkfst

panfeed

parentd

picnic1

picnic2

pizzagal

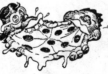
pizzaguy

pizzapar

pizzaxtr

pndparnt

poolpart

prgdin1, 2

promnite

rentakid

Volume 1: Fantastic Activities Disk 3

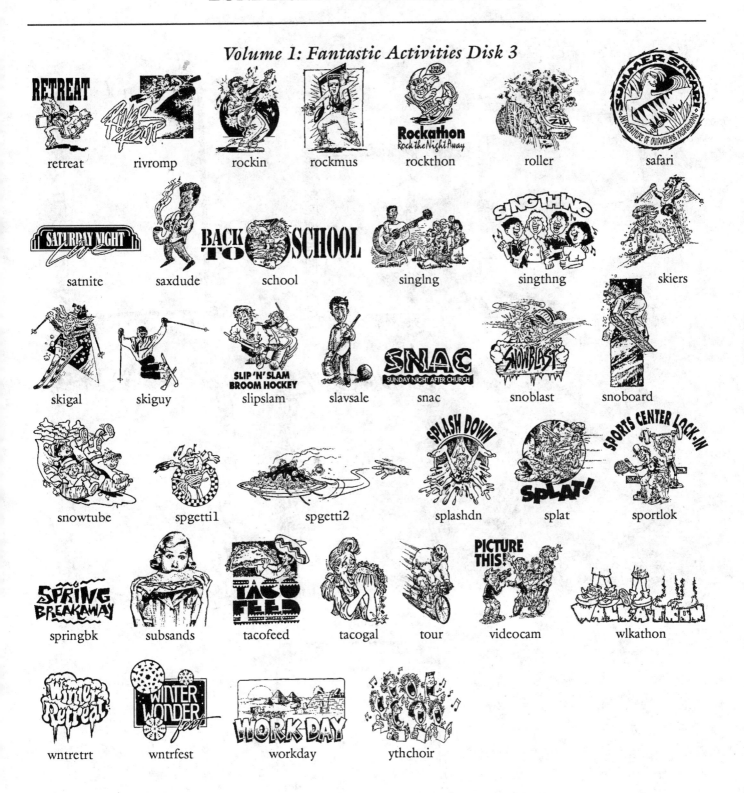

retreat   rivromp   rockin   rockmus   rockthon   roller   safari

satnite   saxdude   school   singlng   singthng   skiers

skigal   skiguy   slipslam   slavsale   snac   snoblast   snoboard

snowtube   spgetti1   spgetti2   splashdn   splat   sportlok

springbk   subsands   tacofeed   tacogal   tour   videocam   wlkathon

wntretrt   wntrfest   workday   ythchoir

Volume 2: Borders, Symbols, Holidays & Attention-Getters Disk 1

brick

caveart

dogs

food

funky

grafitti

lizard

Volume 2: Borders, Symbols, Holidays & Attention-Getters Disk 2

mod   nose   rad

shout   snow   sumfun

splash

Volume 2: Borders, Symbols, Holidays & Attention-Getters Disk 3

summer   surf   tires

zany1   zany2   zany3

Volume 2: Borders, Symbols, Holidays & Attention-Getters Disk 4

biblbolt	biblgal	biblguy	boombox	brainguy	candle1
candle2	celbrson	cowboy	cross1	cross2	cupid
dove	easter1	easter2	firecracker	fireman	galpals
getbusy	haldude	hands	harvpar	hearts	holly
Jesus1	Jesus2	jrhigh	july4	laborday	ladybubl
ltngbolt	mindblowr				

Volume 2: Borders, Symbols, Holidays & Attention-Getters Disk 5

newyear1

newyear2

phonebth

phonedir

phonekids

phoneline

prayer

preturkey

pumpkin

rabbit

radgal

radgroup

radguy

readbibl

risen

savebuck

shadeguy

sheepgrp

skatebrd

srhigh

sunglgal

sunglguy

sunsmile

surfbubl

teenbubl

thankgvng

thanxrad

thnxday

tpmummy

valheart

wow

ythgrp

Volume 3: Sports Disk 1

aerobics	basket	batgirl	batlogo
batman	benchbum	biff	bigdrive	bigdude

blockgal · bodyknot · bonecrush · bsktmove · catch · cheergal · cheers · dblplay

dig · digger · discus · dribbler · driblgal · dumbbell · endrun · exergals

fallkick · fieldgl · finisher · flagball · flagpass · flyer · football · freethro

frisbee1 · frisbee2 · galcatch · goalkick · goalrun · golf

guycatch · hatbat · headhit · headpass · headshot · heavyhit · highkick · hitter

hiyaah · homer · hookshot · hoops · huddle · hurdles · javelin · jumpgal · jumpshot

Volume 3: Sports Disk 2

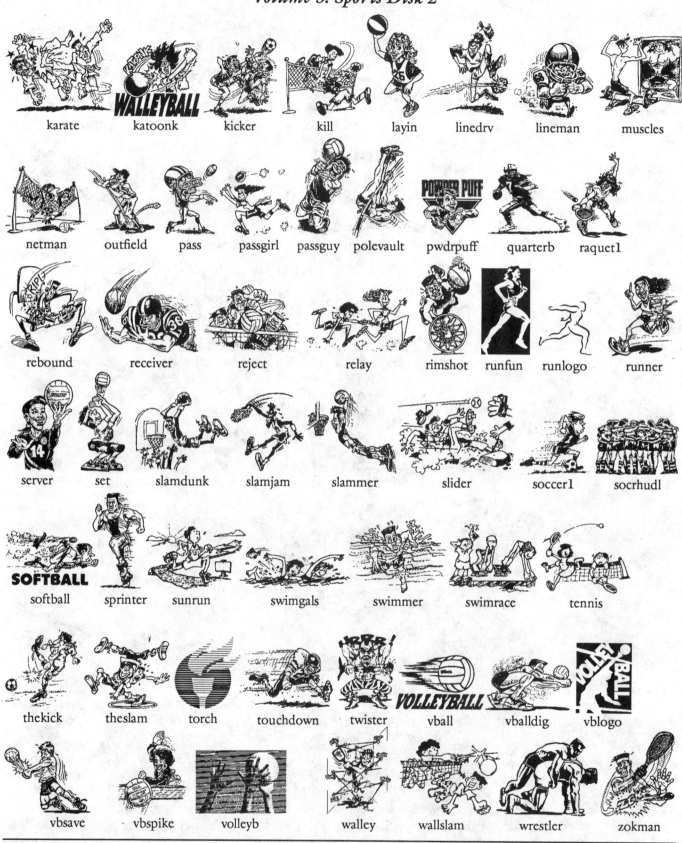

karate	katoonk	kicker	kill	layin	linedrv	lineman	muscles
netman	outfield	pass	passgirl	passguy	polevault	pwdrpuff	quarterb	raquet1
rebound	receiver	reject	relay	rimshot	runfun	runlogo	runner
server	set	slamdunk	slamjam	slammer	slider	soccer1	socrhudl
softball	sprinter	sunrun	swimgals	swimmer	swimrace	tennis
thekick	theslam	torch	touchdown	twister	vball	vballdig	vblogo
vbsave	vbspike	volleyb	walley	wallslam	wrestler	zokman

Volume 4: Phrases & Verses Disk 1

1cor620	1cor924	1john217	1pet315	1pet57	1tim412	2cor129	2cor517

2tim22 · attchurch · attaway · attractn · bigtime · awesome · bchtrp · bestrong · bethere · biblbox

birthday · brgbible · bring · brngfrnd · campus · coming · check · comingmo · comingwk

concert1 · concert2 · entertmt · deut316 · dontforget · dontmiss · fridaynt · godsays

james117

goodfite · goodjob · greater · hapbir · happnin · heb1025

heb135 · inthegym · invited · isa2816 · jesus · john157

lovehim · mark1122 · matt1626 · matt2819 · matt2820 · matt516

Volume 4: Phrases & Verses Disk 1 (continued)

meet

m issedu

missions

music

mourn

nextweek

new

news

Volume 4: Phrases & Verses Disk 2

nxtmonth

postponed   ourgod

outrage

phil16

parents

I PRESS TOWARD THE GOAL

phil314

phil29

palmtree

phil212

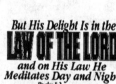
power

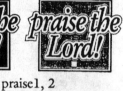
praise1, 2

prov910

psalm119

psalm12

psalm461

rad
tonight

tonight

refuge

rejoice

rom1210

rom828

ythpastor

rom831

setfree

signup1, 2

snowtrip

stuff

whatobrng

suprsumr

sword

takinit

thismnth

thisweek

today

walk

walktalk

wednite

WHAT NOT TO BRING
whatnot

wordout

wrestle

zero

INDEX

Aardvark, LET-13
Abacus, CAR-13, TMK-20
Acacia, LET-17
Accordion, UND-14
Accountant, CAR-9, INN-6, THR-20
Ackee, LET-19
Acorn, IMA-23, MUL-7, SUN-54,
    THR-7, UND-1, UND-8
Acorn squash, LET-19, MUL-5
Acrobats, ENZ-12
Adam and Eve, UND-28
Adding machine, THR-12
Adhesive tape, MUL-6
Adonis, SUN-17
Advertising logos and trademarks,
    INN-9–12
Aerobics, THR-15, TMK-12, ZON-9
Aerosol can, CAR-5
Africa, FMW-3, STU-16, SUN-3
    map, CAR-10, IMA-7, MAG-4
African mask, SUN-3
African violet, LET-5

Agriculture. *See* Farm
Air pollution, CAR-5
Airbrush, CAR-4
Aircraft
    aircraft carrier, STU-5
    airline passengers, FMW-7, MET-4,
        TAC-2
    airliner, ELE-7, HIR-15, MAG-2,
        MET-18, STU-11, STU-22,
        TAC-1, TAC-5, THR-8,
        THR-14, THR-15, THR-20,
        TMK-7, TMK-8
    biplane, CAR-7, CAR-21, MET-3,
        THR-14, TMK-8, TMK-21,
        TMK-24
    blimp, CAR-21, THR-14, TMK-7
    Concorde, FMW-2, TAC-5
    F-4 jet, CAR-21
    glider, TMK-14
    hang glider, CAR-19, TMK-15
    harrier jet, ELE-9
    helicopter, CAR-21, CAR-5, ELE-9,
        INN-5, MAG-4, MET-4,
        STU-11, STU-22–23, STU-25,
        TAC-5, TMK-17, TMK-7
    hot-air balloon, CAR-21, FMW-7,
        STU-5, THR-15
    jets, TMK-18-19
    Lear jet, TAC-5, THR-17
    military, IMA-21, STU-22–25,
        TMK-17–19

    pilot, CAR-10, FMW-19
    private jet, BES-3, THR-13
    private plane, HIR-15
    Space Shuttle, MAG-4, TAC-1
    stealth bomber, TMK-18
    symbol, CAR-5, IMA-17, INN-2,
        INN-5, MUL-2, STU-20
        TMK-20
Airliner, ELE-7, HIR-15, MAG-2,
    MET-18, STU-11, STU-22,
    TAC-1, TAC-5, THR-8,
    THR-14, THR-15, THR-20,
    TMK-7, TMK-8
Alarm clock, STU-5, TAC-5, TMK-26
Albacore, LET-3
Albatross, LET-1
Alexander the Great, SUN-29
Alfa Romeo, FMW-18
Ali Baba, DUB-5, SUN-39
Aliens, COM-1
Alligator, FMW-7, LET-15, SUN-35,
    UND-25
Alligator clip, TMK-17
Aloe, LET-17
Alpha and Omega, UND-7
Alphabets. *See* Letters
Ambulance, TMK-18
American flag, BES-1, ELE-7, FMW-1,
    HIR-4, HIR-8, HIR-15, INN-8,
    MAG-1, MAG-3, MET-11,
    STU-16, THR-15, TMK-20

IND-1

Amphibians, LET-15–16
Anchor, CAR-13, IMA-17, INN-1,
    STU-5, STU-20, TMK-12,
    UND-7, UND-19
Anchovy, LET-3
Anemone, LET-11
Angel, CAR-7, DUB-4, HIR-5,
    MET-15, MUL-7, SUN-5,
    SUN-14, SUN-16, SUN-19,
    SUN-21, SUN-41, THR-8,
    UND-1, UND-4
Angelfish, ELB-13, CAR-1, LET-3,
    THR-9
Anger, IMA-22
Animals, DUB-2, DUB-3, IMA-17,
    INN-5, LET-13–16, SUN-6-7,
    SUN-36, SUN-46, SUN-51,
    SUN-54, THR-7, TMK-1–3,
    UND-11–12, UND-17. *See also*
    Birds; Dogs; Insects; Fish
  aardvark, LET-13
  alligator, FMW-7, LET-15, SUN-35,
    UND-25
  amphibians, LET-15–16
  anteater, SUN-36
  ape, TMK-3
  armadillo, ELB-11, LET-13
  bat, THR-8, UND-19
  bear, DYN-2, GRA-10, IMA-17,
    LET-13, MUL-7, STU-5,
    SUN-51, THR-11, THR-14,
    TMK-1, TMK-8, UND-8,
    UND-9, UND-11, UND-12
  bearded dragon, LET-15
  beaver, LET-13
  bighorn sheep, TMK-3
  boar, LET-14
  buffalo, DUB-3, INN-5, LET-13,
    SUN-4
  bull, DYN-2, IMA-6, STU-6,
    SUN-36, SUN-54, THR-11
  bullfrog, LET-15
  burro, DUB-3
  calf, DUB-1, IMA-6, SUN-4
  camel, COM-4, DUB-1, DUB-3,
    LET-13, MET-15
  caribou, SUN-51
  cat, BES-8, CAR-1, CAR-4, CAR-9,
    CAR-13, , CAS-1, DUB-2,
    ELB-7, ELB-8, ELB-9, ELB-10,
    ENZ-11, ENZ-13, ENZ-6,
    FMW-18, INN5, LET-13,
    MAG-1, MAG-3, MUL-7,
    SUN-36, TMK-1, UND-2,
    UND-3,UND-4, UND-12,
    UND-28
  chameleon, LET-15, SUN-51,
    ZON-4
  cheetah, DUB-3, LET-13, SUN-3,
    TMK-1
  chimpanzee, LET-13, TMK-3

chipmunk, LET-13, SUN-51,
    UND-19
  chuckwalla, LET-15
  coati, LET-13
  cobra, LET-15
  coral snake, LET-15
  cougar, FMW-2
  cow, ENZ-13, IMA-6, INN-5,
    LET-13, SUN-46, TMK-1,
    TMK-9
  coyote, GRA-11
  crocodile, LET-15
  deer, CAS-3, DUB-2, FMW-1,
    INN-5, LET-13, LET-14,
    STU-20, STU-26, THR-7,
    TMK-1, ZON-8
  dolphin, CAR-1, CAR-13, DUB-8,
    HIR-13, INN-5, LET-3, MAG-3,
    TMK-2, UND-21
  donkey, DUB-3, FMW-11, INN-3,
    INN-5, LET-13, SUN-44,
    SUN-7, THR-11, TMK-8,
    TMK-20, TMK-25, UND-2,
    UND-11, UND-24, UND-28
  duck-billed platypus, LET-14
  elephant, CAR-1, CAR-7, ENZ-7,
    FMW-1, FMW-11, IMA-5,
    INN-5, LET-13, SUN-36,
    SUN-40, SUN-46, THR-11,
    TMK-8, TMK-20, TMK-25,
    UND-1, UND-11, UND-17
  flying dragon, LET-15
  fox, GRA-10, LET-13, SUN-6,
    SUN-7
  frilled lizard, LET-15
  frog, COM-1, ENZ-7, LET-15,
    MAG-3, STU-10, SUN-6,
    SUN-7, TMK-2, UND-16
  gavial, LET-15
  gecko, LET-15
  gila monster, LET-15
  giraffe, CAR-1, IMA-17, LET-13,
    SUN-36, SUN-51, TAC-3,
    TMK-2, UND-11
  goat, IMA-6, TMK-2, UND-24,
    UND-26
  gorilla, LET-13
  hippo, LET-13
  horned lizard, LET-16
  horse, ELB-7, ELB-8, ELB-9,
    ELB-10, CAT-2, DUB-1,
    DUB-2, ENZ-4, FMW-19,
    IMA-2, IMA-6, INN-3, INN-4,
    INN-5, LET-13, MAG-1,,
    MUL-9, STU-11, STU-20,
    SUN-4, SUN-16, SUN-19,
    SUN-38, SUN-39, SUN-46,
    TAC-3, THR-21, TMK-13,
    TMK-2, TMK-15, UND-3,
    UND-8, UND-10, UND-11,
    UND-12, UND-17, UND-22,

UND-27, UND-28
  iguana, LET-16
  jaguar, CAR-1
  kangaroo, CAR-1, DUB-2, DUB-8,
    INN-5, LET-13, MAG-2, TMK-2
  killer whale, COM-4, THR-15
  kingsnake, LET-16
  knight anole, LET-16
  koala bear, CAR-1, LET-13
  komodo dragon, LET-16
  leopard, CAT-2
  leopard, DUB-3, DUB-7, LET-14
  lion, CAR-1, ENZ-7, INN-8,
    LET-14, MAG-1, STU-12,
    SUN-7, SUN-9, SUN-36,
    TMK-2, UND-5, UND-9,
    UND-11, UND-12
  lizard, GRA-10, LET-15–16, THR-7,
    TMK-2, UND-3, UND-19
  lynx, SUN-51
  mink, LET-14
  moloch, LET-16
  monkey, CAR-1, CAR-14, CAR-17,
    ENZ-13, LET-14, SUN-7,
    TMK-3
  moose, LET-14
  mountain lion, FMW-2
  mouse, BES-1, DUB-8, LET-14,
    MAG-1, THR-14, TMK-2,
    UND-11
  mudpuppy, LET-16
  musk ox, DUB-3
  newt, LET-16
  orangutan, DUB-7
  orca, COM-4, THR-15
  ox, ENZ-11, SUN-14
  panda, DUB-3, LET-14, SUN-36
  panther, LET-14
  paw prints, INN-5, MAG-1
  pig, IMA-6, INN-5, LET-14,
    STU-14, TMK-10, TMK-3,
    UND-5, UND-12, UND-27
  platypus, LET-14
  polar bear, UND-12
  porcupine, ELB-12, LET-14
  possum, DUB-8
  prairie dog, ELB-12
  rabbit, CAR-8, CAS-2, ELB-5,
    ELB-6, ENZ-8, ENZ-13, HIR-7,
    INN-3, LET-13, LET-14,
    MAG-1, MET-3, MET-8,
    MET-12, MUL-7, STU-14,
    SUN-6, SUN-7, THR-8, TMK-1,
    TMK-3, TMK-24, UND-28
  raccoon, LET-14
  ram, TMK-3
  rat, LET-14
  rattlesnake, LET-15, MAG-3
  reindeer, CAS-3, DYN-1, IMA-14,
    LET-14, STU-15, THR-8,
    UND-5, UND-10

INDEX

reptiles, LET-15–16
rhino, CAR-7, LET-14
salamander, LET-16
seal, CAR-7, DUB-2, DYN-1,
　INN-5, LET-14, TMK-3
sheep, DUB-4, sheep, INN-5,
　LET-14, TMK-3, ZON-8,
skink, LET-16
skunk, LET-14
snake, LET-15–16, MAG-3, SUN-6,
　SUN-46, SUN-51, TMK-3,
　UND-6, UND-7
squirrel, ELB-12, LET-14
tadpole, LET-16
tiger, CAT-1, COM-4, LET-14,
　MAG-1, MAG-1, STU-17,
　UND-8, UND-12
toad, LET-16
tuatara, LET-16
turtle, ELB-11, CAR-1, DUB-3,
　DUB-7, GRA-10, INN-3,
　LET-15, LET-16, STU-18,
　SUN-7, SUN-51, TMK-3
walrus, DUB-8, LET-14
water buffalo, DUB-3, LET-14
whale, CAR-1, DUB-4, LET-4,
　MAG-3, SUN-36, THR-15,
　TMK-3, UND-4
wolf, FMW-13, FMW-14, SUN-36,
　UND-12
zebra, HIR-3, LET-14, TAC-3
Ant, INN-5, LET-9, LET-10, SUN-50
Anteater, SUN-36
Antherium, DUB-8
Ape, TMK-3
Aphrodite, SUN-17
Apollo, UND-8
Apple, CAR-4, DAV-11, INN-8, LET-7,
　MUL-5, TMK-3, UND-7
　blossom, UND-15
　core, ELE-1
AppleTalk connector, ELE-5
Apricot, LET-7
Arcade game, ZON-1
Archelon, ELB-11
Archery/arrows, CAR-7, CAR-19,
　DAV-8, INN-4, INN-8, MAG-1,
　SUN-11, TAC-2, TMK-12,
　UND-8, UND-24, UND-26
Architectural surfaces, ADO-8–16
Armadillo, ELB-11, LET-13
Arrows, ADO-14–15, ADO-17, ELB-1,
　BES-8, CAR-4, ELE-7, ELE-10,
　FMW-7, FMW-13, HIR-9,
　IMA-1, IMA-12, IMA-17,
　INN-2, MAG-2, STU-1, STU-2,
　STU-20, TMK-8
Art Deco, ART-14, BER-1, BER-2,
　CAR-2, MET-2, THR-2, THR-7
Art Nouveau, DUB-5, IMA-23, SUN-1,
　SUN-2, SUN-8, SUN-24,

SUN-25, SUN-26, SUN-45,
　SUN-47, SUN-58, THR-1,
　THR-6, THR-7, UND-8
Artichoke, HIR-3, LET-19
Artist, CAR-7, CAR-13, ELE-3,
　THR-16. See also Artist's tools
Artist's tools, CAR-4, CAR-6, CAR-7,
　IMA-16, IMA-8, INN-3, MET-3,
　MUL-4, STU-13, THR-12,
　TMK-9, UND-20
Arugula, LET-19
Ash, LET-17
Ashtray, FMW-1, IMA-13, STU-16
Asia map, MAG-4
Asparagus, LET-19
Assassin, UND-2
Astrology, CAR-17, IMA-17, INN-1,
　MAG-1, SUN-9, UND-19
Astronaut, ELE-9, IMA-19, STU-5,
　THR-13, THR-20
Astronomer, CAR-10, UND-24,
　UND-25
Astronomy, INN-1, STU-13
Athena, SUN-17
Atom, CAR-5, ELE-7, IMA-21, INN-2,
　MAG-4, STU-5, STU-16,
　THR-13, TMK-5
Atom bomb, IMA-21
Attache case. See Briefcase
Auction, INN-1
Auctioneer, MUL-3
Australia map, CAR-10, MAG-4
Automated teller, THR-16
Automobiles. See Cars
Autumn, BES-2, CAR-16, CAS-2,
　THR-8, TMK-3, TMK-10,
　UND-22, ZON-1
Avocado, LET-19
Award, CAR-7, STU-5, TMK-22. See
　also Ribbon; Trophy
Axe, FMW-13, FMW-14, UND-23
Azalea, ART-12, ELB-13, SUN-27
Aztec face, STU-5

Baby, CAR-11, DUB-2, DUB-7,
　DUB-9, FMW-3, MAG-2,
　MET-10, MET-14, MUL-6,
　MUL-8, SUN-30, SUN-30,
　THR-19, THR-19. See also Stork
Baby bottle, CAR-4

Baby carriage, CAR-4, FMW-17, STU-5
Babylon, SUN-29
Backgrounds, ART-1–16, CAR-2,
　COM-5, ELE-10, ELE-6, ELE-8,
　IMA-20
Backhoe, INN-2, THR-20
Backpacking, MET-19, THR-18,
　TMK-15, ZON-1, ZON-2
Bacon, MET-7
Badge, TMK-6
Badminton, ELE-1, TMK-14
Bag, TMK-8 Sack, TMK-8, UND-2
Bagpipes, SUN-41, UND-10
Bakery, MUL-5
Balance. See Scale
Ball and chain, CAR-9, FMW-7, ZON-3
Ballet, ELE-3, IMA-13, INN-6,
　SUN-18, THR-16
Balloons, CAR-9, COM-4, COM-5,
　DUB-5, ELE-7, FMW-2,
　MAG-2, MET-11, THR-8,
　THR-15, TMK-8
　hot-air, CAR-21, FMW-7, MET-12,
　STU-5
Bamboo, CAT-1, ENZ-13, ENZ-6,
　LET-17, LET-19, THR-1
Banana, LET-7, TAC-4
　leaf, LET-17
Bandaid, CAR-4, CAR-14, IMA-2,
　STU-20
Band leader, MUL-8
Bandit, FMW-1
Banker, CAR-9
Banner, CAS-1, CAR-7, CAR-9, DUB-5,
　ELB-1, ELE-8, ENZ-4, HIR-9,
　HIR-10, MAG-1, MAG-2,
　STU-5, STU-16, THR-4
Barbed wire alphabet, GRA-9
Barbell, CAR-7
Barbeque, CAR-8, IMA-15, MET-8,
　STU-5, TMK-8, TMK-26
Barber, CAR-9
　pole, INN-1, MAG-3
Barley, TMK-1
Barn, CAR-14, THR-15, TMK-20
Barnacle, LET-11
Barracuda, ELB-11, LET-3
Barrel, CAR-4, STU-5
Baseball, BES-7, CAR-19, CAR-7,
　CAR-9, COM-2, ELE-1,
　HIR-15, IMA-1, INN -4,
　MAG-3, MET-2, MUL-9,
　STU-5, THR-8, THR-21,
　TMK-8, TMK-12, TMK-13,
　TMK-16, ZON-9, ZON-10
Basket, GRA-4–5, MET-7, MET-8,
　MUL-5, MUL-7, STU-5,
　SUN-26, UND-1, UND-7,
　UND-15, UND-16
Basketball, BES-7, CAR-7, CAR-19,
　CAR-20, HIR-15, IMA-1,

Cab, CAR-6, MET-13, THR-15, TMK-20
Cabbage, LET-19
Cabin, MAG-1
Cactus, ELB-5, CAR-4, GRA-10, LET-17, LET-18, TMK-1
Cadillac, FMW-18
Caduceus, BES-8 , CAR-11, INN-3, INN-5, STU-12, STU-21, THR-12, TMK-6, TMK-18, UND-7
Cake, CAR-8, HIR-8, IMA-13, MAG-1, TAC-4, THR-9
Calculator, CAR-3, CAR-9, STU-7, TAC-5
Calendar, CAR-3, INN-6, MAG-3
Calf, DUB-1, IMA-6, SUN-4
Camcorder, ZON-3, STU-19
Camel, COM-4, DUB-1, DUB-3, LET-13, MET-15
Cameo, STU-7
Camera, CAR-4, CAR-16, COM-1, DUB-9, ELE-9
    film, HIR-12, IMA-8, IMA-12, IMA-15, IMA-17, IMA-8, INN-3, INN-6, STU-9, STU-21, TAC-2, TMK-8
    lens, TAC-4
    movie, CAR-6, TMK-9
    photographer, IMA-19
    video, CAR-3
Camper, INN-5, INN-8
Campfire, CAR-4 Fire, CAR-4, ELE-7, INN-3, STU-20, ZON-1
Camping, CAR-5, CAR-7, INN-4, MET-19, STU-17, STU-20, STU-26, TAC-2, THR-15, TMK-13, ZON-1
Can, STU-7
Canada map, CAR-10, IMA-7, MAG-4
Canary, LET-1
Candelabra, STU-7, THR-8, UND-1, UND-6
Candle, CAR-4, CAR-13, DAV-1, ELB-3, ELB-4, ELE-4, FMW-18, HIR-5, MAG-3, MET-15, STU-7, SUN-8, SUN-32, SUN-54, UND-1, UND-2, UND-3, UND-5, UND-6, UND-7, UND-9, UND-10, UND-13, UND-18, ZON-7

Candy, ZON-1
Candy cane, ELB-3, ELB-4, HIR-5, IMA-14, INN-6, MUL-7, STU-4, STU-7
Cane, CAR-14
Cannon, MAG-1, STU-7
Canoe, ZON-1, DUB-3, INN-4, TMK-12
Cantaloupe, LET-7
Canyon, ART-10
Cap, DUB-2, STU-11
Caper, LET-17
Capitol building, INN-6, MAG-1, MUL-2, STU-16, THR-15, TMK-20
Car phone, BES-8, CAR-4, MUL-3, THR-16
Card file. See Rolodex
Cardinal, ELB-11, LET-1
Carhop, IMA-21
Caribou, SUN-51
Caricatures, CAR-9–10, IMA-18
Carnation, LET-5, SUN-27, UND-15
Carnival, SUN-30, SUN-45
Carolers, CAR-8, SUN-16
Carousel, CAR-14, CAS-1
Carpenter, DUB-9, IMA-21, THR-20
Carriage, SUN-29
Carrot, LET-19
    and stick, UND-24
Cars, CAR-4, CAR-21, FMW-1, FMW-18, IMA-21, INN-1, INN-5, MAG-2, TAC-1, TAC-5, THR-13, TMK-7, ZON-2. See also Truck
    accident, INN-3
    Alfa Romeo, FMW-18
    antique, CAR-21, FMW-18, MET-18, MET-2, SUN-8, TAC-1, UND-2, UND-17, UND-4, UND-24
    BMW sedan, BES-6
    Buick, IMA-21
    Cadillac, FMW-18
    car phone, MUL-3, THR-16
    car rental symbol, INN-5
    car wash, ZON-1, TAC-2
    carhop, IMA-21
    carpool symbol, INN-3
    Corvette, HIR-15
    delivery van, FMW-7
    Don't Drink & Drive symbol, THR-12
    driver, IMA-21
    engine, TAC-1
    ferry, INN-8
    four-wheel drive vehicle, CAR-21
    gas pump, INN-3, MET-2, THR-20, TMK-20
    Lamborghini, ELE-9
    license plate, IMA-21
    off-road vehicle, INN-5, STU-21
    oil change, COM-2
    Porsche , ELE-9, TMK-10
    racing, CAR-21, INN-8, MET-19, STU-14, TAC-1, TMK-15

    racing flags, FMW-8, INN-8, TAC-4, STU-7
    seatbelt, CAR-15, INN-5
    spark plug, STU-16
    sports car, CAR-21, INN-8
    taxi, CAR-6, MET-13, THR-15, TMK-20
    Testarosa, BES-6
    tire, STU-17
    traffic light, CAR-17
    traffic symbols, INN-6
    transmission, INN-6
    van, MAG-2
    Volkswagen Bug, CAR-9, IMA-8 MAG-2
    windshield, IMA-21
Cart, STU-10
Cartographic patterns, ADO-11
Cartouche, SUN-9, SUN-24, SUN-39, UND-19
Caryatid, UND-9
Cash register, MAG-2, STU-7, THR-20
Cassette tape, ELE-1, TAC-5, TAC-6
Castle, CAS-3, FMW-14, STU-7, SUN-33, UND-2
Cat, BES-8, CAR-1, CAR-4, CAR-9, CAR-13, CAS-1, CAS-4, DUB-2, ELB-7, ELB-8, ELB-9, ELB-10, ENZ-11, ENZ-13, ENZ-6, FMW-18, INN-5, LET-13, MAG-1, MAG-3, MUL-7, SUN-36, TMK-1, UND-2, UND-3, UND-4, UND-12, UND-28
Caterpillar, DUB-1, LET-10, LET-9, SUN-35, SUN-46, SUN-50
Cauliflower, LET-19
Cave man, FMW-13, FMW-14, IMA-4, SUN-38
CD, ELE-1, IMA-6, INN-6, MUL-2, TAC-5
CD player, ELE-9, IMA-8
CD ROM drive, ELE-5
Cedar branch, LET-17
Ceiba tree, SUN-34
Ceiling fan, TAC-2
Celebrities, IMA-18
Cello, SUN-41
Celtic designs, SUN-1, SUN-2, SUN-46, THR-6, THR-7, UND-7
Cement mixer, INN-2
Cement worker, DUB-9
Cemetery, UND-23
Cent sign, TMK-19
Centaur, SUN-17
Centipede, LET-9
Central America map, CAR-10
Certificate, IMA-2, MET-3, THR-5
Chain, MAG-3, STU-3, STU-7
Chair, CAR-13, ELE-2, IMA-3, SUN-43, TAC-1, TAC-2, TAC-6, TMK-8

grapes, CAR-5, ELB-6, LET-8,
    STU-10, SUN-47, SUN-48,
    SUN-58, TMK-3, TMK-9, UND-7,
    UND-15, UND-16, UND-20,
    UND-22
guava, LET-7
honeydew melon, LET-7
jack fruit, LET-7
kiwi, LET-7
kumquat, LET-7
lemon, LET-7, TAC-4
lime, LET-7
lychee, LET-7
mandarin orange, LET-7
mango, LET-7
mangosteen, LET-7
nectarine, LET-7
orange, CAR-4, INN-8, LET-7,
    LET-8, MUL-5, STU-13
papaya, LET-8
passion fruit, LET-8
peach, LET-8, TAC-4
pear, CAR-6, CAR-15, LET-8, TAC-4,
    TMK-3, UND-7
persimmon, LET-8
pineapple, DUB-8, LET-8
plantain, LET-8
plum, LET-8
pomegranate, LET-8
poppy, LET-8
prickly pear, LET-8
prune, LET-8
rambutan, LET-8
raspberry, LET-8
sapodilla, LET-8
sorrel, LET-8
starfruit, LET-8
strawberry, ELE-1, INN-8, LET-8,
    MET-7, STU-16
tamarind, LET-8
tangerine, LET-8
ugli, LET-8
watermelon, LET-8, STU-19, TMK-3
Frying pan, MET-7
Furniture, DUB-9, IMA-4, INN-6
Fuse, TMK-17

Games, TMK-14
Gang, FMW-1
Garage sale, ZON-2

Garbage can, STU-10, TMK-20
Gardening, MET-3, MET-8
Gargoyle, DUB-5, SUN-40
Garlic, TMK-3
Gas mask, TAC-2
Gas pump, CAR-5, INN-3, MET-2,
    STU-20, STU-26, STU-27,
    THR-20, TMK-20
Gate, ENZ-6
Gavel, CAR-3, DYN-1, INN-1, MUL-3,
    THR-12, TMK-4, TMK-20
Gavial, LET-15
Gazebo, UND-20
Gears, BES-3, HIR-14, INN-1, STU-10,
    TMK-5, TMK-6
Gecko, LET-15
Geisha, CAR-14, SUN-13
Geology, IMA-17
Geranium, LET-5
German shepard, TMK-2
Ghandi, Mahatma, IMA-18
Ghost, IMA-14, MAG-3, MUL-7
Gift, CAR-5, CAR-9, CAS-4, HIR-6,
    INN-1, INN-6, MAG-1, THR-9,
    TMK-24, TMK-25
Gila monster, LET-15
Giraffe, CAR-1, IMA-17, LET-13,
    SUN-36, SUN-51, TAC-3, TMK-2,
    UND-11
Gladiators, SUN-29
Glass, INN-6
Glasses, CAR-5, COM-2
Glider, TMK-14
Globe, BES-6, CAR-5, CAR-11, ELE-4,
    FMW-1, HIR-9, HIR-15, INN-4,
    INN-8, MAG-1, MAG-3, MET-11,
    MIC-3, SUN-31, TAC-8, THR-8,
    THR-13, TMK-2, TMK-4–5,
    TMK-20, UND-7
Globefish, LET-3
Gnome, MET-1
Goat, IMA-6, TMK-2, UND-24, UND-26
Goblet, CAR-5
Goblin, FMW-13
Goby, LET-3
Goldfish, CAR-1, CAR-5, LET-3, TMK-2
Golf, BES-7, CAR-20, COM-2, ELE-3,
    FMW-19, IMA-5, INN-2, INN-4,
    INN-8, MAG-2, MET-2, MET-6,
    MUL-9, STU-10, TAC-4, THR-18,
    TMK-9, TMK-12, TMK-13,
    TMK-14, TMK-16, ZON-9
    Jack Nicklaus, IMA-18
    miniature, ZON-2
Gondola, INN-8
Goose, CAT-2, DUB-2, DUB-4, ENZ-6,
    LET-1, SUN-6, SUN-7, SUN-10,
    UND-11, UND-12, UND-24,
    UND-28
Gooseberry, LET-7

Gooseneck barnacle, LET-11
Gorbachev, FMW-3
Gorgon, SUN-17
Gorilla, LET-13
Gourami, ELB-14
Government, TMK-20, TMK-25. *See also*
    Presidents
    Capitol building, INN-6, MAG-1,
        MUL-2, STU-16, THR-15,
        TMK-20
    White House, THR-11
Grable, Betty, CAR-15
Graduation, BES-9, CAR-9, FMW-3,
    IMA-14, MET-3, MET-9,
    MET-12, MUL-4, STU-10,
    THR-8, THR-15, TMK-24,
    ZON-2
Gramophone, MET-12
Grand Canyon, ART-10
Grandfather clock, STU-10
Grapefruit, LET-7
Grapes, CAR-5, ELB-6, LET-8, STU-10,
    SUN-47, SUN-48, SUN-58,
    TMK-3, TMK-9, UND-7,
    UND-15, UND-16, UND-20,
    UND-22
Graph, BES-3, BES-8, CAR-3, CAR-7,
    ELB-2, FMW-7, FMW-8, FMW-9,
    IMA-3, IMA-15, INN-1, MET-13,
    MUL-2, MUL-3, STU-10, TAC-5,
    TMK-4, TMK-22
Grass, ART-10
Grasshopper, LET-10, UND-17
Grass hut, DUB-8
Grave, CAR-5, FMW-2, SUN-19,
    UND-23
Gravel, MAG-4
Great dane, FMW-17
Greece, ancient, CAR-8, SUN-17,
    SUN-29, UND-5, UND-8,
    UND-17, UND-20
Green pepper, LET-19
Gretzky, Wayne, IMA-18
Greyhound, BES-8
Grim reaper, FMW-13
Grocer, CAR-9, FMW-2
Grouper, LET-3
Grunion, LET-3
Guava, LET-7
Guitar, CAR-15, ELE-1, MAG-1,
    THR-16, ZON-2, ZON-3
Gum machine, MAG-3
Gun, CAR-14, DUB-1, FMW-1, FMW-8,
    FMW-10, IMA-21, MAG-3,
    STU-8, TAC-4, TMK-6, UND-25.
    See also Hunting
Gym bag, MET-6
Gym locker, DYN-1
Gymnastics, CAR-19, CAR-20, INN-4,
    TAC-4, THR-21, TMK-15

INDEX

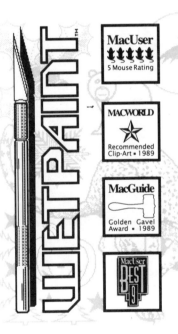

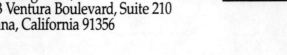

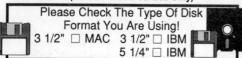

ALMOST FREE Clip Art
AND AN ILLUSTRATED HOW-TO BOOK

Send:
1) This mail-in certificate; **and**
2) **$20.00** to cover shipping and handling.
   International (Outside U.S. & Canada Only)

Please Check The Type Of Disk Format You Are Using!
3 1/2" ☐ MAC   3 1/2" ☐ IBM
5 1/4" ☐ IBM

Shipping and Handling Charge Must Be Enclosed

Name _____

Company _____

Address _____

City _____

Country/Postal Code _____

To: Studio Advertising Art
International "Almost FREE" Clip Art Offer
P.O. Box 43912, Las Vegas, NV USA 89116

We'll Send you:
1) **30 FREE** High Quality Click & Clip Illustrations in Encapsulated PostScript (EPS) format; **and**
2) A 30 page *"How-To"* book on Electronic Clip Art, showing many creative ways you can manipulate this high quality EPS Clip Art.

ORDER TODAY!

B

Click & Clip Illustrations must be used with a page make-up, draw, or word processing programs that will accept EPS Files. This mail-in certificate must be completed in full. Please make sure that you indicate which computer system you are using. $20.00 in U.S. funds for International shipping and handling must be included with this card or your order will not be filled.

IMAGES WITH **Impact!**™

People 1 Save $40

3G GRAPHICS

Mail to:
3G Graphics, Inc.
11410 NE 124th St.
Suite #6155
Kirkland, WA 98034
(206) 367-9321 FAX your orders to (206) 364-3736

800-456-0234

EXCLUSIVE $40 OFF COUPON FOR CANNED ART CUSTOMERS ONLY

☐ **Please send me information on Images With Impact! products.**

☐ **Please send me People 1 at your Special Price of $149.95**

Choose your format: ☐ Mac ☐ IBM (contains both 5.25" & 3.5" Disks)

METHOD OF PAYMENT: U.S. FUNDS ONLY PLEASE. Add $5 for U.S. shipping, $10 Canada, $20 for all other destinations; WA res. add 8.2% sales tax.
Enclosed is my check for $ _____ Payable to 3G Graphics.
Charge my credit card: ☐VISA ☐Mastercard ☐Amer. Express

Acct. # _____ Expir. Date: _____

Signature on Card: _____

SHIPPING INFORMATION: All U.S. orders are shipped via UPS ground. (Call for other shipping options and prices.) Please include street address only. UPS cannot deliver to P.O. Boxes.

Name: _____

Company Name: _____

Street Address: _____

City/State/Zip: _____

Country: _____

Canned Art: Clip Art for the Macintosh

ALL STAR SAMPLES DISKS

As a special supplement to this book, the companies represented have donated over 60 samples of their best work—in all, over 2.0 megabytes of clip art. They are provided in compressed format along with a decompression utility.

To receive the sample disks, send a check for $10 (covering shipping, handling, disk duplication, and the licensing fee for the decompression utility) to Peachpit Press. Sorry, no credit cards or purchase orders accepted.

———————————Please fold along line and staple or tape closed———————————

☐ **Yes**, please send the ALL STAR SAMPLES DISKS to the following address. Enclosed is my check for $10.

NAME	
COMPANY	
ADDRESS	
CITY	
STATE	ZIP